WOMEN

The Bible Study Textbook Series

NEW TESTAMENT

New Testament & History By W. Wartick & W. Fields Vol. I - The Intertestament Period and The Gospels	The Gospel of Matthew In Four Volumes By Harold Fowler	The Gospel of Mark By B. W. Johnson and Don DeWelt
The Gospel of Luke By T. R. Applebury	The Gospel of John By Paul T. Butler	Acts Made Actual By Don DeWelt
Romans Realized By Don DeWelt	Studies in Corinthians By T. R. Applebury	Guidance From Galatians By Don Earl Boatman
The Glorious Church (Ephesians) By Wilbur Fields	Philippians - Colossians Philemon By Wilbur Fields	Thinking Through Thessalonians By Wilbur Fields
Paul's Letters To Timothy & Titus By Don DeWelt	Helps From Hebrews By Don Earl Boatman	James & Jude By Don Fream
Letters From Peter By Bruce Oberst	Hereby We Know (I-II-III John) By Clinton Gill	The Seer, The Saviour, and The Saved (Revelation) By James Strauss

OLD TESTAMENT

O.T. & History By William Smith and Wilbur Fields	Genesis In Four Volumes By C. C. Crawford	Exploring Exodus By Wilbur Fields	Leviticus By Don DeWelt
Numbers By Brant Lee Doty	Deuteronomy By Bruce Oberst	Joshua - Judges Ruth By W. W. Winter	I & II Samuel By W. W. Winter
I & II Kings By James E. Smith	I & II Chronicles By Robert E. Black	Ezra, Nehemiah & Esther By Ruben Ratzlaff & Paul T. Butler	The Shattering of Silence (Job) By James Strauss
Psalms In Two Volumes By J. B. Rotherham	Proverbs By Donald Hunt		Ecclesiastes and Song of Solomon — By R. J. Kidwell and Don DeWelt
Isaiah In Three Volumes By Paul T. Butler	Jeremiah and Lamentations By James E. Smith		Ezekiel By James E. Smith
Daniel By Paul T. Butler	Hosea - Joel - Amos Obadiah - Jonah By Paul T. Butler		Micah - Nahum - Habakkuk Zephaniah - Haggai - Zechariah Malachi — By Clinton Gill

DOCTRINE

The Church In The Bible By Don DeWelt	The Eternal Spirit Two Volumes By C. C. Crawford	New Testament Evidences By Wallace Wartick	Survey Course In Christian Doctrine Two Bks. of Four Vols. By C. C. Crawford
New Testament History—Acts By Gareth Reese	Learning From Jesus By Seth Wilson		You Can Understand The Bible By Grayson H. Ensign

WHAT THE
BIBLE SAYS
ABOUT

WOMEN

By

Julia Staton

College Press Publishing Company, Joplin, Missouri

Library of Congress Catalog Card Number: 80-66128
International Standard Book Number: 0-89900-079-7

Scripture quotations, unless otherwise noted, are from the New American
Standard Bible, © The Lockman Foundation, 1960, 1962, 1963, 1968, 1971,
1973, 1975.

Dedication

To my mother,
who is a fine
example of motherhood.

Table of Contents

Preface   vii

Introduction: Women, Their Roots   1

PART I WOMEN AND GOD'S INTENTIONS   5

Chapter One God's Intentions in Creation   7
Chapter Two God's Intentions After Sin   18
Chapter Three God's Intentions and Culture   28

PART II WOMEN AS IMPORTANT INDIVIDUALS .   43

Chapter Four Women as Important Individuals: .   48
In the Old Testament
Chapter Five Women as Important Individuals: .   80
In the New Testament

PART III WOMEN AS WIVES AND MOTHERS   145

Chapter Six Women As Wives   151
Chapter Seven Women As Mothers   211

PART IV WOMEN AS LEADERS IN THE
CHURCH AND COMMUNITY 259

Chapter Eight Women As Leaders   262

PART V WOMEN, THEIR INNER SELVES   283

Chapter Nine The Characters of God's Women . .   285
Chapter Ten Becoming God's Women   348

Bibliography   373

Topical Index   375

Index of Bible Women   395

Index of Scriptures   397

Preface

You, the reader, need to know from the outset where I, the author, "am coming from." You need to know my prejudices, my philosophy, and my faith in order to understand how I interpret what the Bible says about women.

First of all, I firmly believe that the entire Bible is the inspired Word of God and that there is no statement within it that contradicts any other statement or principle within it. The Bible says a great deal about women—about their natures, their roles, their relationships, their characters—but much that is said is thought by many scholars and writers to be contradictory. Some say that Paul was a male-chauvinist whose thoughts about women were diametrically opposed to Jesus' thoughts. Others say that the women of the Old Testament times were supposed to be "stepped on" by men because they were under the Law and because of Eve's sin, but that women in the New Testament were freed from male-domination as well as from the Law. I do not agree with these conclusions, for I believe that the Bible is consistent throughout.

Secondly, I believe the intentions of God at the time of creation (explained in Chapter One) remain true and constant throughout all of God's Word. His intentions, however, were perverted by sinful men (meaning mankind as a whole); and as a result, women have not been treated well. They have been victims of a sin-oriented society; but God did not intend it to be so. God does not consider women to be inferior, stupid, liars, or manipulators—but much of society does.

Thirdly, I believe that to relieve the confusion in our society about women, we need to return to the basic foundational principles made clear in the Bible. I will point out these principles time and time again and seek to relate them to our lives today.

Fourthly, I want you to know that I am a woman, a wife, and a mother of four children. I will not try to "snow" you by saying that this study is totally objective. It cannot be, for I have certain presuppositions (stated in the foregoing paragraphs) and I view life from the standpoint of a Christian woman. However, I have tried to let the Scriptures speak to me rather than letting my culture determine what the Scriptures say.

I am interested in drawing out the truth rather than pouring into the Bible what *I* think; therefore, I have researched words in key verses as to their meaning in the original language; I have considered the context of the passages; I have studied the culture of the people at the time the Scripture was written; I have read multitudes of books and periodicals with varying views on women in our world today; and I have consulted with my husband who is a true Bible scholar.

Now that you know me better, I hope you have as enlightening an experience reading the book as I did writing it.

Julia Staton

Introduction

WOMEN, THEIR ROOTS

Finding one's roots is a fad these days, part of the nostalgia craze. Such a fad is yet another expression of what people in every generation want to know — Who am I? Why am I here? Where am I going? We can come to understand who we are by taking a glimpse at the lives of those who lived before us, especially those linked to us by heredity. We can come to understand our purpose and function in life and can better influence our future if we know and understand those who went before us. If we know about our ancestors, we feel more secure about our place in time; we feel we are worthy and are meant to be where we are. Many of our fears about the future are calmed by a knowledge of our heritage. Looking for our roots is a "looking back," a becoming aware of all the forces that make us who we are.

As never before, women in our nation need this "looking back" to come to grips with what is going on in our society. Women are now in the spotlight after being in the background for so long. Their natures, their roles in society, their abilities, their self-worth — everything about them is being discussed and debated. Some women are demanding what they feel they have been denied, while others are doubting and wondering about their true worth and what they should be doing with their lives. Changes in the status and expectations of women are causing many of them to be afraid or to feel pressured to make some kind of change. Many women are retreating further inward, fearing they will be suddenly thrust out of their familiar cocoon of home and family.

Women are asking questions:

"Am I a worthy person in my own right or just in so far as I'm connected with others?"

1

"Am I equal to man in all ways, in some ways, or in no way?"

"Am I superior to man, or am I inferior to him?"

"Am I to allow a man to treat me as a sexual object?"

"Am I to have a career, or should I stay home to serve my husband and children?"

"Should I try to be a homemaker, a wife, and also a career-person?"

"Is having a career the only way I will be completely fulfilled?"

"Should I demand my individual rights?"

"Does God consider me equal to man?"

"What does God wish for me to do with my life?"

"What should be my relationship to God, my husband, to other women, to children, to the community, to the job, to the church?"

"Is a woman always to be the servant, or can she exercise authority and be a leader?"

"Is there any meaningful work that a woman can do in the church?"

Women need the answers to these questions. They are upset, worried, and afraid as well as excited by all the changes and emphases in our world today. To help clear away the confusion, to help establish a secure base upon which a woman can stand assured, to help encourage a sense of worth and value, to discover what God's intentions and wishes are for a woman, and to furnish some clues as to a woman's relationships and roles now and in the future — it is quite appropriate and necessary to trace woman's roots, her ancestry, her heritage.

2

Many answers to these questions are floating around us today, but we want to approach the matter from a Christian perspective and seek to know God's will. Therefore, we will search for woman's roots in the greatest book of all—the Bible, the history of God, man, and woman from God's perspective—and we will seek to apply the principles and truths found therein in order to answer women's questions.

Part I

WOMEN AND GOD'S INTENTIONS

To trace the heritage of women accurately, we must start at the very beginning with God, the creation event, and God's intentions for His creation. We could liken our study to the construction of a building—we begin with the foundation and then build and expand upon it until the structure is completed and comfortable. Part I of this book lays the foundational principles and truths for the study of women's history. Then as the heritage of womankind unfolds through the study of the entirety of God's Word (which is considered in the remainder of this book), those principles and truths are organized, expanded upon, and bolted together with applications for a woman's life in our present time. The result is a stable, secure, comfortable structure in which a woman today can understand herself, her surroundings, and God's desires for her.

Chapter One

GOD'S INTENTIONS IN CREATION

Out of nothing that existed before, God made the heavens and the earth. Out of the void, the emptiness, and the darkness, God made a beautiful world filled with life-giving and life-sustaining elements. Then God created man and woman to live in that world; they were the highpoints of His creation.

Woman's Nature

God created the man (male person) first. Then He created the woman (female person), forming her from the rib of man. They were two distinct individuals with different physical anatomies. They were both created in the image or likeness of God: "And God created man in His own image, in the image of God He created him; male and female He created them" (Genesis 1:27). The Hebrew word translated as "man" and referred to by the pronoun "him" in the first two phrases of the verse means "mankind" or "human being," a very general term; then in the last part of the verse the term is made more specific, "male and female." It would be the same as saying, "man plus woman equals mankind; and they were copies of God in their spiritual natures."

No animal was found to be a suitable companion for the man, showing the superiority of both man and woman over the animals: "And the man gave names to all the cattle, and to the birds of the sky, and to every beast of the field, but for Adam there was not found a helper suitable for him" (Genesis 2:20). In the act of creation, man and woman were equal in nature, essence, and worth. They were physically different in order to complement each other sexually and fulfill their responsibilities. God was very pleased with His

7

creation, declaring it all very good: "And God saw all that He had made, and behold, it was very good" (Genesis 1:31). Woman was in no way imperfect or inferior as some contend, since God was delighted in His creation; He would not have been so pleased with a botched creation.

Woman's Responsibilities

God gave the man and woman certain responsibilities. They were to be "fruitful and multiply"—to have many offspring, to fill the earth with people, to complete God's creation (Genesis 1:28). The function of peopling the earth was a vitally important one, and God made the man and woman in such a way that they could only perform it *together.* Man and woman would have to be dependent upon each other to fulfill this responsibility—this is the way God designed them. God never intended for the man or woman to go off by themselves and do "their own thing." From the very beginning He expected them to be together and need one another.

Man and woman were also to "subdue" the earth, which means they were to control, to rule, to have dominion over the rest of God's creation (Genesis 1:28). They were to work in and watch over the Garden of Eden: "Then the Lord God took the man [mankind] and put him into the Garden of Eden to cultivate it and keep it" (Genesis 2:15). Theirs was not a life of perpetual leisure, but one of fulfilling labor. God wanted His creation to be beneficial to man and woman, to sustain their lives and their offspring. He wanted them to work together to keep it beautiful and functioning. He did not want the world to become unruly or "go to seed."

Woman was given an additional responsibility. God saw that it was not good for Adam to be alone (Genesis 2:18).

8

The Hebrew meaning for the word "alone" is a sense of helplessness and restlessness. Thus, God made Eve to be a helper "suitable" or "fit for" Adam (Hebrew meaning: corresponding to). The woman was adequate to meet the man's needs as well as being equal to the man so as to be his friend and companion. Spiritually, the woman corresponded to Adam's nature; physically, she was made to fit "what was before him" (Hebrew translation). She was made to be his supplement (his partner), and she was made to house and bear the children that would result from that partnership.

Woman's Relationships

To Man. Adam was extremely delighted with his counterpart: "And the man said, 'This is now bone of my bones, and flesh of my flesh; she shall be called woman, because she was taken out of man'" (Genesis 2:23). The English translation loses the excited and happy tone of Adam's speech which is inherent in the Hebrew. Adam was really saying, "Whoopee!!" The first man-woman relationship began on an extremely amiable note. They were partners, reaching out to one another, yearning for one another. Soon the first marriage was consummated: "For this cause a man shall leave his father and his mother, and shall cleave to his wife; and they shall become one flesh" (Genesis 2:24).

Their relationship superseded the relationship of parents and children as denoted by the word "leave." This word means "cutting the ties" between parent and child. Not that the child no longer respects or values his parents or no longer spends time with them, but it does mean that the child leaves the dependent relationship to form a new interdependent relationship with his (or her) mate. The man and woman leave their families to begin a family of their own. Of course,

9

Adam and Eve had no parents, but the insertion of this verse by Moses is to show God's intention for marriage.

The man and woman were to "cleave" to one another. This descriptive word means "cling," "stick together," "glued together," or even more accurately — "cemented together." It is such a close relationship that no one is to try to pry them apart (Matthew 19:6). It is a total commitment, including loyalty and affection. It is a binding relationship that is not to be terminated.

In the cleaving, they became "one flesh." Obviously, this does not mean that two physical bodies became one physical body. It means that the two people became related, that they owned each other's bodies (I Corinthians 7:4), and it denoted sexual intercourse. It emphasized the close partnership of the marriage — two people with the same goals, with a unity of purpose, so closely aligned that they seem as one. The sexual act intensified and fulfilled the close relationship.

Of course, "one flesh" was not referring to casual sex or a "one night stand." These latter situations are certainly not preceded by leaving and cleaving! Neither does becoming "one flesh" mean that the identities of two persons merge so that the woman takes on the man's identity and loses what is uniquely hers. Both the husband and wife are individuals; they are both of worth and value. They are both seeking to meet the other's needs, to fulfill one another. They are both giving of themselves — physically, spiritually, and emotionally — in total commitment. They become a unit ("He created them male and female, and He blessed them and named them Adam [lit.] . . ." Genesis 5:2), working together, depending on each other, needing each other.

Some conclude that since Eve was made *for* Adam and was made secondly that woman is inferior to man. There is no indication that Eve was inferior to Adam; the *order* of creation has no bearing on intrinsic worth. If it does, then the animals who were created before Adam would be superior to him. According to the creation narrative, the woman was an individual made in God's image just as Adam was. She was given the same responsibilities and was a personality equal to him.

In woman's additional function of being a helper for the man, being his companion, and being his counterpart sexually, the woman was the completion of the man. Without her, God realized man was incomplete (Genesis 2:18). The woman was not of less worth than the man but was correspondent to his needs. Adam could not perform his God-ordained functions without her. The man was dependent on the woman, and the woman was dependent on the man. This interdependence was not a sign of one person being inferior while another is superior. It was the outcome of two equal persons bound together in a sharing, caring relationship.

We cannot ignore Paul's insight into God's intentions in creation:

> For man does not originate from woman, but woman from man; for indeed man was not created for the woman's sake, but woman for the man's sake. Therefore the woman ought to have a symbol of authority on her head, because of the angels. However, in the Lord, neither is woman independent of man, nor is man independent of woman. For as the woman originates from the man; so also the man has his birth through the woman; and all things originate from God (I Corinthians 11:8-12).

Paul pointed out that woman was made for man's sake (benefit), not vice versa; therefore, the man should have authority over the woman (which in this context meant the wife would show her submission to her husband by covering her head in the worship service, which was the custom of the time).

The translation of the Greek word for "authority" (or power, *exousia*) in verse 10 is very important when considering the relationship between husband and wife. This is not the word that denotes "might," "strength," "rule," "dominion," or even the "ability to exert strength." It means "the privilege of being in a leadership role." Thus, the husband does not have the authority or leadership over the wife because he is stronger, more intelligent, or superior to her; but simply because God gave him the special privilege to be the leader in the marriage relationship. In this way the partnership would run smoothly and in an organized way. The marriage was not to be a dictator-servant relationship. Neither was it to be a relationship of two leaders or two authority-figures. Such a relationship would only result in a power struggle or each person going his or her separate ways. Such a relationship would certainly not be the harmonious, sharing relationship that God intended for marriage to be.

Paul also pointed out that the husband and wife are to be dependent on one another; they are not to be independent of each other. He made it clear that the husband and wife need each other to fulfill God's intentions in creation. The Hebrew and Greek words for "man" (when being distinguished from the female) and "woman" are the same words that are used to denote "husband" and "wife." Thus the context of the passage of Scripture determines the meaning of the words. Ephesians 5:22 ("Wives, be subject to your own husbands, as to the Lord"), I Timothy 2:12 ("But I do not allow a woman to teach or exercise authority over a man, but to remain quiet"), the creation passage, and the passage in I Corinthians 11 which we just considered are all talking about husband and wife relationships. Thus we cannot conclude from these passages that *all* women are to be in subjection to *all* men, except in the sense that all Christians are to be subject to other Christians. We *can* conclude that wives are not to accept the leadership role that God intends for husbands to have.

To God. God gave the Garden of Eden to Adam and Eve, providing them with all the necessities to sustain life (Genesis 2:16; 3:2). They had fellowship with each other and evidently talked with God often as He walked in the Garden (Genesis 3:8). God sought their companionship and love. He could have insisted that they love Him, but that would not result in the spontaneous and free expression of their feelings that He desired. He wanted them to *want* to love Him, to freely choose to love Him. He wanted them to know that they could freely choose to escape His presence and fellowship. They were not prisoners in the Garden; neither were they God's robots or slaves.

God designed only one way to test their true feelings toward Him. They could freely choose to obey His rule or disobey it. They were not to eat (or touch) the tree of the knowledge of good and evil. If they obeyed the rule, they would be showing their trust in and love for God; and they could enjoy the resultant blessings. If they disobeyed, showing their distrust and disregard for God's will, the consequences would not be pleasant: the Spirit within them (God's own Spirit) would die, for they would be cast out of God's presence (Genesis 2:16, 17).

Both Adam and Eve knew of the choice they had, as is shown by Eve's response to the serpent:

13

And the woman said to the serpent, "From the fruit of the trees of the garden we may eat; but from the fruit of the tree which is in the middle of the garden, God has said, 'You shall not eat from it or touch it, lest you die'" (Genesis 3:2, 3).

If Eve were of inferior intelligence, as some contend, then would God have entrusted such a decision to her? If Eve had fewer mental capacities than Adam, wouldn't God have given her a second chance by explaining the rule to her again? If Eve was inferior to Adam, the fact that she convinced him to eat of the fruit does not say much for Adam's moral strength or mental capacities. How could a man of superior abilities and reasoning powers decide to follow Eve's example?

It is clear that Adam and Eve were both intelligent and able to make decisions. They both had equal opportunity and equal responsibility to make the right decision. Eve listened to the pretty words and promises of Satan. She used the senses God had given her, sized up the tree, and saw that the fruit was quite desirable. She thought that God might be deceiving them, seeking to keep them under His control. The idea of being like God and being able to understand all things (Genesis 3:6 — "make one wise") was quite attractive to her. She decided to trust Satan rather than keep her trust in God. Without consulting her partner to whom she had been given and for whom she had been created, she took the initiative and disobeyed God. She acted independently of her mate which was not within God's intentions for marriage.

Paul, when writing to Timothy, discussed why a husband should be the leader in the home by referring back to Adam and Eve's relationship and how Eve disturbed that relationship: "For it was Adam who was first created, and then Eve.

14

And it was not Adam who was deceived, but the woman being quite deceived, fell into transgression" (I Timothy 2:13, 14).

Paul made clear in I Corinthians 11:8-12 that the husband and wife were not to act or be independent of each other and that God gave the husband the privilege of having authority or leadership over the wife because the wife was created for the man's sake. God created an orderly universe out of chaos, thus it is reasonable that He meant for the first human relationship to be orderly and organized — meaning that the man was to be the leader in the marriage relationship. When Eve thwarted that leadership, an imbalance in the universe and in the marriage relationship resulted.

Even though Eve did not consult her husband before acting, she still loved him and felt close to him; for she wanted him to join her in her action (Genesis 3:6). She exerted her influence over him and convinced him to eat of the fruit. We do not know how she persuaded him; neither do we know whether or not he argued very long about it. Thus we cannot assume that she used her sexuality or feminine wiles rather than logical reasoning to convince him; neither can we assume that he did whatever she wished because he was blindly in love with her. Neither can we say that Eve was a weak and inherently evil person. If so, what would we say about Adam's strength and evilness? We can only guess what the result would have been if the serpent had approached Adam instead of Eve. Adam and Eve were simply persons who had a choice to make and made the wrong one. Eve was wrong in acting independently of her husband (I Timothy 2:11-14), and Adam was wrong in giving in to her wishes instead of trusting in God's words (Romans 5:12-21).

15

The fact that Adam listened to Eve points up again that their relationship was not that of a dictator and servant. If it had been, he would not have even listened to what she had to say. God did not punish Adam for *listening* to her, but for *hearkening* (meaning "acting" upon her words, Genesis 3:17) to her.

Both Adam and Eve were responsible to God for the decisions they made. God had hoped and intended that they would both choose to obey Him. In conclusion, we can ascertain that Eve had a one-to-one relationship with God, and she knew what He expected of her; yet she chose of her own free will to disobey Him.

Summary

God's intentions for women are made clear in the opening chapters of Genesis. So that there will be no question or confusion about God's intentions, they are summarized as follows:

1. God made woman to be a unique individual, made in God's image, and equal to man.
2. God made woman with the capacity to bear children, to meet her husband's many needs, and to make individual intellectual decisions.
3. God made man and woman to need each other and expects them to be interdependent.
4. God intends for man and woman to live together in a committed partnership called marriage. The man was given the privilege of leadership in that relationship, and the woman is to submit to that leadership and respect him.
5. God intends for woman to be obedient to Him and not follow her own selfish desires.

16

DISCUSSION QUESTIONS:

1. What Scriptural evidence do we have in the creation passages that women are equal in nature and worth to men?
2. Why did God make men and women different physically?
3. What responsibilities have men and women shared from the time of creation?
4. What additional responsibility were women given?
5. At the time of creation, how would God describe His intentions for the marriage relationship?
6. What is the husband's leadership role in a marriage and why did God give it to him?
7. What conclusions about women can be drawn from Genesis 3:1-6?
8. State reasons why being made second does not make Eve inferior to Adam.

Chapter Two

GOD'S INTENTIONS AFTER SIN

Adam and Eve yielded to their selfish desires and failed to trust in God; thus sin entered into God's beautiful creation, and the bitter consequences of sin were made a reality. Yet God's love for the man and woman and His intentions for them did not change.

Adam and Eve soon realized what they had done and were ashamed and afraid. They had lost their innocence and their pure spirits; they tried to cover their now-apparent nakedness (Genesis 3:7). When God came to fellowship with them in the Garden, they hid (3:8). When God confronted them with their sins, Adam blamed Eve and God who had made her, and Eve blamed the serpent (3:12, 13). Then God told them (the serpent, Adam, and Eve) individually the results of their disobedience.

The Consequences of Sin

The Punishment for Eve. Eve was punished individually for her sin, but the results extend to all women: "I will greatly multiply your pain in childbirth, in pain you shall bring forth children" (Genesis 3:16a). God created the woman's body to house and nurture children; but after Eve sinned, the privilege and responsibility were complicated and made more difficult by additional pain. This pain refers not only to the pangs of the labor pains at the time of birth, but also to all the physical and emotional difficulties that accompany the child-bearing function (menstruation, irritability, etc.). I feel this was the totality of the woman's *specific* punishment.

The rest of verse 16 ("*Yet* your desire shall be for your husband, *and* he shall rule over you") was given by God not as a punishment but as a protection for the woman, for the family, and for the future of the human race. I base this conclusion on the study of the words in the Hebrew text, the context of the verse, and upon the totality of God's revealed Word.

The small Hebrew connecting word that precedes the two phrases is translated "and" in the King James Version. It is such a small word, but it can have many different meanings. It can mean "in addition to" or "at the same time" (would have the same meaning as *also*), or "in contrast with" (would have same meaning as *or*), or it can connect contrasted ideas (would have same meaning as *but, yet,* or *although*). Some translators and scholars feel the word in Genesis 3:16 means "also" or "in addition to," concluding that sexual desire for the husband and the husband's rule over the wife are part of Eve's punishment. Others feel that only the husband being named ruler over her is Eve's curse, while the first phrase means she will have desire for her husband "in spite of" the resulting pain. Neither of these conclusions make sense to me as I study the whole of God's revelation.

I believe the word should be translated "yet" (or "although") as it is in the Revised Standard Version, the New American Standard Bible, and in the Jerusalem Bible. I believe the two phrases at the end of verse 16 are being contrasted with the punishment described in the first part of the verse (pain in childbearing).

It is not logical to think that sex was only instituted after the sin and was to be a curse to Eve. God created woman to be a helper *fit for* the man, which referred to how she was physically made to satisfy man's sexual needs. The woman's body was made for the purpose of having sex and bearing children. Surely God would not tell them to be "fruitful and multiply" (Genesis 1:28), and then not expect them to have sex!

Some say that Genesis 4:1 shows that sex came about after sin entered the picture: "*Now* the man had relations with his wife Eve, and she conceived and gave birth to Cain . . . ." "Now" is translated "and" in the King James Version and is that same small connecting word as is in 3:16. This verse is simply stating that in this act of sex a child was conceived (meaning that the sexual relations before sin did not result in pregnancy).

I feel that sex was God's intention from the very beginning and was not to be thought of as a curse to anyone. In Matthew 19:4, 5 Jesus made clear that God's intention in creating male and female was for the marriage relationship and that that relationship included sex (became "one flesh"):

> And He answered and said, "Have you not read, that He who created them from the beginning made them male and female, and said, 'For this cause a man shall leave his father and mother, and shall cleave to his wife; and the two shall become one flesh'?"

Sex was God's means for cementing the marriage relationship and for the continuance of humanity upon the earth. He did not think it up as a means for punishing sin; sex was one of God's intentions for man and woman from the very beginning.

If God had increased the pain of child-bearing to such a great intensity that Eve would no longer wish to remain in the marriage relationship and would not wish to continue in sexual relations, then the human race would have been annihilated. Instead, God limited the pain while increasing it. He was telling Eve in Genesis 3:16 that *although* she would have pain, the pain would not be so intense that she would no longer have any sexual desire for Adam. God was protecting His created design that a man and woman would get married, have sex and children, and thus people the earth. Genesis 4:1 shows that this conclusion is valid, for we read that Adam and Eve had sexual relations. The pain was limited so Eve still had desire for her husband and remained in the marriage relationship.

The Husband's Leadership. God was also protecting the woman, the marriage relationship and the family structure by stating that the husband was to continue to be the head or leader in the relationship ("rule over you") as he was meant to be from the beginning (as we discussed in Chapter One). If the pain of the punishment would be so great that Eve would not submit to Adam's leadership, then there would be anarchy within the family structure. God desired order and decency when He created the universe; I hardly think that He would desire that order be absent in the family. Giving Adam (and thus all husbands) the privilege of leadership in the marriage was God's way of maintaining order, *not* a way of punishing Eve (and thus all wives).

Now we must consider in depth the meaning of the word "rule" and seek to discover what type of leadership God intended for the husband to exercise. The Hebrew word translated as "rule" in Genesis 3:16b is also used when the Scriptures speak of a ruler of a nation, how God rules over the earth and His people, prophecies concerning Christ being a ruler, and even how a person rules over his own spirit. Hebrew synonyms for the word are "have dominion" and "subdue" as in Genesis 1:28 when Adam and Eve were told to *control* God's creation. Synonyms for "ruler" are "guide" and "overseer" (KJV), "chief" and "officer" (NASB) as in Proverbs 6:7.

The Greek use of the term in the New Testament is consistent with the Hebrew usage but also adds: Christ's relationship with His followers ("Lord," "Master," "Teacher," "head"), and the relationship of the elders ("overseers") to the church. I conclude that God expects the husband to exercise authority over his wife in the same way a ruler has dominion over a nation (a good ruler, that is), in the same way God and Christ rule over the church, in the same way the elders lead the church, and even in the same way each person is expected to rule over or control himself.

But how specifically does God expect the husband to rule? What kind of leader does God wish him to be? God spoke directly to the issue in II Samuel 23:3 when He said a ruler must be just and fear God. God made it clear that He was to be the ruler's guide; God was to have the final word. In Proverbs a good ruler is said to be diligent (12:24) and righteous (29:2). A wicked ruler was compared to a "roaring lion" and "a rushing bear" (28:15). I wonder how many husbands could be described in the same way by their wives?

In the New Testament, Jesus contrasted the way the rulers of the world acted with the way His followers were to act:

> You know that the rulers of the Gentiles lord it over them, and their great men exercise authority over them. It is not so among you, but whoever wishes to become great among you shall be your servant, and whoever wishes to be first among you shall be your slave (Matthew 20:25-27).

Jesus was saying the rulers of the world do not follow God's way, do not act justly, and treat others as slaves; but that Christians who rule over others are to be different — they are to be ministering to others' needs; they are to be serving those whom they rule over. Then He cited Himself as the example of this type of leadership: "Just as the Son of Man did not come to be served, but to serve, and to give His life a ransom for many" (Matthew 20:28).

22

Again in John 13, Jesus demonstrated this principle in His relationship with His disciples when He washed their feet. Foot-washing was a common practice and a needed one, for the people of that day and in that land walked over dusty roads in sandals. But it was usually such a menial task that each person washed his own feet. Sometimes servants in a household would do it for the guest or the master, but a servant could refuse to do the lowly job and be within his rights. Yet Jesus, the Lord and Teacher, washed His followers' feet and commanded them to minister to others' needs with the same humble attitude (John 13:13-15).

Paul expressed the same principle in Ephesians 5 when he compared Christ's leadership over the church with the husband's leadership over the wife: "For the husband is the head of the wife, as Christ also is head of the church, He Himself being the Savior of the body" (v. 23). Headship certainly denotes leadership, but we cannot stop there. We must continue reading and discover that this type of headship consists of unselfish loving and giving:

> Husbands, love your wives, just as Christ also loved the church and gave Himself up for her, that He might sanctify her, having cleansed her by the washing of water with the word . . . so husbands ought also to love their wives as their own bodies. He who loves his own wife loves himself; for no one ever hated his own flesh, but nourishes and cherishes it, just as Christ also does the church . . . let each individual among you also love his own wife even as himself (Ephesians 5:25-33).

Thus, we can conclude that the husband is to "rule" over his wife but in a loving and giving way, meeting his wife's needs, and nourishing and cherishing her. The wife, in turn, is to be subject to her husband's leadership ("Wives, be

23

subject to your own husbands, as to the Lord" v. 22) and respect or reverence him ("And let the wife see to it that she respect her husband" v. 33). Paul's use of the word "authority" in I Corinthians 11:10 (discussed on pp. 11-13 in chapter one) as meaning the "privilege" of leadership rather than a harsh rule over the wife coincides with his teaching in Ephesians 5.

Paul emphasized the same thoughts when he described the character of a good leader in his instructions to Timothy about choosing elders to guide the church in I Timothy 3:1-7. He used the term "overseer" and attributed many of the same qualities to the leader as God did in the Old Testament and as Jesus did in His teaching. The qualities could be summarized as follows: righteous, temperate, prudent, gentle, uncontentious, and a good manager. Peter also expressed the same thoughts when admonishing the leaders of the church: "not lording it over those allotted to your charge, but proving to be examples to the flock" (I Peter 5:3).

God's intentions for a husband's leadership in marriage have remained consistent throughout the Bible. As is clear in Genesis 3:16, God intended for the man to rule over his wife; but not in a harsh, dictatorial way or as a master over a slave and not as a punishment for sin. No, the man's leadership in the home is for the woman's protection as well as the family's protection.

There is no doubt that God desires the husband to be the leader in the home; but in that leadership role, the husband is to be a guide and protector. He is to care for his wife and minister to her needs. He is to give of himself to her and love her unselfishly. He is to be obedient to God and have himself under control. He is to be a good example of Christian character. Only a wicked leader steps on others, considers others second-rate, rules unjustly and harshly, treats others as slaves or property, and neglects another's needs.

It is also clear that God intended for Eve to be in submission to her husband's leadership and that it was God's intention from the very beginning. She was to live within the framework of her husband's guidance and leadership. This does not mean she was in any way inferior to Adam, but that she was to do her part to maintain a harmonious marriage by not living independently of his guidance.

Shared Consequences. Adam was also individually responsible for his disobedience, and the results of his sin extend to all mankind. God cursed the ground so that useless weeds would hamper the growth of helpful plants. Then Adam would have to spend his days in hard toil just to provide enough food for his family. No longer would he be able to pick food off the trees; his environment would suddenly be hostile and difficult (Genesis 3:17-19).

Adam and Eve were both cast out of the Garden of Eden, after God in His loving mercy made clothes for them (Genesis 3:20-24). They were still together and were to continue their marriage relationship, but now they would face many problems and sorrows because all of nature was thrown out of balance by their sin. God's perfect creation was no longer perfect; it was tainted by sin. They would have to struggle to survive in foreign and antagonistic surroundings. They would no longer be able to enjoy the beauty, comfort, and the security of the Garden and God's presence (Genesis 3:24). They would be without God's intimate fellowship.

Yet all hope was not lost. God had devised a plan whereby they could (through their descendants) return to the Garden and have God's Spirit residing within them. He promised them that through the woman's seed someone

25

would be born who would crush Satan's power. Through Eve, a Savior would be born: "And I will put enmity between you and the woman, and between your seed and her seed; He shall bruise you on the head, and you shall bruise him on the heel" (Genesis 3:15, speaking to Satan).

Summary

Adam and Eve's sins and the consequences for those sins did not nullify their intrinsic worth, their individual equality, their roles in life, or the partnership of their marriage. They were still likenesses of God; Eve was still to be a wife and mother; Adam and Eve were still to subdue the earth; they were still expected to people the earth; they were still to act as a unit in the marriage relationship. Even though thrust into a cruel, dark, and lonely environment, Adam and Eve had each other and God's guidance. They continued to depend on each other and to reach out to each other in love. They had children and continued in their marriage relationship. They were still responsible to God and communicated with Him as is evidenced by Eve's comment in Genesis 4:1 that God had helped her when their first child was born and by God's subsequent conversations with Cain and Abel in that same chapter. They were still expected to obey God's leading, but they still retained their freedom of choice and did not always choose to follow God.

And so it is with all of us. We have been created in God's image; within our physical bodies there is a spiritual nature. We also have minds and the freedom to make decisions as we choose. Because God is our Creator, we are to be responsible to Him. He desires that we obey Him and enjoy the resultant blessings. But we all decide at one time or another to go our own way and turn our backs on God. We decide to depend on ourselves instead of God, or we decide to trust the world instead of His Word. Adam and Eve started these tendencies, and we continue in them.

Because of the universality of sin and because of the results of the sinning, our reality is tainted, marred, and imperfect. God's intentions are often not carried out in our daily lives, and thus our lives are not as ideal and complete as He desires for us. This does not mean that His intentions are wrong for us or impossible for us to live out. God's intentions for us *all* are good, right, and will lead to fulfilled lives, for God wants only what is best for us. To prove it, He sent us His own Son to take away the sin and sent His own Spirit to reside within us. Because of Christ we have the hope that the life God intended for us can be achieved.

Yet the difficulties of an imperfect world, evil societies, and sin-tainted cultures loom ahead of us and affect women adversely. Next we will consider the influences of culture, and how the living out of God's intentions has been made more difficult.

DISCUSSION QUESTIONS:

1. What was the totality of Eve's punishment for sin?
2. Why should sexual relations not be considered a punishment?
3. What type of leadership function and attitudes did God intend for the husband to exercise?
4. What is to be the wife's response to a husband's loving leadership?
5. List all the consequences of Adam and Eve's sin.
6. How does sin affect our world today in these areas:
   a. nature
   b. relationship to God
   c. relationships between men and women
   d. woman's feeling of worth

27

Chapter Three

GOD'S INTENTIONS AND CULTURE

Societies and cultures change; and as they change, so do the thoughts and feelings of the people within that society or culture. What we think, what we do, and what we feel are greatly influenced by the basic philosophies of the culture within which we live. We are also influenced by what we were taught as children — the values, the philosophies, and the prejudices of our parents which were formulated in a large part by the society in which they were living as well as by what their parents taught them. And so the cycle continues, generation after generation.

It is logical to assume then that our understanding of God's will is influenced by our culture, just as the thoughts and actions of the people of Bible times were influenced by their culture. Therefore, it is very important that before we study in detail the lives of the women of the Bible, we must understand the culture and society in which they lived.

At the same time, we must realize that all the customs and practices of their culture were not from the mind of God. They were shaped in a world filled with evil and formed in the minds of men who were stained with sin. We know this is true because Jesus Christ, the very incarnation of God, showed us by His life and words in the New Testament what God's thoughts, intentions, and wishes were. Many of them were diametrically opposed to the customs and traditions of the time (Mark 7:6-8). His own family did not understand; His disciples were puzzled many times by His strange words and actions. In fact, it was because of Jesus' opposition to the customs and traditions of the time that He was crucified. He threatened the very culture and society of the time by seeking to break down the barriers that men had erected through hundreds of years.

28

Discovering God's Intentions

Because of the effect of culture, we can only be certain about God's intentions or His will for us through His direct communications to people, through Jesus' example and words, and through the inspired writers' interpretations of Jesus' words and example — all of which are contained in the Bible. Just because a great man or woman (such as Abraham, Sarah, or David) thought or did something does not mean they were doing what God intended, for they were affected by sin.

We might ask, "If all the gruesome, cruel, violent, and sinful things that are recorded in the Bible were not God's intentions, then why did God have men record them?" We can find the answer in I Corinthians 10:1-11:

> For I do not want you to be unaware, brethren, that our fathers were all under the cloud, and all passed through the sea; and all were baptized into Moses in the cloud in the sea; and all ate the same spiritual food; and all drank the same spiritual drink, for they were drinking from a spiritual rock which followed them; and the rock was Christ. Nevertheless, with most of them God was not pleased; for they were laid low in the wilderness. Now these things happened as examples for us, that we should not crave evil things, as they also craved. And do not be idolaters, as some of them were; as it is written, "the people sat down to eat and drink, and stood up to play." Nor let us act immorally, as some of them did, and twenty-three thousand fell in one day. Nor let us try the Lord, as some of them did, and were destroyed by the serpents. Nor grumble, as some of them did, and were destroyed by the destroyer. Now these things happened to them as an example, and they were written for our instruction, upon whom the ends of the ages have come.

These happenings were recorded to be examples for us to teach us the folly and destructiveness of sin. We can see with our own eyes through the lives of these people who lived long ago what sorrow and pain accompany actions resulting from pride and selfishness. We can see that even though many of these people lived close to God, talked to Him directly, and witnessed many signs and wonders, they still made mistakes and suffered from them. Neither the mistakes nor the suffering were God's will or intention for them; instead He worked out His purpose and plan *in spite of them.* God allowed human practices that were against His will to show their folly. For after all, people have never been God's robots or puppets.

A major portion of the Bible is the recording of history — a recording of human culture, societies, ideas, and events — as well as clear, direct statements from God as to what He wished. We must be careful as we study God's Word to always distinguish between God's revealed will and the customs of the time.

A Man's World

The culture or society surrounding the women of Bible times was definitely man-dominated; as is evident when the literature of the historians, ancient manuscripts, and the text of the Bible itself are studied.

Jewish Culture. [1] The husbands (fathers) were the leaders in the family structure. The inheritance (family reputation, name, and possessions) was passed on through the males in the family; the genealogies in the Bible from Genesis 5 on were mainly recorded by the listing of the male family members (although women were included in Jesus' genealogy

---

1. The major source concerning Jewish culture is Josephus in his *Antiquities.* Another helpful source is *Jerusalem in the Time of Jesus* by Joachim Jeremias (Philadelphia: Fortress Press, 1969).

in Matthew 1). This male leadership in the family was consistent with God's wish for order in the home and with God's original intention concerning the marriage relationship.

Yet because of sin, God's intentions were distorted and perverted. Men went to extremes in their leadership roles. Some of them became domineering brutes who treated women as slaves rather than as persons who were their partners and equal to them in worth and dignity. God intended for a man to have only one wife, but many men had as many wives and concubines as they could support. Even some of the greatest leaders in the nation of Israel failed to obey God's intentions for marriage (Jacob, David, Solomon, etc.).

According to the Bible and the Mishnah, women were often treated as men's property. Men used their wives to protect their own lives, as did Abraham and Isaac, when they told the kings that their wives were their sisters and let the foreign kings include them in their harems. This was not favored by God; in fact, He intervened to protect the women (Genesis 12:11-20; 20:1-3).

Forcible rape was condemned, but prostitutes were common. Pretty women were considered spoils of war, and the victors could "have their way" with them. A concubine was raped, killed, and then cut into pieces which shows the utter disregard by some men for the life of a woman (Judges 19, 20—please note that God did not command that this woman be treated in this way). She was a victim of the confusing and violent times during one period of Israel's history as were the four hundred virgins of Judges 21 who were captured at a feast to become some men's wives.

Fathers had supreme authority over their daughters. At times, fathers sold their daughters into slavery in order to pay off debts. At marriage the authority over the woman was given to the husband. The average Jewish girl was betrothed at 12 to 12-1/2 years of age to a man of her father's choosing. From the moment of her betrothal, the woman was as legally committed as if she were actually married. The betrothal could only be broken by a divorce.

The husband was to receive the wife's inheritance, and any money that she made would belong to him. In New Testament times, the wives were expected to wear veils (or wear their hair up in a knot or braids) in public to show they were under their husband's authority (I Corinthians 11:10). A woman was expected to be faithful to her husband and morally pure, but the husband was allowed to go to prostitutes and "play around" (Note: this was not God's wish or command, but an outcome of a sin-perverted culture). Adultery was considered to be a crime against the husband (committed by the wife), and a woman could not divorce her husband. In a few rare cases, a woman did demand that her husband divorce her, and it was allowed. If a husband got jealous, the wife would have to pass a test of faithfulness; but there was no such recourse for the wife.

According to one Jewish school of thought (Shammai), the only reason a man could divorce a woman would be adultery or unchastity. But the more popular thinking (Hillel) was that a man could divorce his wife for any cause and at any time that she displeased him. The most popular reasons were: transgressing a Jewish law or tradition, giving her husband untithed food, having marital relations while ritually unclean, failing to fulfill a vow, going into the street with her hair unbound, spinning in the street, talking with a man, raising her voice so the neighbors could hear, burning the food, or the husband found a woman that pleased him more.

The society did have high respect for motherhood and the role of the wife as homemaker. There was strong compassion for widows and orphans; yet women without men to protect them or provide for them materially were numbered among the poor and were often in dire straits. Women were most honored and respected in their position in the home, especially when they became mothers. Women with children were considered to be especially blessed by God. There was strong belief in family solidarity, and the woman's place was to support the man by being a keeper at home.

Women's daily routine of activities could be listed as follows: Looking after sheep (also a man's job) — Genesis 29:6; drawing water — Genesis 24:11, 15-20, I Samuel 9:11, John 4:7; churning butter and preparing meals — Genesis 18:6, II Samuel 13:8, John 12:2; grinding grain for flour — Deuteronomy 24:6, Job 41:24, Proverbs 31:15, Matthew 24:41, Judges 9:53; opening home to guests and the needy — Judges 4:18, I Samuel 25:18, II Kings 4:8-10; spinning wool and making clothes — Exodus 35:26, I Samuel 2:19, Proverbs 31:19, Acts 9:39; harvesting in the fields — Ruth 2:2; and, of course, the basic domestic chores of laundry, dishes, making beds, etc. A wife could have slaves (maidens) to help her; but she was to keep busy, for the rabbis taught that "idleness led to unchastity."

Some women were allowed to be shopkeepers in the market place, and many could move about in public, but all public activity was restricted. A woman was not to talk seriously or at length with a man (other than her husband) in public or privately.

In the religious realm, a woman could not be a priest. We are not certain why, but it is thought that her role as mother and homemaker would restrict her religious activity. Her uncleanness every month (menstruation — Leviticus 15:19-33) would also restrict the times she could serve.

A woman could offer no sacrifices and was only allowed in certain areas of the temple grounds. She could not enter the Holy Place, the Holy of Holies, or the court of men; and she could only use certain gates. Even the synagogues which were used later contained separate galleries, one for men and one for women. She could participate in some of the religious festivals but was not required to attend the Passover, Pentecost, or the Feast of the Tabernacles as the men were. Women were not to be instructed in the Law.

Many rabbis considered women to be wanton and wild; they thought every action and word of a woman was to manipulate man or was sexually motivated. Women were encouraged to stay inside most of the time and to go to the temple late in the day after the men had finished. Men thought women were liars; thus their testimony was not accepted in court.

There were some women who were strong and courageous, who stepped outside these restrictions, and rose above men's prejudices to become great leaders, blessed and guided by God — but they were the exceptions, not the "norm."

We must note that God did not place these domestic and religious restrictions on women. His intentions for women were that they would be good wives and mothers, but also that they be unique individuals able to think, able to be responsible, and able to respond to Him. He did not shut women out, as is proven by His encouragement of women leaders in the Old Testament, by Jesus' attitudes, actions, and teachings concerning women, and how women were looked upon in the early church. But in the society of the time, men who were stained by sin sought to restrict women's thoughts and activities.

Greek and Roman Influence. We need to consider the effect of Greek and Roman ideas concerning women because these ideas were part of the culture of the New Testament times.

The beautiful and wealthy women were admired; and respected, devoted mothers were well thought of; but most women were thought to be agents of evil. Women's activities outside the home had been quite restricted, but as time went on, they were allowed to express themselves through music, art, and literature. Women became enthralled by the performances at the theater and the games as they were allowed more and more freedom.

Religiously, there were goddesses as well as gods and priestesses as well as priests. There were some goddesses whom only women could worship. One religion was presided over by Vestal Virgins, who were young women who remained virgins for thirty years and devoted themselves to their religious festivals and the performance of their official duties. Many women were intrigued by the cults of the East which had sexual immorality as an integral part of their practices.

Some women were rulers of countries and some were leaders in battle, but these women were out of the ordinary. Most women exerted their main influence as wives and mothers. Women were recognized as being strong influences upon men and were even taught how to seduce men. Many wives traveled with their husbands and advised them about politics, governmental policies, and about the value of various literature. There is even some evidence that there were some "henpecked" husbands. Women became more and more bold and articulate and began speaking in public as well as at home. And as women began to hold property, they became even more powerful.

One Greek writer spoke of marriage as a partnership with the men and women having different roles. The husband was to work outdoors, provide for the family economically, and be the protector; while the wife was to work indoors, nurture the children, and learn from her husband. Women who drank, attended the theater or the games, who nagged or gossiped, or who treated their husband's friends harshly were said to be intolerable wives. Another writer said the women were expected to be morally pure, but the husbands could "play around" freely. He felt the women should be educated because of what they could do for the "state" (government), but they were definitely inferior intellectually.

Children were desired and were thought to make the home complete. Women who had no children were quite distressed, for the husbands could divorce them if the condition remained. However, the ability to adopt children alleviated the problem somewhat. Children were to be dependent on their parents and to be obedient to them; in most cases, their marriages were arranged by the parents; although, in some instances, the arrangements had to be changed because of "falling in love" complications.

There was much immorality and materialism in the Greek and Roman cultures. There was much pre-marital sex, many extra-marital affairs, and a great deal of emphasis on riches. Some women would go from man to man according to what material gifts he could bestow upon her. And riches gave women more luxuries and more leisure time, causing many of them to lead lives of immorality.[2]

---

2. These and additional details can be found in Chapters 2 and 3 of Frank and Evelyn Stagg's book, *Woman in the World of Jesus* (Philadelphia: Westminster Press, 1978).

While the Greeks and Romans retained a small vestige of the sanctity of marriage and the home, their society was perverted by sin to a great extent which in turn affected the way women were treated and looked upon. The writings of the New Testament point out the errors of the culture and make clear God's will for women who live in that time.

For Us Today

Let us take a thoughtful look at the views of our culture today and consider how they may be influencing our thoughts. And at the same time, let us consider how we can seek to change those views and not let them overpower us.

Many women today feel that God is biased toward men and against women because of much of the language used in the Bible and because of many of the situations recorded there. They point to the masculine designation for God (His being our Father, not Mother), the laws of the Old Testament being given to man and concerned mainly with men, the use of masculine pronouns in the sermons of Jesus and the apostles, and the fact that Jesus chose twelve *men* to be His apostles and excluded women from His intimate group.[3]

These women's rights' advocates are failing to distinguish between God's intentions, His direct commands, His revelation of His mind and character through Jesus, His instruction through the inspired writers of the Bible, and the perversion that sin had caused in the society of Bible times. Neither are they using their common sense. They are nit-picking (majoring in little details) and in doing so are missing the whole point of God's revelation and how Christian principles are active in the world today.

---

3. Discussion on this point in Chapter Five, page 102.

The Language. We have seen how the culture of Bible times was tainted by sin. We must realize that the language spoken at any given time will reflect the beliefs and customs of the culture of that time, tainted though the culture may be. God wanted to be understood by the people of that culture; thus He had to use language that was familiar to them. He had to use the terms they were familiar with and had to structure His sentences so as to be understood by them. Even though the use of the masculine nouns and pronouns would seem to refer to only men, the majority of the time they referred to the general populace — men and women. (Writers today also use the terms "men" and "he" to refer to all people.) At other times, the directions were given to the men because they were the heads of their households. One of their responsibilities was to teach their families the word of the Lord.

The fact that many of the laws of the Old Testament pertained to men is reflective of the more ambitious and aggressive roles that men were expected to fulfill. Yet even with that thought in mind, many of the laws referred to the general populace. Even though the masculine terms were used, the meaning was all inclusive.

In the New Testament times, the Greek language was used in that culture. In the Greek, the masculine and feminine designations of the pronouns were not referring to sex differentiations at all; they are simply language forms.

As we continue our study, we will discover that the Bible was written to all people and about all types of people. With God there are no distinctions — no Jew or Greek, no male or female — just people in need of God. The main distinctions that were made were about men and women's different roles in life in the culture of that time.

Living in our Culture. Christianity works within a culture, not above it or outside of it; how else could it influence the lives of men and women in that culture? Christians are in the world and are somewhat restricted by the laws and customs of their culture. They are, of course, to seek to overcome the *sin* of that culture rather than be overcome by it. In overcoming the sinful tendencies of our culture we are told in the Bible that God is not as concerned about certain rules and regulations as He is about attitudes, life-styles, and that a Christian not be a reproach in any way to Christ—the Person he represents. Thus, we must study God's Word more than we study modern philosophy; we must experience God's help for our troubled souls more than we turn to modern psychology; we must determine to do things more God's way than the way of our peers.

We must not swallow the modern views of women who say that God and the Scriptures are biased against women. We must study the Bible for ourselves and discover how wrong they are. We must realize that there are other ways to be happy and fulfilled than finding a career outside the home or opening a business. We must not accept the words of women who hate men, downgrade them, and say, "We need men like a fish needs a bicycle." We should be wary of those who espouse complete independence for women. We were not created for that. We must realize that much of the current emphasis on "finding yourself" is totally self-centered in orientation and leaves little room for the attitude of humble service that God wishes for all of us to have.

Neither should we believe those who say women are to be *only* in the home, chained to the stove and washing machine, and are not to have any active role in the church. Neither should we believe those who say wives are to obey their husbands no matter what they ask. We must not believe those who say women are here solely for the amusement and enjoyment of men. Neither are we to believe that marriage is old-fashioned and soon to be a thing of the past. God has never said those things!

We must recognize that the views and ways of our world today (our culture) are not the ways of God. They will result in discontent, confusion, and unhappiness. Let us determine to overcome the sin-tainted culture in this world by studying God's Word and way — thus renewing our minds and lives so we can fulfill God's will. The apostle Paul said it this way:

> I urge you therefore, brethren, by the mercies of God, to present your bodies a living and holy sacrifice, acceptable to God, which is your spiritual service of worship. And do not be conformed to this world, but be transformed by the renewing of your mind, that you may prove what the will of God is, that which is good and acceptable and perfect. (Romans 12:1, 2).

Summary

The following truths were emphasized in this chapter:

1. Culture affects the thoughts, actions, and values of all people.
2. The Bible states God's intentions in His direct statements to men, through Jesus' example and words in the New Testament, and through the interpretations of Jesus' words and actions by New Testament writers.
3. The Bible records how man changed and perverted God's intentions.
4. Some of the practices and customs of the culture are in accordance with God's will and some are not. We must distinguish between them to ascertain God's will for women.

40

DISCUSSION QUESTIONS:

1. Discuss the various ways that Jesus was opposed to the customs and traditions of His day.
2. What guidelines can we use to be sure we do not allow our culture to wholly determine our understanding of God's will?
3. Why did God include problems and mistakes of mankind in the Bible? Why didn't He include only the perfect ideals of Christianity and the perfect actions of Jesus?
4. How did men in the Jewish world look upon women?
5. In what ways had they strayed from God's original intentions of how women were to be seen and treated?
6. Why is a concern over the use of masculine designations throughout the Bible "nit-picking"?
7. What is our responsibility in our culture today?

Part II

WOMEN AS IMPORTANT INDIVIDUALS

To stem confusion amidst our fast-paced, ever-changing society, women must know themselves, their own value as persons in this world, and how God views their personhood.

Introduction

Everyone wants and needs to feel important. Being loved and being needed are involved in the feeling of importance, but there is more. I think most people would echo the following words: Being important is not only my "being there," but it is that I am influential. I am valuable, I am significant, I am meaningful, and I am esteemed. My being there makes a difference. Because of *me* circumstances and people are influenced and changed. If I am not there, I would be missed. I am not someone who can be pushed aside and ignored without something or someone else being affected. I have a spot in this world, and a significant one at that. Without me taking up that spot, the world will be the loser.

It is not that I am important only because of what I *do*. I do not want to feel that my value lies just in keeping some floors clean, some beds made, some cookies baked, some clothes washed. Or in bringing home the paycheck, doing the yard work, or in greasing the car. No, I want to feel that I am important because of *who* I am, because of my individual personhood. I am a person. I have a soul. I have a mind. I have rights and I have needs.

I do not want to be thought of as second-class, as trivial, as dispensable, or as inconsequential. I do not want to be thought of as a body who can meet someone's sexual needs — only. I do not want the world to see me as a non-essential. I want to stand forth as an essential — absolutely vital — individual, not because of a certain role that I play but because I exist.

Women Today

Currently, women are verbalizing these very thoughts. They no longer want to be treated as second-class citizens in our society. They have been looked upon as people (which is better than being looked upon as animals or property), but as inferior people — who are needed because they meet man's sexual needs and can produce children. Women are rebelling against this impersonal and degrading view. They are angry; they are hurting; they are sad. They are just beginning to realize that they are indeed important, not for just what they do but because of who they are — and they want the whole world to know it.

But as so often happens, many women have gone to extremes. Instead of reaching out to men seeking to better the relationship between them, they are shutting the men out of their lives. They are running away from the men, stepping on them on the way out. They are seeking to be independent and alone.

Instead of turning to God for His guidance and support, they are shutting God out and believe that because He is male He has nothing to say to them. Women are on the warpath, demanding their rights, demanding that their significant personhood be recognized. Their violence and brash outspokenness is getting attention, but women will never reach their full potential of happiness and satisfaction with these attitudes and methods. Woman can never be truly happy or content until she feels her value and importance *within herself*, regardless of the external circumstances. Outside forces and recognition will help, but will never fulfill that inner longing to feel worthy. Only God can meet that need.

God's View

God has consistently recognized the value and the importance of women. He did not change His mind after the creation or after Eve sinned. He thinks women are special and has always treated them as such. He has always treated them with loving care and concern. He considers women to be intelligent persons and holds them responsible for their actions. He praised women consistently in the Scripture when they fulfilled their roles of wives and mothers and when they excelled in bravery, wisdom, trust, or leadership. There was never any doubt in God's mind that women are influential human beings. God acknowledged overwhelmingly that women were essential parts of His plans and have contributed to the course of history.

But there is no need for you to take just my word for it. Let us consider the Scriptures carefully in the next few chapters and discover these conclusions.

Chapter Four

WOMEN AS IMPORTANT INDIVIDUALS: IN THE OLD TESTAMENT

After Adam and Eve's mistakes in the Garden of Eden, God promised that eventually evil would be crushed and good would triumph. "I will put enmity between you and the woman, and between your seed and her seed; He shall bruise you on the head, and you shall bruise him on the heel" (Genesis 3:15). Absolutely essential to God's plan was the sending of a Savior, and God chose a woman to bear that precious child. If God had changed His mind about the value of woman, He would have decided to bring the Savior to earth in another way.

He also had the perfect chance to repopulate the earth without women when He destroyed the world by the flood. Instead He decided to use the same system He had created in the beginning — man and woman in partnership, repopulating the world and carrying out His purpose. The degradation of the world before the flood did not mean that God's intentions or purposes for man and woman needed to be changed; they were perfect in the beginning. But it did mean that mankind's heart needed to be changed.

Women and a Special Nation

To change man's heart and to make him a blessing to all the earth, God decided to build a nation of people who would look to Him as their God, who would love and obey Him, who would show the rest of the earth God's thoughts and wishes, and through whom God would send the Savior. God cleansed the earth through the flood, and then man and woman began to repeople the earth (through Noah, his wife, and family). God chose Abram and Sarai (whose names were later changed to Abraham and Sarah) to begin His special nation.

48

God desired that this nation wholly trust and lean on Him, thus the father and mother of that nation had to learn to fully trust in Him. It took many years and many situations for Abraham and Sarah to learn this vital lesson. God had to restate His promise to make a great nation from them several times before they were fully convinced. He had to personally intervene several times to correct their mistakes of selfishness and impatience so that His purpose could be fulfilled. God was patient and forgiving, and finally they "grew up" to depend fully upon Him. God's people and plan were begun.

Sarah. It was not only through Abraham that the earth would be blessed, but also through Sarah. She was his partner. Without her, God's promise would not come to pass. In Genesis 18:10 and in Romans 9:9, it was emphasized that Sarah was important to God's plan: "At this time I will come, and Sarah shall have a son." God emphasized that Sarah would be the "mother" of the nation. When He changed Abraham's name, He also changed Sarah's name to seal the covenant (promise):

> Then God said to Abraham, "As for Sarai your wife, you shall not call her name Sarai, but Sarah shall be her name. And I will bless her, and indeed I will give you a son by her. Then I will bless her, and she shall be a mother of nations; kings of people shall come from her" (Genesis 17:15, 16).

Abraham and Sarah's marriage was a good one; Abraham loved Sarah and was sensitive to her needs. But, at times, he loved himself more. When they went down to Egypt to escape the famine at Negeb, Abraham was afraid the king would notice Sarah's beauty and want her for his own. He was afraid if the king knew she was Abraham's

49

wife, he would kill Abraham in order to be free to take Sarah. So Abraham asked Sarah to pose as his sister (Genesis 12:10-13). He wanted to save his own skin at Sarah's expense. He treated her as expendable property, not as if she were a full and equal partner in the marriage relationship. He was not trusting in God's promise either. He should have known that God would not allow him to be killed.

But God cared about Sarah's predicament. He did not want her to be used by men in such a demeaning way — as a body to be passed around to meet man's needs. He sent plagues upon the Pharaoh and his house, which made the Pharaoh realize that he should not have taken Sarah (Genesis 12:17-20). God intervened on Sarah's behalf. Sarah's purity both of her person and her marriage was very important to God. God not only stepped in to save Sarah this one time, but He did it again (Genesis 20).

God also cared about Sarah's feelings. Even though Sarah had made the mistake of giving her handmaiden to Abraham so that a child could be born because of her own insecurity, impatience, and lack of trust in God's promise, God understood her violent emotions about the presence of Hagar and her son (Ishmael).

Hagar felt superior to Sarah because she had borne a son when Sarah could not. Then after Isaac was born as the fulfillment of God's promise (Genesis 21:1, 2), Hagar's feelings of superiority and spite were seen in the attitude and actions of her son in his reactions toward Isaac (21:9). Sarah was afraid for the peace and solidarity within the family. What would happen between two men who both felt they were the first-born of Abraham? She could see only strife, hatred, and bitterness ahead.

She asked Abraham to send Hagar and Ishmael away (Genesis 21:10). Abraham was distressed; because according to custom whenever a servant produced children by the master, she could never be sent away. God intervened and told Abraham it was best to send them away and to not fear for them, because Ishmael would become the leader of another nation and would do well (Genesis 21:12, 13).

God also thought of Sarah as an individual. He wanted her to have faith and trust in Him, just as much as He wanted Abraham to do so. It was evident that Sarah knew of the promise and her part in it, for she became frustrated when she felt she was not able to fulfill her responsibility. God's gentle rebuke of Sarah when she doubted for a moment that she could have a child (because of the couple's advanced age) showed that God expected her to trust Him as an individual in her own right: "And the Lord said . . . 'Why did Sarah laugh, saying "Shall I indeed bear a child, when I am so old?" 'Is anything too difficult for the Lord?'" (Genesis 18:13, 14). Sarah was personally responsible to God. It was not that she found her identity from being Abraham's wife and only in that way was she known to God.

When Sarah's faith had matured as it should have, God recognized it and praised her: "By faith even Sarah herself received ability to conceive, even beyond the proper time of life, since she considered Him faithful who had promised" (Hebrews 11:11). The mention of Sarah in other Scriptures shows how important God felt she was:

Look to Abraham your father, and to Sarah who gave birth to you in pain; when he was one I called him, then I blessed him and multiplied him (Isaiah 51:2).

For it is written that Abraham had two sons, one by the bondwoman and one by the free woman. But the son by the bondwoman was born according to the flesh, and the son by the free woman through the promise. This contains the allegory: for these women are two covenants, one proceeding from Mount Sinai bearing children who are to be slaves; she is Hagar. . . . And you brethren, like Isaac, are children of promise . . . . But what does the Scripture say? "Cast out the bondwoman and her son, for the son of the bondwoman shall not be an heir with the son of the free woman." So then, brethren, we are not children of a bondwoman, but of the free woman (Galatians 4:22-24, 28, 30, 31).

For in this way in former times the holy women also, who hoped in God, used to adorn themselves, being submissive to their own husbands. Thus Sarah obeyed Abraham, calling him lord, and you have become her children if you do what is right without being frightened by any fear (I Peter 3:5, 6).

Hagar. Even though Sarah was quite important to God's plans, He did not favor her and at the same time disregard Hagar. Hagar was a lowly handmaiden (slave), but God cared about her and treated her as an important individual. When she fled because of Sarah's harsh treatment before her child was born, God appeared to her and told her to return and to submit herself to Sarah's authority (Genesis 16:8, 9). In this way she would be protected until her son was born and grown. A pregnant woman alone in the wilderness was a fearsome prospect, and God wanted only the best for her. He promised Hagar a future for her son — he would be a leader of a nation (16:10-12).

Then later when God told Abraham to send Hagar and Ishmael away, He did not forsake her (Genesis 21:17-19). In the wilderness when Hagar was despairing for her and her son's lives because their water supply had run out, God set a well in their midst to meet their needs. He calmed Hagar's fears by repeating the promise that Ishmael would be leader of a nation. The mother and son were able to find a homeland; Hagar found Ishmael a wife; their lives were full (21:20, 21).

Lot's Wife. God also cared about Lot's wife, indeed his whole family. When, because of strife, Abraham and his nephew, Lot, came to part, Abraham allowed Lot to have first choice of the land. Lot chose selfishly the best land (Genesis 13:10) which was toward Sodom. He lived in Sodom with his family. Sodom was so evil (13:14) that God decided to destroy it, but He wanted Lot, his wife, and his daughters to get out of the city safely. He sent angels to help them escape before the fall of the city, but Lot and his family were reluctant to leave. The angels had to take them by force and ordered them not to look back to the city but to escape to the mountains (Genesis 19:17).

Even though God had expressed His concern for her, Lot's wife chose not to obey the Lord. As the fire and brimstone fell upon Sodom, she looked back. Her action signified a distrust in God and a longing for her life-style in an evil city. God held her individually responsible for her actions. He looked upon her as an important and thinking individual who could make her own decisions. Notice He did not punish Lot for her disobedience; He punished *her* immediately by turning her into a pillar of salt (Genesis 19:26). God expected this woman's individual obedience; when she failed to obey, He punished her.

Rebekah. Isaac's wife, Rebekah, was considered a vital part of God's plan for His nation. She talked to God on an individual basis; for when her pregnancy was physically troublesome, she asked the Lord for the reason. God answered her directly with a very important promise:

> Two nations are in your womb, and two peoples shall be separated from your body; and one people shall be stronger

than the other; and the older shall serve the younger (Genesis 25:23).

We should notice that Rebekah did not go to her husband and ask him to talk to the Lord on her behalf. She related to God personally, and God treated her as an important individual. Rebekah's actions in her later life were not pleasing to God, but He worked out His plan in spite of that fact.

Rebekah's importance is pointed out in Romans 9:10-13:

> And not only this, but there was Rebekah also, when she had conceived twins by one man, our father Isaac; for though the twins were not yet born, and had not done anything good or bad, in order that God's purpose according to His choice might stand, not because of works, but because of Him who calls, it was said to her, "the older will serve the younger." Just as it is written, "Jacob I loved, but Esau I hated."

Leah and Rachel. Isaac and Rebekah's son, Jacob, inherited the leadership of God's nation. His wives, Rachel and Leah, were troubled at times because of their barrenness. According to the cultural views, the most important responsibility of a Jewish woman was to bear children. When women were not able to do so, they felt cursed and unworthy. They felt they were letting their husband down.

Leah was not loved by Jacob (as a husband should love a wife), and she felt this lack keenly. To comfort her in her emotional distress, God enabled her to bear many children. "Now the Lord saw that Leah was unloved, and He opened her womb, but Rachel was barren" (Genesis 29:31). God was concerned about her well-being.

Later God showed the same concern for Rachel; He "remembered Rachel" and enabled her to bear children (Genesis 30:22). God cared for these women, not for what they could do for His nation, but because they were individuals

54

who had special needs. He did not want them to feel unworthy or ashamed in the culture in which they lived. They were certainly honored to be the mothers of the twelve patriarchs, the leaders of the chosen nation.

Hebrew Midwives. Through varying circumstances, God was working out His plans to develop His special nation. He used the situation of Joseph's (Jacob's son) being sold into slavery to save His people from annihilation through famine. While Jacob's descendants were in Egypt, their numbers increased greatly which added quantity to God's nation.

Then a Pharaoh came to power in Egypt who had forgotten what Joseph had done for the Egyptians and why his descendants were residing there (Exodus 1:8). The Egyptian ruler seized the opportunity to make slaves of the Hebrews, compelling them to build for him. Yet their numbers increased steadily, alarming the Pharaoh. He was afraid they might rebel or join with Egypt's enemies. He told two midwives (scholars are uncertain whether they were Egyptian or Israelite) named Shiphrah and Puah to kill any Hebrew males that were born (Exodus 1:15, 16).

These women respected God and His purposes, however, and did not obey the king (Exodus 1:17). They risked their lives to help the Hebrew people and lied to the king about their actions (1:18, 19). God appreciated their efforts and was good to them (1:20), for because of them His nation was allowed to increase even further. He rewarded them by establishing households for them (provided families for them, 1:21). These women defied a man's orders — a king's no less — to protect God's interests. God did not overlook their bravery; He treated them as very special individuals.

Jochebed. God allowed His chosen people to remain in bondage for several years in order to impress upon the people the terribleness of their bondage, to encourage them to turn to God for help, to demonstrate His power spectacularly, and to develop the proper leader for them. He wanted them to turn to Him in complete trust, so they would have a solid basis for the beginning of their pilgrimage to the land He had chosen for them.

Their leader was to be Moses. The Scripture does not reveal how Jochebed (Moses' mother) knew that Moses was a special child, although it is mentioned that he was a goodly or beautiful child (Exodus 2:2). Perhaps it was a mother's instinct, a vision from God, or simply a mother's deep love for her child that prompted her to think so creatively as to keep him hidden from the murderous soldiers of the Pharaoh for three months after his birth.

Then when she knew she could not hide him safely any longer, she thought of putting him in a water-tight basket and placing the basket in the exact place on the River Nile where the Pharaoh's daughter came daily to bathe. How innovative! And it was a stroke of genius to place her daughter in the reeds nearby, so she could seize the opportunity to tell Pharaoh's daughter that she knew of a nurse who could care for the child — his own Hebrew mother. Jochebed had much courage and a great faith in God; she knew God would protect her son.

In rewarding her faith, God met the need of a loving mother. He spared the life of her son and arranged it so she could be with him in his most formative years and teach him of the Hebrew God and the Hebrew ways. Some might say all these circumstances were coincidental, but I can see God's direction and guidance in the events even though

His part in them was not expressly stated. God's way of developing Moses into a leader as seen in the ensuing chapters of Exodus bears out my belief.

Jochebed was a thinking individual, and one who was very important to God — so important that He includes her in the list of the faithful in Hebrews 11:

> By faith Moses, when he was born, was hidden for three months by his parents, because they saw he was a beautiful child; and they were not afraid of the king's edict (11:23).

Women and The Law

God's leadership of His nation was done mainly through the men. This was the logical and natural approach, since the men were the leaders and the protectors of their families, since the family name and the sense of history was passed down from generation to generation through the sons, and since the women supported the activities of their husbands. But God did not forget or ignore the women.

The women and children were included in the exodus from Egypt because they were vital parts of God's plan and because they, too, suffered from the bondage. The women were also included in the specific laws that God gave to His people. Women were considered to be individuals with needs and responsibilities. They were not discarded or left out. God was just as concerned for them as He was for the men. He designed laws especially for the women, concerning their relationships and roles in life.

To understand how the Law affected women in that point of time, we must first study the Law itself — its purpose and content. God did not devise a system of law just to keep the people under His thumb or to spoil all their fun. He wanted this nation to be special and unique; He wanted them to be an example of purity, goodness, and decency for all the other nations of the world. Because God was their leader, the other nations would realize by the example of Israel that God was holy and pure. Because of Israel's devotion to God in conduct and worship, other nations would conclude that God was worthy of worship and the only true God.

God knew if Israel was going to make an impact on the world by showing the true character and power of God, she would have to be organized, have laws, and be devoted wholly and faithfully to Him. So He made a covenant with the nation (an agreement, a promise) — if Israel would consent to be used as God's special instrument, would be faithful and obedient; then God would bless them, and from their nation the Savior would come.

God gave them the Law for their guidance and to make clear to them His will for their lives. The Law established a guide for moral actions, for showing love and compassion for others, for common sense practices of cleanliness and health, for right attitudes and practices of worship, and as a means of protecting those who might be taken advantage of by unthinking mankind.

But God did not force Israel to accept His Law or the covenant-relationship. It was a decision that they had to make. If they chose to follow God and establish the covenant, then they would be expected to fulfill their part of the agreement. God left no room for doubt or questioning about His intentions or desires; He made them very clear. Neither did He leave any doubt about what would happen to them if they decided to follow other gods or laws.

A good summary of God's intentions and purpose of the Law is found in Deuteronomy 30:11-18:

> For this commandment which I command you today is not too difficult for you, nor is it out of reach. It is not in heaven, that you should say, "Who will go up to heaven for us to get it for us and make us hear it, that we may observe it?" Nor is it beyond the sea that you should say, "Who will cross the sea for us to get it for us and make us hear it, that we may observe it?" But the word is very near you, in your mouth and in your heart, that you may observe it. See, I have set before you today life and prosperity, and death and adversity; in that I command you today to love the Lord your God, to walk in His ways and to keep His commandments and His statutes and His judgments that you may live and multiply, and the Lord your God may bless you in the land where you are entering to possess it. But if your heart turns away and you will not obey, but are drawn away and worship other gods and serve them, I declare to you today that you shall surely perish. You shall not prolong your days in the land where you are crossing the Jordan to enter and possess it.

It is evident from the preparation of the people to receive the Law, the directions that God gave to Moses, and the content of the Law that God's covenant was meant to include the entire nation of people — women and children as well as men (Exodus 19 and 20). The women were just as responsible for obeying the Law as the men were. The women brought their jewelry to Aaron for him to make the golden calf while Moses was on Mt. Sinai and were held just as responsible for their sin as the men were (Exodus 32).

It is significant to note that after the wilderness wanderings and just before the nation was proceeding to conquer the promised land, Joshua read the Law to the whole congregation of Israel, with "women and the little ones" specifically named and included (Joshua 1:14). He also exacted promises from the *whole* nation that they would serve the Lord only; He made a covenant with *all* the people (Joshua 24:19-25).

We will also see that the women personally benefited from the provisions of the Law. Even secular history records that the Israelite women were better treated than any heathen nation because of the Law.

The Decalogue (Ten Commandments). All of the ten commandments applied to the women as well as the men, but two of them were related specifically to women's roles in life. The *fifth* commandment—"Honor your father and your mother" (Exodus 20:12; Deuteronomy 5:16)—placed the responsibility onto the children to respect both parents, not just the father. Such respect would result in obedience. In Exodus 21:15 and 17, the command was amplified by the imposition of the death penalty upon a person who struck or cursed his or her parents.

Leviticus 19:3 expresses the same essence using the word "fear"—"fear every man his mother and his father"—meaning to "reverence." It was the same word used when referring to the fear of God in numerous places in the Scripture.

God's emphases make evident His high regard for family life and discipline. He recognized the role that both the father and mother play in the rearing of the children and desired that the responsibility for good behavior also rest upon the children themselves.

In the *seventh* commandment—"You shall not commit adultery" (Ex. 20:14; Deut. 5:18)—God made clear what He thought of marriage. His intentions for marriage had not changed since His institution of it in the Garden of Eden. He desired that the husband and wife remain faithful to each other and to their commitment in their partnership; a pure and satisfying relationship would result. He sought to protect the marriage relationship and to place responsibility for the relationship on both partners. The punishment

60

for adultery was stoning, again pointing out God's aversion for such unfaithfulness and His high regard for marriage.

Many say after reading the *tenth* commandment that God compromised with the cultural influence and referred to the wife as just another piece of the man's property:

> You shall not covet your neighbor's house; you shall not covet your neighbor's wife or his male servant or his female servant or his ox or his donkey or anything that belongs to your neighbor (Exodus 20:17).

The Hebrew word for "house" should be translated "household," meaning one's family and all his possessions. It did not denote the physical structure as we think of it today. The wife is distinguished from the property and is listed first, indicating her importance.

In Deuteronomy 5:21 (the parallel phrasing of this commandment):

> You shall not *covet* your neighbor's wife, and you shall not *desire* your neighbor's house, his field or his manservant, his ox or his donkey or anything that belongs to your neighbor. (Italics mine)

The wife is listed by herself, first, and with a different Hebrew verb than what was used to refer to the man's property. The different verb denoted a special and intimate relationship that was not present between the man and his slaves and possessions. We must take the parallel passage into account and realize that God is not saying women are simply the property or possessions of men. Instead they have a distinct, unique relationship with their husbands.

Laws for Women's Protection. In the latter chapters of Exodus and in the next three books (Leviticus, Numbers, and Deuteronomy) God expanded in detail on the ten general commandments and made His will in everyday matters quite clear. In my study of these laws, I could not find that God discriminated against women or pointed out the superiority of men. In the instances when issues concerned women specifically, God showed great compassion and made quite clear the importance He placed on womanhood.

Most of the laws pertaining to women were for their protection. It was indeed a man's world in those times, and it was easy for sinful men to over-emphasize their leadership responsibilities and mistreat those who were entrusted into their care or those who had different roles and responsibilities than they did. God knew their sinful tendencies and thus emphasized how He wanted the women to be treated.

In Exodus 21 specific guidelines were given concerning the handling of *female slaves*. Although slavery disgusts our sensibilities, slavery of both men and women was a common custom of the society in Bible times. A slave was considered a man's property and was often treated as a member of the family and not considered to be of less worth than any other person (that is, in Jewish culture; this was not true in other cultures). A person usually became a slave when his or her father needed money and sold him or her to another man to serve in his household for a time.

Often a female slave became the other man's wife, concubine, or his son's wife or concubine. Having concubines is also a distasteful practice and was a perversion of God's original intention for the man-woman relationship, but it was a fact of life, a custom of the time, that God allowed to exist.

God wanted the female slave to be treated properly. The master was to take care of the physical needs of the slave. If he did not want a slave for his wife or concubine, he could sell her to someone else (not a foreigner, because a foreigner might not treat her fairly), give her to his son, or let her go free. In this way God was legislating that the female slaves be taken care of and not be simply cast off when they did not please the men. Neither were the slaves to be beaten (Exodus 21:20, 26).

If a foreign woman was captured as a spoil of war, the man could keep her as his wife. He was to allow her to have a period of mourning for her lost family. He was not to sell her or mistreat her. The children would be raised as Israelites. If the man decided he didn't like her, then he was to set her free (Numbers 31; Deuteronomy 21).

God also designed laws to protect pregnant women from harm (Exodus 21:22), to protect women from being gored by an ox (21:28-32), to protect women from rape (22:16 — the man must marry her or pay fee to her father), and to protect widows from being afflicted (22:22).

Women also had to be protected from their husbands, for *divorce* was a custom of the time (even though God expressed hatred for it). Some husbands could accuse their wives falsely in order to get out of the marriage. A husband might say his wife was not a virgin when he married her. God devised a law (Deut. 22:13-21) whereby the situation must be brought before the judges. If the parents can prove the man is lying, then he must be punished, fined, and not allowed a divorce. But if the woman was found to have been sexually intimate with another man before marriage, then she would be punished.

Divorces were gotten easily and often in the biblical world. Adultery was forbidden and punished by death (Deut. 22:22; Leviticus 18:20; 20:10), so evidently the "some indecency" mentioned in Deuteronomy 24:1 is referring to something other than adultery:

63

> When a man takes a wife and marries her, and it happens that she finds no favor in his eyes because he has found some indecency in her, and he writes her a certificate of divorce and puts it in her hand and sends her out from his house.

"Indecency" literally means "any sexual perversion." Many husbands used almost any excuse to divorce their wives, so God devised a rule to act as a deterrent to hasty divorces and thus protect the women. God required the husband to go before a judge and get a document to present to her. Then the woman would be free to remarry anyone other than her first husband (Deuteronomy 24:2, 4). Marriage was the only means a woman had in that culture to have her physical needs met (other than prostitution or slavery), thus it was devastating to a woman to be cast off by her husband anytime he felt like it. Making a divorce harder to get forced the husbands to think about what they were doing and prevented harsh and rash decisions.

Even though God allowed divorce, we know that it was in no way within God's plans for marriage. Jesus made that point clear:

> Have you not read, that He who created them from the beginning made them male and female, and said, "For this cause a man shall leave his father and mother, and shall cleave to his wife; and the two shall become one flesh"? (Matthew 19:4, 5).

Why then did God allow provisions for divorce in His Law? Jesus continued:

> Because of your hardness of heart, Moses permitted you to divorce your wives; but from the beginning it has not been this way (Matthew 19:8).

64

God allowed divorce to exist because of man's sinfulness, even though it was not His intention or desire. And He did seek to protect the women from wholesale divorce and the harsh after-effects.

The fact that the *inheritance* was always passed down through the sons made it difficult for some women. God provided that when a man dies, his brother should take his widow as his wife and the resulting children would carry on the dead brother's name (Deuteronomy 25:5, 6). This was called the levirate law.

In Genesis 38 we read of Tamar whose situation came under this law. She married two brothers, both of whom died. Her father-in-law, Judah, was afraid to give another son to her for a husband, so he kept putting her off. The younger brother was to have married Tamar, but she could see that Judah was not going to live up to the law. The years were ticking by, so she took matters into her own hands, became pregnant by Judah, and had his two sons. She escaped death and economic deprivation in this way and forced the family line to be continued.

In another instance, Zelophehad had only daughters as his offspring (Numbers 27:1-11). So who would receive the inheritance when he died? The daughters told of their plight to Moses and other leaders of Israel and asked that they be allowed to receive the inheritance. Moses took the matter to the Lord who agreed that the women should have the inheritance. Then God designed a law that would deal equitably with such a situation from that time on (Numbers 27:7, 8). In Numbers 36:1-13 an addition was made to the law, saying that the daughters who received an inheritance could only marry within their tribe, thus keeping the inheritance within the family. Through these instances we can certainly conclude that God really cared for the women.

65

Laws Pertaining to Women's Health. God was also concerned about the physical health of women. He made laws providing for purification and rest after childbirth (Leviticus 12:1-8), as well as sanitary measures to be taken after sexual intercourse and menstruation (Leviticus 15). Leviticus 18 and 20 list many sexual prohibitions which would protect the men, the women, and the families from physical and emotional destruction which would be caused by incest, illicit sexual activities, and bestiality. Daughters were not allowed to become prostitutes (Leviticus 19:29). Illicit sex and rape were prohibited, and punishment was set for a rapist (Deuteronomy 22:22-30). Again the concern of God for women is evident.

Women's Responsibility Toward God. God has always considered women as individuals with intelligent minds and mature wills capable of making decisions. He included women in the provisions of His Law concerning attitudes and rituals of worship. He did not exclude them from worship. When He gave the detailed orders about the building of the tabernacle, the women were to help sew and were to bring offerings (contributed mirrors, Exodus 38:8). The sacrificial system included the women as well as the men, even though the priests could only be men.

The women were allowed to make vows (to promise to give something to God or abstain from something, Numbers 30:3). However, their vows could be annuled by their fathers or husbands if they were not deemed proper (30:5, 8), as a way of protecting them from over-strict vows and to insure that they remained under the leadership of the men in the family. Women were allowed to make the Nazarite vow (abstinence from certain food and drink and from having their hair cut) with no conditions added (Numbers 6:2).

Neither did God exclude women from the accountability to Him for their sins. They would be punished for sexual impurities (Leviticus 21:9; 20:10; 19:29; chapters 18 and 20) and for being a wizard or witch (20:27). And, of course, women were responsible for living out all the Law that God had given in a general sense. When He did not spell out whom the Law was pertaining to specifically, it pertained to all of Israel.

Miriam. A good example of God's expectation that women obey His Law is seen in the life of Miriam, the sister of Aaron and Moses. Miriam was courageous, intelligent, and faithful. She was considered to be one of the leaders of the nation of Israel: "Indeed I brought you up from the land of Egypt, and ransomed you from the house of slavery; and I sent before you Moses, Aaron, and Miriam" (Micah 6:4). She was called a prophetess and led the women in a song of praise and triumph after the crossing of the Red Sea (Exodus 15:20), which also points out that women worshipped God freely.

But in Numbers 12, we read that Miriam spoke against Moses because of his Ethiopian (or Cushite) wife (thought to be other than Zipporah, the wife he had in Midian). We do not know if she was envious of his wife or if she was being rebellious and quarrelsome, but we do know that God held her responsible for her actions. He punished her by afflicting her with leprosy (a most dread disease of the times) for seven days (Numbers 12:10, 15).

God thought of Miriam as an individual, spoke to her directly from a pillar of cloud about her sin of doubting the authority of Moses (Numbers 12:5), and punished her. She was held accountable to God for her personal actions. If she were of inferior intelligence or importance, God would not have bothered speaking to her, would not have punished her in such a dramatic way, and would not have allowed her to lead the people.

Women During Conquest of Canaan

Rahab. Rahab was a harlot or what we would call a prostitute or "lady of the night." Men paid her for sexual favors. Her residence was situated on the wall of the city of Jericho and was easy access to the many who passed through the city gates. She lived apart from her family and evidently made linen (flax was laid out on her roof, Joshua 2:6).

The Israelites led by Joshua were preparing to conquer the promised land, and Jericho was the first city on the list. Spies were sent ahead to determine what they were up against. Strangers who went into Rahab's house would not be questioned, so they went there to stay. Rahab had heard of this nation of the Jews and the many wonderful and powerful things the Lord they worshipped had done for them. She knew of the wickedness of her own people and the relative powerlessness of their gods. She asked for the safety of herself and her family, knowing full well what destruction was in store for Jericho. The spies promised she and her family would be spared in exchange for their safety.

But even before she declared her faith in the Hebrew God and extracted the promise from the spies, she faced certain death by lying to the king's soldiers who came to question her about the two strangers who were seen going into her house. She sent the soldiers on a "wild goose chase," hid the spies on her roof, and then let them down over the wall by a cord when the danger was past. She stepped out in faith and courageously helped the enemies of her people.

God rewarded her courage and faith. She and her family were saved from the devastating destruction and lived with the Israelites the rest of their lives (Joshua 6:25). Rahab married Salmon, and had a son named Boaz who married Ruth. From this family line came King David and then Christ (Matthew 1:5).

Rahab's faith justified her in the sight of God ("Likewise also was not Rahab the harlot justified by works, when she had received the messengers, and had sent them out another way?" James 2:25). Even though she was a heathen, a member of an idolatrous, immoral nation and a prostitute besides, God took notice of her and cared for her.

Women During the Period of the Judges

The period of the judges was one of the lowest in Israel's history. The Israelites had captured most of the land that God had promised them, but they were not as yet united as a nation. There was much violence and anger between the tribes and in Israel's relationships with her heathen neighbors. There was a wildness and a confusion that fed the instability of the people. They would turn away from God and then be beaten into submission by a foreign power. They would cry out to God for help; He would always answer their pleas by choosing a leader to unite them, encourage them, and lead them to victory over their oppressors.

Women were much abused during this period of Israel's history; many times they were treated as mere pawns in the wars and feuds (examples: sacrifice of Jephthah's daughter in Judges 11, the murder of the concubine in Judges 19, and the kidnapping of the 400 virgins in Judges 21). But these gross and crude actions toward women were not by God's design—they were the results of the sinfulness of mankind. In stark contrast to the men's attitude toward the women, God considered them to be valuable individuals who were indispensable to His plans.

Deborah. She was a married woman with housewifely duties, but God chose Deborah to lead the Israelite nation to victory over the Canaanites. Deborah was close to God and a counselor to her people. God spoke to her directly, giving instructions about how the Canaanite army could be defeated (Judges 4:5, 6). God chose men to be valiant leaders in those dark times, but the fact that He chose a woman for such a role emphasizes that He considers women to be equal to men as distinct individuals with many capabilities. Some commentators suggest that God chose her because no men were available; that seems highly unlikely since a man, Barak, was the leader of her army. The fact that Barak would not make a move without Deborah's guidance and leadership shows the extent of her abilities (Judges 4:8).

Manoah's Wife. Samson's mother was not named, but God considered her to be quite important — so important that He appeared to her twice through angels and gave her specific instructions about the special child she was to bear (Judges 13:3-5, 10-14). Her son was destined to become a great leader of Israel. God's guidance and personal communication to this woman emphasizes again His high regard for women and their positions as wives and mothers.

Women During the Period of the Kings and Prophets

In this period of history, the nation of Israel was solidifying and coming closer to being united. But the process was very slow; violence, wars, and battles were still very much a part of the lives of the people. God's people decided that the only way they could become a full-fledged nation that would demand respect was to have an earthly king as their neighbors did. God was upset that they were so impatient and lacked the trust and commitment to their covenant, but He allowed them to have a king.

He personally chose the kings and communicated His will to them. Whenever they obeyed His will, things went well for the nation. When they rebelled against God, the nation got in trouble. The nation rose to its zenith of wealth and power under the reign of Solomon, but the latter part of his reign signaled the end of the united nation. With a superficial reading of this period of history, one might conclude that God had forgotten about the women. But upon a closer examination, we can see that the role of being a wife and mother was still vital to the nation of Israel and God's purposes and that women were still considered to be precious individuals. Though not spoken to directly by God as in times past (except for Huldah), women were still influential persons, especially as they touched the lives of the kings, leaders, and prophets of the nation.

Hannah. Hannah, the wife of Elkanah, demonstrated the close relationship she felt with the Lord in I Samuel 1. As was the custom, she traveled with her husband to the temple to worship (note that women were not shut out of opportunities of worship). At this particular time, she was greatly distressed because she had no children (a mark of blessing in that culture, I Samuel 1:10). She made her agony and deep emotions known to the Lord as she prayed and wept. She felt such a close relationship with God that she even bargained with Him, saying that if He gave her a son, she would dedicate him wholly to the Lord (1:11). She was so fervent in her praying that the priest thought she was drunk. She explained her deep yearning to him, and the priest expressed his desire that her prayer be answered. God cared for Hannah and acknowledged her overwhelming desire for a child (1:19) by giving her Samuel, who became a major spokesman for the Lord and a guide for the kings of Israel. Hannah rejoiced because of God's blessing, prayed a great prayer of praise (I Samuel 2:1-10), and kept her promise.

Abigail. She was a godly and beautiful woman, although her husband, Nabal, was a churlish man. Abigail exercised her God-given intelligence to persuade David not to shed blood unnecessarily (I Samuel 25). According to the customs of the time, David had been insulted by Nabal and could, by all rights, kill him and his household. Abigail convinced him that the Lord would not wish him to do so. Her frequent references to the Lord, her humble attitude, and her diplomacy suggest to us her closeness with the Lord, her desire for peace rather than violence, and her concern for the future king of Israel as well as for her husband. She, though a woman and a stranger to him, influenced David greatly. He was so impressed that when the Lord struck Nabal with death, David asked Abigail to be his wife (I Samuel 25:39).

Woman from Tekoa. During David's reign he was continually having family problems. His own son was a rascal and a rebel (Absalom), but David loved him dearly. He grieved while Absalom was in exile because of the treacherous murder of his own brother (Amnon). Joab thought of a plan to bring father and son together and used the services of a woman of Tekoa to accomplish the feat. She was well-known for her wisdom and ability to speak well. She appealed to David's deep-felt emotions for his son and convinced him to ask Absalom to return rather than continuing to punish him. Thus David could enjoy his presence in the years that remained (II Samuel 14:1-20).

David was impressed with her and her reasoning powers; he decided because of her influence to terminate Absalom's banishment. This again points out the influence of a woman on the king and illustrates the intelligence and eloquence of a woman even in those male-dominated times.

A Wise Woman. Although she was not named, a brave and intelligent woman convinced Joab (David's general) not to punish a whole city for the rebellious actions of one of its inhabitants (II Samuel 20:16-22). Joab asssented to her logic and agreed to leave the city intact if they would deliver the miscreant to him. She spoke to the people of the city; they found the man, killed him, and threw his head over the wall to Joab. A whole city was saved because of the wise counsel of a woman.

Woman of Shunem. A prominent, influential woman ministered to the physical needs of the prophet Elisha, even providing a room for him to stay in whenever he was in the area. This enabled Elisha to be much more comfortable while doing the Lord's work. This woman was rewarded by God enabling her to become a mother and then by enabling Elisha to heal her son when he died of a heatstroke (II Kings 4:8-37). Though this woman was not named, God cared for her and made a special effort to meet her needs.

Israelite Girl. A maiden captured by the Syrians was able to influence a whole family because of her trust in God and concern for her master. Her master, Naaman, was the captain of the Syrian army; but his position did not shield him from having troubles and sorrow. He discovered he had leprosy, a disease that disfigured and eventually killed its victims. Of course, he was greatly distressed and had tried *every possible cure.* The maiden told Naaman's wife about the prophet in Israel who could cure him. Naaman went to Elisha and was cured of his leprosy (II Kings 5:1-19). Although God did not personally speak to this young girl, she showed the close relationship she had with the Lord even while a slave in a foreign land.

Jehosheba. During Queen Athaliah's evil reign and purge of her family members, a brave and godly woman, Jehosheba, saved Joash from being murdered by hiding him and his nurse in her bedroom for six years (II Kings 11:2, 3). Because she was willing to risk her own life, a man who was faithful and true to God was saved. When the time was right, he was made king. Though not specifically stated, we know that God's hand must have been in her actions.

Huldah. Huldah was a prophetess during the reign of King Josiah. When the book of the Law was found, she was consulted (rather than any of the male prophets) to attest to the genuineness of the scroll. Because of her position, she received messages from God and communicated them to the people. Her speaking resulted in the people repenting and turning back to God (II Kings 22:14-20).

Esther. We must acknowledge Esther who was in the right place at the right time to save the Israelites. The opportunity was hers because she was the Queen; yet she did not accomplish the feat because of her position but because of who she was as an individual. The King had the power to have her killed if she came into his presence without being invited (even if she was the Queen), but she took that chance because her cousin Mordecai had convinced her of the necessity of that action to save her people. Haman had tricked the King into making a proclamation that all the Jews be killed on a certain day. She asked all the Jews to pray and fast for three days, as she would do, in order to have the strength to do what had to be done (Esther 4:16). She knew that whatever happened God was with her and approved of what she was doing; she was willing to die to accomplish God's will. God rewarded her bravery and humility; Haman was hanged. Mordecai was honored, and all the Jews were saved from death.

Widows: In these times, widows had an especially rough life because of their economic situation. But God cared for them (Isaiah 1:17; Jeremiah 7:6) and in specific instances provided for their needs. The widow of Zarephath was preparing to fix the last meal for herself and her son and then wait to die, when God directed Elijah to her. Her willingness to share the meager meal with Elijah was rewarded by their having enough food to eat each day and by Elijah's miraculous healing of her son (I Kings 17).

When Elisha was prophet, a widow was deep in debt. She was bereft because her children were about to be taken as slaves to satisfy the debt. She had only one pot of oil left in the house, but Elisha miraculously multiplied the oil for her so she could sell it and pay the debt (II Kings 4:1-7).

Wives and Mothers. God, through the poetic and prophetic writings, makes clear His high opinion of good wives and mothers. In Psalm 144:12, He refers to women as being cornerstones. In Proverbs He extols the teachings and wisdom of good mothers (1:8; 29:15; 30:11; 6:20; 10:1; 15:20; 17:25; 19:26; 23:22; 2:2-5; 3:13-18; 4:6-9; 8:1, 11; 9:1-6). He urges husbands to delight in and be satisfied with their wives (Proverbs 5:18-20; 12:4; 18:22; 19:14), thus emphasizing the importance of the wife to her husband.

God praised the gracious woman (Proverbs 11:16) and the wise (14:1). God's view of womanhood is wonderfully expressed in the beautiful story of the loving and caring Ruth and the treatise in Proverbs 31:10-31 about the virtuous woman. He pictured woman as a devoted wife and mother whose priorities were her family and the service she could perform for others. She was skillful and diligent. She was intelligent and had interests and abilities that extended beyond her home and family. She feared God and allowed her husband to be the leader in the home and at the gates of the city. There is no hint of a down-trodden, unhappy wife and mother who feels like a man's property or as a slave to her family. Even within the cultural situation, she was happy and fulfilled—just what God desires for every woman.

Evil Women. God extolled women and recognized their intellectual and leadership abilities; but He also made clear that women were responsible for their actions, and He did not approve of evil attitudes, words, or activities. The negative influence of some women did not go unnoticed or unpunished by God.

Bathsheba influenced David to commit adultery and murder (II Samuel 11). They both suffered the loss of the child that resulted from that relationship. Solomon's downfall can be traced directly to the influence of his hundreds of wives and concubines who turned him away from God and toward their gods. He wanted to please his wives, so he built high places for their gods; then he became enmeshed in their life-style (I Kings 11:4).

Jezebel, a staunch idol-worshipper, influenced her husband, King Ahab, to institute idol worship in Israel and led in all sorts of atrocities and immoral acts (I Kings 16-21). She was killed as violently and horribly as she had lived. Athaliah was an evil ruler who became known for her murders and also met with a horrible death (II Kings 8:26; 11:1, 3).

Even when using symbolic language in poetry and the prophecies, God made clear the qualities of women that would lead to ruin. Proverbs describes the deceit and folly of an adulterous woman (2:16; 5:3, 6; 6:24-35; 7; 22:14; 23:27, 28; 30:20). Babylon is compared to a woman who is puffed up with pride in Isaiah 47:1-15. He speaks of deceitful prophetesses in Nehemiah 6:14 and Ezekiel 13:17, 18, pointing out their error and fate. The whole book of Hosea compared Israel with the adulterous wife of Hosea (Gomer) and illustrates the final degradation of such sinning.

Women Who Were Victims. Women were used and abused by sinful men during this period of history: Michal was used as a pawn between David and Saul (I Samuel 18:20, 21); Tamar was raped by her own brother (II Samuel 13); Abishag was a young virgin who was used to comfort King David with her body as he was dying (I Kings 1); Rizpah was a victim of violence perpetrated on her sons (II Samuel 21); daughters were sold into bondage (Nehemiah 5); and women were the victims of wars and violence (Nahum 3:5, 10).

We must remember, however, that God did not condone these actions, nor did He wish them on women. They are simply the results of sin's activity in the world. The godly women of these times overcame these trials and problems and lived the best lives they could with trust and faith in God. Though the surrounding circumstances were difficult and though many men did not treat the women properly, we must see beyond these externals and know that God still loved them and viewed them as valuable human beings, just as He did at creation.

77

Summary

We can ascertain the following truths from a study of the Old Testament:

1. God considered women to be of great importance and value.
2. God considered many women to be vital parts of His plan for mankind.
3. God considered women to be intelligent individuals, capable of making their own decisions. He held them responsible for their actions. He expected and desired their trust and obedience.
4. God considered women to be influential, having a definite effect on the world around them.
5. God showed His loving concern for women and sought to meet their needs.
6. God praised the brave, faithful, and righteous women and their roles of wives and mothers and chastised women when they sinned.

DISCUSSION QUESTIONS:

1. Using Old Testament Scriptures, cite evidence for the following truths:
   a. God does not want women to be treated as property.
   b. God demands that women be responsible to Him.
   c. God cares about a woman's emotional well-being.
   d. God's love and care is not given out with regard to a person's status in life.

    e. God treats women as if they are intelligent, thinking individuals.

    f. God expects and desires that women speak to Him personally.

    g. God cares about women's physical well-being.

    h. God rewards women who follow His way.

    i. God instituted the Law for women as well as men.

    j. God has a high regard for motherhood and the sanctity of marriage.

    k. God believes women have leadership ability.

2. What was the purpose of the Old Testament Law?

3. Why did God make special provisions for divorce?

4. Discuss how women influenced Biblical history.

5. Compare the influence that women had on men in Old Testament times with the influence they have on men today.

Chapter Five

WOMEN AS IMPORTANT INDIVIDUALS: IN THE NEW TESTAMENT

The Birth of Jesus

Even though Israel as a nation failed to communicate God's will and purposes to the world, and even though sin had a stronghold on the lives of men, God deemed the time was right to send His Son into the world. Through God's words and actions surrounding this momentous event, we can see how He looked upon women with great favor and respect.

Mary. God chose a young woman, Mary, to bear His beloved Son. Worldly logic would say God should have chosen a wealthy, socially prominent, older woman who had previous experience in rearing children. But God chose a virgin, a teenager, who came from a poor family that lived in the obscure village of Nazareth. She did not live in a palace; she did not command attention as she walked through the streets. She was simply a sweet, young girl who was highly favored by God (Luke 1:28, 30), regardless of (or perhaps partially because of) her humble background. Her husband-to-be was a lowly carpenter. When they took the infant Jesus to the temple, the young couple could afford only a pair of pigeons for the offering—the more wealthy would have used goats or lambs.

Mary, herself, was astounded that God would choose her to bear the Savior (Luke 1:47, 48). She gave thanks to the Lord—"for the Mighty One has done great things for me" (1:49)—and was elated because the promise that was given to Abraham would be fully completed through her (1:54, 55).

We can ascertain God's respect for Mary as a person because of the kind and understanding way He spoke to her through the angel. Mary was troubled by the appearance of the angel (as each one of us would be), but he told her, "Do not be afraid, Mary" (Luke 1:30). Then the angel explained that she had found favor with God and would bear His Son. But Mary was confused and was wondering how the birth could come to pass: "How can this be, since I am a virgin?" (1:34). The angel gave her reassurance and comfort, stressed the power of God, and mentioned that her relative Elizabeth would also play a part in God's plan (1:35-37). The mention of Elizabeth prompted Mary to visit her; the visit comforted Mary even more because of Elizabeth's testimony of how God was blessing her and her confidence (through God's revelation to her) in the greatness of Mary's child (1:42-45).

God also intervened to protect Mary from possible harm and probable disgrace by speaking to Joseph in a dream, assuring him of God's part in her pregnancy and that she had been chosen to bear the Savior. Joseph had the right as the injured party of an engagement contract (which in those times was as binding as marriage) to hold Mary up for public shame and punishment, for he would have assumed she had been sexually intimate with another man while engaged to him. Such an action was strictly forbidden. Or Joseph could have quietly gotten out of the engagement contract by divorcing her. But because of his dream and God's assurance that she was pregnant because of the Holy Spirit, Joseph took Mary as his wife.

Elizabeth. God also showed His concern for Mary's relative, Elizabeth. She was a righteous woman (Luke 1:6), the wife of a priest (1:5). But she was getting old and had no children as yet. Because of the emphasis on motherhood in that culture, she was humiliated by her barrenness. But God gave her joy and happiness when He informed her husband that they would have a child (Luke 1:13, 14) and emphasized how great that child would be. Elizabeth did not feel slighted that God did not speak to her directly but instead felt that God had indeed looked upon her with favor (1:25). Her joy was full to overflowing when she realized the part her son, John, would have in fulfilling God's will on earth. What an honor to bear the man who would be likened to the prophet Elijah, would be called the forerunner of the Savior, and would turn men back to God (1:15, 16, 76). And how privileged she felt to be aware that the child within her relative Mary was the Savior (1:41-45).

Anna. Amidst all the momentous and exciting events surrounding Jesus' birth, there was an elderly widow who served faithfully in the temple (Luke 2:36-38). She was the prophetess Anna who fasted and prayed continually. She was a proclaimer of God's truth and well aware of God's many statements about the coming of Christ. Her main hope in life was to see the fulfillment of that promise. What joy she felt when God made it possible for her to hear Simeon's proclamation about Mary and Joseph's child, see the Savior with her own eyes, and then immediately proclaim the Christ to everyone she saw. God did not overlook this faithful and trusting woman.

Jesus and God

In the first chapter of John, Jesus is called the Word and the Light. These word-images show clearly Jesus' purpose for coming to earth in the form of man. Words are the basic forms of communication from God to man and from man to man. Jesus, as the Word (John 1:1), is the communication to man of what God thinks, desires, and feels — the communication of who God is, of what God is really like. The nation of Israel had only given a partial and distorted view to the world of who God is. Jesus came to give the complete and perfect view of God's character, intentions, and loving concern.

Jesus was also the true Light (John 1:9). Light illuminates the darkness and reveals the true nature of things. Jesus came to penetrate the darkness of sin with the truth from God and came to reveal the true nature of God. Through Him, men and women could receive God's Spirit and be called God's children. In short, Jesus came to explain God to mankind (John 1:18) as well as to save mankind.

How could Jesus explain God fully and completely? Because Jesus was in the beginning at creation, was with God, and was (is) God (John 1:1). He was in the very bosom of God (John 1:18). Thus whatever Jesus thought, felt, said, or did was an explanation — a revelation — of what God thinks, feels, says, and does (John 5:30; 8:38; 12:49).

It follows then that Jesus' treatment of women would reflect what God thought about women and how they should be treated. Jesus' compassion for women would be an accurate reflection of how God cares for women as individuals. And Jesus' teaching concerning women and related subjects would be God's thoughts, desires, and intentions.

Through the following study, we will see that Jesus' actions toward and attitudes about women will be consistent with God's caring and intentions concerning women which were evident in the Old Testament. We will also notice how Jesus rose above the cultural and traditional practices of the day to elevate women's status and free her personally from the sinful aspects of male domination.

Jesus and Women

His Mother. Jesus' relationship with His mother can certainly give us a good indication as to what He thought of women. Mary must have been a competent mother, for Luke 2:52 tells us that "Jesus kept increasing in wisdom and stature, and in favor with God and man." Such growth would not take place if He were deprived of opportunities or of love and caring.

Yet we might wonder about Jesus' seeming rebuke of His parents in Luke 2:49: "And He said to them, 'Why is it that you were looking for Me? Did you not know that I had to be in My Father's house?'" The family had made the journey to Jerusalem to participate in the Feast of the Passover. On the way home from the festivities, Mary and Joseph realized that Jesus was not with the group. They hurried back to Jerusalem in a state of panic and searched for Him. They found Jesus conversing with the teachers in the temple. Even though amazed at the conversation and insights of her son, Mary reveals her anguish and worry by blurting out, "Son why have you treated us this way? Behold, your father and I have been anxiously looking for you" (Luke 2:48).

Jesus did not yell or scream at them; He did not hide from them; He did not act as a rebel. He calmly reminded them of His true parentage and wondered why they had been worrying. They should have realized that He would have been in the temple. Jesus' words were not an agitated rebuke, but were gentle reminders of who He was and His mission. We read later that Jesus was in subjection to His parents (Luke 2:51); and many times we are reminded in the Scripture that Mary pondered about the ways of her special child and "treasured all these things in her heart" (2:51).

Jesus' manhood continued to develop, and He prepared Himself for His ministry. He began to travel and chose His disciples. Just as it is with many others, Mary was not fully aware of His manhood. When Jesus and His disciples went to a wedding feast (where His mother was also in attendance), Mary automatically turned to Jesus when the wine ran out. He said, "Woman what do I have to do with you? My hour is not yet come" (John 2:4).

Jesus was not being disrespectful or bawling His mother out. The word "woman" in the Greek was a customary and respectful mode of address. It was the same as the word for "wife." A husband would call his wife "woman" in an affectionate and respectful way. Jesus could have called Mary "mother," which would have been simply another means of address. Today we would have good feelings about the term "mother" used as a form of address, but we would not be pleased with the use of the word "woman" in that way. But we must remember that in Bible times "woman" was used customarily as an address. Jesus was simply making it clear to His mother that He must go off on His own now and no longer be dependent on her. He was in effect "untying the apron strings," asserting His independence, and looking expectantly toward His public ministry.

Mary's feelings were not hurt by Jesus' words, so His words were not said in a stinging or sarcastic way. She was not dismayed that He talked to her in such a manner — thus the remark was not as harsh as it may sound to us. She simply turned to the servants and said, "Whatever He says to you, do it" (John 2:5) and stepped out of the picture.

85

She was certain of Jesus' powers and His inclination to meet needs; she also was beginning to get the idea that she was no longer Jesus' protector or boss. There was no rift in their relationship, for they all (Mary, Jesus, His disciples, His brothers) went to Capernaum together after the wedding (John 2:12).

Like most mothers, Mary still worried about Jesus, even though He was out on His own. She wondered if He was eating properly; she worried that He was working too hard (Mark 3:21). She was aware of how the leaders of the people disliked Him and tried to discredit Him in front of the multitudes. One particular time just after He had been accused by the Pharisees of being of the devil, Mary requested to speak with her son (Matthew 12:46). But Jesus said the apron strings must be severed; He had a job to do; He could not return to her loving breast and protective arms. He had to face the harsh realities of the world with His new family—His disciples: "And stretching His hand toward His disciples, He said, 'Behold, my mother and my brothers'" (12:49).

Then He placed the responsibility of His mother's individual faith and conduct at her own feet—"for whoever shall do the will of my Father who is in heaven, he is my brother and sister and mother" (12:50). It was Mary's responsibility to seek to do God's will herself, by "letting go" of Jesus and allowing Him to accomplish God's plan. Only then would she be His spiritual as well as His physical mother. Jesus was not being cruel or shutting His mother out. He was inviting her to do her part by allowing His ministry to continue "full speed ahead."

Jesus showed His deep love and concern for His mother as He was dying on the cross. Even though He was suffering much physical pain and emotional agony, He was concerned that His mother be taken care of (for she was apparently a widow by this time). He knew she would also need financial security. He told John to take her as his responsibility (John 19:25-27).

We can conclude that Jesus respected and loved His mother, gently reminded her from time to time of His special mission, and recognized that she was an individual with a mind, a person who could take responsibility for her actions, and one who had a deep emotional need as she viewed Him dying on the cross.

Women With Spiritual Needs. Jesus had great compassion for sinful women, which was a new experience for those women. Women of such poor reputations could not expect respect or caring from the men who knew them; they could only expect to be used by them or judged harshly by them.

(1) One such woman was the Samaritan whom Jesus met at a well near Sychar (John 4). Jesus was alone because His disciples had gone into the city to get food, and He was too tired to go with them, meaning it was probably evening.[1] In those times, the women usually went to the well to draw water in the morning or in the late evening. But most women would use the well in the center of town rather than this one located outside the town. Since this woman came alone to this less-used well, it may signify that she did not want to face the other women of the community because of her bad reputation. She did not want to be the subject of the stares, the nudges, and the harsh words that would probably accompany her shameful behavior.

---

1. In Jewish time, the "sixth hour" would be noon, but it is generally accepted that John used Roman time which would mean 6 a.m. or 6 p.m.

She had had five husbands (probably divorced each time) and was then living with a man without the ties of a marriage bond (John 4:16-18).

She was known by all the community to be sinful; yet Jesus, the Holy and Pure One, spoke to her and even asked something of her! To make matters even more complicated —Jesus was a Jew; the woman was a half-breed. The two peoples despised each other. The Jews usually bypassed Samaria when going to Galilee; and when they had occasion to step on Samaritan land, they quickly shook the dust of the land off their feet. And they certainly would not eat with a Samaritan, for they could not even touch one without being ceremonially unclean. And if that were not enough, she was a woman. According to the rabbis, Jewish men were not supposed to speak to a woman in public.

Jesus was truly not behaving like a "normal" Jewish male; He was rising above the traditional prejudices of the day. He decided to pass through Samaria instead of going around the country. And not only that—He spoke to a woman for quite a long time and asked her for a drink. Jesus had nothing with which to draw water from the well and He had no cup with which to drink, so actually He was asking to share the water and cup of a Samaritan woman! How unthinkable! How could He wish to share a cup of water with a "dirty Samaritan"!

The woman was amazed at Jesus' request (John 4:9). She hated Jews and did not trust men, but this man was different. The disciples were also amazed, not so much that Jesus would be talking to a Samaritan (for He had decided to go through Samaria, some type of contact would have been expected) —but that He would be talking to a woman (4:27)! It is quite obvious that Jesus was doing the "unconventional thing" in reaching out to a lonely, troubled woman.

When we study their conversation, we can note Jesus' compassion for her and His seeking to meet her need. We can see that He considered her to be a thinking individual of great worth despite her reputation. After showing her that He was not bound by the prejudices of the current culture (by speaking to her and asking for a drink), He sought to speak to her of spiritual matters; for He knew that to be her innermost need. If He had considered her to be of inferior intelligence and not able to speak of intellectual matters (as most men thought in those times), He would not have spoken to her in symbolic terms (living water, John 4:10) or even considered answering her question about the place of worship (4:21).[2]

Jesus prodded relentlessly but gently and kindly. She was evasive and tried to shrug off the penetrating truths. She even jested about getting some of the living water so she would not have to come to the well anymore (John 4:15). She did not want to talk about her inner problems and needs, but Jesus pointed out the basis of her need — her guilt about her past and present sins. He revealed to her His knowledge of her situation without having been told of it:

> "Go call your husband, and come here." The woman answered and said, "I have no husband." Jesus said to her, "You have well said I have no husband; for you have had five husbands; and the one whom you now have is not your husband, this you have said truly" (John 4:16-18).

Her perception of Him was becoming clearer and clearer — He was of God, some kind of prophet (4:19)! This woman was a half-breed and sinful, but she was not stupid!

---

2. Those who feel this woman was dense intellectually because of her answers and questions will have to concede that the disciples were also dense when Jesus spoke to them of spiritual terms (John 4:32, 33) on the same occasion. And how can we explain the *man* Nicodemus, a teacher, who did not know what the spiritual term "born again" meant (John 3)?

She tested Jesus even further by asking Him about the proper place to worship — which was one of the main lines of contention between the Jews and Samaritans. The Samaritans thought of themselves as Jews; they worshipped the same God and built a place of worship which they felt was every bit as good as the one in Jerusalem; but of course, the Jews found the feelings and views of the Samaritans about worship contemptible. "How would *this* Jew react to such a question?" she wondered.

Jesus' kind and compassionate answer (note the use of "woman" as means of respectful address, see page 85) reveals His love for her and His respect for her as a person:

> Woman, believe Me, an hour is coming when neither in this mountain nor in Jerusalem, shall you worship the Father. You worship that which you do not know; we worship that which we know; for salvation is from the Jews. But an hour is coming and now is, when the true worshippers shall worship the Father in spirit and truth; for such people the Father seeks to be His worshippers. God is spirit; and those who worship Him must worship in spirit and truth (John 4:21-24).

He pointed out to her the importance of the Jewish nation (the nation from which salvation — the Messiah — would come) but wanted her to know that to God one's race and one's place of worship made no difference. What mattered to God were one's motives and attitudes. Jesus was saying, "God will accept you. To God you are not considered lowly because you are a Samaritan, a woman, and a sinner. God loves you." He was telling her that she was a very special, worthy person.

She got His point about the Messiah right away (John 4:25), again pointing out her intelligence. Jesus stressed her specialness even more when He revealed to her that He was the Messiah (4:26). He had expressed that fact to only a few people thus far in His ministry.

She was so thrilled with Him and His words that she left hurriedly for the city, leaving her water pot behind. She could not wait to tell everyone about her experience. She wanted others to meet Him and see if her feeling that He was the Messiah was correct (John 4:29). She forgot about her shameful reputation amidst the joy of her discovery, as did many other Samaritans. Jesus showed this woman respect, love, and consideration. He thought of her as a person with a need. And, as a result, she became a new woman — a leader and an evangelist.

(2) Jesus was a guest for dinner at the home of a prestigious Pharisee, but that did not mean He would look down upon or turn away "a woman of the city, who was a sinner" (Luke 7:36-50). The word "sinner" used in this way usually referred to sexual unchastity (when referring to women). Evidently her unsavory reputation was known, for Jesus said, "Her sins, which are many, are forgiven, for she loved much; but he who is forgiven little, loves little" (7:47). The custom at the time was that at special festive dinners, the doors of a home could not be barred; thus many times people came in off the streets to observe the festivities.

A prostitute, a woman of the streets, came inside the Pharisee's home. She was humble and probably ashamed of her status in the eyes of the guests, but she was compelled to minister to Jesus. She had evidently heard about Jesus and about His compassion. She knew that He treated women with love and respect, unlike the other men she knew. She had no doubt heard of His healing of the son of the widow of Nain — perhaps she had even been in the crowd and witnessed His compassion for this woman first-hand.

She came into a house with a flask of ointment and with the intention of washing Jesus' feet and showing her appreciation for Him. The washing of another's feet was a necessary task in those lands of dusty streets, but it was the lowliest task there was. The slaves were usually delegated to do this task; but even they could refuse to do so, meaning the guests would have to wash their own feet. Evidently Simon, the host in this instance, did not provide a slave or even water to minister to his guests' needs (Luke 7:44).

Even though she had no water or towel, this sinful woman was determined to honor Jesus. She was so touched by the love and the purity she had seen and sensed in Jesus that her tears provided the water needed to wash off the dust from His feet. She used her hair to wipe His feet dry. She kissed His feet which in that time was an expression of the deepest respect. She poured ointment on His feet—an expression of bestowing great honor.

The Pharisee (Simon) showed through his calloused words his utter disregard for this "low-life" woman and was shocked that Jesus would allow her to even touch Him (Luke 7:39). Jesus pointed out Simon's entire lack of sensitivity as to how to meet another's needs and his inability to show respect and honor to someone else, by comparing his laxity with this woman's deep devotion and caring. How appalled Simon must have been to have been unfavorably compared to a woman and to an immoral woman at that! Jesus was again rising above the prejudices of this society, by showing that this woman was worthy of high praise instead of disdain and disrespect—and, in this instance, superior in her character and understanding to a highly religious *man*.

But Jesus did not stop there. He did not just talk *about* her or use her actions to make an instructive application. He spoke directly to her, releasing her from her sins and the guilt she felt because of them (Luke 7:48). He ministered to her deepest spiritual need. He freed her to turn her life around and live righteously. The faith she had in His character and power would save her from further sinning, enabling her to relate to God once again as a friend, rather than as a guilt-ridden enemy (7:50). He propelled her into a new type of life. Jesus emphasized to us all this woman's intrinsic value and worth as a human being, regardless of her status in society.

(3) The religious leaders of the day did not appreciate (and that is putting it mildly) Jesus' continual disregard for their traditions and customs and His assertions of His unique relationship with God. They took advantage of any opportunity to make Him look foolish, treasonous, or irreligious in front of the people who thronged after Him. They even *manufactured* opportunities.

The leaders could not wait to thrust the adulterous woman in front of Jesus (John 8:1-11).[3] With devilish glee in their manner, they asked, "What should be done to this obviously sinful woman? Moses said we should stone her" (8:4, 5, paraphrase mine). These self-righteous men were using a woman to entrap Jesus. They cared nothing for the woman; they didn't care what she was feeling while her shame was on public display. They used her as if she were a piece of property to make Jesus squirm and stutter around. If He said she should be stoned, He would not be showing the love and mercy He preached about. If He said she should

---

3. Although this incident was not included in the earliest manuscripts, it is wholly consistent with the attitudes and life-style of Jesus. It must have been believed by the early church, because it was passed down orally through the years and included in the later manuscripts.

be freed, He would be encouraging men to break the Mosaic Law and to commit adultery. Neither response would be palatable to the people.

However, Jesus did not worry about His answer; instead He was concerned for the woman. She must have felt great shame — being caught in sin, and then being paraded like a dirty animal before the accusing crowd. We do not know why Jesus stooped down and wrote on the ground, but perhaps it was to relieve the tension of the moment — to get the piercing eyes of the critics off of the terrified woman in their midst. He knew the accusers would automatically look down to see what He was doing.

Neither do we know what Jesus wrote on the ground. Perhaps He wrote, "Where is the man?" To be the sin of adultery there had to be a man involved. According to the Mosaic Law (Leviticus 20:10), both the man and woman were guilty and to be stoned; yet these same leaders who liked to spout forth the Law had in essence changed the Law to apply to women only. Men in this culture could get by with loose sexual morality. Perhaps Jesus quoted the Law on the ground and was pointing out to them the injustice of their accusations, in that they were accusing the woman but letting the man go free.

The second time Jesus wrote on the ground perhaps He listed the individual sins that He knew each person in the accusing circle had. Whatever He wrote, the accusers left quietly, one by one. A tumultous, angry scene was changed to a silent one. The woman was probably hunched down on the ground, noticing the passing shadows of the people as they left. She must have looked into the eyes of Jesus in utter incredulity. Just a moment before, she was afraid for her life, feeling the hatred and contempt of her accusers;

now she was left alone with a soft-spoken man who did not accuse her, though she had been caught in the very act of adultery.

If Jesus had been simply using this incident to teach a lesson, He could have walked away without saying a word. He could have left the woman to deal with her own guilt. But He cared about the woman as an individual; He considered her to be worthy and of value. He spoke directly to her and told her that He did not condemn her (John 8:11). He made her aware of the forgiveness she could have and told her to go her way and live a different type of life. He gave her back her dignity, her awareness that she was of value, and her motivation to go on living—but this time to live in a better way. He fulfilled her innermost spiritual need and gave her the impetus to change her lifestyle.

Women With Physical Needs. Jesus also rose above the prejudices of His day in His dealings with the sick. Sick persons were considered to be sinners. "Why else would they be sick, unless God was punishing them?" thought the Jews. But in Jesus' caring and compassionate treatment of the sick, we can know that sickness grieves God. God wants it relieved; He does not desire it for His people. Physical illness and infirmity are the consequences of the permeation of sin into men's lives, not a punishment from God. They are the natural consequences of the imbalance of all of nature and the results of sin in society.

The Scripture mentions several instances of Jesus' healing ministries to sick men, women, and children. Although more healings of men are recorded, there is no basis for the theory that Christ discriminated against women in this area. Just as there were women and children in the crowds who were fed miraculously, there were undoubtedly many women and children in the multitudes who thronged Him for the healing of their infirmities. Just as Jesus did not ignore or turn away from women who had reputations of being grossly sinful, He did not turn away from those women who needed His healing touch.

(1) Jesus and His disciples came to stay with Peter in his home, which was evidently used as a teaching and ministering headquarters (Luke 4:40). Peter's mother-in-law (probably a widow) was sick in bed with a fever (Luke 4:38, 39). Jesus touched her, and the healing was immediate and complete. She began to minister unto the physical needs of the guests, so they could soon receive the crowds of sick people who came at sunset (v. 40). Jesus realized her physical need and met that need, so she could serve others. How could Jesus and the disciples expect this woman who had been so ill to cater to their needs to eat? Were they being unfeeling? There is no record that they asked her to serve them or even expected her to. The point is that her healing was so complete that she felt great and was more than willing to help her daughter with the responsibility of being a good hostess.

(2) As has been stated before in this book, a widow's plight in the culture of Biblical times was pitiful indeed. A widow's main hope was that someone in her family would be responsible for her economical support. Thus when Jesus and His disciples came upon a grieving widow walking in a funeral procession near the gates of the city of Nain (Luke 7:11-18), Jesus had compassion for her. Her only relative — her son — had just died. Her family had disintegrated, no doubt leaving her emotionally as well as financially deprived.

Jesus put Himself in her place, knowing how lost and lonely she felt. He reached out with His words to comfort her saying, "Do not weep" (Luke 7:13). Then He reached out with His hands and touched the coffin (which would probably have been a type of stretcher). He did not worry about the rule concerning touching the dead; He knew He would not be polluted. He was only aware of the pollution in the life of this woman that this death would cause.

Then came the stirring command, "Young man, I say to you, arise!" (Luke 7:14). The effect was immediate. The widow's son sat up and began speaking. The son had been taken from her, but Jesus had restored him to her (7:15).

What a touching and clear example of Jesus' caring and compassion! The widow thought her life was finished, but then she met Jesus. Jesus was busy; He had places to go and people to see. He could have walked on by that funeral procession; He could have not given a second thought about an insignificant, grieving woman. Yet He stopped, He comforted, He ministered. This woman was important to Jesus.

(3) The woman with an issue of blood was considered "unclean" by the society in which she lived. Just as a leper and someone who had contact with the dead, she was supposed to isolate herself from people (according to the law, Leviticus 15:25ff.). She had been sick for twelve years and had never been able to find anyone to help her (Luke 8:43). She had spent all her money and had tried all the doctors (Mark 5:26). But she had heard about the powers of a certain man called Jesus. She had seen His miracles of healing as she stood on the outskirts of the crowds who followed Him. She believed He could help her.

But because of her uncleanness and the embarrassing privateness of her condition, she did not want to ask for His help. And she certainly did not want to be the focus of attention; for if others found out she was unclean and yet milling around among the throngs, she could receive harsh treatment. Yet she was willing to risk discovery, for she felt Jesus was her last hope. She pressed forward with the crowd, pushing through till she was behind Him. She stooped down and reached out to touch the hem of His garment. The healing was immediate (Luke 8:44).

The incident was not over, however. Even though hundreds in the crowd were touching Jesus, He felt some of His power being used (Luke 8:46). Somehow He sensed that a person needed His special attention, not just the physical healing attention.

The woman realized she could not hide what she had done; and, of course, feeling quite grateful and exhilarated to be freed of the awful burden, she told the crowd about her problem and how she had been healed. Jesus reached out to her in love by calling her "daughter" (probably meant the same as "daughter of Abraham" in Luke 13:16); He emphasized that she was no longer to be cast out or despised by society. He praised her for her faith and encouraged her to receive comfort from the fact that she would no longer be burdened by the physical malady. He stressed that her relationship to God was intact; now she could start a new life (Luke 8:48). Just as Jesus had done with the sinful women, He made her realize her true worth as an individual and encouraged her to live a new life in God. Because of the healing she received, she would no longer live in despair or be ashamed of who she was. She no longer had to live on the outskirts of the crowds; she was a new woman!

(4) With all these examples of Jesus' love and compassion that we have considered thus far, it would be hard to imagine that Jesus would turn His back on anyone or pretend that He did not hear someone crying out to Him with a need.

Yet when a Gentile woman cried out to Him to heal her demon-possessed daughter, He seemingly did just that (Matthew 15:21-28; Mark 7:24-30).

Jesus was tired and wanting to rest; He did not want anyone to know where He was (Mark 7:24). Only those who are constantly in the public eye can really understand His need to be relieved of the incessant needs of the crowds who thronged Him daily. A Gentile woman whose constant cries annoyed the disciples (Matthew 15:23) humbly placed herself at Jesus' feet and implored Him to help her daughter. At first, Jesus did not respond to her; then He rebuked her:

> Let the children be satisfied first, for it is not good to take the children's bread and throw it to the dogs (Mark 7:27).

The Jews habitually called the Gentiles "dogs," but the term Jesus used was the diminutive form meaning "little dogs" or "house pets." Thus His rebuke was not as harsh as it may appear on the first reading. Still it was a rebuke, and it is puzzling to commentators and scholars as to why Jesus responded to this woman in this way.

Jesus had just finished speaking to the scribes and Pharisees after they had been criticizing His disciples for eating with unwashed hands. Jesus pointed out their inconsistencies and deceitfulness in what they said and did. I'm sure He had His fill of them. Then as He was seeking to get away awhile for a short rest, an imploring woman cries out for His help. Jesus was never too tired or too busy to meet someone's need, so why did He turn a deaf ear to her? Perhaps Jesus was putting her off to test her sincerity and to show in a dramatic way to His disciples that there were people who honestly had faith in Him, quite unlike the leaders from whose presence they had just sought escape. Perhaps He wanted to show to His disciples that she was not just another seeker of miraculous signs.

The disciples would have looked upon this woman with distaste because of her sex and because of her race. Jesus' reference to the children of Israel in contrast to the "dogs" made clear to the woman and the disciples alike that He must go first to the Jews and seek to win them. He could have decided to go to the Gentiles at this point and might have been better received, but He knew His mission had to be fulfilled among the Jews first — and He was committed to that mission. Not even a sincere, needy woman could deter Him from that mission. [4]

The woman's reply showed her sincere faith, her humility, her unselfishness, her determination, and her intelligence: "Yes, Lord, but even the dogs under the table feed on the children's crumbs" (Mark 7:28). She understood Jesus' meaning and was assuring Him that she was not desiring to deter Him in His mission but was sincerely and simply seeking help for her daughter. She emphasized that she knew He could give her that help, and that she was asking for nothing more.

Jesus was pleased with her reply and her expression of belief (Matthew 15:28). He answered her request and healed

---

4. God's plan from the very beginning was to win the world through His chosen people, the Jews. The Jews failed miserably, but God always remained faithful to His covenant-relationship with them. Jesus, of course, would carry out His Father's intentions and plans. He knew He was to reach the Jews first and then through that nucleus reach the rest of the world. He chose Jews (twelve of them, modeled after the twelve patriarchs) to form the nucleus of the New Israel. The Gentiles would have received Jesus well; this was probably a source of great temptation to Jesus — why not leave these tradition-bound, hypocritical Jews and go to the Gentiles who might receive Him with open arms? But Jesus knew that this was not God's wish; it would not be fulfilling God's promise to His people.

her daughter. He showed her that He thought that she and her daughter were important.

Jesus tested the woman both for her benefit and for the benefit of the disciples. He wanted them to know of His mission priorities (even in the face of the needs of the Gentiles), of the importance of sincere faith, and of the necessity of meeting real needs. He wanted the woman to know that she was an individual from whom faith and responsibility were required; He refused to do as she asked just to get rid of her, much as one might brush a fly off his shoulder. Even though very weary, He took the time to point out God's truths.

(5) Jesus was continually thwarting the teachings of the religious leaders, which infuriated them. On one such occasion, Jesus was teaching in the synagogue (Luke 13:10-13). In the same place, there was a woman who had been crippled for eighteen years. She was grotesque; she was bent double; she could not straighten her back. How uncomfortable she must have been. How difficult life must have been for her to have to continually be in the bent-over position. But she did not blame God, for she was worshipping in the synagogue.

When Jesus saw her, He cared. He knew the physical and emotional pain she suffered daily. He thought not about what day of the week it was. He only thought about this woman's discomfort and how He alone could help her. He called her to Him and talked to her personally, comforting and assuring her: "Woman, you are freed from your sickness" (Luke 13:12). He touched her; immediately she was able to stand erect, and almost as quickly she was excitedly glorifying God (13:13). What freedom! She could walk normally; she could see people instead of feet and the ground!

In the midst of such happiness, the synagogue official was very upset (Luke 13:14) because Jesus had healed her on the Sabbath — a day set aside only for worship and rest. The official was more concerned about his rules and rituals than about a person with a need. Jesus pointed out the callousness and emptiness of such an attitude. He mentioned that they will untie an animal and water that animal on the Sabbath because they sympathize with the animal's need. Yet they felt no compassion for this Jewish woman, a descendant of Abraham (they loved to boast about their relationship to Abraham), who was in dire need (Luke 13:15, 16). Why were they so upset that He would untie her from her burden? Jesus was stressing that this woman was much more important to God than any animals or any holy day. Jesus restored to the woman her dignity and health and publicly defended her value as an individual. People, even women, were first with Jesus and thus with God.

Women as Jesus' Friends. Jesus chose only men to be His followers who would continue His mission and be named specifically as His disciples. Why did He not choose a woman? We could just as well ask, "Why did He not choose a Gentile?" Neither choice would have been conducive to the carrying out of His mission to reach the Jews first. In such a man-dominated culture, a woman would not have been accepted readily as a leader and speaker among the Jews. Men were the dominant and aggressive leaders in that time; that was their role in life. Whereas women were basically to keep the home and children. Also women in the group that traveled over so many miles would probably have given rise to suspicions of immorality.

Even though there were no women in the innermost group of disciples, Jesus did have women numbered among His followers and friends. (1) Mary and Martha of Bethany were sisters of Lazarus and very dear friends of Jesus (John 11:5). He was welcome in their home and often enjoyed refreshment and relaxation there.

On one such occasion, Martha was busy with the preparations for the meal. There would be much to do to feed the large group (His disciples were with Him, Luke 10:38). Mary chose to sit at Jesus' feet and listen to Him teach. The phrase "seated at His feet" was the term used to denote the relationship of a student and teacher. That Jesus would allow a woman to take on the position of a student would have been quite innovative; in those days, women were not encouraged to study and learn in the manner of formal education. They were encouraged to learn housewifely duties and leave the intellectual pursuits to the men.

Martha felt the most important thing at the moment was to get the meal ready, and she was angry that her sister was oblivious to that necessity and was making no move to help her with the serving. She was so incensed that she interrupted Jesus' teaching to complain and to request that He ask Mary to help with the serving (Luke 10:40). If Jesus felt that a woman's only role was to be in the kitchen serving others (as many felt in that day), then He would have asked Mary to fulfill her role and get busy serving.

Instead He rebuked Martha for having her priorities mixed up and for being worried about the unnecessary. He said, in essence, that the most important concern at the moment was His teaching, that Mary had chosen to listen, and He could not ask her to discontinue that good behavior and attitude (Luke 10:41, 42). Jesus was asserting Mary's right to listen, to learn, and to think about spiritual matters. Jesus was saying Mary was an intelligent individual, a valuable person, and had just as much right to study and learn as the men in His group.

At the same time, Jesus was not saying that women's role in the kitchen and in the area of service was wrong. He was not condemning Martha's activities; He was disappointed only in her attitude. He appreciated the many ways that Martha ministered to Him and His disciples, and no doubt Mary joined her sister in serving them many times. Jesus' use of the words, "Martha, Martha," showed His affection for her and the gentleness of His rebuke (Luke 10:41). He did not say she was letting the cares of the world destroy her spiritually or that because of her selfishness she would no longer have a part with Him. He merely told her she was too bothered and worried about the least important things at that particular moment. In Martha's anxiety, she was trying to force her sister to do what Martha thought she should do. Jesus was saying, "The meal can wait; allow Mary to be the individual she is. Allow her soul to be fed, before we feed our physical bodies."

We can tell that Martha had also been a student of Jesus by her responses at the time of Lazarus' death (John 11:24-27), so the problem was not that Mary never chose to serve or work in the kitchen but always chose the more cerebral occupations (notice her lowly acts of service in John 12:3), or that Martha always worked in the kitchen and never chose to learn spiritual truths from Jesus.

This occasion did not hurt the relationship of the sisters with Jesus, for when Lazarus got sick they sent word to Jesus immediately. They did not even request that He come to them; they knew of Jesus' love for Lazarus (John 11:3) and knew that He would be concerned and come soon.

When Jesus finally did come (after Lazarus' death), Martha left immediately to greet Him (John 11:20). Neither sister understood why Jesus had waited so long. They both greeted Him with these words, "Lord, if you had been here, my brother would not have died" (11:21, 32). They both recognized Jesus' authority (called Him Lord) and His power to heal, but they did not grasp why He had allowed Lazarus to die. This does not point out the stupidity of the women, for even Jesus' disciples did not understand Jesus' actions (11:11-16).

Jesus took the time to comfort Martha in her grief by assuring her of Lazarus' resurrection (John 11:23); she thought He meant the final resurrection at Judgment, but she expressed her unswerving faith in Jesus as the Son of God (11:27). Here again, Jesus treats a woman as an important individual and asks for her testimony of belief in Him (11:25, 26). He never thought of her as simply someone to meet His physical needs; He thought of her as a person with a mind and a capacity to think and reason.

Martha was not dense or stupid; she was a very logical, common-sense person. When Jesus asked that the stone be rolled away, she automatically thought of the practical consequences—the stench of a four-day-old corpse. It was not that she was stupid for not realizing what was going to happen. No one else knew what to expect either, as is shown by the questioning of the people (John 11:37) and by the reaction of everyone after the raising of Lazarus (11:45).

Mary was sitting in the house weeping, while Martha was greeting Jesus. It is interesting that Jesus asked to see Mary (John 11:28), pointing out again Jesus' treatment of women as valuable individuals. She came to Him immediately, and He reached out to her with compassion. He went with her

105

to the tomb where His emotions were expressed in weeping with all those there (11:33-35). He cared because His friends were hurting—the fact that two of them were women is important for us to note. Jesus' compassion knew no limits.

After the spectacular event of the raising of Lazarus from the dead, they were all gathered at the house again and Martha was serving (John 12:2). Unlike the earlier occasion, she went about her work and allowed Mary to choose her activity, which was the anointing of Jesus' feet. Judas Iscariot objected to Mary's action because the ointment was so expensive (12:4, 5). Jesus defended Mary's action, emphasized the humble devotion she showed, and expressed His appreciation for her thoughtfulness (12:7, 8). Again, Jesus pointed out Mary's value as a person and the rightness of her actions:

> Truly I say to you, wherever this gospel is preached in the whole world, what this woman has done shall also be spoken of in memory of her (Matthew 26:13).

Besides these very close friends, Jesus also had many women as His followers. They followed Him from place to place. Some had been healed by Him; some simply desired to support Him and His disciples financially (Luke 8:1-3). Joanna, Susanna, and Salome were of this group as well as Mary Magdalene. Mary, the mother of James and Joses, the other Mary, the sister of Jesus' mother, and the wife of Cleopas or Alphaeus (Matthew 27:56; Mark 15:47) are all mentioned as being in the group; but it is not known if this was referring to the same woman or different individuals. The Scriptures do not make clear all the women as to their roles or names; but we do know that these women followed Jesus, were at the cross, and were at the tomb.

(2) Joanna, the wife of a nobleman, had been healed by Jesus. She followed Him from place to place and ministered

to Him. She was present at Jesus' death; she stood "afar off" with the other women, and was no doubt with the group of women who prepared spices to take to His tomb (Luke 23:55, 56), took the spices to the tomb, and discovered its emptiness. She and the other women reported the reality of the empty tomb to the disciples (Luke 24:10).

(3) Salome, wife of Zebedee and the mother of two of Jesus' disciples (James and John), was also included in this group of women. She was nearby at His death and reported His resurrection.

As any mother, she was ambitious for her sons; but she found that her ambition was based on the wrong motives and on misunderstandings of Jesus' mission. She was rebuked by Jesus (Matthew 20:20-23) as were her sons (Mark 10:35-40). She mistakenly thought of Jesus as destined to be an earthly ruler with an earthly kingdom and wanted to be assured of special places of honor for her sons. Jesus made it clear that she did not understand what she was asking (Matthew 20:22). The rebuke was not out of anger, for Jesus knew the mistaken ideas of His followers and knew they would not fully understand till much later. Even after His resurrection, the disciples were expecting Him to declare Himself King of Israel (Acts 1:6).

But Jesus did use this opportunity to teach His disciples what it meant to be His followers, what suffering lay ahead, and who the truly great were—those who serve, not those who seek special honors or power. Jesus did not kick Salome or her sons out of the group of His faithful followers; instead He patiently taught them and impressed upon them the responsibilities that were theirs. He included both men and women in His call to be servants for Him and all mankind.

(4) Mary Magdalene who had been possessed by seven demons was freed to start a new life because of Jesus' caring

for her. We do not know the details; we only know that her new life included following Jesus from place to place and ministering to Him.

She and the other women followed Him to Jerusalem in His last days and watched Him die on the cross (Mark 15:41). She took note of where He was buried (15:47). Mary was puzzled by the rolled away stone and saw the empty tomb. She ran to tell Peter and John about the empty tomb; the two disciples came to investigate for themselves and returned home (John 20:1-10). But Mary remained at the tomb weeping and wondering where Jesus' body could be. Her deep love for Jesus was evident in the distressful tone of her response to the angels (John 20:11-13). She was not frightened or even surprised by the angels' appearance; she cared only about the body of her Lord.

Jesus chose to appear to Mary Magdalene and sought to comfort her in her grief (John 20:14-17). He related to her personally to relieve her grief, but He also gave her a job to do. He chose her to personally witness His resurrection. This is quite significant, since women were thought to be liars and were not trusted to testify in a courtroom.[5] Jesus again rose above the cultural prejudices and commanded Mary, a woman, to report to the disciples about His resurrection. It was the most important event in the history, the very basis of Christianity, and He chose a woman to first tell the good news about it! But the disciples acted as most men of that time would; they did not believe Mary (Mark 16:11). Even when she related how she had seen Him alive, they distrusted her testimony.

Jesus cared about Mary Magdalene and was concerned about her grief, but He emphasized to her and to the world

---

5. Joachim Jeremias, *Jerusalem in the Time of Jesus*, pp. 374, 375.

how much value He placed upon her as an individual when He chose her to be the first to see Him raised from the dead and to be the first proclaimer of the good news.

Jesus definitely related to women differently than any other man. He treated them with great compassion. Even as Jesus was being led to His death, He was concerned about the women who mourned in the streets for Him; He knew what pain the fall of Jerusalem would bring to them (Luke 23:27-29). He did not belittle women or treat them as inferiors. He did not condescend to them, but treated them as equals. He often emphasized to them how important they were. It is no wonder that the women were so faithful to Him during the misery of His death, were the first ones eager to minister to His body in the tomb, and the first to tell others of the risen Christ.

Summary

Through observing Jesus' attitudes and behavior toward women, it is not difficult to conclude that He thought of women in the following ways:

1. As worthy, valuable persons deserving of His love and concern,
2. As intelligent, thinking individuals capable of faith and obedience,
3. As persons with physical and emotional needs which He sought to fulfill,
4. As persons equal to men in worth,
5. As persons deserving of praise and sometimes of rebuke, but never to be ignored.

All of these attitudes are consistent with God's thoughts and intentions which were made clear in the Old Testament;

and since Jesus was "God in flesh" we can know that God thinks about women in the same way that Jesus did.

Jesus' Teaching About Women

Now we turn to a consideration of specific teachings of Jesus about women. Of course, we can expect His teachings to remain consistent with His attitudes and behavior.

Women's Role. Jesus did not teach specifically about a woman's role in life. He gave no commands that applied to women only. His teachings were directed to men and women equally, except for those times when He taught the disciples by themselves. He gave no directions about housekeeping or about a woman's place in the synagogue.

Of course, society at that time said woman's role was to be a wife and mother. Jesus did not teach that women should not continue in the roles of wives and mothers, but He made it clear that they were not to be considered as pieces of property or as inferior beings. Jesus accepted the services of women in several different instances (Luke 8:2, 3; Matthew 8:14, 15; Luke 10:38-42; John 12:1-8, etc.), but He never taught that only the women were to serve others or that women were to be confined to only those tasks. His concept was that each person is to serve others, regardless of sex, race, or station in life.

He directed His disciples to serve the crowds when He miraculously fed the five thousand (John 6:11-13). Notice He did not ask a group of women to come and serve everyone. He asked Peter and John to prepare the room and food for the Passover meal, not His women followers (Matthew 26:17-19; Luke 22:8-13). And who can forget His demonstration and teaching of humility and service when

110

He washed the disciples' feet and told them to serve others (John 13). He Himself prepared breakfast for His disciples after His resurrection (John 21:9) instead of asking His women friends to do so. Jesus taught by word and example that we are *all* to humbly serve one another.

But I must hasten to add that Jesus did not ignore the needs, problems, and attributes of women in His teaching. Jesus praised women publicly for their faith, devotion, and love and took these opportunities to teach those who were near at hand about these qualities. He praised Mary of Bethany for choosing the best activity and for anointing Him; He praised the "woman of the street" for honoring Him and the Syro-Phoenician woman for her faith. He praised a poor widow for her devotion and sacrificial giving (Mark 12:43, 44).

Jesus was concerned that wives be treated properly as is shown by His teachings on divorce. He taught that adultery, both in the overt action and in the lusting, was destructive to marriage and was a sin:

> You have heard that it was said, "You shall not commit adultery"; but I say to you, that everyone who looks on a woman to lust for her has committed adultery with her already in his heart. And if your right eye makes you stumble, tear it out, and throw it from you; for it is better for you that one of the parts of your body perish, than for your whole body to be thrown into hell. And if your right hand makes you stumble, cut it off, and throw it from you; for it is better for you that one of the parts of your body perish, than for your whole body to go into hell. And it was said, "Whoever divorces his wife, let him give her a certificate of dismissal." But I say to you that every one who divorces his wife, except for the cause of unchastity, makes her commit adultery; and whoever marries a divorced woman commits adultery (Matthew 5:27-32).

111

By stressing that "lusting after" was also a sin, He was teaching that women are not to be treated or thought of as mere sex objects. In Matthew 5:31, 32 Jesus placed responsibility upon the husband saying he would be wronging his innocent wife if he divorced her, regardless of the law about a bill of divorcement.

The society of that time considered adultery to be a sin if a woman committed it, but men were allowed to be unfaithful. Husbands were allowed to divorce their wives whenever they pleased, causing grave hardships (both physical and emotional) on the women. Jesus emphasized in this teaching that women had rights also. He sought to restore justice in this area of the Jews' thinking and sought to protect the women:

> And some Pharisees came to Him, testing Him, and saying, "Is it lawful for a man to divorce his wife for any cause at all?" And He answered and said, "Have you not read, that He who created them from the beginning made them male and female, and said, 'For this cause a man shall leave his father and mother, and shall cleave to his wife, and the two shall become one flesh?' "Consequently they are no more two, but one flesh. What therefore God has joined together, let no man separate." They said to Him, "Why then did Moses command to give her a certificate and divorce her?" He said to them, "Because of your hardness of heart, Moses permitted you to divorce your wives; but from the beginning it has not been this way. And I say to you, whoever divorces his wife, except for immorality, and marries another commits adultery." The disciples said to Him, "If the relationship of the man with his wife is like this, it is better not to marry." But He said to them, "Not all men can accept this statement, but only those to whom it has been given. For there are eunuchs who were born that

way from their mother's womb; and there are eunuchs who were made eunuchs by men; and there are also eunuchs who made themselves eunuchs for the sake of the kingdom of heaven. He who is able to accept this, let him accept it" (Matthew 19:3-12).

In this passage, Jesus emphasized the necessity for marriage to be a strong and permanent union as God intended for it to be from the beginning of time. He stressed that division and separation were man's work, not God's. He pointed out that the allowance for divorce was because of the great sinning of men. It was to protect the women who were being unfairly treated by their husbands and was to control the husbands' actions.

Jesus did not side with any Jewish school of thought on the issue, but pointed the listeners back to God's desire for permanent marriages and to the equality of man and woman in creation. Jesus was, in essence, calling for an end to discrimination against women in this area of life.

Jesus also defended women in other instances. He stressed that a woman's individuality, personhood, and obedience were much more important than her physical properties or her role in life:

And it came about while He said these things, one of the women in the crowd raised her voice, and said to Him, "Blessed is the womb that bore You, and the breasts at which You nursed!" But He said, "On the contrary, blessed are those who hear the Word of God, and observe it" (Luke 11:27, 28).

He also defended the widows against the cruelties of the hypocritical Jewish leaders (Matthew 23:14).

Jesus also included women and their everyday activities when illustrating truths. He spoke about the Queen of Sheba (Luke 11:29-32), the effect of discipleship on both men and women (Luke 12:51, 53), the effect of the end times on both (Matthew 24:40, 41), and how a woman has pain at the birth of a child (John 16:20, 21). He included women and their activities in several of His parables: The woman and the meal (Matthew 13:33), the ten virgins (25:1-7), the woman and the yeast (Luke 13:19-21), the lost coin (15:8-10), and the importunate widow (18:1-8). He in no way ignored women and their place in society.

We can discern from a consideration of Jesus' teachings that He recognized the presence of women and how they were contributing positively to the society. He considered them equal to men in dignity, worth, and in need. He desired that their rights be considered and that they be protected from injustice.

Women and the Early Church

When Jesus left the earth to return to His heavenly home, He did not intend for His message or mission to be forgotten or finished. He commissioned His band of followers to go throughout all the world, tell the good news, and make disciples of all nations (meaning all mankind, Matthew 28:18-20). No longer was God's message to be restricted to the Jews; it was to be extended to all people.

The book of Acts records the beginning of the church (the organization of Jesus' followers, called those of the Way, the brethren, the saints, Christians, etc.), the church's growth, the spread of the Christian message, and the work of particular preachers, evangelists, and leaders. The Epistles

114

(letters) shed even more light on the life of the early Christians, the joys and problems within the church, and the persecution from without. These writings give specific instructions for solving problems, encourage the Christians in the face of persecution and false teaching, and exhort them to live in Christ's way no matter what happens in the world around them.

Jesus fully intended that His attitude and behavior toward women be the example for those of the early church; He intended for the Christians to continue His efforts to elevate the status of women, to think of them as important individuals, and to expect them to contribute in many ways to His cause—the evangelization of the world. He expected the Christians to continue to treat women with love, respect, and compassion as well as allow them to study and work in the ministry of the church.

Thus we can expect that the record of the activities of the early church and the teachings of the Epistles are consistent with God's intentions and desires for women as well as with Jesus' example and teachings concerning women.

Women as Believers. We can know assuredly that women were among Christ's followers at the very beginning of the church (Acts 1:14) and were among the multitudes of people who heard the Christian message. We have abundant evidence that women responded to the message, became active Christians, and were thought to be equal to the male Christians in worth and dignity.

There are direct statements that both men and women believed, were baptized, and were added to the church (Acts 5:14; 8:12). It is evident from the use of the word "souls" (persons) in Acts 2:41 that women were included in that number that responded at the close of Peter's sermon

115

on Pentecost. There are references to whole households believing and being baptized, which would certainly include women (Acts 11:14; 16:33; 18:8). Saul, when persecuting Christians, did not discriminate; he sought to throw both men and women Christians into prison (8:3; 9:2; 22:4). The widows were numbered with the saints as friends of Dorcas and were no doubt among those who believed as the result of Dorcas' healing (9:41, 42). Surely women were included in the "all who lived at Lydda and Sharon saw him (Aeneas), and they turned to the Lord" (9:35).

It is stated directly that Timothy's mother was a believer (Acts 16:1) as was his grandmother (II Timothy 1:5). We have the undisputable record of Lydia's conversion (Acts 16:14, 15). Leading women of Thessalonica were persuaded and joined Paul and Silas (17:4); prominent women in Berea believed (17:12); and a woman named Damaris from Athens believed (17:34).

In Romans 16, Paul greeted many women Christians: Phoebe, Priscilla, Mary, Narcissus, Tryphena, Tryphosa, Persis, Julia, mother of Rufus, sister of Nereus, and perhaps Junias (might be a man). He exhorted two women in the Philippian church to be united (Philippians 4:2). He spoke of Claudia in II Timothy 4:21 and greeted Nympha of a church near or in Laodicea (Colossians 4:15). He greeted Apphia in Philemon 2, and he answered the communication from Chloe about the problems in the Corinthian church (I Corinthians 1:11). John wrote to an "elect lady" in II John 1. He could have been writing to a church; but after noting the parallel of his address to a man in III John 1 with that to the "lady," many scholars are inclined to think he was writing to a woman.

Women were held responsible (as they are now) as individuals before God for their sins. "For all have sinned and fall short of the glory of God" (Romans 3:23). Sapphira was held just as responsible for her lie as Ananias was for his (Acts 5:1-10).

But women also had (and still have) equal access to God and to the saving grace of Jesus:

For as in Adam all die, so also in Christ *all* shall be made alive (I Corinthians 15:22).

For there is one God, and one mediator also between God and man [mankind], the man Christ Jesus, who gave Himself as a ransom for *all* . . . (I Timothy 2:5, 6).

. . . Since, she is a woman; and grant her honor as a *fellow-heir* of the grace of life, so that your prayers may not be hindered (I Peter 3:7b).

As Jews, women were not allowed to participate in the rite of circumcision, to study Law, to become a priest, or worship with the men. But as Christians, the women were equal before God, could participate in baptism, could gather with the men for worship and study, and could become full members of Christ's body, the church:

For *all* of you who were baptized into Christ have clothed yourselves with Christ. There is neither Jew nor Greek, there is neither slave nor free man, there is neither male nor female; for you are *all* one in Christ Jesus (Galatians 3:27, 28).

Women as Workers in the Church. The female Christians were expected to participate as full members of the church's ministry (Romans 12:3-8; Ephesians 4:6-16, note the use of the word "all"). They would have participated in the church's activities of teaching, fellowship, prayer, breaking of bread, taking meals together, selling possessions, and sharing their wealth (Acts 2:42-47; 4:34-37; 5:1).

117

Women were present at the first prayer meeting of Jesus' followers in the upper room and took part in the selection of Matthias (Acts 1:14). Many Christian women were hostesses to church meetings held in their houses. Peter went to a prayer meeting of Christians at the house of Mary (mother of John Mark) after his miraculous release from prison (12:12). Lydia extended hospitality to Paul and his friends after her conversion (16:15); Paul returned to her house (after he was let out of prison) where evidently the church was meeting (16:40, note the term "saw the brethren").[6] A church near or in Laodicea was meeting in Nympha's house (Colossians 4:15). Priscilla and her husband started churches in their home (Romans 16:5; I Corinthians 16:19).

Women led in doing acts of charity, the best example being Dorcas (Acts 9:36-39). Women evidently performed special acts of service and perhaps held specific offices in the church organization in order to perform these services. Phoebe was called a helper or a deaconess, in Romans 16:2. Paul asked that she be treated with the same kind of consideration that he asked for the male leaders and elders (I Thessalonians 5:12, 13; I Timothy 5:17). Because of the similarity of the verbs, connecting words, and the phrasing in I Timothy 3:1-12 concerning the overseers, deacons, and women, some conclude that there might have been a special group of women formed for specific functions. I Timothy 5:9-12 lends some credence to the thought that perhaps there was a special group of widows formed to do certain functions. Indeed there is a reference in a secular source

---

6. It is interesting to note this church begun by this woman convert was the only church that supported Paul financially continuously (Philippians 4:15).

from the second century about deaconesses in the early church (Letters of Pliny), but we have no definite proof that women held these specific offices. We can conclude, however, that women performed many necessary services. At Tyre, the wives helped escort Paul out of the city and prayed with him (Acts 21:5) — showing their willingness to serve and how close-knit the family relationship of the church was.

We do know that women of that time had definite leadership abilities and influenced the life of the early church. Priscilla was a friend of Paul's, was definitely a leader along with her husband, and even taught a man about Christ (Acts 18:2, 18, 26; Romans 16:3, 5; I Corinthians 16:19; II Timothy 4:19). Chloe must have had influence to have Paul respond to her communication (I Corinthians 1:11). Euodia and Syntyche must have been key members of the church of Philippi (Philippians 4:2).

In Peter's sermon on Pentecost, he made clear that women would have a part to play in the beginnings of the church when he quoted Joel's prophecy about daughters prophesying as well as the sons, and handmaidens as well as manservants (Acts 2:15-18). Luke recorded that Philip's four daughters did prophesy (Acts 21:9), and Paul mentions the practice of women prophesying in the worship service (I Corinthians 11:5) and its commonness.

Acts 8:1 states, "they were *all* scattered" (referring to the church which would certainly include women). Verse 4 of that same chapter refers to those who were scattered saying, they "went about preaching the word." This could mean women proclaimed the good news as well as the men.

In Revelation 2:20, John mentions that the church is tolerating a woman called Jezebel who calls herself a prophetess.

119

He was not upbraiding them because they allowed a woman to preach, but because they were tolerating false teaching which was leading to immorality. This reference points out that women speaking in the church was a common thing.

The church continued living out the compassion of Jesus as they helped the brethren in Judea during the famine, as they shared their wealth with each other so that none lacked, in healing physical infirmities, and looking out for the needs of others, including the needs of women. Some of the widows were being neglected in having their daily physical needs met, so the people chose others who would have the time to help them (Acts 6:1-3). James included the care for widows in their distress as part of pure religion (James 1:27).

To prove further that women were full and active members in the early church, we have the instructions from the writers of the Epistles about the conduct and relationships of women. Paul dealt with their conduct in worship services and their marriage relationships (I Corinthians 11, 7, 14:33-35; I Timothy 2:9-14; Titus 2:1-10; Colossians 3:18, 19; Ephesians 5:21, 22). Peter admonished women about their attitudes and conduct at home and about their witness for Christ (I Peter 2:13 — 3:7). Of course, all the instructions and principles about living the Christian life found in the Epistles were as applicable to the women as to the men, except those that specifically applied to men, such as for husbands, elders, and deacons.

Women and Paul. It is important that we explore the attitudes, motivations, and teachings of Paul concerning women not only because he was a great leader and teacher in the early church and wrote the majority of the Epistles in the New Testament, but also because many scholars and women think Paul was a male chauvinist. Many will agree with most of what I have said thus far about how God looks at women, how Christ looks at women, and how influential women were in the early church; but they will not agree with what I have to say about Paul.

They feel that Paul showed in his teaching that he thought women were inferior, were to be put down and held down, and should be restricted in their activities simply because of their sex. Some say Paul did not have a full understanding of Christ's desire to eliminate the prejudice against women and his eyes were clouded by the trends of his culture. Others say he was often confused about the role of women and thus changed his mind about them often—perhaps because he was single and not experienced with women's ways. Others say he did not completely set aside his strict Pharisaical upbringing so that his old views and patterns of thought about women crept into his teaching from time to time.

I feel all these views could be summed up in one word—hogwash! As I stated in the preface, I believe the Bible, the entire Bible, is consistent and expresses God's desires for mankind. And I believe the *whole* Bible, though written by sinful men and about sinful men, is the inspired revelation from God. Paul was a man guided by the Holy Spirit; he sinned, of course, by his own admission many times, and he had to grow from a babe in Christ to maturity just as anyone else. But his words that were included in the Holy Scripture were written by a mature man of God and were not tainted by sinful thoughts or by his old life-style. In fact, he wrote that all the aspects of his past life he counted as rubbish or garbage (Philippians 3:8); in the context of that comment, we can conclude that he "threw out the garbage" or cast off his old ways and thoughts.

121

Paul wrote that in Christ there are to be no distinctions between male and female (Galatians 3:28). He was not saying that there are no differences between the sexes, but he was saying that being in Christ transcends all distinctions —yes, all prejudices—in this earthly life. He had been a devout and committed Jew, a part of the strictest sect of the religion; yet he was able to set aside his prejudices about the Gentiles when Christ sent him on a special mission. It follows, then, that Paul was also able to put aside his prejudices against women.

Paul emphasized again and again a woman's personal access to God as well as her responsibilities to God and her part in the activities of the church. As we have already seen, he recognized women as his friends and co-workers in the gospel; he evangelized women; he never intimated that their ministries were inferior to his or any man's (I Cor. 12, Romans 12). Paul called Priscilla a fellow worker in Christ Jesus (Romans 16:3), praised her, and gave thanks for her efforts on his behalf (16:4). The word "fellow worker" means helper and was the same Greek word he used to refer to Timothy (Romans 16:21) and to Luke (Philemon 24).

In Philippi, Paul showed his compassion for a slave girl who was possessed by an evil spirit and used cruelly by her masters to make money for them (Acts 16:16). She followed Paul around, crying out after him continuously. We are not told why she did this. Was she seeking for Paul's help? Or was she fully at the mercy of the demon within her and seeking to disturb Paul's attempts at evangelism in that city? Whatever the reason, Paul became very grieved and cast the spirit out of her (16:18, 19), freeing her of her distress and making her owners quite angry. Some translations say Paul was angry or annoyed with the girl, but the Greek word does not give us that idea. The word "grieved" (*diaponeomai*) means to labor through grief, meaning a high intensity of being troubled or grieved but not the idea of being angry or vexed.

Paul did write some difficult passages of Scripture concerning women. But if we keep in mind Paul's inspiration, the real meaning of the Greek words he used, the context of each passage, and the many passages in which he implied the equality of women with the men, we should be able to understand these difficult passages more easily. In the following paragraphs, Paul's writings that pertain specifically to women will be quoted and his views discussed.

(1) I Corinthians 7:1-5:

> Now concerning the things about which you wrote, it is good for a man not to touch a woman. But because of immoralities, let each man have his own wife, and let each woman have her own husband. Let the husband fulfill his duty to his wife, and likewise also the wife to her husband. The wife does not have authority over her own body, but the husband does; and likewise also the husband does not have authority over his own body, but the wife does. Stop depriving one another, except by agreement for a time that you may devote yourselves to prayer, and come together again lest Satan tempt you because of your lack of self-control.

a. Considering the context and the phrasing in the Greek in verse 1, Paul was responding to their question about whether they should have marital sex or not. The sentence "It is good for a man not to touch a woman" should be in quotation marks and have a question mark following it, because it is a question that the people have asked Paul. In the remaining verses, he was answering that question. The Christians were confused because in the heathen religions from which they had come, sex was a part of the worship. They did not want in any way to be going back to their old ways and were wondering whether marital sex was right or not. Paul assured them that sex between married partners is quite acceptable and desirable.

b. Paul addressed the wife as well as the husband and emphasized that the wife had claims on the husband's body just as much as the husband had on hers. He pointed out that the duty of sex is mutual and reciprocal. It is clear that to Paul marriage was a partnership in which the husband and wife were to communicate and make decisions together.

(2) I Corinthians 7:8, 9, 39, 40:

> But I say to the unmarried and to widows that it is good for them if they remain even as I. But if they do not have self-control, let them marry; for it is better to marry than to burn . . . A wife is bound as long as her husband lives; but if her husband is dead, she is free to be married to whom she wishes, only in the Lord. But in my opinion she is happier if she remains as she is; and I think that I also have the Spirit of God.

a. Paul affirmed that he preferred the single life and preferred that widows and widowers not seek to remarry, but that was to be strictly their own decision—both men and women were free to decide for themselves.

b. Paul made clear that divorce was not to be the natural course of events, but that the partners were to be bound to each other for life (v. 39). Saying that the woman was bound does not mean that the man was free to divorce while the woman was not. This thought would be inconsistent with God's wishes in all the rest of Scripture and would not fit into the context of this chapter in which Paul is clearly speaking to both partners in the marriage relationship and emphasizing their equality.

124

c. In 7:25-35, Paul made his preference for singleness known (for both men and women) but said, "make up your own minds."[7]

d. In 7:37, 38, Paul allowed fathers the choice of whether to give their daughters away in marriage or not—a practice which would be in keeping with the Jewish custom.

e. In 7:10-17, Paul treated both the husband and wife equally in the question of whether or not to divorce when married to a non-Christian. He told them both to remain with the mate if the mate agrees and assured them that the children resulting from the union would not be tainted by the non-Christian. Paul's main concern was that the Christians do what was best in order to win the non-Christian.

(3) I Corinthians 11:3-15:

> But I want you to understand that Christ is the head of every man, and the man is the head of a 'woman, and God is the head of Christ. Every man who has something on his head while praying or prophesying, disgraces his head. But every woman who has her head uncovered while praying or prophesying, disgraces her head; for she is one and the same with her whose head is shaved. For if a woman does not cover her head, let her also have her hair cut off; but if it is disgraceful for a woman to have her hair cut off or her head shaved, let her cover her head. For a man ought not to have his head covered, since he is the image and glory of God; but the woman is the glory of man. For man does not originate from woman, but woman from man; for indeed man was not created for the woman's sake, but woman for the man's sake. Therefore the woman ought to have a symbol of authority on her head, because of the angels.

7. For a more detailed discussion of the state of singleness versus marriage, see Chapter Six on Women as Wives.

However, in the Lord, neither is woman independent of man, or is man independent of woman. For as the woman originates from the man, so also the man has his birth through the woman; and all things originate from God. Judge for yourselves; is it proper for a woman to pray to God with head uncovered? Does not even nature itself teach you that if a man has long hair, it is a dishonor to him, but if a woman has long hair, it is a glory to her? For her hair is given to her for a covering.

a. The women in Corinth were evidently unsure about how to handle their new-found freedom in Christ and needed some guidance concerning their conduct and example to others in the church and in the community.

b. In verse 3, Paul's view about the relationship of husband and wife (same words as for "man" and "woman," so we must depend on the context to determine the meaning; this passage is speaking of the marriage relationship and the conduct of married persons in the worship service) is consistent with God's view which was discussed in detail in Chapters One (pp. 11-13) and Two (pp. 22-25). The man has the privilege of leadership over the wife; he is to be her loving leader, protector, and guide. This relationship promotes harmony in the home and in no way indicates the husband's superiority over the wife.

c. Paul was speaking about the conduct of both mates in the worship service. He recognized that the wives could pray and prophesy as well as the husbands (so how could he think that women could not speak in church services?).

d. In verses 5-10, was Paul speaking about veils, hats, or a certain way of fixing a woman's hair? Scholars are not sure. The Greek word could mean any one of them, and the context could point to any one of them. At this point,

126

we need to consider the customs of the time: (1) When in public, married women wore veils or their hair done up in a knot or braids on top of their heads ("covering on her head" could mean either). This was a sign to all that she was not available but belonged to and was under the leadership of her husband. (2) Available, unmarried women and prostitutes did not wear veils and wore their hair loose around their shoulders. (3) A woman had to shave her hair (or cut it off short) if found guilty of adultery.

The Christian women of the Corinthian church may have gone to extremes to show their new status in Christ and let their hair hang loose or go without veils in the worship service. Paul was concerned about their example and witness. He said if they were going to by-pass the custom, they might as well shave their heads because they were showing to the world and their fellow Christians that they were available. But, in fact, they were married. They were acting as if they were ready to become adulteresses. He was saying they needed to retain this custom of the veil or hair-do in order to show their purity as Christian wives and not be poor witnesses for Christ in the community. He was making a practical application of his thoughts just preceding this passage — that they should live in order to save others (I Corinthians 10:31-33).

We can understand verses 7-10 better if we remind ourselves of the study of creation (Chapters I and II). Both men and women were made in the image and likeness of God and were to reflect God's character in their lives. We also know that the wife had the additional responsibility of completing and helping the husband. Paul was probably repeating this concept in verse 7, rather than downgrading women or placing them under men. When he said that woman originated from man, he was not referring to her subordination to man. Man was made from the dust of the earth, but he would not be considered subordinate to the earth. When Paul said "the woman is the glory of the man," he meant the wife is the reflection to the world of her husband's character because of the unique relationship of marriage and her responsibility to support him in his leadership role in the home. This understanding sheds light on verses 8-10 and means that Paul's teaching remained consistent with the rest of Scripture.

In essence, Paul was saying: if a wife appears to the community as a loose woman, she is reflecting dishonor upon her husband's character as well as her own. A loving, caring, Christian wife would not wish to do such a thing; she would instead want to show to the world her pure relationship with her husband (v. 10).

e. In verses 11 and 12, Paul emphasized the interdependence between the mates in the marriage relationship; neither mate was to act independently of the other, and God was to guide all their actions because He is their Creator.

f. Paul then told them to judge for themselves what their proper witness should be (v. 13).

g. Paul repeated the necessity to adhere to the customs of the time because of their witness to others, by stating what the people in that culture thought of certain hair styles (verses 14-16).

h. Paul's reference to angels in verse 10 is difficult to understand; the scholars have no answers. An angel is a messenger or agent from God, which could mean a person as well as a heavenly being, so Paul could have been referring to leaders in the church. Or could Paul have been thinking about the rebellion of the angels in the beginning of time? He could have been saying that the wives should seek to be good examples of submission—even to those hosts in heaven. Elsewhere we find indications that the angels of heaven are watching the church to discern God's plan (Ephesians 3:10, I Peter 1:12).

(4) I Corinthians 14:34, 35:

> Let the women keep silent in the churches; for they are not permitted to speak, but let them subject themselves, just as the Law also says. And if they desire to learn anything, let them ask their own husbands at home; for it is improper for a woman to speak in church.

a. We can ascertain from the context that Paul was speaking about conduct within a worship service. Members were speaking simultaneously and causing confusion during the service. They were anxious to use their gifts of the Spirit, but were forgetting that they were to seek to edify the church not themselves (vs. 12, 17-26). Paul was giving them instructions in order to have a peaceful and edifying worship service, not an individualized confusion (v. 33).

b. It was obvious that Paul was talking to wives (note— "husbands at home" v. 35).

c. "Let the women keep silent," v. 34. The Greek for "keep silent" (*sigao*) means to act quietly. It is not the word (*phimoo*) which means to muzzle, to shut up, to silence. "It is improper for a wife to speak in church," v. 35. The Greek word for "speak" (*laleo*) can mean arguing, chattering, or questioning, which fits the context of this passage. The wives were (in this context) evidently chattering or asking questions during the service, adding to the confusion. Paul was simply saying, "Don't disturb the worship service; ask your husbands at home your questions about what was said."

Paul could not have meant that women were never to say a word in church because of his statement in I Corinthians 11:5 (prophesying was not done only in private — 14:24-26, 29, 31), because he encouraged all Christians to prophesy (14:1-5), and because such a view would be inconsistent with all the rest of the Bible.

d. The reference to being "subject" (*hupotasso*) in verse 34 meant to "set in array under" or "to set in order." Paul was saying "get yourselves in order so there won't be confusion and noise in the worship service." Paul used the word "law," which can refer to a custom (as well as an ordinance), which fits the context.

e. Paul was making his guidance specific by pointing out those who were causing the problem — those speaking in tongues, those prophesying, those praying out loud, and some chattering or questioning wives (14:34, 35).

(5) I Timothy 2:9-15:

Likewise, I want women to adorn themselves with proper clothing, modestly and discreetly, not with braided hair and gold or pearls or costly garments; but rather by means of good works, as befits women making a claim to godliness. Let a woman quietly receive instruction with entire submissiveness. But I do not allow a woman to teach or exercise authority over a man, but to remain quiet. For it was Adam who was first created, and then Eve. And it was not Adam who was deceived, but the woman being quite deceived, fell into transgression. But women shall be preserved through the bearing of children if they continue in faith and love and sanctity with self-restraint.

a. Paul is dealing with the husband-wife relationship in this passage also. Notice the close parallel of this passage with I Peter 3:1-6. Both deal with women's outer adornment, women's behavior, and submissiveness, and both give an

130

Old Testament example of a husband-wife relationship. Paul also refers to child-bearing in verse 15. He surely was not speaking about single women!

b. Paul's guidance about the adornment of women (v. 9) was not meant as a "put-down." He was simply telling the wives to not be as other women in the pagan culture who were overly concerned with their appearance, but to be wise and moderate in their adornment and thus show their uniqueness as Christians. They would be showing to the world their wisdom and where their values lay. They were to be more concerned about the good they could do for others than about the money and time spent on their appearance.

c. Paul recognized that women could study and learn, showing he had put aside his Jewish thoughts about women (v. 11). When Paul spoke of submissiveness, it is in the context of the marriage relationship and consistent with God's intentions. He was not saying that *every* woman must be submissive to *every* man, nor that *no* woman can teach *any* man.

d. In verse 12, Paul was still speaking about the marriage relationship. The phrase "teach or exercise authority" in the Greek means acting independently and domineering over. It is the picture of the wife becoming a dictator in a marriage and acting wholly without her husband's guidance or leadership. She would be acting outside of God's guidelines established at creation, and she would get into trouble just as Eve did when she acted independently of her husband (verses 13, 14). To "remain quiet" did not mean "do not speak" in the Greek. It meant self-restraint, tranquility, and a quiet life-style. The thought fits in with Paul's comments about moderation in dress (v. 9) and is the same

131

word used in verse 2 of the same chapter: ". . . in order that we may lead a tranquil and quiet life . . ." (also used in II Thessalonians 3:12, translated "quiet fashion"). Makes one wonder why the translators translated it properly in two places but improperly when pertaining to wives, doesn't it?

We can see that Paul was in no way prohibiting a woman from speaking in the church or in the home, but was simply admonishing wives to be prudent, moderate, submissive to their husbands, and self-controlled.

e. "Preserved through the bearing of children" is another troublesome phrase about which the scholars are not certain. If we consider the context, it is very unlikely that he is talking about a woman's eternal salvation. It seems logical that he was talking about a wife's relationship with her husband as he was in the preceding verses. He was probably saying a wife is not to be ruling her husband but to be concerned with her children and her proper behavior, thus preserving her womanhood as God created her to be.

(6) Colossians 3:18, 19:

> Wives, be subject to your husbands, as is fitting in the Lord. Husbands love your wives, and do not be embittered against them.

a. Paul addressed the wives directly, evidently considering them to be responsible persons just as he considered the husbands to be. He told the wives to voluntarily submit to the husbands' leadership. The idea in this sentence is active. It is not the idea that the husband does to the wife and she just sits back and endures. It is the idea of the wife actively yielding to the husband's leadership; the concept is wholly consistent with God's intentions for marriage.

132

b. Husbands are to "love" (*agape*) their wives. This type of love is the unselfish, caring love, the putting-another-first love, the doing-what-is-best-for-the-other-person love. There is no hint in Paul's statement of a dictator-slave type relationship that many say Paul was advocating. "Embittered" means being "sharp or pointed" in the Greek (*pikraino*) and is also used in Revelation 10:10. It could be referring to a "gouging" of the wife either physically or emotionally. Or it could mean "do not let the responsibilities of headship become a sharp pain to you." Paul hardly sounds like a male chauvinist in this passage where he stresses the loving and caring for the wife's needs.

(7) Ephesians 5:21-33:

And be subject to one another in the fear of Christ. Wives, be subject to your own husbands, as to the Lord. For the husband is the head of the wife, as Christ also is the head of the church, He Himself being the Savior of the body. But as the church is subject to Christ, so also the wives ought to be to their husbands in everything. Husbands, love your wives, just as Christ also loved the church and gave Himself up for her; that He might sanctify her, having cleansed her by the washing of water with the word, that He might present to Himself the church in all her glory, having no spot or wrinkle or any such thing; but that she should be holy and blameless. So husbands ought also to love their own wives as their own bodies. He who loves his own wife loves himself; for no one ever hated his own flesh, but nourishes and cherishes it, just as Christ also does the church, because we are members of His body. For this cause a man shall leave his father and mother, and shall cleave to his wife; and the two shall become one flesh. This mystery is great; but I am speaking with reference to Christ and the church. Nevertheless let each individual among you also love his own wife even as himself; and let the wife see to it that she respect her husband.

a. Paul was stating the general principle that each Christian is to be submitted to every other Christian. We must be willing to yield (an active verb) to one another; we must seek to put others first. The rest of the passage (which extends into chapter 6) discloses the specific practical applications of that principle.

b. Application to the wives: Just as God intended at creation, wives are to submit to the leadership of the husbands. The relationship is like that of Christ and the church; the church recognizes Christ's leadership and submits to it. "In everything" would be "in every" if translated literally. Paul could not have meant that a wife must submit in every situation. Otherwise, why was Sapphira punished for submitting to her husband? (Acts 5:1-10). We must consider the context and go back to verse 22 to the phrase "as to the Lord" and to the parallel passage in Colossians 3:18 ("as is fitting in the Lord"). Wives are to submit in all situations that are under the Lord's guidance. This would fit in with the context of the husband being under the Lordship of Christ (I Corinthians 11:3). Peter also referred to such submission but qualified it by mentioning *chaste* behavior, meaning a woman was to submit as long as she could remain pure in that submission (I Peter 3:2).

c. Application to the husbands: As Paul stated in Colossians 3:19, husbands are to love (*agape*) their wives. Paul explained this self-sacrificing type of love by comparing it to Christ's love for the church and showed to what a great extent Christ was willing to express His love for the benefit of the church — He gave His own life. Husbands are to love

134

their wives that much also. They are to love their wives as much as they love themselves, thus thinking of their wives' needs as well as their own (v. 28). "Nourish" is from the Greek root word (*trepho*) which means to bring up, or as we would say it, "look after" (v. 29). "Cherish" (*thalpo*) means to soften or to treat tenderly and carefully, emphasizing the sweet tenderness of a husband's love.

d. Paul's reference to Genesis 2:24 points out his intention to make clear God's desires for the marriage relationship. If all that he said had been contrary to God's original desires, he would have hardly quoted that Scripture which points out the closeness and unity of the relationship based upon the equality of two persons committed to becoming a partnership.

(7) I Timothy 5:9-15:

> Let a widow be put on the list only if she is not less than sixty years old, having been the wife of one man, having a reputation for good works; and if she has brought up children, if she has shown hospitality to strangers, if she has washed the saints' feet, if she has assisted those in distress, and if she has devoted herself to every good work. But refuse to put younger widows on the list, for when they feel sensual desires in disregard of Christ, they want to get married, thus incurring condemnation, because they have set aside their previous pledge. And at the same time they also learn to be idle, as they go around from house to house; and not merely idle, but also gossips and busybodies, talking about things not proper to mention. Therefore, I want younger widows to get married, bear children, keep house, and give the enemy no occasion for reproach; for some have already turned aside to follow Satan.

a. We don't know what the "list" was that Paul was referring to. These widows could have been a certain group set aside to perform certain functions, or they could have been on the list to receive economic aid from the church, or a combination of both as verse 16 might indicate. Whatever it meant, those women on the list were to be older widows with good reputations and characters and attitudes of humble service.

b. The younger widows were not to be on the list because they would still be of marriageable age and would not be able to carry through with their vows or their way of functioning with others on the list. Paul's language may sound strong here, but he was emphasizing that women should not lock themselves into something that they would not be able to uphold or would not want to in the future. He was actually freeing the young widows so they could have a future in marriage.

c. Paul pointed out that the most desirable role for these young women (the women of that culture would have agreed with him) was for them to become wives and mothers. He was also pointing out how important and demanding a role that was, for without this "work at home" they would have extra time on their hands and would be tempted to yield to Satan's ways.

d. Again Paul was emphasizing that Christians should be alert to how their examples for Christ are affecting their environment.

(8) Titus 2:1-5:

But as for you, speak the things which are fitting for sound doctrine, older men are to be temperate, dignified, sensible, sound in faith, in love, in perseverance. Older women likewise are to be reverent in their behavior, not malicious gossips, nor enslaved to much wine, teaching what is good, that they may encourage the young women to love their husbands, to love their children, to be sensible, pure, workers at home, kind, being subject to their own husbands, that the word of God may not be dishonored.

a. Paul was concerned that Christians have the proper life-styles and values and thus be proper witnesses for Christ in the community. He included the women as well as the men in his instructions.

b. Paul recognized the ability and the responsibility of women to teach (v. 3).

c. The older women were to encourage the younger women to love their husbands and children, to be sensible, pure, and kind. They were to encourage them to be "workers at home" which meant those who keep their houses and make their family a priority. Paul nowhere says that is *all* that women are to do. His comments on women teaching and prophesying would not be consistent with the idea that women were to be at home *only*.

d. Again, he says the young women should be *subject* to their husbands, which literally means "to set in order" and comes from the same Greek root word as "submission." The wife is to strengthen the order and harmony in the family by submitting to the husband's leadership. Note that Paul said "to their own husbands"; Paul did not say *every* woman is to be subject to *every* man.

e. "That the word of God may not be dishonored" literally means "to speak injuriously of." Paul was concerned that no one have a cause to speak badly of the Word of God. Because of the wife's unwillingness to behave in all these ways, she could be causing great harm to the cause of Christ.

f. Consider verses 1, 2, 6-8 in this chapter and notice that Paul did not single out women and give them instructions because they were more sinful or because they were so weak that they needed extra help. He gave just as many instructions to the older and young men. Many of the guidelines were the same for both sexes. The differences have to do with differences in roles, not in value or ability.

Summary. We have discovered that Paul was not down on women. He did not think of them as inferior beings who were to act as slaves or as the property of men. He did not ask them to never speak in church, to never teach, and to always remain at home. He considered them equal to men in value and contribution to the cause of Christ.

Although Paul preferred the single life for himself, he recognized the necessity for marriage and upheld the validity of God's intentions and desires for the relationship. He in no way promoted the idea that wives are to be the slaves of a dictator husband. He stressed the loving-giving, interdependent relationship in quite eloquent terms.

Paul was concerned that the worship services be handled in decency and in order and admonished the women to do their part to promote peace instead of confusion. Paul's main concern throughout the majority of his writing was the effect of the Christians' witnessing upon the world. In all that he said to women, he was concerned that they conduct themselves properly in all their relationships so that no one outside the church had reason to accuse the way of Christ but would instead be won to Christ.

For Women

You are a woman. You are somebody special. No matter where you are or what you are feeling at this moment, you are important. You are just as important to your family, to your community, and to the world as is your husband, father, or brother. You are a unique and beautiful individual created in the image of God. You have intelligence, you have deep-felt emotions, you have a spirit, you have a physical body that is wonderfully made.

Someone cares about you and knows how important you are — God. He knows everything about you and yet He loves you. He wants the best for you. He wants you to be happy, to be secure, to be content, to be fulfilled. He created you, so He knows what will benefit you the most. He does not want you to be lonely, to be depressed, or to feel inadequate.

He made you to be feminine. He made you to be different from men, so that you could form a complementary relationship with a man (unless you have the gift of celibacy), so that you could each "fill in" where the other lacked, so that a partnership of equals could be formed, so that families with children could be established. In God's plan, you are of great value and worth; and in the scheme of things, your happiness and fulfillment depends on your submission to His will for you. But He does not force you to go His way. He knows you have a mind and can make decisions for yourself. You are nobody's puppet — not even God's. But He does hope that you will decide to love and obey Him.

No matter how man or society treat you or look at you, you can know that God loves you and cares for you. He considers you to be indispensable to His work on earth. He considers you so important that He sent His Son to earth to die for you, and He makes available His own Spirit to live within you to give you the strength to live as the person He knows you can be. And He gives to you the written Word which spells out the guidelines for you to have a fulfilling life.

You may not be proud of the person you are this very minute. You may not like the way you look at times. You may not like the way you behave at times. But you should be proud of and love the person God designed and intends for you to be. You should be thankful for the physical body you have, the intense emotions you feel, and for the wonderful mind you have with which to think and reason. You should be thankful for God's love and for how He looks at you. You should be thankful for the opportunities you have to exercise your mind and your abilities.

If you are truly thankful, you will take care of your physical, emotional, and intellectual being. You will not participate in habits or activities that will harm your body or mind. If you are truly aware of God's love for you and how speical He thinks you are, you will turn to Him in obedience. You will respond to His love and will reach out to others with that same kind of love.

You must seek to not allow worry, frustration, and confusion to become the habit-pattern of your life and bog down the great woman you can be. You must look beyond yourself and your external circumstances to the victory that you can have as a Christian seeking to live like Christ. You must take advantage of every opportunity to improve and grow physically, socially, emotionally, intellectually, and spiritually. You must seek to allow the Holy Spirit to work God's miracle within you — the miracle of growing daily into Christ-likeness.

When you realize what a valuable person you are, when you realize how much you can contribute, when you realize the full breadth of God's love for you, you will not feel the need to criticize or downgrade others in order to make yourself look better. You will not gossip, make sarcastic remarks, or seek to destroy another person. You will feel no need to whine, to complain, or to pout because of your lot in life. You will not stoop to deceitful methods to get your way; neither will you push, shove, or step on others. You will not feel the need to demand your rights or your way. You will not act out of pride or selfishness. Instead you will think of others and seek to meet their needs.

You will not seek to become the "boss" in your family or seek to become independent of what men can contribute to your life. You will not seek to escape your responsibilities; you will accept whatever they are without a rebellion or resentment.

You will seek to make the best use of your capabilities, serving God with your whole being. You will serve Him as a teacher, musician, doctor, engineer, hostess, saleslady, mother, or as a floor scrubber—wherever your abilities and interests lead you. You will know that God is with you and for you in whatever you want to do—as long as you keep your priorities straight. You will seek to further the cause of Christ in your contact with all those whose lives you touch. You will never need to apologize or be ashamed because you are a woman and not a man.

YOU ARE WOMAN

You are somebody special
You are wonderfully made
You are feminine
And for you also, God's plans were laid.

You are worthy and unique
No one is the same
You are female
And for you also Christ came.

You can laugh, you can cry
You can dream, you can sigh
But only God could care so much
That for you also His Son should die.

You are somebody special
You are not an insignificant clod
You are beautiful and complex
You are a woman made by God.

DISCUSSION QUESTIONS:

1. Explain what John meant when he wrote, "In the beginning was the Word, and the Word was with God, and the Word was God" (John 1:1) and tell how this verse relates to Jesus' purpose on earth.
2. Describe Jesus' relationship with His mother.
3. Cite all the incidents in which Jesus rose above cultural restrictions to minister to women.
4. What evidence do we have of the intelligence of the woman at the well in John 4?
5. How was Jesus a friend to women?
6. How were women influenced in their contacts with Jesus?
7. What do the incidents in Luke 7:36-50, Luke 13:10-16, 8:1-11 show us about the Jewish cultural view of the value of women? What do they show us of Jesus' view of women?
8. How did Mary and Martha differ? How were they alike?
9. Cite instances of Jesus' patience in His relationships with women.
10. Jesus did rebuke women at times. When and why did He do so?

11. What evidence do we have that Jesus expected both men and women to have *serving* ministries?
12. What conclusions can be derived from Jesus' teachings concerning those things that touched women's lives?
13. Summarize how the early church viewed women.
14. Many say that Paul was a male-chauvinist and that his writings should be taken out of the Bible. How does such thinking affect one's view of the Bible? What evidence do we have that Paul was not down on women?
15. What was Paul's view of marriage?
16. Make two columns on the chalkboard. Entitle the first column — God and Jesus' view. Entitle the second column — Paul's view. Then compare the views on each of the following points:

    a. Are women equal to men?
    b. Are women to be allowed to be leaders in the church?
    c. Are women to be encouraged to study and learn God's Word?
    d. Are women allowed to pray to God publicly and privately?
    e. What rights do women have?
    f. What responsibilities do women have?
    g. Are women worthy beings?
    h. Should women ever work outside the home?

Part III

WOMEN AS WIVES AND MOTHERS

To feel secure in a highly-mobilized and transitory world, a woman must have commitments and responsibilities; she must come to understand why God put her on this earth and how she can make her life most fulfilling.

Introduction

THE PROBLEMS

Family life in our nation today is threatened on every side and is facing many problems. The following make-believe incidents illustrate some of the problems:

Todd and Susan have three children — a son in the first grade of school and twin daughters, age three. They live in a small city in the Midwest. Todd works at a local factory on an assembly line. Susan is a homemaker. Her days are filled with the household chores of cooking, cleaning, and laundry. Todd, Jr. is active in school and takes piano lessons. The twins are inquisitive and "into everything" as the saying goes. Supper is an especially hectic time — Todd, Jr. wants to tell about his day at school, the twins are fussy and hungry, and Todd, Sr. is home from work, dirty and tired. When the dishes are finally done and the twins are bathed and in bed, Susan would like to talk to her husband to find out what he is thinking, how his work is going, and to share some of her own thoughts and feelings. She has been in a child's world all day and needs some adult conversation. But the same scene recreates itself every night — Todd, Jr. is sitting in front of the television, eyes glued to the screen; and Todd, Sr. is in his chair, with the newspaper spread out over his chest, fast asleep. Susan is beginning to wonder if this is all there is to life.

Duane and Valerie live in a large city in California with their two teenage sons. Duane is a very successful executive with a large firm. His job requires that he travel all over the country; he is away from home an average of twenty days each month. Valerie has her own interior-decorating business and is doing quite well. They own a large home, have a pool, and have membership in the country club. Their

146

sons each have a car and active social lives. They do well in school and in sports activities. Each person in the family goes his or her own way; each follows his or her own interests. The family tries to get together once a year in the summer for a few weeks to enjoy the cabin on the lake that they purchased several years ago, but each year it gets harder to pick the right time to go. They will probably not go at all this year.

Betty and Joe have one two-year-old daughter. Betty is afraid she may be pregnant again and is unhappy about it. Joe is a farmer and a good one. Betty had always been a city girl, but when Joe's father died and left him the large farm, the move to the country seemed the logical thing to do. They are both active in the church and involved in the community activities, but Betty still feels as if she is an outsider. She has nothing in common with the other women. Her child is demanding and cross most of the time, causing Betty much frustration. She feels caged in; she has no interest in the garden or in housekeeping. She would really love to get her old job back and drive into the city every day, but Joe will not hear of it. He says, "A wife is to stay at home and raise the kids."

Bill and Jane have no children and do not intend to have any—ever. They feel children would restrict their life-style. They live in a luxurious apartment in New York City. They both work for the same publishing firm as photo-journalists. They travel a great deal, maintain large wardrobes, and "party" in their free time. They belong to a club that switches sexual partners once a week. They say their lives are quite modern and exciting; but when alone, Jane admits that she is afraid she is losing Bill.

Roger and Kim are in court today. They are getting a divorce. The court hearing is to decide who gets custody of the four children and how the assets are to be divided. Roger and Kim had a good life together, but they are simply "not in love" with each other anymore. The children are confused and worried about what is going to happen to them.

John and Diane live together in a small duplex not far from the university where they both attend. They say they are committed to one another but feel that marriage is of no value. They don't need to sign a piece of paper; they *feel* married and that is good enough for them. John works at a gas station, and Diane works part-time at the library. They don't have much money, but they share in everything. They are both looking forward to their separate careers. They don't know what the future holds, but they are happy right now.

The problems inherent in these situations — a lack of communication, a lack of understanding, a lack of togetherness, the desire for independence, wrong priorities, the desire to be free of responsibility, the misapplication of roles, the readiness to divorce to solve problems, and the lack of commitment — are faced either directly or vicariously by all of us.

Many people are doubting the traditions of the past about marriage and family life. Many are asking questions: Is marriage really relevant today? Should we be making divorce easier and more painless? Should both parents be pursuing careers? Should we have written contracts for marriage that can be renewed or revoked every three years? Are adulterous affairs the way to sexual excitement? Should the husband be expected to share in the housework and child care? What do we do when we do not *feel* passionately in love with our mate? Should young couples live together to see if they are compatible before marriage? Wouldn't it be more fulfilling not to have the responsibility of children?

The Sources

The problems and questions arise from three basic sources:
(1) The fast-paced society in which we live. Everyone is on
the move; no one has time to spare. Too many meetings;
too many places to go and things to do. There's no time to
care or get involved with others. (2) The emphasis on materialism. Many have the idea that "things" make one successful.
People-relationships take second place to the acquiring of
property and things. (3) The emphasis on the individual
and the "now." We are told we need to find ourselves. We
need to "pull our own strings." We must strike out on our
own, be free of all ties, and "do our own thing." It matters
not what others think or how others feel. We are told, "Don't
worry about the future; just live for the present moment."

Each of these emphases or philosophies are contrary to
God's will for us. Psychologists and sociologists are just beginning to see how unfulfilling and damaging these trends
are. They are realizing that people cannot live happily unless
they look outside of themselves, find a worthy cause to be
committed to, and seek to live out certain responsibilities.
People must be involved in the lives of others and feel a
closeness and unity with others. And they are finally ad-
mitting that the marriage and family relationships are the
best environment for such needs to be met.

Many of those who have been involved in divorce, "free"
sex, the career world, "going their own way," fulfilling their
selfishness, and who have given up the care of their children, etc. are now saying, "Marriage is the only way I can
find true happiness. I need the sharing that accompanies
marriage and parenthood. I need to be needed. I need to
have someplace I can call home with someone whom I can

call mine. I need the companionship, the security, the intimacy of marriage and parenthood. I need someone to really care when I get the flu. I need to feel committed and involved with others and causes outside myself."

God's View: God is not surprised by these statements, for that is how He created us to be. He has known all along what will make us happy. He has consistently made clear to us in His Word that we are to get out of ourselves, leave our selfishness behind, and seek to serve others out of hearts of love and compassion. He designed marriage and the family to provide for each person's fulfillment and security, to eliminate loneliness, and to provide an avenue for our needs to be met — the need to be intimate, the need to have responsibility, the need to be committed and involved, the need to love and be loved.

When God designed family relationships, He did not wish or intend for them to be saturated with problems, heartaches, pain, or sorrow. But mankind's disobedience has taken its toll; the wonderful relationships God intended have been changed continuously to satisfy human selfishness. Thus tragedies have multiplied in the family life of mankind all through history. To help us get out and stay out of the messes in life caused by sin, God has set forth certain attitudes, character attributes, and practical guidelines in His Word.

Let us discover together from God's Word how we can make the important marital and family relationships right again and how God expects a woman to fulfill her responsibilities as a wife and mother.

Chapter Six

WOMEN AS WIVES

A Committed Relationship

After God created the first man and woman, He explained how marriage was to function: "For this cause a man shall leave his father and mother, and shall cleave to his wife; and they shall become one flesh" (Genesis 2:24). One family relationship (parent-child) was to be loosened in order to tighten another (husband-wife; for further discussion of this verse see Chapter One, pp. 9, 10). The new relationship was to be one of sharing and of thinking of another's needs. Two people were to act as a unit, as a partnership with less individual selfishness.

A Joining. The word "cleave" (*dabaq*) provides for us a clear picture of what God meant marriage to be. It means to adhere, to stick together as with cement, to be attached, to be united, to be bound. It includes loyalty, affection, and the idea of physical closeness. The term was used by the psalmist to describe adhering to God's commandments — "*cleave* to God's testimonies" (Psalm 119:31), and when speaking of how a "tongue *cleaves* to the jaws" (22:15). The word was used to describe how "bone *clings* to skin," (Job 19:20), how "fish *cling* to scales" (Ezekiel 29:4), how "a waistband *clings* to the waist of a man" (Jeremiah 13:11). In the same way, husbands and wives are to become so joined that they cling to one another.

Jacob's wife, Leah, knew what cleaving meant. She was unhappy in her relationship with Jacob but was pleased when she had children, for she hoped that as a result her husband would "*become attached*" (*lavah*, cleave) to her

151

(Genesis 29:34). The "cleaving" relationship was obviously not referring to just the sexual relationship. Much more was involved.

Jesus used the word "cleave" (*kollaomai*) and the word "joined" or "yoked" (*suzeugnuo*) when referring to the marriage relationship (Matthew 19:5, 6). He stressed that two persons became one, that God joined the husband and wife, and that only death could separate them.

Paul used similar words to describe how Christians in the church should relate to one another, placing the accent on partnership and unity: "*be made complete* [katartizo] in the same mind and in the same judgment" (I Corinthians 1:10). He warned the Christians about being tied too closely with unbelievers: "do not be *bound together* [heterozugeo] with unbelievers" (II Corinthians 6:14). Paul was not saying they were not to have any dealings at all with unbelievers, but that they were not to have a cleaving relationship or a partnership with them. Paul also mentioned that a wife (or in the context, a husband as well) was *bound* (*deo*) as long as her husband lived (I Corinthians 7:39), stressing the close and permanent ties of marriage.

In God's view, marriage involves a unity, a sharing, a working together of husband and wife. It is not only to be a "living together" situation, but there is to be much communication as well as physical and emotional togetherness between the mates.

Oneness to God means two people sharing their whole selves with one another. It means telling each other about the everyday, mundane things. It means letting the mate feel a part of each other's lives. The two are to make decisions together and solve problems together. They should

152

openly discuss disappointments and irritations as well as feelings and needs. They should share in hobbies and interests as much as possible. And, of course, they should pray and worship together.

It is clear that God intends for marriage to be a very closely knit relationship, one in which the two mates are joined together so that they feel, think, and act as a unit. They are two separate persons but are to have the same goals and values. He wants them to be so bound up with or tied to each other that their unity will be visible to everyone. The happiness that can come from such a relationship is described in Ecclesiastes 4:9-12:

> Two are better than one because they have a good return for their labor. For if either of them falls, the one will lift up his companion. But woe to the one who falls when there is not another to lift him up. Furthermore, if two lie down together they keep warm, but how can one be warm alone? And if one can overpower him who is alone, two can resist him. A cord of three strands is not quickly torn apart.

Marriage partners are to be joined or coupled together, much as a team of oxen are yoked together. The two oxen are separate with minds and wills of their own. When the farmer places the yoke upon them, they are united in the eyes of the world. But unless they pull together and work toward the same goal, they are not in unity and they will accomplish nothing.

If each had in mind a different goal (a different part of the field to plow) and each tried to go his own direction to fulfill his own desires, the yoke would begin to chafe against their necks inflicting pain. Neither goal would be reached, and bitterness and resentment between the two would be inevitable. Each would blame the other because they were not "getting anywhere." They would probably feel that the only solution is to be separated. They want to go their own ways; they want to break the yoke. Though united by the yoke, they were not acting as a team.

It is easy to see the analogy extending to the marriage situation. Just being legally united in marriage does not ensure the unity of a joined relationship. Each person has to put forth effort and has to yield at times. And without the unity of goals and desires, the end of the yoking situation looms ahead.

God wants marriage to be a binding, yoking relationship in which two individuals are united and then learn to live in unity — learn to live and work together as a team. Teamwork is a complementary relationship. The two individuals seek to fulfill the same goal, and together they work to reach that goal. The goal cannot be reached if the husband and wife are competing with each other, seeking to have their own needs met first and at the expense of the other. Instead they must seek to fill in the spaces where the other lacks. Their only competition is to be with the world, not with each other.

God wants husbands and wives to be stuck together with "super-glue" so that no one or no situation (except the death of the mate) can separate them. He wants marriage to be a partnership in which each mate is committed to live for the well-being of the other and is committed to the permanency of the relationship. He wants them to work in unity, each in their own special way, to achieve their agreed-upon goals. In this way, family responsibilities can be met, goals reached, and both men's and women's needs for security, love, and companionship can be fulfilled. Such unity or yoking together could be pictured in this way:

God

Husband   Wife

The apex is God; the husband and wife are joined together in obedience to God's will. They act as one. Neither individual loses his or her identity. Neither is subordinate in value to the other. The triangle does not rock or tilt to one side or the other but remains firm and stable as long as the relationship remains within God's will.

The example of the marriage of Ahab and Jezebel in the Bible clearly teaches the danger of being yoked with someone who has different spiritual values and is not living in obedience to God. Ahab was a worshipper of God, but Jezebel worshipped Baal (I Kings 18). The historians have written that the greatest crime of King Ahab was in marrying Jezebel. When she became Ahab's wife, she brought into Israel an entourage of prophets and the practice of worshipping the idol Baal. She had a special hall built for the prophets of Baal and established a grove near the palace for the sacrifice of virgins.

After Elijah, the prophet of God, warned Ahab of his punishment because of the murder of Naboth, Ahab tore his clothes, fasted, and prayed to God for forgiveness. God noted his humility (I Kings 21:27-29), so Ahab did have some redeeming qualities. But the influence of his evil wife

155

turned him from the Lord. We must be warned that the results of being joined with someone who has no regard for God are most likely to be disastrous.

On the other hand, one of the best examples of a "glued tight" marriage relationship that was based on obedience to God's will is that of Priscilla and Aquilla. They worked together as tentmakers (Acts 18:3) and in the Lord's work by hosting churches in their home (Romans 16:3, 4, 5), by teaching others about Christ (Acts 18:26), and by being Paul's co-workers (Romans 16:3) and traveling companions (Acts 18:18). They traveled together wherever they felt the Lord was leading them (Acts 18:2). They were truly of the same mind, having the same goals and values. When one was mentioned, the other was automatically mentioned also.

Of course, many in our modern society would react with repugnance to the idea of such a binding relationship. They advocate that couples should live together for awhile first to see if they are truly suited to one another; if not, each can then go his or her own way and find someone else. They have the philosophy, "If things aren't just the way you like them, you can always get a divorce."

They also feel a successful marriage could be described as follows: Husband and wife have their own individual causes, go their own way, and hardly ever do their purposes meet. Each individual pursues his or her own interests with little togetherness or sharing. Such a marriage in God's eyes is simply two people who may have a marriage license and who may get together occasionally for a meal or sex, but they are certainly not cleaving together as God wants a husband and wife to do.

The importance of such a unified, cleaving relationship must be considered in one's selection of a mate. A Christian should choose a mate with whom he or she can live and work within unity. It would be very difficult to build the cleaving relationship of marriage if there was no foundation for oneness, or if the two people had little or nothing in common.

The following questions will help to point out areas that should be discussed and thought about before marriage:

1. What books does each person read? Is the newspaper read regularly? What magazines are read?

2. What types of entertainment does each enjoy? What television programs does each watch? What type of music does each like?

3. How much education does each have? What is each person's attitude toward education? How well did each one do in school and/or college?

4. Is the couple able to discuss weighty matters or current events together?

5. What is each person's special interest? What kind of parties does each like? Do they both like the outdoors and sports or do they have more sedentary interests?

6. Can each write a personality profile of the other, listing both strengths and weaknesses? Can each determine how they complement each other?

7. Over what matters does the couple disagree or argue?

8. What is each person's relationship to God? Attitude toward the church? Attitude toward and acceptance of Christ?

9. What is each person's idea of success? What are their life-time goals? Attitude toward material things?

10. Is each mate attached to the other physically? What is the attitude of each toward sex? What are their expectations in this area?

11. What is each person expecting from the marriage relationship? What do they feel is the function of the wife? Of the husband?

If the two persons do not agree on the answers to many of these questions, there may not be an adequate foundation for the unified, teamwork relationship of marriage. Of course, people can change. People can develop new interests if the motivation is strong enough. But very few people will change their basic values, goals, and attitudes (except through conversion to Christ). No one should expect to change another person to please themselves, not even after the vows have been said and eternal love has been pledged. After the excitement and passion subside, most individuals return to their basic personalities and characters. Be alert and be aware.

A Covenant. God had a covenant-relationship with His people and compared that relationship to that of marriage many times in His Word. A covenant is an agreement, a contract, or a promise made between two parties. Both parties commit themselves to live out the terms of the agreement. God promised to bless His people (the nation of Israel) if they would promise to obey Him, and He promised to punish them if they rebelled. The Israelites accepted the terms of the agreement and promised to obey. Each party involved in the covenant accepted a commitment—God was committed to care for and bless His people, and His people were committed to obey His directions.

It was very serious business! It was not a contract that could be taken lightly or accepted as an afterthought. God repeatedly showed His people how serious the covenant was and how they were held responsible for fulfilling it.

In Isaiah 54:4-8, God's relationship with His people was described as being like that of a husband and wife. God said He rejoiced and delighted in His people and felt that He was married to them, just as a husband is to a wife (Isaiah 62:4, 5). God described Himself as being a husband to His people (Jeremiah 31:32) and said He had betrothed the nation to Himself (Hosea 2:19).

When Israel broke the covenant, the prophets likened the break-up to that of a divorce (Malachi 2:16). Israel was said to be like an adulterous wife who had taken strangers rather than being true to her husband (Ezekiel 16:32), like a harlot who has many lovers and then wants to return to her husband (God) after the divorce (Jeremiah 3:1), or like a husband who dealt treacherously with his wife (even though she was his companion by a covenant, Malachi 2:14, 15).

The book of Hosea paints the picture quite graphically of how God thought of the covenant-relationship as that of a marriage relationship. Hosea and Gomer were married just as God and His people were married (Hosea 1:1-11). But Gomer left Hosea for other lovers (as Israel left God and went to other gods). Then when Gomer was being sold as a slave by her "lover," Hosea bought her back for his own and said, "take no more lovers" (3:1-5), just as God had done for the nation of Israel.

Not only was the *old* covenant-relationship compared to marriage, but the *new* covenant-relationship between God (Christ) and the church was also likened to the marriage relationship. John the Baptist referred to Jesus as the bridegroom (John 3:29); Jesus referred to Himself as the bridegroom (Matthew 9:15). Paul spoke of the cleaving relationship as well as the love and commitment between Christ and the church and compared the relationship to that of a husband and wife in marriage (Ephesians 5:31, 32). The apostle John talked of the marriage of the church to Christ, the joy and purity that would be part of the marriage, and referred to the church as the Bride (Revelation 19:7-10, 22:17).

In God's view, marriage is to be considered as a serious commitment between a husband and wife. It is to be treated as a covenant, a promise, and a contract. Marriage is not to be the result of an impulsive action or the whim of a fleeting desire. It is a public commitment that a man and woman will be partners and act as a unit, rather than acting as two separate individuals who go their own ways. It is a covenant before God, between themselves, and before men.

Just as God wanted His people to commit themselves to keep the covenant as a sign of their love and regard for Him, so He expects marriage partners to carry out their commitments to one another because of the love and concern they feel for each other. God did not want His people to obey Him out of fear or out of a sense of burdensome duty. Neither does He want a marriage to be held together by fear or by duty only. Husbands are to seek to understand and honor their wives, realizing they are their equals (I Peter 3:7). Wives are to love their husbands in an affectionate way (Titus 2:3, 4). Husbands are to love their wives in a self-giving way, and wives are to respect and honor their husbands (Ephesians 5:22, 33). Marriage is to be a covenant-relationship—a commitment in which two people are bound together by love and respect.

Broken Covenants. There is a saying, "promises are made to be broken." But that is not God's philosophy, nor was it His intention when He designed marriage, anymore than it was when He designed the covenant with His people. Yet because of sin, mankind has perverted God's intentions and stepped all over His promises, shattering the covenant to pieces time and time again. There are many examples of broken marriage covenants in the Bible:

(1) Cause—Independent Attitude. The marriage relationship was on the forefront of the first shattered covenant. Adam and Eve had made a covenant to act as a unit and to be partners, but Eve decided to act independently of her husband. She was not fulfilling her commitment to Adam or to God and convinced Adam to forget his responsibility to God as well (Genesis 3:6).

(2) Cause—Polygamy. It is clear that God intended for a man to have only one wife, and a woman to have only one husband (Genesis 2:24). Yet Lamech, a descendant of Cain, took *two* wives, perverting the close relationship God intended for marriage to be (Genesis 4:19).

God allowed polygamy and the taking of concubines to exist—even among some of Israel's greatest leaders—but He never approved it or encouraged it. Instead, in His Word we find several examples of how disruptive such a practice was to family relationships. Consider the heartaches, the bitterness, the hatred, and the discord that was present in the following triangles: Abraham, Hagar, Sarah; Jacob, Rachel, Leah; Elkanah, Hannah, Peninnah. Much of King David's problems and unhappiness can be traced to his marriage relationships and his concubines; Solomon's downfall was attributed to his many wives (II Samuel 5:13; I Kings 11:1-3). The practice was especially harmful to the women who were often traded back and forth as pawns in wars and amidst deceitful transactions.

Jesus' comments about marriage always referred to the husband and wife in the singular; He assumed monogamy to be the natural state of marriage, just as Paul and other writers of the New Testament did. Paul made it clear that the leaders of the church (who were to be examples to all) were to be monogamous (I Timothy 3:2, 12; Titus 1:6), regardless of the practices of the culture.

161

(3) Cause — Trading Partners. Abraham and Sarah had a loving covenant relationship. Abraham was sensitive to her needs, and Sarah was anxious to please him. But Abraham did not fulfill his part of the marriage covenant when he asked Sarah to pose as his sister to save his own life (Genesis 12:10-13). Abraham broke the cemented relationship by allowing Pharaoh to take Sarah into his harem. Sarah also violated their commitment by asking Abraham to take Hagar to produce an heir (Genesis 16:2).

(4) Cause — Deceit. Isaac and Rebekah allowed their twin sons to become a divisive force in their marriage which resulted in deceit and manipulation. Instead of discussing who should rightfully get the father's blessing, Rebekah tricked Isaac into blessing Jacob instead of Esau (Genesis 27).

(5) Cause — Not Unified in Faith. Zipporah, the wife of Moses, was not a Jew and evidently did not share his beliefs because their son had not been circumcised. As the family was departing from Midian to Egypt, God showed His displeasure about the omission. In anger, Zipporah circumcised their son. She showed her disgust and bitterness with such force that she and her children separated from Moses and went back to Midian, while he went on to Egypt to lead the people. Their covenant-relationship was broken (Exodus 4:24-26). When Moses was with the Israelites in the wilderness, Zipporah, their sons, and her father came for a visit, but the unity of the marriage was not reinstated (Exodus 18:5, 6).

(6) Cause — Legal Dissolvements. God originally intended for a marriage to be terminated only by natural death, but the sins of mankind brought up so many other situations that God allowed marriages to be dissolved for other reasons. In the Old Testament, a marriage could allowably be ended

because of the execution of one of the mates or because of divorce. Divorce was just the opposite of being joined in a covenant-relationship; it was the releasing of the mates from the relationship. They would then both be free; they would no longer be partners.

Those who were found guilty of sexual perversions, such as incest (Leviticus 20:11), homosexuality (20:13), sex with an in-law (20:12, 14), sex with animals (20:15, 16), and sexual infidelity of a married person (adultery, 20:10; Deuteronomy 22:22) were executed. Being sexually intimate with someone else besides the married partner destroyed the covenant-relationship in God's eyes. Such a harsh punishment made clear how strongly God felt about the relationship of marriage.

Evidently in Moses' time, the men were dismissing their wives quickly and often, leaving the women without protection or any way to make a living. They could not remarry or their husbands could accuse them of adultery. The only way they would make money would be to become harlots which would also result in the charge of adultery and consequent execution.

God, through Moses, was guarding against such heartless actions by commanding the men to get a bill of divorcement, a legal piece of paper saying the woman was free of her marriage and could remarry. She could then make a new relationship and be taken care of.

Divorce was permitted for the reason of "indecency" (Deuteronomy 24:1). Many of the men in the Jewish culture interpreted this to mean "anything the husband did not like." But men were clearly prohibited from divorcing when they falsely accused their wives of infidelity. And when a man forced himself upon a virgin, he would have to marry her and could never be divorced. This was a definite deterrent to pre-marital sex and rape (Deuteronomy 22:13-19, 28, 29).

In the New Testament, Jesus re-emphasized God's original intentions for marriage (Matthew 19:4-6), and told why Moses and God allowed divorce (19:7, 8). Instead, Jesus allowed for divorce when sexual immorality was present. Contrary to many in His culture, He said that was to be the *only* reason for divorce: "I say to you that everyone who divorces his wife, except for the cause of unchastity, makes her commit adultery" (Matthew 5:31, 32).

The Greek word He used for "unchastity" (*porneia*) was not restricted in its meaning to refer to pre-marital or extra-marital sex. It referred to "any sexual perversion," such as incest, homosexuality, bestiality, or adultery. Jesus was saying that in God's eyes only sexual immorality was a just cause for a divorce. It was the only thing besides death that could break the covenant-relationship legally. When the relationship was broken for that reason, a divorce was allowed; and both persons could remarry. Just as Moses had done, Jesus was seeking to protect the women from being abused and used by the men who were divorcing them whenever they felt like it (See Chapter Five, pp. 111-113 for discussion).

Paul also reaffirmed God's original intentions for marriage. He desired that only death break the covenant-relationship (Romans 7:2, 3) and emphasized the cemented relationship of marriage (I Corinthians 11:11). Paul also gave another reason for which divorce could be allowed. A new situation had arisen among the early Christians that needed to be spoken about—Christians and non-Christians were married partners. This problem had not arisen in Jesus' time which explains His silence about it.

Paul exhorted the Christians to seek to carry out God's will for the marriage relationship by not initiating a divorce from a non-Christian mate (I Corinthians 7:14); but he went on to say, "Yet if the unbelieving one leaves, let him leave; the brother or the sister is not under bondage in such cases" (I Corinthians 7:15).

We can see that acting independently from each other, acting in anger or in deceit, polygamy, sexual immorality, death, and possibly being married to a non-believer are actions that break the covenant-relationship of marriage that God designed. But only divorce and death are the public affirmations that divide a husband and wife; divorce is the public dissolvement that results from a private action that broke the relationship.

Many in our society believe that when problems occur in a marriage, divorce is the easiest available answer and in some cases the only solution. In contrast to that popular belief, God says clearly that marriage should be for always, a firm commitment that should not be broken except in the most devastating circumstances.

Adam and Eve had a definite problem in their marriage, but their love and commitment to each other prevented their marriage from being dissolved. Abraham and Sarah had many problems, but they remained together and were able to grow together as they matured in the faith and enjoyed its fruition when Isaac was born in their old age. Sarah might have asked for a divorce when Abraham was willing to give her away to another man, but her love and commitment won out for the benefit of them both.

It would seem that Isaac and Rebekah had irreconcilable differences, but they did not divorce. Moses and Zipporah were separated but, as far as we know, did not divorce. David and Michal experienced many turbulent times but did not divorce. David and Bathsheba were both guilty of adultery and murder—hardly a good basis for the start of a marriage—but they were able to endure the rocky times. Hannah was very unhappy in her marriage (because of her barrenness and her husband's other wife), but Elkanah was a loving husband who helped her through the rough times and rejoiced with her when Samuel was born, instead of getting impatient with her and divorcing her.

There is no doubt that there will always be problems in any marriage, but there are many solutions other than divorce. There is *agape*-love (acting for the well-being of the other, regardless of how it affects oneself), forgiveness of the wrongs of the mate, sharing in communication in order to reveal problems and discuss solutions, determined commitment, complete trust in the Lord, and simply "hanging in there." These other options must be considered if the commitment of the marriage relationship is to be within God's will.

But what about those who have divorced already, whose marriage covenant was broken publicly for some other reason than what God had expressly allowed (sexual immorality or an unbeliever who desires divorce)? God has said that He hates divorce for any reason (Malachi 2:16). He does not wish for any marriage to be broken. He allows divorce because of the hard-heartedness of mankind and how wretchedly we treat each other. He allows divorce as a "way out" for innocent victims in horrible situations. And God is a forgiving and loving God. Even those who have been divorced can find God's forgiveness through repentance.

God repeatedly forgave the nation of Israel for their rebellion and the atrocities they performed on each other. God forgave Abraham of his indiscretions and lack of faith; God forgave His leaders who were polygamists. God forgave those who launched out on their own, leaving God

166

out of their lives. God forgave David of his immoralities. Jesus forgave the woman who was living with a man and who had been married five times (John 4). Jesus forgave a woman caught in the very act of adultery (John 8). He forgave a prostitute and a crooked tax collector. He forgave the impulsive acts of selfishness as well as the unbelief of His disciples. God forgives sinners; He always has. A sinner who confesses his sin, repents, and turns back to God will find a loving Father with His arms outstretched, ready to welcome him. God's grace even extends to those who have broken their marriage covenant when they should have tried to work it out.

Of course, this does not mean we should rush right out and get a divorce. We should not do that anymore than we should go out and murder or commit incest, knowing that God may forgive us. A mature Christian will seek to do God's will in all matters and try not to misuse God's grace. A mature Christian will do everything possible so that God will not be hurt or disappointed. He will also treat others who have been touched by divorce with the same type of love and forgiveness that God shows.

A Submissive Relationship

What is Submission? Submission (*hupotage, hupotasso, hupakouo*) is an aspect of one's character as well as an overt behavioral action. It proceeds out of the attitude of humility, which is the esteeming of others before oneself (Philippians 2:3). Submission is being concerned about others' needs and being able to yield one's own rights for the benefit of others.

Jesus exhibited this characteristic better than anyone else. He lowered Himself—He was God in heaven and on the throne—by becoming a fleshly man. As that man, He was obedient even though He was still God. Jesus continually subjected Himself to God (I Corinthians 15:28) and lived according to God's will, not His own (Luke 22:42), even though He was equal to God. He was humble and submissive—even when that submission led to His death—for the salvation (and thus benefit) of all mankind (Philippians 2:5-8).

God makes it clear in His Word that we are all to follow Jesus' example and be submissive. He points out many relationships that require submission:

(1) We are to submit to God and His laws or commands (James 4:7). One way to glorify God is by our submission to the gospel (II Corinthians 9:13). Going our own way or being hostile to God are opposite actions of submission to God (Romans 8:7; 10:3). We are to be as obedient children, obedient to the truth (I Peter 1:14, 22). Abraham was pointed out as an example of submission when he went where God told him to go, even though he knew nothing about the location (Hebrews 11:8).

(2) We are also to submit to Christ (Ephesians 5:24), just as all authorities and powers have submitted to Him (I Peter 3:22), just as the winds and waves submitted to His voice (Matthew 8:27), and just as the demons obeyed Him (Mark 1:27).

(3) We are to submit to higher authorities of our communities and nation (Romans 13:1, 5; Titus 3:1; I Peter 2:13) as well as the leaders of the church (I Corinthians 16:16; Hebrews 13:17; I Peter 5:5).

(4) Servants are to submit to their masters (Ephesians 6:5; Titus 2:9; I Peter 2:18).

(5) All Christians are to submit to one another (Ephesians 5:21).

(6) Wives are to submit to their husbands (Ephesians 5:22; Colossians 3:18; Titus 2:5; I Peter 3:1, 5) and are to receive instruction submissively (I Timothy 2:11).

(7) Children are to submit to their parents (Ephesians 6:1; Colossians 3:20; I Timothy 3:4).

In God's view, submission is not the result of an action of a powerful person (or persons) conquering others by the use of force and demanding that they submit. It is not done with a war-like attitude—"I won, ha! ha!, now you must submit to me." Instead, submission is a voluntary yielding coming from an attitude of humility—"I am happy to serve you."

The contemporary world's view is so contrary to God's will. In the desire for freedom and independence, many have gone to extremes and say we must do "our own thing" without being responsible to anyone else. They say we don't need others; we can make it on our own, and we can do it "our way." It is the idea that "I will do whatever I want, whenever I want. Let everyone and everything else go hang." With such selfishness and meism, it is no wonder that the idea of submissiveness and service for others is repugnant to so many people today.

It is little wonder that husbands and wives today are so confused about what rights are theirs and how their own individual needs can be met. It is little wonder that there are so many problems in America's families and that the divorce rate is increasing daily. There is no way people can get along peacefully and constructively if each person is selfishly seeking to do his or her own thing without regard for anyone else. Life then becomes a battleground with wars to be won and persons to conquer. People become objects for manipulation rather than persons to love and help. The world's way leads to confusion, loneliness, and dissatisfaction. But God's way of humble submission leads to order, contentment, and fulfilling relationships.

Let's look at God's way more closely, discovering how submission fits into the marriage relationship.

The Husband's Role. Even from the time of creation, God intended for the husband to be the leader and protector of the marriage team. He gave the man the leadership role in the marriage, not because the man was superior in any way to the woman and not because God did not favor women, but to promote order, peace, and security in the relationship (see Chapters One and Two). Because people have different feelings and ideas, if there is no leader in a relationship — whether it be marriage, or at work, or in a friendship — many decisions will not be made and many responsibilities will not be fulfilled. Time will be wasted, and insecurity and confusion would result. Both lives in the relationship would become ineffective.

Because of the emphasis on individual rights and freedom in our society today, many women have developed a type of paranoia when anyone talks about the leadership of the husband in the home. They say they should not have to submit to any authority in the marriage relationship. Yet in all of our relationships, we have to be submissive at times. If we work at a job outside the home, we must be submissive to the boss, manager, or board of trustees. If we drive, we must submit to the traffic laws. If we take college classes, we must submit to the school rules and to the teachers. And none of these actions of submission have anything to do with one person being superior to or more powerful than another.

170

A circuit court judge friend of ours illustrated the principle this way: "While I am in the court room, I am the final authority (the "head") in the relationship there. Everyone else in the courtroom must submit to me. I am not the "head" because I am superior to everyone else, but because that is my role or position—that is my job in the judicial system. But when I leave the court room and drive down the street toward my home, I have to submit to the school crossing guard. That young child is not superior to me, but in that situation, the child is the authority (the "head") and I must submit to him."

It is time that women thought out this principle instead of reacting in anger and irritation or thinking that God "has it in for them" because he expects them to submit to their husbands. As we have already discovered (pages 168, 169), God expects men, women, and children to submit in many relationships to encourage peace and order. Wives, themselves, are to be the authorities in many situations—over their children, over the students in their classes, over the members of the club in which they are leaders, over the workers that are placed under their supervision at work, etc. We do not appreciate the chafing, complaining, or rebelling of those over whom we have authority. We expect them to recognize and submit to our leadership; we should do the same for our husbands.

Regardless of how we feel or what we think about the husband's role, it is clear from Scripture that God intends for husbands to be the "heads" in the marriage relationship: "But I want you to understand that Christ is the head of every man, and the man is the head of a woman, and God is the head of Christ" (I Corinthians 11:3). Notice that Paul was comparing three relationships in this verse: the personal

171

relationship with Christ, the marital relationship, and Christ's relationship with God.

We have already considered Jesus' submission to God. Paul was being consistent with the rest of Scripture by saying God was Christ's leader (head). Christ and God had an intimate relationship; in fact, they were fully equal—in intelligence, in value, in every way—but there had to be a guiding leader in the relationship to establish order and to accomplish the goals of the God-head. The "headship" had nothing to do with one's superiority over another or the diminishing of another's personality. Jesus was not less God because He submitted to the Father. God was not a dictator and did not force Jesus to submit; Jesus submitted voluntarily. Neither did Jesus decide to assert His independence from God or demand that His rights be considered; He sought instead to do God's will.

The husband is to submit to his "head"—Christ. He is to yield to Jesus' way and life-style. He is to take on Jesus' attitudes and thoughts. He is to treat his wife as Jesus would, which means he would love her, seek to meet her needs, act unselfishly for her benefit, and yield to her rights as a Christian individual at times (Ephesians 5:21).

In Ephesians 5, Paul made the same emphasis comparing the marriage relationship with Christ's relationship to the church:

> For the husband is the head of the wife, as Christ also is the head of the church, He Himself being the Savior of the body. But as the church is subject to Christ . . . husbands, love your wives, just as Christ also loved the church and gave Himself up for her that He might sanctify her, having cleansed her by the washing of water with the word, that He might present to Himself the church in all her glory . . . So husbands

172

ought also to love their wives as their own bodies. He who loves his own wife loves himself; for no one ever hated his own flesh, but nourishes and cherishes it, just as Christ also does the church (Ephesians 5:23-29).

Christ is the church's leader; the members are to look to Him for guidance, protection, support, and strength. But look what Jesus did *for* the church: He provided eternal salvation (v. 23), loved her, gave Himself up in death for her (v. 25), cleansed her from sin (vv. 26, 27), nourished and cherished her (v. 29). Jesus loved the church so much that He gave Himself completely; He died for the church's welfare. But He did not stop there. He continuously nourishes and cherishes (feeds, encourages) the church even to this day.

The husband is to be the same kind of leader for his wife. He is to be strong enough that she can look to him for guidance, protection, and support. He is to care enough for his wife that he would even give his own life for her benefit; he will probably not have to die physically for her, but he is to die to his own selfishness in order to provide for her needs (not just physical needs but all her needs). The husband's acting in this way, of course, is the very essence of the Christian life — dying to selfishness to serve others in love. The apostle Peter added that the husband is to seek to understand his wife, treat her with tenderness and respect, remembering that they are equals in sharing the grace of God. When a husband acts in this manner toward his wife, his prayers will not be blockaded from God's attention (I Peter 3:7).

Nowhere in any of God's guidelines for marriage do we get the idea that husbands are to be the dictators over the slave-wives or obedient-subjects (wives). Doing things God's way leaves no room for the conquering, demanding attitude of a despot. There is no room for seeking to manipulate others to meet one's own needs. There is no room for the harsh barking out of orders that must be obeyed immediately without question. There is no room for the attitude that "I am better and stronger than you, woman, so you must do as I say or else" or "God says that I am your head, so you must obey me." There is no room for the trying to keep a woman under the husband's thumb or to keep her "in her place." Headship does not mean locking a wife up as Peter did in the nursery rhyme: "Peter, Peter, Pumpkin Eater had a wife and couldn't keep her, put her in a pumpkin shell and kept her there very well."

The Wife's Role. It is clear from Scripture that God intends for wives to yield to their husband's leadership to promote peace, security, and order. Having two leaders would be just as bad as having no leaders (which we discussed earlier). Each would seek to have his or her own way, and the war would begin. The home would become a battlefield with all the pain, bitterness, and hurt that would naturally result.

Wives are told repeatedly by God to submit to their husbands, both at home and in the worship services, as long as it is fitting and proper in God's eyes. He does not expect the wife to do immoral or unkind acts for her husband. She is to remain "chaste" in her submissive behavior (I Peter 3:2).

Wives are to respect their husbands (Ephesians 5:33). Paul said to Timothy that the wives should learn to receive instruction from their husbands in submissiveness (I Timothy 2:11). Wives are not to dominate in the marriage relationship and are not to act independently of their husband's wishes. They are to exercise self-control and live quietly (2:12). In essence, wives are to yield or "give in" to their husbands' leadership.

Many times such submission may be against the wife's better judgment. But she must think of what will benefit her husband and the family, what will promote peace and unity, rather than what she wants to do. In this way, the marriage will not be filled with strife, confusion, or two opposing forces turning away from each other—pulling and pushing in order to get their own way.

To do things God's way means the wife will not be "calling the shots," manipulating the husband to do her wishes, or be the domineering force in the home. She will not be screaming or demanding her rights. She will not go off to do her own thing, forgetting her family. Instead, she will be seeking to do what is best for her husband and family. God does not mean that the wife is to be a slave, doing all the giving and serving. Neither is she to be a door-mat, stepped on, used, or abused by her husband. We have already discovered that the husband is to be a giving, loving, and serving leader, and that submission is a mutual exercise (Ephesians 5:21).

Submission does not mean the wife is not to express her ideas or make any decisions. The couple is to be a team; they are to act as partners, which means they will both share their ideas and feelings, take turns listening and talking, and work together to make the best decisions possible. The responsibilities of leadership and submission do not negate the joining and the commitment of the marriage relationship; instead they enhance the partnership, the complementing action.

Just as any good leader, the husband will delegate authority to his wife and allow her to make decisions relating to her unique abilities and role. He will also want her counsel and advice on many major decisions and should ask for it.

175

A wife can hardly be a "helpmeet" in the fullest sense of the word if her husband never consults her. The wife should think the issue through carefully, express her thoughts honestly and respectfully, and express her doubts, worries, and concerns. The husband should do the same. They should pray together, and then decide together what is to be done.

How does a wife's submission work out practically if a decision must be made and the partners have discussed the issue, but they do not agree on what should be done? If possible, they should wait, pray, and seek advice from others who can be objective, and get more information. Then they should discuss the matter again. If no agreement can be reached or the decision must be made quickly, the husband should make the decision and take all the responsibility for the consequences. The wife, in turn, should abide by his decision with no back talk, bitterness, or fretting. She should trust that he is doing what he thinks will benefit them both. If the decision turns out to be wrong, they should not argue about it but behave in a loving manner. The wife should not constantly bring it up or say "I told you so."

Agape-love is the Basis. In order for a marriage to follow God's design, the husband and the wife must love each other with *agape* (a Greek term for love). Only with this type of love will it be possible for the husband to lead as he should and for the wife to submit as she should. This love is not the passionate, tingling kind that is present during courtship and the early days of marriage. It is not the love that expects the other person to fulfill all your desires. It is not even a mere friendship love (although husbands and wives are to have this kind of love for one another also). It is the type of love that God has for us and the kind that Jesus had for the church (Ephesians 5:25). It is the type of love that God desires for each person to have for every other person. It is the kind of love that puts the other person first, the kind that loves the unlovely, the kind that continues loving regardless of the response. It is the kind of love that we must have if our marriages are to endure the many hardships and problems that are caused because we are sinful people living in a sinful world. It is the kind of love that is shed abroad in us as Christians by the Holy Spirit.

The qualities and/or attitudes that are included in *agape*-love are best described in I Corinthians 13:4-8:

> Love is patient, love is kind, and is not jealous; love does not brag and is not arrogant, does not act unbecomingly; it does not seek its own, is not provoked, does not take into account a wrong suffered, does not rejoice in unrighteousness, but rejoices with the truth; bears all things, believes all things, hopes all things, endures all things.

In order to fully understand this type of love and how it fits into the marriage relationship, we must consider the meaning of each of these attitudes and then apply them to the day-by-day living of a husband and wife. Although all of these are just as applicable to the husbands, we will zero in on the wife's actions and reactions.

(1) "Love is patient" (*makrothumeo*). Being patient in the Greek meant putting up with people for a long time. It also meant not seeking revenge for a wrong. If a wife is patient, she will put up with the faults, idiosyncracies, and annoying habits of her husband. She will not seek to pay him back when he does her wrong.

What if he picks his nose or throws his socks under the bed? Put up with it. What if he always squeezes the tube of toothpaste in the wrong place and never puts the toilet paper in the holder? Put up with it. What if he refuses to take out the garbage and never hangs up his clothes? Put up with it. What if he never shuts the cupboard doors and leaves lights on all over the house? Put up with it. And put up with it all in a cheerful spirit. Don't nag, gripe, or complain about his thoughtlessness. Don't get angry, either inwardly or outwardly. Simply accept him for the way he is and fill in the spots where he lacks. Put the toilet paper in the holder, close the cupboard doors, turn off the lights, and take out the garbage yourself. Adjust to his imperfections, and be thankful when he adjusts to yours.

Many men are immature no matter what their chronological age may be. At times they expect to be pampered and watched after as if they were little boys. Some men need time to realize their responsibilities and to fully live up to them. A patient wife will understand his "little boy" tendencies and will give him time and opportunity to grow up. She will refrain from criticizing him, but will instead generously praise any efforts he puts forth. She will not order him to do this or that, but she will lovingly suggest how he might help her with the house or the children. She will let him know that she needs him and appreciate any help he is willing to give. A wife who feels that she is the only one "who can do things right" will never help her husband grow up. She will probably develop a martyr-complex and become very difficult to live with, while her husband will never feel he is adequate enough to help her with the house or children.

(2) "Love is kind" (*Chresteuomai*). Kindness means doing what is beneficial to others and being sweet about it. It is refraining from doing and saying anything that would be harmful to another. It is putting aside one's own thoughts and feelings and doing what is best for another.

Kindness also includes a tender, affectionate type of love which Paul referred to in Titus 2:4, "encourage the young women to love their husbands." Many wives are kind and affectionate to almost everyone else except their husbands. They complain and forget to consider their husband's feelings. They react with sarcasm or silence instead of showing their appreciation for their husbands.

A kind wife will think of what will help and please her husband. She may rub his back after a hard day's work. She may lay out his clean clothes and fix the bath water for him. She may make him some coffee before he has to ask her for it. And she will do all these little services for him without any inner resentment. She will not hold these favors over his head or expect any favors in return.

Consider this situation: The husband does not mind the heat of the summer, but the wife is very uncomfortable in the heat and wishes to turn on the air-conditioner. He says she is being silly and is going to run up the electricity bill. She says the heat makes her sluggish and irritable. The kind wife will do as her husband wishes, even though she may continue to explain to him how the heat makes her feel. Then if and when he does yield, she will turn on the air-conditioner only when absolutely necessary and will seek to save electricity in other areas.

(3) "Love is not jealous" (*zeloo*). A person with *agape*-love will not be envious or begrudge what someone else has or does. She will be content with her own situation. Many women live their entire lives thinking the "grass is greener" in other places or situations or wherever they are not. They tend to think that everyone else has life better, and they become filled with bitterness or resentment about their lot in life. A woman who continues in this attitude will never find the happiness and contentment that life can give her.

A wife who is not jealous will not bemoan the fact that her husband gets to travel all over the country in his work meeting interesting people, while she stays at home with her housework and children. She would realize that her work is just as important and worthwhile as his and she would find ways to make her life at home interesting and exciting. She would also realize that her husband's work is filled with loneliness, pressures, and fatigue, and not as exciting and glamorous as it may seem to someone who does not have to experience it.

(4) "Love is not arrogant, not a braggart" (*perpereuomai, phusioo*). *Agape*-love is not filled with pride and egotism, does not feel better than others, and does not boast about oneself. No wife should feel she is superior to her husband. Oh, she may do some things better than he does, but she must realize that in intrinsic worth and value, they are equal. She may be more educated or have better taste or more of the social graces, but she must see her husband from God's point of view, not the world's. And she must not seek to build up her own self-esteem at his expense. Pointing out his faults or inadequacies privately or in public will undoubtedly erode his own self-image and cannot help but erect barriers between the marriage partners, even though at the moment such criticism may make the wife feel good about herself.

(5) "Love does not act unbecomingly" (*aschemoneo*). To not act unbecomingly means to not act disgracefully or in a disorderly manner but in politeness and with courtesy. We can all remember to "mind our manners" out in public, but how many of us forget to do so at home? It is good manners to always try to make things pleasant and easier for the other person. It means seeking to curb certain irritating habits that we may have. It means speaking in a kind tone

of voice and using such words as "thank you," "please," and "I'm sorry." A polite wife will not interrupt her husband when he is speaking, or finish his stories, or tell the punch line of his jokes. She will not continue in a habit that she knows irritates him. She will think of his needs and wants before her own.

(6) "Love does not seek its own" (*zeteo*). A person with *agape*-love will not desire or require that her own needs be met first. She will not think of what others owe her but of what she can do for others. She will put aside thoughts of herself to think of others. How many wives can honestly say that they concentrate on their husband's interests and needs before their own? Too many of us whine because our own needs are not met, instead of seeking to meet our husband's needs.

How money is spent in a family is usually a good indication of whether everyone's needs are considered or just one person's needs. Is the wife never satisfied with her home, the furniture, the car, or her husband's pay check? Is she always conniving or hinting for more money? Does she buy things without her husband's knowledge? When we constantly think of material things and of our own selfish desires, it is not long before we are caught up in "possession-itis" and the "I've got to have more" syndrome. It is a horrid disease that eats away at our good judgment and common sense. It often destroys our system of high ideals and proper values, for it appeals to our basic selfish lusts. Soon we are seeking to fulfill those lusts with little regard for anyone else, and our possessions or "what we want" become the most important part of our lives.

If we are not seeking our own, we will be actively seeking to help our husbands reach their full potential as worthy individuals—not worrying about their monetary success.

181

What we have means very little to God; it is *who* we are that makes the difference.

If we are not seeking our own, we will be unselfish and think of the other person first. A wife who has this quality will not be seeking to break away from her family and responsibilities to satisfy her own selfish desires or to manipulate others to get her own way. She will not seek to make decisions independent of her husband's wishes. She will not seek to dominate the home. She will not constantly be pressuring her husband to do and achieve more, so that her social or financial status can improve.

(7) "Love is not provoked" (*paroxunomai*). This quality refers to basic self-control. We must not become irritated or angry easily; we must not allow ourselves to become so exasperated that disgust or rage results. We must not give in to feelings of anger and allow them to control our words or actions.

Suppose the husband forgot for the fourth time to pick up the bread and milk on his way home from work. The wife should not look at him with daggers in her eyes or slam doors or throw dishes. She should instead go get the groceries herself, or calmly ask her husband to go back and get them before supper, or do without. She should not allow the anger she feels to build up inside her so that later in the evening she "blows up."

Suppose the husband sold the car and bought a new one without the wife's knowledge. Should she scream and call him an insensitive clod? Should she shut herself up in the bedroom the rest of the evening and pout? Should she announce that she is going on a wild spending spree herself? Should she demand that he take the new car back? Or should she just seethe inside while she bangs the pots and pans around? No, she should be patient, loving, and kind. She might tell her husband that she is disappointed that he did not allow her to help him pick out the new car or that his impulsiveness worries her, but she should not let her feelings turn to resentment or rage or allow her actions to be that of an angry, selfish child. She should probably smile and ask to be taken for a ride in the beautiful car he picked out!

(8) "Love does not take into account a wrong suffered" (*logizomai*). *Agape*-love means one forgives *and* forgets. It means we don't write down every wrong done to us by our husbands in a mental record book and then turn to it when we need it for ammunition in an argument. Many wrongs will be suffered by both mates in a marriage, but love demands forgiving and forgetting all about them, wiping the guilt away, and starting with a clean page every day.

Forgiveness is not just mouthing the words "I forgive you." If we have truly forgiven and forgotten the wrong, our behavior will show it. A wife who says she forgives but refuses sexual intimacy when her husband desires it has not forgiven. A wife who says she forgives but won't speak to her husband for the rest of the week has not forgiven. A wife who says she forgives but gets revenge against her husband in various subtle ways has not forgiven. We must not continue to hold our hurt feelings and grudges fast in our hearts, for bitterness will result, and resentment will drive a wedge in the relationship.

(9) "Love rejoices in the truth, not in unrighteousness" (*chairo, aletheia, adikia*). We must be truly happy about what is good and true and honorable; we must not delight in deception or any aspect of sinfulness. A loving wife will not seek to deceive or manipulate her husband. She will not influence him toward bad habits or immorality. She will seek to be pure and righteous and will encourage him to be

righteous. She will not pressure him so much that he feels he must be dishonest to get her what she wants. She will seek to remove all corruptive influences from their home and life-style and will seek to accomplish God's will.

(10) "Love bears all things" (*stego*). *Agape*-love seeks to preserve and protect the object of her love. The Greek gives us the picture of putting a roof over the head of our loved ones for their protection. A loving wife will not wish to have the rain fall upon her husband's head; she will want to protect him from the harsh things in life. She will want others to think well of him, thus she will not criticize him or cut him down with sarcastic remarks in public; she will instead praise all his good qualities and tell others how much she appreciates him. She will wait for the right time to burden him with her problems instead of dumping them on him when he is tired and grumpy. She will seek to help him in his responsibilities so he will not feel overburdened or bewildered by them. A loving wife can be a true suitable helper (Genesis 2:18) by attending to the minute details, such as telephone calls, making appointments, running errands, and writing letters for him; she can be what might be called a "live-in" secretary and be such valuable support to him. There is much truth to the saying that behind every successful man is a woman—a helpful and supportive woman.

(11) "Love believes all things" (*pisteuo*). Such belief means a wife will rely on her husband. She will be dependent on him; she will fully trust him; she will adhere to him. She will be confident that he will take care of her and do what is best for them. She will not be constantly worrying and fretting, for this would be a sign that she did not trust his judgment. She will leave the leadership role to him and not try to infringe upon it. She will always seek to believe the best about him.

(12) "Love hopes all things" (*elpizo*). A wife who has hope will not give up but will be determined to keep going, no matter how bad things get. What if your husband is an alcoholic or in a mental institution? What if he is unfaithful to you? *Agape*-love is filled with optimistic outlooks and positive thinking. You must keep on hoping and keep on praying that the situation will improve in time. But this is not to be a passive hope; you must not sit back and expect God to take care of everything. You must be actively seeking help and counsel from Christian friends and do all in your power to make things better. You must be assured that God is in charge and will not allow you to be faced with more than you can bear (I Corinthians 10:13).

(13) "Love endures all things" (*hupomeno*). "Endure" means to remain under and comes from the same root word as submission. It gives us the picture of a floating buoy in a stormy sea—it remains afloat no matter how severe the storm because of what it has inside it. We, too, can remain afloat or remain under the protection of God if we are submissive to God and believe in His promises. There are many horrible tragedies that can befall us in this life. You or your husband could be an invalid. Your child could be deformed. Your house could burn down. On and on the list could go, but we know we can endure any difficult circumstance triumphantly if we are living in God's way and with His love inside of us. And this type of endurance is not a passive resignation that says, "This is the way things are, we just have to grin and bear it." It is not the way of defeat but of victory.

If we would put all of these characteristics of *agape*-love into practice, I'm sure almost all of us would agree that our marriages would last longer and be more fulfilling. When each person puts out the effort to benefit the other, it is hard to go wrong. Attitudes and actions of unselfishness will enable a marriage to endure many rough times and will allow both mates to feel content, even in those times when the emotional, passionate form of love is absent. We may not always "feel" that we are in love; but if we continue to act out the aspects of *agape*-love, the "feel" will return. Of course, this love is not achieved overnight; it takes much effort and time to accomplish it to its fullest extent. But God expects each Christian to make *agape*-love an active part of his or her life.

Biblical Examples

A. Submissiveness and mature love are not qualities of life that are just idealistic and theoretical. They can and do work out in a practical way in marriages as the Scriptures point out:

(1) Peter cited Sarah as being an example of submissiveness to her husband (I Peter 3:6). He referred in particular to her calling Abraham "lord." The only recorded instance of her doing so was when the three men from God came to visit and told them that they would have a child in their old age. Sarah became excited and called Abraham "lord" (Genesis 18:12) as she was contemplating the pleasure that was about to befall them.

Her respect and submissiveness in that instance was best seen in her actions when the men came. She prepared a meal for the visitors when Abraham asked her to do so (18:6). We wives all know how Sarah would have felt having to prepare food for unexpected guests. She could have fussed and fumed about having to do it; or she could have refused to do so, thinking Abraham was expecting too much of her on such short notice. How would God have felt if Sarah had refused to be hospitable to the men He had sent to give her the news she had awaited for so long? But Sarah showed that she was humble, submissive, and loving.

We should also note that Abraham put forth a great deal of effort toward being hospitable. He saw that the guests' feet were washed and that they were able to rest in the shade of a tree. He chose the best calf from the herd, instructed the servant how to prepare it, and prepared a drink for the guests (Genesis 18:4-8). He was not the type of inconsiderate husband who brings home guests and then does nothing to help. He was showing love and concern for Sarah as well as for the guests.

Probably the greatest test of Sarah's submissiveness was when Abraham told her that God had instructed him to sacrifice their only son (Genesis 22). Sarah loved her son and showed how protective she was of him by her request to send Hagar and Ishmael away (21:10). Then after all the waiting, after all the promises, after all the inherent problems and heartaches of rearing a child, her son was going to be taken away from her? She must have questioned Abraham and wondered about God's instructions. Abraham no doubt comforted her and encouraged her to trust in God. How her heart must have ached as Abraham and Isaac started up the mountain! Yet she did nothing to stop them or to change God's directions. She submitted.

(2) Instead of trusting in God to provide for him and his family during the time of famine, Elimelech decided to move to Moab and live amidst foreigners (Ruth 1:1). Naomi, his wife, was submissive and went with him. She would not have desired to live among idol-worshippers whose thoughts and customs were so different from hers; and it is obvious that she thought fondly of Judah, for she wanted to return

187

there when her husband and sons had died (1:6, 7). But she trusted her husband and yielded to him.

(3) Mary showed her submissiveness to God when she responded to the announcement that she would bear the Savior with these words: "Behold, the bondslave of the Lord; be it done to me according to your word" (Luke 1:38). And this attitude carried over into her marriage relationship.

Women were not required to go with their husbands to register for the census. However, Joseph took Mary with him, though it would have seemed unwise since she was in the later stages of pregnancy (Luke 2:4-6). We don't know why Joseph decided that she would accompany him. Whatever the reason, Mary went along willingly, though she must have been very uncomfortable and inconvenienced by the trip.

When they arrived in Bethlehem, there was no room for them to lodge for the night. We read no indication that Mary grew irritated at Joseph's thoughtlessness of not reserving a room ahead of time, or that she grew angry, or that she felt sorry for herself. She trusted that Joseph would make the decisions that were beneficial to them both. She did not weep or grow hysterical when she saw where they would stay for the night — in a stable! She was humble and did not feel put out to be in the meager surroundings. Mary is certainly a good example of a person who practiced self-restraint, who was patient, who was not easily provoked, and who did not seek her own way.

B. The Bible also provides us with examples of what results in a marriage when the wife does not practice submission based on *agape*-love:

(1) Eve struck out on her own. She did not even discuss with Adam what her plans were. She simply acted independently and rebelled by satisfying her own selfishness

and then convinced Adam to do the same. If she had been humble, submissive, and had practiced mature love, she would not have brought sin into the world. (See Chapters One and Two for fuller discussion.)

Many wives are tempted to do as Eve did. The lure of what the pleasures of the world have to offer has caused many women to turn from their husbands and families and seek to make it on their own and get a "piece of the action." Women need to feel special and important, and they sometimes feel a career or a taste of the jet-set style of life will fulfill those needs better than a life of service at home. But they find, just as Eve did, that the desirable bait has a deadly hook within it.

(2) When Abraham asked Sarah to pose as his sister, she yielded to him. But God did not praise her for that action, for her submission in that instance was not based on *agape*-love. Seeking to be pure and righteous was not a part of her decision. She should have known that God would not want her to yield and be a party to immorality and deception. Neither was she thinking clearly about Abraham's welfare. She should have encouraged him to trust that God would keep him safe and alerted him to the dangers of deception. She should have reminded him of their marriage covenant and its seriousness.

God does not expect us to be blindly obedient and do whatever our husbands say. He does not want us posing for pornographic material, covering up for our husband's lies, or robbing banks — even though our husbands may tell us to do so. Our first obligation is to be righteous before God, and in that way we can influence our husbands to be righteous — which means there may be times when we will have to refuse to do what our husbands desire us to do.

(3) Rebekah and Isaac's marriage started out well. It was obvious that Rebekah was a humble person, eager to serve others (Genesis 24:17-19). But after the twins were born, the marriage began to disintegrate. Because of the feelings she had for Jacob, Rebekah changed from a respectful, submissive wife to a conniving, manipulative woman. And because Isaac favored the other son, the problems in the marriage grew. Rebekah thought God was taking too long to fulfill the promise He had made about Jacob, so she took matters into her own hands and acted independently of her husband and God. Yet all the while she rationalized that she was doing what was best.

She took advantage of her husband's weak and blind condition and tricked him into believing he was giving his blessing to his favored son Esau when actually it was Jacob in disguise (Genesis 27). Rebekah was being selfish and dishonest. Her deceit grieved and angered her husband and caused the two brothers to hate one another. Rebekah's unwillingness to be submissive and to trust caused her later life to be one of separateness and sadness, for Jacob had to leave the family for his own safety. We have no record that she ever saw Jacob again.

Many wives today feel just as helpless, as frustrated, and as impatient as Rebekah did, and many react just as she did—with deceit and manipulation—in order to get their way. Some wives put purchases on their credit cards and then conveniently forget to tell their husbands about it. Some wives laze around the house or spend time on the phone all day, but right before the husband returns home, they arrange things so it looks as if they have been working hard. Some wives pout and cry so their husbands will give in to their whims. Some wives hide the purchases they make.

On and on, the list could go. We must realize that such actions are selfish; they do not result from humility, submission, or *agape*-love. If wives truly respect their husbands, they will do nothing that would hurt them and will not seek to do things behind their backs.

(4) Michal, King Saul's daughter, loved David, but it turned out to be a selfish love — not *agape*. She loved David when he was a great soldier and esteemed by the people (I Samuel 18:20-28), and she helped him to escape from her father Saul who was seeking to kill him (19:11-17). But as time went on, it became apparent that she thought only of herself and did not share David's dedication to the Lord (II Samuel 6:16-23). She was sickened by David's celebration that the ark of the covenant was returned to the city, despised him in her heart (I Chronicles 15:29), and told him of her disgust. Her love was not mature and unselfish and thus could not withstand the passage of time. Perhaps Michal had never forgiven David for using her as a pawn in his dealings with Saul and allowed her resentment to build within her heart (II Samuel 3:13, 14).

A superficial, selfish love can never maintain a good marriage relationship and will not help a woman learn to be submissive. Loving someone when he is successful and handsome or because of how he makes you *feel* or because of what he can do for you is not the love that promotes a cemented relationship. It is a fleeting love and will not last through difficult times. When the first problem arises, the wife with this type of love will think only of herself and her needs. When the husband does not seem so attractive or successful, her love dims and she wants out of the marriage relationship. If she remains in the marriage, often hate and disgust become her main attitudes, and submission will be non-existent.

191

(5) Jezebel was certainly not a humble, submissive wife. She became the master of her husband Ahab and ruled over Israel. She was determined to destroy the prophets of God and change the religion of Israel to Baal-worship (I Kings 18:4, 13). Her foremost opponent was the prophet Elijah; but in the face of her evilness and power, even he fled at times.

Her power over Ahab was illustrated best in the incident of Naboth's vineyard. Ahab wanted the vineyard that was close to the palace, but Naboth (the owner) refused to sell. Ahab pouted about it; but Jezebel reminded him of his kingship, told him to quit pouting, and said she would get the vineyard for him (I Kings 21:7). As we read the passage, we get the picture of a hardened, ruthless woman disciplining a blubbering, little-boy husband.

Jezebel wasted no time and arranged for Naboth's murder. When Ahab went to take possession of the vineyard, Elijah met him there and told him of the punishment that would come to them both because of their evil. And then the Scripture includes a verse which shows how much harm the domination of Jezebel caused: "Surely there was no one like Ahab who sold himself to do evil in the sight of the Lord, because Jezebel his wife incited him" (I Kings 21:25).

After Ahab's death, Jezebel continued to exert her evil influence causing political intrigue, death, and the turning away of many in Israel from God to Baal. Her horrible death was vividly described (II Kings 9) as a warning about the results of such wickedness, just as her life illustrates how living totally for self is against God's will.

God created women to live for others and to be guided by a leader in the home; when they step out of that design, they cannot be satisfied and content in their womanhood. Of course, not every domineering wife is as evil as Jezebel was, but in usurping the authority that God gave to the husband, a wife will soon lose respect for her husband. She will become disgusted with his ineptness; her concern for his well-being will be replaced by what she must do to preserve herself. She will feel she has to treat her husband as a little boy (as Jezebel did with Ahab). She will make all the decisions and take care of all the responsibilities, while the husband lives out his days silently in a corner of a room watching television or working on a hobby. It is a sad and tragic scene which is being lived out in many homes, but what is most tragic — the wife often has no idea that she took over the leadership of the home that was to be the husband's. She felt she was doing the right and logical thing because her husband was making so many mistakes. Of course, this is an *extreme* description of a dominating wife. Many wives do not go that far but dominate only in certain areas. Yet we must be aware of its dangers and realize where we could be heading.

No matter how difficult it is, wives must allow their husbands to make mistakes. Husbands must realize that they will not always make perfect decisions. The way husbands can mature, gain wisdom, and realize what it takes to function as a leader in the home is to make mistakes. This is a very difficult part of submission. When the husband flounders and flops around, when he seems to be getting nowhere, making wrong decisions right and left, it seems only proper that the wife step in and make things right — but she must not! Instead she must encourage and support her husband in his decisions (unless they are evil or immoral) and not neglect to act as a partner with counsel and advice.

(6) Ananias and Sapphira had a partnership-type marriage, but it was not based on God's will. Sapphira was submissive

to her husband, but her submission was not based on *agape*-love — thus she was not pleasing to God.

Ananias and Sapphira agreed to lie to the apostles and to God about the amount of money they received for the land they sold. They wanted the appreciation and acclaim for being generous and helping fellow Christians, but they also wanted to hang onto some of the money and use it for their own selfishness. Sapphira yielded to her husband's desires, but she was not thinking of his spiritual welfare. She was not thinking about being righteous (Acts 5:1-10).

In this instance, God showed beyond a shadow of a doubt that decency and honesty are parts of being a submissive wife, for He punished them both for their evil. God does not want wives to be blindly obedient. He wants them to act with the well-being of their husbands in mind.

C. Now we come to a terrifically difficult question — "What are wives to do when their husbands do not live as God intends for them to or when their headship is not within God's will?" We can again turn to examples in the Scripture for guidance:

(1) Leah's marriage was based on the deceit of her father (Genesis 29), and Jacob, her husband, did not love her. He loved her younger sister (Rachel) who also became his wife. Leah was not pretty, had weak eyes, and was unloved by the husband whom she loved dearly. She kept hoping as she bore Jacob sons that he would begin to love her and be the husband he should be (29:32, 34; 30:20). He provided for her physical needs and the needs of their children, but he never met Leah's emotional needs.

Yet Leah was always loyal and submissive to him. She did not resort to complaining or deceitful actions. She never exhibited the irritability or jealousy of the pampered Rachel

194

(30:1, 8), and she did not have the loyalty to foreign gods that Rachel had (31:19). Leah remained faithful in a trying situation; she did not leave nor divorce Jacob; neither did she become an embittered woman, taking out her resentment and frustrations on others.

There are women today who are in the midst of one-sided, unfulfilling marriages. May they learn from Leah. May they practice her patience and learn to hope and endure all things. [1]

(2) Abigail's husband, Nabal, was very rich but was also very selfish and difficult to live with. He was described as being harsh, evil, and churlish (I Samuel 25:3) in direct contrast to his wife, who was described as being intelligent and beautiful. When David asked nicely for Nabal's help, Nabal refused in a very insulting way (25:5-8, 10, 11); thus David decided to seek revenge with violence upon Nabal and his family. It is thought by scholars that Abigail had often been the peacemaker in such situations, saving Nabal's life many times. She understood her foolish and worthless husband (25:25), and was submissive to him in the way that God would have her to be—she did what she had to do to save his life and the life of her family; she thought and acted upon the basis of his well-being.

Abigail brought gifts to David and used tact and resourcefulness to appease David's feelings. Nabal would not have approved, but she was acting in his best interests. When Abigail returned home, Nabal was in the midst of a drunken feast (25:36), so she waited till the next morning to tell him

---

1. I am not saying that a woman today should remain in a bigamous marriage, for such a marriage is against the laws of our land. In the days of Leah and Jacob, having more than one wife had become a custom or an accepted practice; God allowed the practice, but we can find no proof that He approved.

what had happened. Some think if she had told him right away in his drunken condition, he would have beaten her.

Abigail's marriage had probably been arranged by her parents on the basis of the wealth Nabal possessed, but no amount of wealth could make up for the misery Abigail no doubt felt being tied to such a man. Yet she fulfilled her duty to him by protecting him ("bear all things") and seeking to solve the problems his temper and selfishness brought on the family. She did not dominate him, neither did she leave him or divorce him. She somehow lived above the chaos of her family life and retained her charm and beauty. She was submissive and acted on the basis of *agape*-love, even though Nabal was very unlovable.

Many women today live with drunken, surly husbands. May they remember Abigail and learn from her patience and endurance in a bad situation.

(3) The setting was a sumptuous and elaborate palace in Persia under the rule of Ahasuerus (Esther 1:5-7). The King was hosting a seven-day banquet in the garden of the palace and was enjoying showing off his riches. He ordered that wine was to be given freely to any and all who wanted it and in any amount they desired. On the last day of the festivities, the king and the guests were no doubt quite drunk. The King wanted to entertain the party and commanded his wife Vashti to come before the drunken, reeling group and display her beauty (historians say he was asking her to make a lewd display, such as a strip-tease dance).

Vashti refused to appear. The King and the other men were outraged that a wife would not obey her husband — a king, no less! They gave no thought at all to how they were seeking to use her to satisfy their drunken lusts. They decided to make an example of her to all wives who might decide to disobey their husbands and removed her from the throne. We do not know what happened to Vashti, but we must admire her for standing up for the principles of morality.

This incident adds additional proof that God does not expect women to allow themselves to be used unjustly or for immoral purposes. Such actions would nullify the purpose of submission which is to encourage the husband to draw closer to the Lord and His way. A wife is not to be a willing partner with her husband when he seeks her to do evil or turn from the Lord, for that would violate the principle of *agape*-love.

(4) Peter also gave some good teaching to wives who had non-Christian husbands:

> You wives, be submissive to your own husbands so that even if any of them are disobedient to the word, they may be won without a word by the behavior of their wives, as they observe your chaste and respectful behavior (I Peter 3:1, 2).

Being submissive, respectful, and morally pure are the ways to win husbands to Christ—not nagging, living independently, making ultimatums, deceiving, or continuously evangelizing. Peter said being quiet and gentle is the more fruitful way (3:3, 4). Respect the husband as an individual. Don't think of him as a hopeless case and begin to store up disgust. Be the wife you should be to him, but know that God will not expect you to act immorally to please him. Don't continually push the Bible and church at him; it will only cause him to rebel further. Win him by your sweet kindness, your politeness, and your considerate, loving behavior —not by your exhortations or haranguing.

D. A Summary. Being a submissive wife and practicing *agape* is anything but easy in our modern society; for it means surrendering our rights, it means yielding to someone else, it means putting others first, it means having a servant's attitude, and it may mean being patient and kind in trying circumstances. All of these attitudes are downgraded and mocked by the philosophies which are flaunted by the media today. But we must decide which way to go —God's way or the world's. Consider the results of each carefully.

A Sexual Relationship

The Joy. Wives have many different views about sex. Some say it is a necessary evil, a curse perpetrated upon all women because of Eve's sin. Others say it is a wifely duty. Some say, "That is all my husband thinks about." Others say, "I don't know what all the fuss is about. Sex is blah; it is boring." Still others say, "It is the only real fun I have in life." And others believe adultery and switching partners regularly is the only way to have an exciting sexual relationship.

No matter what we think about it, God designed marriage to include sex. Man did not think up sex; God did. It is a special gift God gives to married partners: "And they shall become one flesh" (Genesis 2:24). Sex is the physical expression of the "cleaving" of a marriage relationship. It is an acting out of the unity of two people (I Corinthians 6:16). It is an overt expression of submission, a surrendering of one's physical self to meet the needs of one's mate, and an outgrowth of love that results in emotional fulfillment and physical affection. The sexual desires of humans and the possibility for those desires to be met in marriage are proofs that God really cares for us and wants the best for us.

Sex is one of the means God uses to bind the husband and wife together. God wanted the first man and woman

198

and all others afterwards to "be fruitful and multiply" (Genesis 1:28); the only way they can do that is to depend upon each other and engage in the sexual act. Sex is one way the husband and wife can complement one another. They can *physically* complete one another; they can enhance and satisfy their God-given desires, together. The husband and wife can complete and satisfy each other with their bodies (I Corinthians 7:4).

Sex gives pleasure—not because of our dirty minds or because of our selfishness, but because God wants us to find pleasure in one another in the marriage relationship. He wants us to know full and abundant joy. Abraham and Sarah had a pleasurable concept of sex, and it was not thought of as sinful in the context of their marriage. When they were told that they would have a child, Sarah did not think of the pain or the inconvenience of pregnancy. She thought mainly of the pleasure they would have in the sexual act (Genesis 18:12).

God even provided in the Law for the full pleasure of uninhibited sex between married partners:

> When a man takes a new wife, he shall not go out with the army, nor be charged with any duty; he shall be free at home one year and shall give happiness to his wife whom he has taken (Deuteronomy 24:5).

The words "give happiness" refer to the sexual relationship.

God also included in the Bible a whole book which contains the sexual intimate talk between a husband and wife —Song of Solomon. One cannot read the book without understanding how these two people delight in one another's body and tell each other so (4:9, 11; 6:1-9; 7:1-10). This book describes the abounding joy that God intends for husband and wife to find in one another.

Proverbs includes some explicit wishes of God for the sexual relationship in marriage:

> Let your fountain be blessed, and rejoice in the wife of your youth. As a loving hind and a graceful doe, let her breasts satisfy you at all times; be exhilarated always with her love (5:18, 19).

Sex also provides a means to relieve tension and anxiety. Isaac was comforted in his frustration, worry, and grief over his mother's death by his sexual relationship with Rebekah, his wife (Genesis 24:67). Many married couples can attest to the fact that sex relaxes them as nothing else can. Many say they can tell when they need such a release, because they begin to get irritable and snipe at one another. The best cure is sexual intimacy.

Sexual satisfaction within marriage also provides spiritual protection from Satan. Satan is a master at taking God-given desires and twisting them into avenues of selfishness. Not depriving your husband of the sexual satisfaction he needs means you are helping him resist the temptations that Satan will throw in front of him (I Corinthians 7:5). So wives should think twice before saying, "I'm too tired; I've got a headache" or before being totally unresponsive.

Within the marriage relationship, sex is normal, right, pleasurable, God-blessed, and God-designed (I Corinthians 7:1-5; I Timothy 4:1, 3). Women need to open their minds to this fact and not remain so inhibited about it. We must have a healthy, positive attitude about sex, so it can really bless our lives and our marriages.

To curb illicit and pre-marital sex, parents and churches have sometimes gone overboard and left the impression that all sex is dirty and sinful. Such an imprint on young girls' minds is hard to erase. Saying the marriage vows and putting on the wedding rings does not automatically unlock one's inhibitions about sexual intimacy. It takes much love, patience, and the proper understanding to mature and find sex to be the glorious experience God intended it to be.

Agape-love is an essential ingredient to a fulfilling sexual relationship in marriage. Always thinking about what the other person likes and needs and being committed to meet those needs is so important. Being able to submit and being able to yield to one's own desires and preferences will enrich the sex-life as well as other aspects of marriage.

A husband with *agape* will be gentle and patient; he will meet the wife's need for tender embraces, sweet talk, and gentle stroking. He will realize that her emotional mind-set is the most important part of sexual intimacy for her. He will shave and shower before asking for sex. He will not force himself on her when he knows she is upset with him, overly tired, or sick. He will conscientiously set aside time to be with her alone on a date often and regularly; he will think of ways to show his love for her (gifts, compliments, praise her in public, etc.). He will encourage honest communication between them about their likes and dislikes in the actual sexual actions.

A wife with *agape* will realize that her husband is stimulated by the sight of her body. She will watch her weight, seek to dress attractively, to smell good, and to not be embarrassed as her husband delights in her nakedness. She will seek to shut out all other thoughts, concentrating on her husband and pleasing him. At times, she will need to surrender herself physically (even though she may not prefer to at that time), because she understands that her husband needs the release, the comfort, and the closeness of sex. She, too, will set aside time to be with him alone; she will free herself of her family and household responsibilities for a few hours regularly. She will learn to communicate openly and honestly about her preferences in the sex act; and if she is not sure what she likes, she will encourage them to find out together.

The Guidelines. God never intended for sexual desires to be evil, to be dirty, to be exploited, to be the means of manipulation, or to be a form of slavery. Sinful men have perverted God's intentions in this area also. Through the Scriptures we can see how God intended for sex to be beautiful, to be pleasurable, and to be a source of binding the marriage relationship. But when sin entered the world, God also had to give some guidelines for the proper use of sex.

We know assuredly that God is against adultery, premarital sex, and all other sexual perversions (Leviticus 20:10, 14, 21; Matthew 19:9; Romans 1:26, 27). He intended for sexual intimacy to be *only* within the bond of marriage (Genesis 2:24; Hebrews 13:4). He encouraged husbands and wives to find *all* their sexual satisfaction with their mates (Proverbs 5:15-17).

Yet in our sinful society, there are sexual temptations on every hand. God does not have His head in the sand; He knows what we are facing (Proverbs 5:1; 6:23; 7:1-5). He has given us Christians His Word and His Spirit to guide us and give us the strength to overcome the entrapments that Satan sets for us. We must realize that there is no temptation that will come to us that is stronger than our ability to control ourselves (I Corinthians 10:13).

God emphasized in His Word the horrible consequences of infidelity. He warned us that even though "having an affair" may be exciting and pleasurable, it is only temporary pleasure and will lead to awful pain and problems later:

Stolen water is sweet; and bread eaten in secret is pleasant. But he does not know that the dead are there, that her guests are in the depths of Sheol (Proverbs 9:17, 18).

Adulterous actions can lead to spiritual death (Proverbs 2:16-19) as well as the death of a marriage covenant. Adulterous relationships are laced with insecurity and end in bitterness (Proverbs 5:1-6). Adultery is foolish and ends in hurting and disgrace (Proverbs 6:32, 33). Such sexual relationships are using and manipulating others to meet selfish needs (Proverbs 6:26). Because of the harmful results of adultery and sexual perversions to persons and to marriages, God forbids them, punishes them, and calls them sin (6:27-29; I Corinthians 6:9; Galatians 5:19; Hebrews 13:4).

But God does not stop with the warnings. He also tells us how to resist and avoid sexual temptations. Of course, the best deterrent is the proper understanding of marriage —as a committed, covenant-relationship, a unity of two persons that allows no person or situation to separate them or threaten their commitment, and as a submissive, loving relationship in which each lives for the benefit of the other. Such a close, sharing relationship coupled with satisfied sexual needs leaves little desire or need for extra-marital activities. But when the temptations do come, or when lustful thoughts protrude into our consciousness, we must exercise self-control. We must push them out, get busy with other activities, and fill our minds with good and pure thoughts (Philippians 4:8; James 4:7).

We must also stay away from bad situations (Proverbs 5:8). We must constantly be on the alert; we must get away from a person who is sending sexual signals. The world is filled with lonely people whose mates are often absent or who are not fulfilling all their needs; without even knowing it, these people are looking for intimacy in other relationships. When a lonely man and a lonely woman find one another, there is real danger! When you feel lonely or depressed, or when you are having problems in your marriage, concentrate on alleviating your problems, not on seeking someone to fill your empty spaces. Don't allow yourself to get into sexually compromising situations. Flee from them!

We also need to be careful about the signals we are sending out. Are we dressing provocatively (Proverbs 7:10)? Are we talking and acting flirtatiously (Proverbs 6:2; 7:5; 16-18)? Do we flirt with our eyes and bodies (6:25; 7:21, 22)? It may be fun, but it may also lead to temptations we never dreamed possible. We must remember to always act as pure and morally upright women; the only time we should behave provocatively or send out sexual signals is when we are alone with our husbands.

The Single Woman

With such an emphasis on the marriage relationship in the Bible, in the Jewish culture, and even in our society today, the single woman might become frustrated and worried about her single status. She might wonder if she is strange or weird or might be thinking of little else but "snaring" a husband, rather than living life to its fullest in her present state. Is the marriage relationship the only one in which a woman's needs can be fulfilled, the only way she can be happy?

The Scriptures teach that some persons are given the gift for singleness from God and thus can be quite happy and fulfilled in that state.

Jesus' Teaching. Right after Jesus spoke about the closeness and the permanent nature of the marriage relationship, the disciples were disturbed. They were surprised that the marriage relationship was to be considered so binding. They commented to Jesus that it might be better for a person not to marry than to get into a relationship that they could not get out of (Matthew 19:10). Then Jesus stressed that the single life was a gift that only certain people had: "But He said to them, 'Not all men can accept this statement, but only those to whom it has been given'" (Matthew 19:11).

Only certain people could remain single and be happy and fulfilled in that state, Jesus said. He was intimating that God gave the capacity for singleness only to certain people and that the demands of the single life were high. Not everyone can fulfill those demands.

Then Jesus gave three causes for the single status:

> For there are eunuchs who were born that way from their mother's womb; and there are eunuchs who were made eunuchs by men; and there are also eunuchs who made themselves eunuchs for the sake of the kingdom of heaven. He who is able to accept this, let him accept it (Matthew 19:12).

a. Some are single from birth. Either they cannot function sexually, have no interest in sex, or are able to control their sexual drives.

b. Some are single because of circumstances of life. In those days men slaves were often castrated so they would not be a sexual threat to the master's household of women. This would also include those who have no desire for sex or marriage because of family or societal influences.

c. Some are single because they choose to devote themselves wholly to God. They choose to control their desires for sex and marriage and are able to do so. Thus they are left free to be completely devoted to the Lord's work.

After this discussion, Jesus repeated the idea that only some people were able to maintain the single status. We can conclude from Jesus' comments that singleness is a valid state in God's eyes. It is not something to be ashamed of or to be worried about. It is just as fulfilling as marriage, but because of God-given sexual desires not everyone can maintain it.

Paul's Teaching. Paul's teaching was consistent with what Jesus taught. He also stressed that singleness was a gift from God to certain people and could be a fulfilling way of life. Paul himself was single, and he encouraged the state for those who could handle it:

> But I say to the unmarried and to widows it is good for them if they remain even as I. But if they do not have self-control, let them marry; for it is better to marry than to burn (I Corinthians 7:8, 9).

Paul was saying that singleness requires great self-control. If a person is constantly thinking of sexual encounters and is "hot with passion," then that person should consider marriage. Don't seek to live against your natural, God-given functions, for you will be wide open to the temptations of Satan in the sexual area of your life. On the other hand, if your desires and thoughts are controlled relatively easily, you may be called by God to be single—"Only as the Lord has assigned to each one, as God has called each, in this manner let him walk" (I Corinthians 7:17).

Paul went on to say (7:18-24) that we should be happy in whatever condition God has placed us. He used the example of the slave. If one found himself a slave, he was advised not to worry about his condition but serve God in that situation. The same is good advice for the single person.

You may not understand why you are single; you may desire to be married, but the opportunity has not yet presented itself. Don't mope around or become frustrated. Don't let life pass you by while you are waiting, hoping, and praying for marriage. Instead, thank God for your situation and make the best of it. Don't get impatient. Let God do His work in your life. Don't try to outguess or manipulate God. Instead, be determined to serve God with all of your talents in your single status. Get involved in the local church and community.

Paul pointed out that both marriage and the single life were valid in God's eyes (v. 28). He stressed the transitoriness of life on earth and how each person must do all he can to promote God's will and cause (7:29-31). Then he emphasized that singleness had some advantages:

> One who is unmarried is concerned about the things of the Lord, how he may please the Lord; but one who is married is concerned about the things of the world, how he may please his wife, and his interests are divided. And the woman who is unmarried, and the virgin, is concerned about the things of the Lord, that she may be holy both in body and spirit; but one who is married is concerned about the things of the world, how she may please her husband (7:32-34).

Paul was not saying the marriage state was inferior; neither was he trying to restrain us from marrying (7:35, see also Chapter Five, pp. 123-125). He was simply pointing out that the single person can be devoted wholly to the Lord; she or he does not have to be tied down by the physical considerations and responsibilities that are inherent in marriage. He can be wholly committed to doing God's work. God's work will be the "cause" that the single person can be involved in. It can be the way a single person can be a fulfilled, whole person. Being single is nothing to be ashamed of; on the contrary, what a great opportunity to have the time and energy to serve God in a full and complete way!

A single woman is not deprived, lacking, or inferior. She can live a full and complete life outside of the marriage relationship. In many cases, being single is a special call from God. A single woman is bound to have many abilities that can be used to full advantage in the local church (Romans 12:6). It is up to the single woman to get involved and be serving, and it is up to the local church to realize her potential and provide opportunities for her to serve.

Summary

God intended for marriage to be a joyous celebration, a relationship of satisfaction, a reward to those who follow His will (Ecclesiastes 9:9). God created marriage (Genesis 2:24) and desires that it be *gratefully* shared by husband and wife alike (I Timothy 4:3). Marriage is good because God made it, and the partnership can be set apart to His purpose through a study of His Word and through prayer (I Timothy 4:4, 5).

The major points stressed in this chapter are as follows:

1. Marriage is to be a committed relationship, a uniting of two people into a unit—so "stuck together" that they act as one.

2. Marriage is to be a covenant-relationship. Death and divorce are two public terminations of the covenant.

3. Marriage is to be a submissive relationship, issuing out of humility and *agape*-love.

208

4. Marriage is to include a joyous and satisfying sexual relationship that spotlights the interdependence between the husband and wife.

5. Singleness is just as valid a state as marriage and is a special gift from God to some people.

DISCUSSION QUESTIONS:

1. Divide the class into buzz groups and assign them the seven situations described in the Introduction (pages 146-148). Have them discuss these points:
   a. What are the basic problems in the situation?
   b. What trend in our society promotes this problem?
   c. What principles concerning marriage found in God's Word would apply to this problem?
   d. How could this situation be changed if God's way was followed?
2. What positive qualities do you think are added to our lives when we are committed to relationships and/or causes?
3. How does unity of goals and values aid in the commitment of marriage?
4. How do our contemporary wedding ceremonies point out the covenant-relationship of marriage? Be specific.
5. Give reasons why God would not approve of polygamy.
6. Why do you think God hates divorce?
7. Why, then, does God allow divorce?
8. According to the New Testament, in what two situations would divorce be a viable solution?
9. If we are to follow in God's way, how are we to treat those who have been divorced?
10. Tell in your own words what God's definition of submission is.

11. Tell what submission (from God's viewpoint) is not.
12. Why is submission a difficult attitude and behavior to fulfill in the marriage relationship?
13. What can happen if a wife is not submissive to her husband's leadership? Give Biblical examples.
14. Have each member of the class share one area of conflict in their marriage and then have the class discuss how that conflict could be solved on the basis of *agape-*love.
15. List the guidelines that God gave us in His Word to keep the sexual relationship pure.
16. What can your church or class do to help enhance the status of a single Christian?
17. Have the class list reasons why marriage is still a relevant life-style today.
18. Have the class summarize the wife's and husband's (separately) responsibilities in a marriage.

Chapter Seven

WOMEN AS MOTHERS

In a country where child abuse and neglect escalate yearly, where abortion is the socially accepted solution to unwanted pregnancies, where runaway mothers have become as common as runaway fathers, where more women are entering careers outside the home and leaving their children with baby-sitters or in day-care centers, where more children are left at home to shift for themselves while parents "party" every night, where the majority of parents told Abigail VanBuren in a survey that if they had it to do over again they would *not* have children, it may seem an anachronism to say, "Motherhood is a great privilege." Yet that is the message we receive from God through the Scriptures.

A Great Privilege

Motherhood. One of the responsibilities that God gave to the first marriage partners was to "be fruitful and multiply, and fill the earth" (Genesis 1:28a). Besides creating sexual intimacy for the pleasure, satisfaction, and the physical expression of the unity of marriage, God created the sex act as the means of providing the earth with new life, new human beings.

God promised that the Savior, the one who would crush the head of Satan, would be born of woman (Genesis 3:15). Christ, the Messiah, would begin life on earth in the womb of a mother and would become a newborn infant. If God had the idea that children were nuisances, the source of all worry and frustration, a cross that parents have to bear, real "pain in the necks," He would hardly have chosen for His Son to become one. He could just as well created a fully-grown man out of the dust of the earth (as He did Adam)

211

and sent Him to earth in that form. And if being a mother is a second-class, inferior position for a woman, why would God have chosen for His Son to be born and reared by such a woman?

It is evident that God had a high respect for motherhood. He made specific reference in His Law concerning the respect and honor that should be given mothers (Exodus 20:12, Leviticus 19:3, note that fathers are included also). The book of Proverbs makes numerous admonitions about respecting and listening to mothers:

Do not forsake your mother's teaching (1:8; 6:20).

A foolish son is a grief to his mother (10:1).

A foolish man despises his mother (15:20).

A foolish son is . . . bitterness to her who bore him (17:25).

He who assaults his father and drives his mother away is a shameful and disgraceful son (19:26).

He who curses his father or his mother, his lamp will go out in time of darkness (20:20).

Do not despise your mother when she is old (23:22).

The eye that mocks a father, and scorns a mother, the ravens of the valley will pick it out (30:17).

Even though the Jewish world of the Bible was very much tainted with sin, it did retain the high respect that God intended for motherhood. The most glorious, wonderful thing that could happen to a woman was to have a child; and the saddest plight for a woman was to be barren. Barrenness was considered to be a curse, while having children was equated to being blessed by God.

Eve said she had received a child with the help of the Lord (Genesis 4:1) and considered her third son, Seth, to be appointed by the Lord as a replacement for Abel who had been murdered (4:25).

Sarah was so distressed at her barrenness that she persuaded Abraham to become intimate with her maid so a child could be born into their family (Genesis 16:1-8). When Hagar had conceived, she looked down upon Sarah who had not conceived. Her attitude shows us the great importance the women placed on motherhood (16:4). There is no mistaking Sarah's happiness when she was told she would have a child at last (Genesis 18:12), and the extreme joy she felt when Isaac was born (21:6, 7).

We cannot forget Rachel who was so vexed and depressed because her sister was having children, while she herself was barren (29:31; 30:1); and how she credited the Lord with blessing her when she finally did have a child (30:23).

Hannah was also greatly distressed because of her barrenness (I Samuel 1). Her husband's other wife treated her as an inferior because she had no children. Hannah wept, prayed ceaselessly, and would not eat. Her husband was concerned and indicated that he wanted to make her happy. "Isn't an attentive, loving husband better than children?" he asked (1:8, my paraphrase). Hannah evidently did not think so. She prayed so fervently in the temple that the priest thought she was drunk. When God fulfilled her great desire to have a child, she gave Him all the glory and honor (2:1-10) and followed through with her commitment to dedicate her child to the Lord's service.

When Mary (the mother of Jesus) conceived, her song of rejoicing and thankfulness was similar to that of Hannah's (Luke 1:46-55) and overshadowed any fear or confusion she felt because she was a virgin and yet was pregnant. Elizabeth (mother of John the Baptist) said that God had removed her own disgrace and looked upon her with favor by allowing her to become pregnant (Luke 1:25).

213

WHAT THE BIBLE SAYS ABOUT WOMEN

In contrast to the Jewish view of motherhood (and God's view) is the view of many in our world today. Many in our society look with disdain on motherhood and completely disregard the life of the fetus in the woman's womb. Many women say, "It is my body, and only I have the right to decide whether or not that unborn person should be born." How callous! How selfish! What about the rights of that person within the womb to have a chance to grow and develop? Does any woman have such infinite and perfect knowledge that she is able to discern what kind of person the child in her womb would grow up to be or what kind of contribution to society that person could become? No, only God knows; so how can any woman dare to throw away that human life as she would throw away a piece of garbage? We will probably never know how many great people were never allowed to be born in our present day.

God creates life; He allows life to become. He designed the process by which humans would be formed. The man and woman are the means or the vessels — but they do not create life. God gives the life that is in the woman's womb, and He considers that life to be a person from the moment of conception. He fully expects that person to be born unless *He* and only *He* decides otherwise. How dare any woman usurp the authority of God by taking the life of a completely defenseless human being?

God considers the life of the fetus within the womb to be very precious. He made special provisions in His Law for the protection of pregnant women (Exodus 21:22, 23) and condemned those who ripped open a woman with child (Amos 1:13; II Kings 8:10, 12; 15:16-18). And He considers that life to be a person from the moment of conception. He indicated this when He told Mary of Elizabeth's conception:

"And behold, even your relative Elizabeth has also conceived a son in her old age" (Luke 1:36). Elizabeth had conceived a *son*, not a thing, a cell, or a blob. There is no hint that God considered what was in the womb of a woman to be anything other than a person — no matter what stage of pregnancy was being discussed.

When speaking of Rebekah's pregnancy, the Scripture says: "But the *children* struggled together within her . . . And the Lord said to her, 'Two *nations* are in your womb; and two *peoples* shall be separated from your body'" (Genesis 25:22, 23). God would hardly consider the children, the nations, or the peoples to be nonentities within her womb. Job considered himself to be a person in his mother's womb (Job 31:15) as did the Psalmist (Psalm 22:10; 139:13). God told Jeremiah that He formed him in his mother's womb and set him apart to be a prophet before He was born (Jeremiah 1:5). John the Baptist was said to have been filled with the Holy Spirit while in his mother's womb (Luke 1:15) and even leaped with joy when Mary came to visit because of the person who was in Mary's womb (Luke 1:41, 42).

Children. Not only does God consider the life in the womb to be precious, He considers children who come from the womb to be special gifts. He considers them to be the most valuable parts of a family, to be the signs of a secure and successful family, and are to be sources of pride as is evident from these passages:

> Behold, children are a gift of the Lord; the fruit of the womb is a reward. Like arrows in the hand of a warrior, so are the children of one's youth. How blessed is the man whose quiver is full of them; they shall not be ashamed, when they speak with their enemies in the gate (Psalm 127:3-5).

215

Your wife shall be like a fruitful vine, within your house, your children like olive plants around your table. Behold, for thus shall the man be blessed who fears the Lord (Psalm 128:3, 4; olive plants were the most prized of plants).

Let our sons in their youth be as grown-up plants, and our daughters as corner pillars fashioned as for a palace; Let our garners be full, furnishing every kind of produce, and our flocks bring forth thousands and ten thousands in our fields; Let our cattle bear, without mishap and without loss, let there be no outcry in our streets! How blessed are the people who are so situated. How blessed are the people whose God is the Lord (Psalm 144:12-15).

Jesus, who made clear God's thoughts, loved children and did not consider them to be nuisances. He took time out of His busy schedule to hold them and speak to them. The disciples thought their great leader should not be bothered with such nonsense as talking to children, and Jesus' reaction was surprising to them:

But when Jesus saw this, He was indignant and said to them, "Permit the children to come to Me; do not hinder them; for the kingdom of God belongs to such as these. Truly I say to you, whoever does not receive the kingdom of God like a child shall not enter it at all." And He took them in His arms and began blessing them, laying His hands upon them (Mark 10:14-16).

Jesus compared the children to those who would be the greatest in the Kingdom of Heaven and warned that anyone who would cause children to stumble spiritually might as well be dead in God's sight, emphasizing the importance He placed on the lives of the children (Matthew 18:1-16).

Summary. From God's viewpoint, we can see clearly that motherhood is a gift to women, a reward, and a blessing

216

to be received with joy and gratitude. The role of mother-hood is to be taken very seriously; it must not be trifled with. Motherhood is a great honor, a position of great importance, and one that deserves respect.

A Great Responsibility

God said motherhood was a joy, but He never said it was easy. Because of sin in the world, we must realize that with motherhood come frustrations and problems as well as happiness and fulfillment. Along with the great privilege of being a mother comes a great responsibility.

I must hasten to add that God considers that the fathers share in that responsibility. Such a belief is consistent with God's view of marriage. If marriage is a partnership, a shar-ing, a united relationship, then it follows that the rearing of children is to be a joint effort. Fathers were very involved in the lives of their children in the Scriptures. They provided for their physical needs, they instructed and disciplined them, and they gave them loving protection. Every principle and guideline that we will consider in the relationship of the child and the mother, God applied to fathers. Since this is a book about women, mothers will be referred to in the remainder of this chapter, but please understand that the applications extend to the fathers as well.

We now turn to the big questions—"What does God expect of a mother? What all is involved in the responsibility of being a mother?"

Jesus implied in His teaching in Matthew 7:9-11 that parents are to give their children gifts; and that many parents, though touched by sin, know how to give the right gifts to their children:

Or what man is there among you, when his son shall ask him for a loaf, will give him a stone? Or if he shall ask for a fish, he will not give him a snake, will he? If you then, being evil, know how to give good gifts to your children, how much more shall your father who is in heaven give what is good to those who ask Him!

Paul also stressed this fact when he was speaking of how he considered the Christians at Corinth to be his children. He mentioned how parents are to save up (*thesaurizo*) for their children (that is, "lay up treasures or gifts," literal translation, II Corinthians 12:14).

But what are these gifts to be? Food, clothing, shelter, money, and the gifts that money can buy? Yes, these are to be given, but there is much, much more that we must give to our children.

LOVE. The first gift that a mother is responsible for giving her children is love — *agape*-style. We might say, "Oh sure, mothers naturally love their children." But do they? If so, then why do mothers abuse and neglect their children? Why do mothers allow their unborn children to be killed (abortion)? Why do mothers go off in their own way and many times literally or essentially give up the responsibility for their children, leaving them to grow up by themselves? Why do mothers think of their children as intrusions into their lives rather than blessings? Why do some mothers say they wish they had never had children or say they resent how their children "tie them down"?

Agape-love does not allow for any of these attitudes or actions. It is a total giving of oneself; it is acting for the benefit of the children, not oneself. Paul expressed it well when he spoke of his love for the Corinthians, how he thought of them as his children, and what resulting actions and attitudes were in his life because of that type of love: "I will most gladly spend and be expended for your souls" (II Corinthians 12:15). According to the Greek, he was saying, "I am willing to be consumed, to be completely spent out for your benefit." He was willing to give his all, not grudgingly or in irritation or frustration, but *gladly*. Mothers who love their children as God directs will give themselves totally to their families (this includes husband, of course) and will do so gladly.

This "giving of oneself" does not happen overnight or magically when the newborn infant is placed in the mother's arms. It involves great effort; it involves a continuous process of growing and maturing.

A mother with *agape* will give of herself to her child no matter what he looks like or what his interests or talents are. She will love him *in spite of* how he behaves, what he says, or what his attitudes are. Many mothers find that difficult. Some tend to love the child who is attractive, the child who seeks to please, the child who is multi-talented, and the child who shares the mother's interests; while they push aside the handicapped child, the ugly child, the child who constantly misbehaves, or the child who is totally different in temperament and interests. Children can sense how we really feel about them. We must love all of our children in our actions as well as our words (I John 3:18). Let us not be sucked into the worldly view of what makes a good and successful person; beauty and talent are not what life is all about.

The Bible provides us with clear examples of the destructiveness of "selective" love in a family relationship. Rebekah favored Jacob because of his quiet nature, while Isaac favored Esau because of his interest in hunting and what he considered to be manly pursuits (Genesis 25:28). This favoritism caused a rift in their marriage relationship, caused Rebekah to practice deceit, caused hatred between the brothers, caused Esau to want to kill Jacob (27:41), and caused Jacob to flee from his family to live in a foreign land for several years.

When Jacob acquired a family of his own, he favored one of his sons over the others (Joseph, Genesis 37:3, 4). The anger and resentment of the other sons built to such a peak that they considered killing Joseph and finally sold him as a slave to the Egyptians.

Favoritism which is seen or felt through the words and actions of the parents will inevitably cause friction and tension within the family, not to mention the harm it does to the self-image of the slighted child. Such children will often do *anything* to get attention and to feel some love directed toward them—they will cheat, run away, steal, cause commotion and confusion, "hang out" with the wrong crowd, etc. Mothers must make a concentrated effort to see the "specialness" in each one of their children, to delight in them as individuals, encourage their good qualities, and discipline their characters.

A mother with *agape* will express in her attitudes and actions to her child all the aspects of love that are listed in I Corinthians 13:4-7. It was probably expected that we consider these characteristics of *agape*-love as we were seeking to establish principles for the marriage relationship (see Chapter Six), but how often do we think of how these same characteristics should be applied to a parent-child relationship? Perhaps we tend to think of our children more as possessions or property than as real persons with a worth and dignity of their own. We women don't like to be considered as property, so let's don't treat our children as such.

(1) Instead, let us be patient. May we put up with our children and learn to wait ("Love is patient," I Corinthians 13:4). Our children may be intelligent, but they still do not have an adult grasp of many facts and concepts. They are forgetful, so we must patiently remind them of their chores, of their homework, and of the necessity of picking up their clothes or toys. When they are having fun, hours can seem like minutes; and they seldom feel the pressure of having to get places on time as we adults do. Thus we must not get so upset when they are late, and our pushing and prodding must be gentle. When they are sitting still or standing in line, minutes seem like hours to them, so we must be patient as they whine, fuss, and fidget.

It is hard for younger children to understand why older brothers and sisters are allowed to participate in activities while they are not; their concept of age and the privileges that go with it is limited, so we need to explain patiently and seek to compensate whenever possible. Children have a limited concept of money—how it is earned and how it is to be spent. They find it difficult to understand how we can go to town, buy groceries, pay the doctor's bill, buy shoes, and buy a lawn mower, but when they want to stop for a coke or want to buy a bicycle that catches their eye, we say, "We just don't have the money." They think having money is as simple as writing a check or asking the bank teller for money. Thus we must patiently explain and help them learn about the intricacies of the world of money.

Children do not fully understand what effort and skill is needed to put a meal together, to mow the yard, or to do well in music and sports. They don't realize that planning, hard work, and much practice are parts of what it takes to be successful. So we must be willing to repeat ourselves, encourage them to work and practice, and put up with their expressions of frustration and irritability. And do the reminding, the encouraging, and the putting up with without irritation or anger.

(2) "Love is kind." Kindness refers to tenderness and affection. When Paul told Titus to have the older women encourage the younger women to "love" (*philandros*) their husbands and children (Titus 2:4), he was stressing kindness and affection. When Paul addressed the Galatians as children (4:19), he was stressing tender affection. When Jesus addressed His disciples as children (John 13:33), He was emphasizing the affection He felt for them. When John addressed his fellow Christians as children, he also stressed this affection (I John 2:1, 12, 28).

Paul compared the relationship between the leaders of the church and the members to that of a mother and her children, using the words "gentle," "nursing," and "cherishing" (or tenderly caring and fond affection, I Thessalonians 2:7, 8). These words were commonly used to refer to the parent-child relationship; and indeed, the word "cherish" (*thalpo*) presents the picture of a mother hen gathering her chicks under her to keep them warm with her feathers.

We can conclude, then, that God considers this type of warm affection to be a must in a family. Children need kind, gentle words of love and concern, and loving embraces and touches in order to feel truly loved. How about the words we speak to our children? How often do we tell them we love them? How often do we praise their efforts? How often do we tell them how we appreciate them? More than likely, we spend more time criticizing them and showing our irritation with their actions and attitudes. We must learn to respect their personhood, be sensitive to their feelings, and remember not to make fun of them publicly or privately. Playful teasing may seem to be enjoyed by all, but we must be very careful. Teasing and things said in fun may cut and hurt the child's inner being.

How often do we touch, kiss, or embrace our children? We've all read the research about the importance of touching and cuddling an infant, but we must realize that no matter what the age of a child, he needs physical affection.

Psychologists are discovering the need of all humans to be physically touched, stroked, and embraced. Many problems that adults have with giving and receiving love can be traced to the lack of physical affection they received as children. "Touch therapy" groups have arisen all over the country in an effort to help adults realize their own identities through receiving physical affection from others and help them to be able to give out physical affection themselves.

Kindness also includes having compassion and being able to comfort one another in time of trouble. God said He comforted His people, had compassion for them, and would never forget them — just as a mother treats her child:

> The Lord has comforted His people and will have compassion on His afflicted. But Zion said, "The Lord has forsaken me, and the Lord has forgotten me." Can a woman forget her nursing child, and have no compassion on the son of her womb? (Isaiah 49:13b-15a).

> As one whom his mother comforts, so I will comfort you; and you shall be comforted in Jerusalem (Isaiah 66:13).

Such compassion and comfort is a seeking to understand the child's feelings and problems and really caring. Certain problems may seem insignificant and of no consequence to an adult, but they may be quite real and devastating to a child. A fear of the dark, a fear of dogs, a fear of water—such things may seem like nonsense to an adult, but they must not be laughed off or made objects of criticism or teasing. Kindness means a mother will care about the child's distress and will seek to comfort him with her presence and assuring words of love.

Such comfort and concern also mean the mother will really pay attention to what the child is feeling or saying. The "kind" mother will look the child right in the eye when he is speaking to her and will put her mind on what he is saying, not on what is simmering on the stove or the list of chores that have to be done. She will cry with him and laugh with him. She will really listen and respect his "side" of an issue.

(3) "Love is not jealous." A mother must not envy the youth, the energy, the activities, or the relationships of her children. She must not seek to look or act as youthful as they are. She must not feel as if she is in competition with their father for their affection and loyalty. She must not seek to attract her daughter's boyfriends to herself. Neither should she be hurt or peeved if her child can do something she always wanted to do as a young person but could not.

(4) "Love is not boastful or arrogant." A mother must not make herself and her problems and needs to be the center of the family's attentions. She must not consider herself to be better than her children. Education and more earning power does not a more important person make.

Neither should a mother be blind to her children's faults and brag about her "wonderful" children to everyone (becoming a bore). She must realize that her children are not perfection personified and that they may be to blame for some of the scrapes they get into. Many mothers are very quick to see how other people's children, the school person-nel, the Sunday School teacher, etc. are to blame for all their children's problems, but are very slow to understand that some blame must be laid at the feet of their own children and that they must be made to feel responsible for their actions.

(5) "Love does not act unbecomingly." A mother should be polite and courteous to her children. I wonder how many of us have thought about this aspect of love. We expect our children to say "please," "thank you," "excuse me," and "I'm sorry," but how often do we treat them with the same politeness and consideration? We don't want our children to interrupt us when we are talking, but we think nothing of interrupting their conversations. We know crude language and saying "shut up" shows disrespect, so why do we sometimes use such terms with our children? We want our children to share their food, toys, etc., but how many times do we guard our own possessions from our children's touch or use? We must be alert to how we are treating our children and determine to be as polite and courteous to them as we expect them to be to us and others.

(6) "Love does not seek its own." A mother should not be selfish and always put herself first. Her children and their needs should come first. A mother should not leave her children uncared for either physically or emotionally in order to pursue her own interests. A mother who feels restrained and unbearably tied down by the responsibilities of her chil-dren is probably thinking of herself first. She will have difficulty coping with the daily drudgery and irritations of being at home. She will think of herself as a slave to her family and resent each bit of service she has to perform and often will make sure everyone around her knows how hard she works. She becomes a martyr of her own making. How much better

it is for a mother to feel that her children are precious gifts of God and that God has deemed her worthy enough to nurture and care for them.

A mother who "seeks her own" may try to live out her fantasies through her children. She may force her children to perform or fulfill roles that she had always wanted as a child but could not do. Or such a mother may make her children so dependent on her that they cannot function without her. In this way, she always feels needed and wanted. She makes her children's decisions, she buttons their shirts, ties their shoes, makes their beds, etc. She treats her children as pieces of property, not as persons who need to learn to become responsible and make decisions. She would not want her children to marry or ever leave her "possession." She would be the type of mother who would never be willing to "cut the apron strings," because the children were filling her empty spaces.

A mother who "seeks her own" might expect her children to be parent-figures to her. She might expect them to always offer comfort and reassurance to her when she is depressed or feeling lonely. She might expect even a very young child to act as an adult and carry adult responsibilities, while she herself remains the pampered child.

A mother who "seeks her own" may decide to keep her child, even though he or she was born out of wedlock. She would refuse to give the child up for adoption, even when this would give the child a more secure family environment. She will think only of her own need for love and companionship rather than what is best for the child. Certainly it is not in the child's best interests to be reared by a resentful grandmother or by a harried mother who cannot offer the security that a child needs because of her own guilt and fears.

Many women these days are in the position of being step-mothers. They, too, must not "seek their own" by favoring their own children over the children of another woman. We are reminded of Jephthah who was the son of a harlot. His mother allowed the father to take the child, for life with a harlot would not be a fit environment for a child (Judges 11:1). But Jephthah's stepmother made certain that her sons knew they were special and that Jephthah was beneath them. Thus as adults, her sons threw Jephthah out of the family. He fled and got in with the wrong crowd (Judges 11:2, 3). His stepmother was not showing *agape* toward the child who was entrusted to her care.

The mother who thinks of her children before her own needs and wants will give of herself and of her time. She will spend time with her children — playing with them, working with them, traveling with them, and communicating with them. She will take the time to listen as well as to share her own thoughts and feelings. She will seek to have the family together for meals as much as possible. She will help them with their homework and go to their school activities. She will not continuously be saying, "I'm too busy," or "don't bother me now." She will not try to fill their hours with so many activities that she will not have to spend time with them. Neither will she think that "things" are an adequate substitute for her physical presence and attention.

The results of various surveys point out that children need and desire the physical and mental presence of their mothers (fathers too). In a recent survey conducted by *Family Weekly,* a group of children were asked what they wanted most that they did not have at the present time. The majority of them answered, "someone at home to talk to."

Mothers can participate in community and church activities, but they must be certain that they are also with their children a great quantity of time. A mother should try to be with her children during these events: when they get up in the morning, when they are sick, when they have had their feelings hurt, when they come home from school, when they participate in activities or perform in public, when they go to bed, when they want to share their dreams and fears. Why do I point out these events? Because these are the most important to children, the times they are the most ready to talk, or the times they are feeling the most vulnerable and need the comfort and security of knowing that their mother is there.

My daughter's teachers asked them to write about their mother for this past Mother's Day. They were to tell what their mother does that they appreciated the most. My eleven-year-old said, "She always is there and takes care of me when I am not feeling good." My seven-year-old said, "She lets me cook and bake with her." I was deeply touched by these comments and reminded again of the simple things that children require. They do not want the pretty clothes or the fancy toys nearly as much as someone who cares about them and spends time with them.

What does this say about a mother who works outside the home? We have no evidence that God is against wage-earning mothers. We have already studied how capable and important God considers women to be, but we have also ascertained that a woman's husband and children are to be her top priorities. Each woman must decide for herself if she can hold down a job and also meet all the needs of her family, for she will be held responsible to God for how she fulfills her role as wife and mother. Every mother needs to ask herself: "Do I have this job for myself (I want to get out of "prison") or for the way it helps my family?" "Does my husband want me to work, or would he rather I didn't?"

"Does our family really need the money this job provides or have I fallen into the materialistic trap?" "Am I spending enough time with my children and husband?" "Do I really know them or am I losing touch because of my new interests and activities?" And every mother needs to realize that love and time cannot be doled out at the beginning of each week as easily as an allowance.

When Paul told Titus that the young women should be taught to be "workers at home," (Titus 2:5), he was not saying women should *only* be at home. But he was indicating that a mother's presence was needed at home a major portion of the time, a presence that manifests love and seeks to guide. The Scriptures do not seem to uphold the popular theory that "quality time is more important than quantity time." On the contrary, *both* kinds of time are needed to fulfill the needs of children.

(7) "Love is not provoked." There will be anger-inducing situations in everyday family life, because no person in the family is perfect. Mistakes will be made, and irritating habits will continue. Appliances will break down, schedules will be in conflict, and not everyone's desires will be met all the time. The Scriptures do not say that a mother must never get angry; she will inevitably get angry at times and "blow her stack." But the Bible does say that anger must not become a habit pattern of her life, that a bad temper must not be the only way she reacts in tense situations, and that physical violence must not be a part of her life.

A mother with *agape* will know how to control her words, her tone of voice, and her actions. She will constantly be seeking to promote peace and harmony in her home. She will be "slow to anger" (James 1:19) and will not let the sun go down while she is still seething in anger (Ephesians 4:26b). She will realize how words spoken in haste and

229

anger can pierce a child's heart. She will not allow material considerations to take precedence over the spirits of her children. A broken glass, muddy footprints on a freshly scrubbed floor, a torn bedspread, a ruined pair of hose — these can all be remedied or mended much easier than can a bruised heart of a child.

(8) "Love does not take into account a wrong suffered." A loving mother will be forgiving. Children can step all over a mother's heart. They can rebel and turn their backs on all that they know is right. They can speak harshly and wound a mother's spirit. They can communicate distrust and hatred by a look in their eyes, a scowl on their faces, a slammed door, an angry shout. They can withdraw into their own world and shut a mother out. They can move away and never make a phone call or send a card to their mother.

But even at that, a loving mother will forget these slights and forgive her children. She will always be ready to receive them back again with open arms and a smile. She may never understand or approve of their different ways and attitudes, but she will always love them. And she will not wallow in self-pity, bitterness, or resentment because her children don't "treat her right."

(9) "Love rejoices in the truth." A loving mother will maintain her honesty and integrity no matter what the circumstances are. Her children will be able to trust her word, and they will know that she will carry out her promises. They will not hear her lying to her neighbor on the phone; they will not observe any deceit being perpetrated by her on their father; they will not hear her gossip; they will not catch her cheating. They will observe her strict observance of traffic laws and will see her pay back the store clerk the few cents she was overpaid. She will not excuse her child's action to

the school teacher or blame others for her children's mistakes. She will encourage her children to pay their debts and take responsibility for their wrong-doing. She will not seek to find loopholes in the laws of the land nor in the commandments of the Lord. She will not tell "stories" to her children to silence their questions or to appease their curiosity; she will tell them the simple truth.

(10) "Love believes all things, hopes all things, and endures all things." Mothers must learn to trust and believe in the potentiality of their children. They must strive to maintain a positive outlook on life, believing that the future will be bright even though the present may be bleak. Mothers must learn to trust in God's will for their own lives as well as for the lives of their children. That means setting aside worries and anxieties. That means believing that God will take care of them and their families. That means setting aside the fretfulness and the nervousness, and letting the peace of God rule in their hearts no matter how turbulent the situation may be.

(11) "Love bears [protects] all things." A loving mother will seek to protect her children and keep them away from what threatens their well-being. She will seek to protect her children's dignity, their health, and their lives. She will seek to develop and maintain a stable, secure environment for the children, which involves removing the threats to the children's peace of mind.

The best way to provide the children with the protection of a secure environment is to have a proper marriage relationship. There is no other single factor as important to enhance a child's feeling of safeness and security. The June 1980 issue of the *Ladies Home Journal* recorded the results of a survey taken from a large group of fourth, fifth, and sixth graders asking the question, "What worries you?" The

231

five most popular answers are very revealing: losing a parent, going blind, being held back a year in school, wetting pants in class, and hearing parents quarrel. Notice that two of the five relate to the relationship of their parents.

An active, responsible father who loves and cares for his wife and vice versa, promotes an atmosphere of love and unity that pervades the whole home life. A husband and wife who are committed to their covenant relationship, who complete each other rather than competing, who daily live out *agape*-love with each other and with their children, and who live as responsible adults in the community will be a constant assurance to the children that their spots in life are secure. They will know that they can be safe from the storms—literal and symbolic—and that they have a haven to go to when they hurt. They will not be living in the constant fear that one of their parents will leave, that there will be a divorce, or that the parents won't want their children around anymore.

Of course, not every home can have the stability of a good marriage. Single-parent homes, which are increasing at a rapid rate in this country, have a definite disadvantage in the area of a secure environment for the children. The single mother must realize the fear and insecurity that the absence of the father will provoke. If the cause is divorce, the mother must be certain the children are not alienated from the father. An all-out effort must be made to allow the children time to be with their father. Often the children are afraid that the remaining parent will also leave, or that they are to blame for the parents' break-up. Reassuring words and being with the children physically with very few absences for awhile will be a tremendous help.

If death is the cause, the single mother must realize how deeply the children are hurting, even though they may seem oblivious to what has happened. The mother must not lean heavily on the children for support or to fill her loneliness. She must realize that the children need to lean on her. Mothers should not selfishly keep their grief to themselves; but must share it with their children, so they can freely share with her. She should explain the finality of death and should not forbid the children from participating in the funeral and arrangements. The children must realize with a certainty that the father will never return to be with them.

Few single mothers can be the "rock of stability" for the children in these crisis situations, for they are hurting and suffering so much themselves. But if their lives are founded on the Rock, Jesus, and they have practiced thinking of their children's needs before their own, they will overcome their inadequacies and provide the protection their children need. They can do so by spending a great amount of time with their children, communicating and sharing with them, engaging in social activities with them, continuing life as much as possible as it was before the tragedy, getting involved in a loving, caring fellowship of Christians, encouraging the children to be active in church activities, and seeking a "substitute father" for the children (someone who can relate to them as only a man can — perhaps a youth minister or Sunday School teacher who could give them special attention).

Biblical Examples. There are many examples in the Bible of mothers who sought to protect their children in various ways:

(1) Sarah sought to protect Isaac's dignity from the mocking harrassment of Ishmael and asked Abraham to send Hagar and her son away (Genesis 21:9, 10).

(2) Hagar became distressed when she felt she could no longer protect her son's life. The water had run out; they were outcasts; they were all alone in the wilderness. How

relieved she was when God came to their aid! (Genesis 21:16).

(3) Jochebed hid her son from Pharaoh's murdering soldiers for three months. When she realized she could not hide him safely any longer, she made a water-proof basket, put Moses in it, placed it in the reeds, and had her daughter watch over him until someone found him. She saved Moses' life, was able to rear him in the palace, and was able to teach him of his heritage (Exodus 2:1-11).

(4) Rizpah was a concubine of Saul. Her two sons were handed over to the Gibeonites and hanged to appease the foreigners for an oath that Saul had not kept. It was a cruel and heartless act. The bodies of the dead sons should have been buried at sunset on the same day they were hanged according to Jewish law, but they were allowed to hang there and rot. It was no doubt difficult for Rizpah to comprehend such cruelty. In an effort to maintain the dignity of her children, she stayed with the bodies many days and nights to keep the birds and beasts from eating the rotting flesh. King David heard of her loyalty and devotion and had the bones buried properly (II Samuel 21:8-14).

(5) Bathsheba protected her son's ascendance to the throne by reminding David of his promise to install Solomon as king before the plot of Adonijah to take over the kingdom could be fulfilled as David lay dying (I Kings 1:17, 18, 21).

(6) Two harlots had babies within three days of each other and in the same house. One baby died. At night the mother of the dead baby exchanged it with the live baby, but the next morning the mother recognized that the dead child in her arms was not hers. The mother would not admit to making the trade, so a quarrel ensued, and the matter came before King Solomon. He knew that the real mother of the live child would seek to protect the child's life at all costs, even if it meant she had to give her child up; so Solomon

threatened to cut the child in half. The true mother did not want the child to die and offered to let the other woman have the child — then the mystery was solved. The child was returned to the right mother (I Kings 3:16-27).

(7) The widow of Zarephath had enough food that she could live for two more days, but she was ready to share her food with her son; thus they both would eat a last meal and die (I Kings 17:12). God through Elijah spared their lives because of her unselfishness and willingness to share their last morsels with the prophet. But how troubled she became when her son became sick later and died, especially since she had faithfully served Elijah. God through Elijah brought her son back to life, which increased the faith of the widow (I Kings 17:17-24).

(8) The woman of Shunem was also severely troubled when the child God had given her died suddenly. But she turned in trust to Elisha who restored her child's life (II Kings 4:27).

(9) Mary was willing to leave her homeland, her comfortable life in Bethlehem, and go far away from her relatives in Nazareth to a foreign land filled with strangers and strange customs in order to protect the life of her son, Jesus (Matthew 2:13-15). When Jesus was older, Mary was extremely worried when Jesus could not be found among the travelers going back to Nazareth after the celebration of the Passover, and she informed Jesus of her anxiety when she found Him in the temple in Jerusalem in the midst of the teachers (Luke 2:48). She also showed her desire to protect Him when she came with her other sons to take Jesus home when the Jewish leaders were accusing Him of being from Satan (Mark 3:21, 31-35).

(10) Salome sought to protect the interests of her sons, James and John. She wanted to be assured by Jesus that

they would be given prestigious places in His Kingdom. Though her understanding was shallow, her efforts for her sons were quite motherly (Matthew 20:20-24; Mark 10:35-40).

(11) The Canaanite woman of the region of Tyre and Sidon came before Jesus pleading that He help her daughter who was demon-possessed. Jesus ignored her at first and then rebuked her, but her faith and persistence were so great that she continued pleading. She put her pride aside for the sake of her daughter who was suffering. Jesus rewarded her faith in Him and her love for her child by healing the child (Matthew 15:21-28; Mark 7:24-30).

In these instances, we clearly understand how mothers consistently sought to protect the lives, health, and dignity of their children. It is hard to comprehend that not all mothers are so caring and unselfish. The numbers of abused and neglected children in our country alone are appalling. It is a tragedy that such a fundamental aspect of *agape*-love — protection — is being denied so many children.

Child abuse is another result of a society that stresses *me*ism, that stresses going your own way regardless of how others might be hurt, that stresses doing whatever feels good. It is the mind-set that says: "If it makes you feel a release from your tension to beat your child, then do it. If sexually abusing your child feels good, then do it. If you want your life to be unencumbered, then leave your child in a parking lot." I shudder to think what other atrocities will be done before our society sees the error in such a philosophy.

Summary. Having *agape*-love for our children is a huge responsibility. No one who fully understands the breadth and depth of the relationship between mother and children would ever be guilty of considering motherhood as an inferior career or inferior position in life. Neither could they feel that being a mother is a snap and only requires a small portion of her time and effort. Being a mother requires all that a woman has to give and all the self-control that she can muster. A mother who is a Christian has the help of the Holy Spirit within her to enable her to live out *agape*-love in her home. She can ask God for the wisdom and strength that is needed to be a loving, self-giving mother; for God has promised He will hear and answer that prayer (James 1:5).

INSTRUCTION. Another gift that mothers (and fathers) are to give their children is the instruction of their minds and spirits, which includes guidance of their attitudes and behavior or the aid in forming their characters. This instruction should issue out of an *agape*-love relationship.

God has always been concerned that the children in a family be instructed properly. He repeated many times to the people of Israel the importance of training their children. But *what* does God expect us to teach our children and *how* are we to teach them?

(1) *The Content.* It is obvious that God expects children to have a basic education. How else could a child *read* God's Word? How could God have expected His chosen ones to *write* God's Word unless they had learned how to write? How could God have expected His people to follow His minute directions about the construction of the tabernacle without being trained in mathematics and measurement?

However, God's foremost concern has always been the spiritual education of the children. Part of God's instructions concerning the observance of the Passover feast included allowing time for the parents to explain what God had done for Israel to their children (Exodus 13:14). He told the parents to teach their children about the importance of the memorial

237

made from stones of the Jordan River (Joshua 4:6, 7, 21, 22). It is clear that God wanted the history of how He had worked with and for the nation of Israel, His laws, and the principles of His way of life to be transferred from generation to generation through the training of the children (Deuteronomy 11:18, 19; Psalm 78:5-8). God's intent has always been that a child properly trained in the wisdom that comes from God will result in the maturing of that child into the person God created him to be: "Train up a child in the way he should go, even when he is old he will not depart from it" (Proverbs 22:6).

Paul, in writing to Timothy, re-emphasized what the writer of Proverbs declared — that the wisdom to live life properly comes from God and His sacred Word:

> You, however, continue in the things you have learned and became convinced of, knowing from whom you have learned them; and that from childhood you have known the sacred writings which are able to give you the wisdom that leads to salvation through faith which is in Christ Jesus. All Scripture is inspired by God and profitable for teaching, for reproof, for correction, for training in righteousness that the man of God may be adequate, equipped for every good work (II Timothy 3:14, 15).

Thus we can conclude that the main content of a child's instruction is to be God's Word which leads to salvation, which reveals God's will and way, and which tells us how to achieve and maintain a pure character and loving attitudes.

(2) *The Method.* But how are we to get this important content into the minds and lives of our children? I don't suppose there are very many Christian mothers who have not wished at one time or another that they could prepare a dishful of Christ-like attitudes and spoon-feed them to their children. Or have wished that their children were puppets

238

with strings that they could pull to make them behave and think as they should. Or would have liked for their children to be as empty glasses which they could fill with God's truth as easily as pouring water from a pitcher. But we all know that children cannot be spoon-fed God's life-style, cannot be manipulated as puppets to do God's will, and cannot have God's truth poured into them. Children are individuals with their own minds and wills; thus their instruction is anything but easy.

God's way of child-instruction includes the living example of their mothers (and fathers) doing God's will in every area of life. God wants us to soak up all of His principles and attitudes, so much so that God's life-style becomes our life-style; then the children would not only learn by our words, but also by our actions. God stressed these points in Deuteronomy 11:18-21:

> You shall therefore impress these words of mine on your heart and on your soul; and you shall bind them as a sign on your hand, and they shall be as frontals on your forehead. And you shall teach them to your sons, talking of them when you sit in your house and when you walk along the road and when you lie down and when you rise up. And you shall write them on the doorposts of your house and on your gates so that your days and the days of your sons may be multiplied on the land which the Lord swore to your fathers to give them, as long as the heavens remain above the earth.

God expects us to speak and write His words in the presence of and for the ears and eyes of our children. He expects us to discuss His principles of living as we go about our daily activities, pointing out how God's truth is to be applied in every facet of life. And most important of all, He expects us to *live* life before the eyes and ears of our children with God's viewpoint and actions, not the world's.

The Bible records for us some instances of how mothers were good examples for their children:

a. Elizabeth was righteous in the sight of the Lord (as was her husband). She "walked blamelessly in all the commandments and requirements of the Lord" (Luke 1:6). And her example was reproduced in her son, John the Baptist.

b. Mary, Jesus' mother, demonstrated repeatedly her submissiveness to God's instruction and even called herself "the bond-slave of the Lord" (Luke 1:38). Jesus followed her example, was in subjection to His parents as well as the Lord, and matured properly (Luke 2:51, 52).

c. Paul mentioned how a real and active faith was passed on from generation to generation in Timothy's family. First, his grandmother Lois demonstrated her faith; then his mother Eunice demonstrated her faith (II Timothy 1:5). She taught Timothy from God's Word (II Timothy 3:15) and practiced her faith right before his eyes, even though her husband was a Greek and did not share her religious faith (Acts 16:1). As a result, Timothy was well spoken of by all the Christian brethren (16:2), became Paul's companion and co-worker, and retained his mother's faith in his own life (II Timothy 1:5).

We mothers must realize the importance of our examples in the development of our children's characters. We must realize that our children can see through the masks we put on. Our inner attitudes and thoughts will be revealed to our children by our day-by-day words and actions. Our children are intelligent and very sensitive; they can pick up moods and attitudes very quickly.

If a mother says prayer is important but her children never see or hear her pray, they will follow her example rather than her words. If a mother says the Bible is an important guide to their living but she never reads the Bible to them or never reads it herself, the children will follow her example not her words. If a mother says, "we should be thankful for all the blessings God gives us," but never takes time to thank God herself in her children's presence, the children will follow her example not her words. If a mother says Sunday School and worship are necessary but does not go herself, the children will follow her example not her words. If a mother says, "God's way is the only right way," but hardly gives God a thought as she goes about her daily activities, her children will follow her example not her words. Yes, God's way of life must be taught verbally, but it must also be *caught* by the children's observing God's life-style at work in our lives.

Another way that God expects us to instruct our children is by the use of correction, warnings, and rebukes. He expects us to direct and guide our chidren; He expects us to discipline them so their characters can continually improve. Such discipline includes verbal reproof and exhortation as well as physical force.

God has never been an advocate of "permissiveness" or allowing a child to determine his own way, for He knows a child is a selfish, foolish individual who cannot be left to decide on his own what he should do in life or how he is to do it. A child left to his own devices will destroy himself and all those who are touched by his life. A child needs discipline (correction) in order to learn to live unselfishly and be a delight to all who know him as these verses point out:

> Stern discipline is for him who forsakes the way; he who hates reproof will die (Proverbs 15:10).

> Discipline your son while there is hope, and do not desire his death. . . . Listen to counsel and accept discipline that you may be wise the rest of your days (Proverbs 19:18, 20).

Foolishness is bound up in the heart of a child; the rod of discipline will remove it far from him (Proverbs 22:15).

Do not hold back discipline from the child, although you beat him with the rod, he will not die. You shall beat him with the rod and deliver his soul from Sheol (Proverbs 23:13, 14).

The rod and reproof give wisdom, but a child who gets his own way brings shame to his mother (Proverbs 29:15).

Correct your son, and he will give you comfort; he will also delight your soul (Proverbs 29:17).

It is evident from these verses in Proverbs that God approves of physical punishment as a means of correction, but we must understand that God does not condone or encourage severe, harsh, or unjust punishment. Physical abuse that results in visible cuts, bruises, burns, or broken bones, and other damage to the child's body would be wholly inconsistent with God's emphasis on love, tender affection, and protection of a child.

The phrase "beat him with the rod" (Proverbs 23:13, 14) troubles some people. The word "beat" (*nakah*) denotes mild striking or smiting. It is not a word that means to crush, to beat down, to bruise, or to beat to pieces. It is not denoting an act of great violence; it was simply a means of correction. The word "rod" was a common term used to refer to any form of correction. God's mouth was called a rod (Isaiah 11:4); and when God used a nation to punish His people, He called that nation a rod (Isaiah 10:5). He called many different types of correction a rod (Ezekiel 20:37).

Some popular lecturers have said that God wants us to use only "wooden rods" to discipline our children, citing the verse in Proverbs as evidence. If they were to be wholly literal, they should also include the use of the "rod of iron"

242

which is also referred to in Scripture (Psalm 2:9; Revelation 2:27; 19:15). It is nonsensical to say that God wants only one particular item used in discipline or only one type of correction method used with our children, for God used many different kinds of correction methods Himself when disciplining His people, depending on the people and the situations.

Children are different, and situations that require discipline are different; thus the method of correction cannot always be the same. My father had to only clear his throat or snap his fingers for us to know that we had better straighten up. Many times, we would have much rather had a spanking from my mother than endure her "bawling us out." She had a way with words and a tone of voice that could "cut" into our very beings with the knowledge of how we had done wrong. We may choose to use a hairbrush, a yardstick, or a belt to provide a spanking; the results will be the same, regardless of what item we use. Perhaps a "sending to his or her room" or a withdrawing of privileges would be a fit punishment for a child in certain circumstances— the method of correction is not "cut and dried." Surely, we realize that the presence of a literal rod or stick in the corner of a room is not going to solve our discipline problems.

We have to know our children as individuals, ascertain the circumstances, be discerning and wise, and pick the item and the method that is most appropriate (the one that will promote the understanding of the child as to what he has done wrong and how it will not be tolerated). God is not particular about the item or method of correction we use; He only specifies that we do discipline our children and that we do it out of love and concern for the child's character.

We must never kid ourselves into thinking that as long as we read the Bible to our children, take them to church and Sunday School, and live committed and moral lives ourselves that they will grow up to be fine Christian adults. We must also guide and correct them. When they do wrong, we must point out their error forcefully, and at times we may have to use physical punishment for emphasis and to help them remember the teaching involved. They must know what they have done wrong, and they must be warned that such actions and/or attitudes are not acceptable to the parent or to God.

The Old Testament gives a good example of what happens to an undisciplined child. Samson received verbal instruction of God's Word, and his parents were upright examples; but evidently he had very little corrective discipline. For as an adult, he acted strictly on the basis of his selfish desires. When he saw a woman he liked, he commanded that his father get her for him (Judges 14:2, 3). When he wanted to eat, he ate, even the honey that lay in the carcass of a lion he had killed (14:9). He demanded his own way many times (15:1), and he found himself consumed by his life of violence and lust (16:1). His lack of self-control led to his destruction (16:4ff).

In the New Testament, the writer of Hebrews pointed out how integral discipline is in a good family relationship when he compared God's discipline to that of a father:

My son, do not regard lightly the discipline of the Lord, nor faint when you are reproved by Him; for those whom the Lord loves He disciplines, and He scourges every son whom He receives. It is for discipline that you endure; God deals with you as with sons; for what son is there whom his father does not discipline? But if you are without discipline, of

244

which all have become partakers, then you are illegitimate children and not sons. Furthermore, we had earthly fathers to discipline us, and we respected them; shall we not much rather be subject to the Father of spirits and live? For they disciplined us for a short time as seemed best to them, but He disciplines for our good, that we may share His holiness. All discipline for the moment seems not to be joyful, but sorrowful; yet to those who have been trained by it, afterwards it yields the peaceful fruit of righteousness (Hebrews 12:5-11).

We can note several truths and principles from this Scriptures about discipline:

a. Corrective discipline is a serious matter (v. 5). It is not to be an afterthought or something done impulsively; it should be considered very carefully and thoughtfully. The individual child's needs and temperament, the situation, and the severity of the wrong must all be considered so that the punishment will be just, fair, and profitable. Those who are being disciplined are also to consider the seriousness of the matter and realize that it is for their benefit.

b. The source of the discipline is love—a heartfelt concern for the child's well-being (v. 6). A loving mother will want her child to have a pure character and righteous conduct. She will seek to do all she can to restore a fallen child to an upright position—both physically and spiritually.

c. Corrective discipline is to be a natural part of a family relationship (vs. 7, 8).

d. The results of corrective discipline are: children will respect their parents and learn to be submissive (v. 9), they will learn to consider others rather than their own selfishness, and they will learn to be holy (or pure, v. 10; and righteous, v. 11).

e. Corrective discipline will hurt for awhile (v. 11). The parents are hurt that the child has done wrong. The child may be hurting phsyically and emotionally; the tears may flow for a short time. But the end result is well worth the momentary sorrow, for a child has been corrected, guided, and directed toward God's way of living.

Paul very adequately summed up God's intentions concerning the importance, results, and methods of discipline in a family relationship:

> Children, obey your parents in the Lord, for this is right. Honor your father and mother (which is the first commandment with a promise), that it may be well with you, and that you may live long on the earth. And, fathers, do not provoke your children to anger, but bring them up in the discipline and instruction of the Lord (Ephesians 6:1-4).

Paul was emphasizing what the Old Testament writers emphasized: children must be trained and guided in order to learn obedience to and respect for others (which God desires). Such training will result in a fulfilled and happy life when he develops into an adult, *if* he obeys the teaching he receives (vs. 1-3).

Paul cautioned parents against using harsh punishment (v. 4, the word "fathers" as it is used here can mean "parents"). The Greek word for "provoke to anger" presents the picture of an unyielding tyrant who inflicts punishment indiscriminately and without careful thought. Such action will only embitter and anger a child. The child may learn to behave properly but only out of fear. His resentment will continue to build, even though he may not voice it. Then suddenly the child will be in a full-scale rebellion (usually in teen-age years), perhaps with violent repercussions.

Sometimes parents have been "in absentia," either physically or emotionally, as their children were growing up. Then when they discover their teen-agers are selfish and unmanageable, they begin "laying down the law" which only results in rebellion and resentment. Children do not adjust well to sudden changes and will be confused and angered by this sudden strictness of their parents. The best way to prevent such rebellion is to establish a relationship filled with love and discipline from the time the child is born until he becomes an adult and/or leaves home. There is no time in a child's development when a parent can take a rest from guiding him onto the right path. It is a continuous and ongoing responsibility.[1]

Not provoking a child to anger also includes treating the child as a person with a mind and will, not as a possession or a piece of property. It includes not belittling the child by calling him or her stupid. It includes not physically or emotionally abusing the child. It includes not screaming or using verbal abuse. It means praising a child when he does right as well as rebuking him when he does wrong. It means requesting and suggesting with words such as "please" and "thank you," rather than demanding with curses and threats. It means being consistent so the child always knows the rules and what is expected of him or her. It means explaining calmly why punishment is necessary.

"Bringing them up in the nurture and admonition of the Lord" (v. 4b, KJV) stresses the tender, affectionate care that is needed ("nurture") as well as the instruction by word

---

1. But the responsibility is not eternal. There also comes a time when the parents must "let go" and allow the child (who has become an adult) to accept and fulfill the responsibilities of being an individual in the world.

and action ("admonition"). Admonishing includes putting truth into one's mind (verbal teaching) and warning (use of corrective discipline) children when they have done wrong (I Corinthians 10:11, Acts 20:31, Colossians 3:16).

What about the children who rebel and turn away from their parents' faith and values, even though the parents have taught by word and example and have used corrective discipline based on love? Such tragedies do occur. We cannot quote Proverbs 22:6 ("Train up a child in the way he should go, even when he is old he will not depart from it") and put all the blame at the feet of the parents. To do that would be to ignore all the rest of God's Word. God makes clear that children have a responsibility to listen and to obey the instruction they receive (Proverbs 19:20; Ephesians 6:1-3; Colossians 3:20; Hebrews 12:5). He warns them of what will happen if they do not listen and obey and tells them how happy and fulfilled they will be if they do obey (Proverbs 1:1-9; 2:1-5; 3:1, 2—these verses are only samplings. Much of Proverbs is on this topic and could definitely be applied to the responsibility of children). He calls those who do not obey foolish (Proverbs 10:1; 15:20; 17:25), shameful, and disgraceful (19:26). He says if they continue in their erring ways, they will destroy themselves (20:20).

We must remember that children are individuals with minds and wills, not puppets or lumps of clay. They will come to a point in their lives when they will decide to handle life in their own way. It may be before they are mature enough to do so, or they may lash out and rebel on the basis of a momentary emotional impulse.

God knows what grief and heartache this causes us (Proverbs 10:1; 17:25), and He shares in our sorrow. He knows what it feels like; for many of us, though we are His children and in His family, rebel against Him and seek to go our own ways at times. We will feel the pain and the sorrow that rebellious children cause, but we must not wallow in guilt, bitterness, or self-pity. We must understand that the children are responsible for their own lives; they will make mistakes, and hopefully will come to their senses.[2]

We can draw comfort from the story of the Prodigal Son (Luke 15:11-32) and realize that it was not the father's fault that the youth wanted to go his own way, that the youth finally did come to his senses, and that the father was lovingly and hopefully awaiting his return, and then gave his forgiveness immediately. The youth did not even have to prove his trustworthiness; he only had to return and acknowledge his mistake.

Summary

As a Christian mother strives to give to her children the gifts of love and instruction, she will find the rewards and blessings of motherhood returning to her in abundance. As she ponders the development of the precious individuals in her household whom she directly influences, she will have the same awe, wonderment, and joy that Mary felt as she watched Jesus grow—"And His mother treasured all these things in her heart" (Luke 2:51b).

The value of children who have been lovingly guided to live in God's way can never be measured by monetary values, by silver, or gold, or jewels. Their value can only be measured

---

2. An exception would be the youth that is lured into a cult by deceit and is kept there by force and brain-washing techniques. In this instance, a parent should do everything possible to free their young person from such evil.

by the godly influence they have on the society and the world in which they live. God considers the job of a godly mother to be a great work for Him and His cause.

The points emphasized in this chapter are as follows:

1. God considers motherhood a gift and a reward to women, and so should we.

2. Children are wonderful gifts to each family, and we should treat them as such.

3. Mothers are responsible (with the fathers) for the development of her children's characters and can fulfill that responsibility through practicing all the aspects of *agape*-love, through the instruction of God's Word and way of life, and through the wise use of corrective discipline.

The Childless Woman

What about the woman who has no children? Does God have something against a woman who desperately wants a child but remains barren? Not at all. There is one incident recorded in the Bible in which God struck women and they became barren as a punishment (Genesis 20:18), and there is evidence that God gave children to women as special gifts in certain situations. But we must remember that God loves us and wants the best for us. He does not purposely withhold from us what would fulfill us and make us happy.

However, sin is in the world, and Satan is active. Because of sin's presence in all aspects of nature, we have to cope with disease, sickness, and physical maladies. The inability to have children is one of these maladies and must be endured by some, regardless of the frustration and the pain.

A childless woman can follow the examples of women in the Bible who were concerned about their barrenness. Most of them went to God in prayer and communicated to Him their great desire to have a child. However, I would hesitate to promote the idea that a childless woman should act the way Hannah did, being overly distressed and bargaining with God. But that may be because it is hard for me to identify with her situation since I have four healthy children and don't have to share my husband with another woman.

Today there are additional avenues of help. Medical help can be obtained to determine why a couple is childless and then remedy the situation. There is also the possibility of adoption. There are also many ways to compensate — becoming foster parents, working as parents in a children's home (institution for child care), and being involved in youth groups and Sunday School classes in order to love young people and be an influence on young lives.

No woman should sit around and feel sorry for herself or be mad at God or her husband because she is childless. There are many ways to be beneficial to children and to receive their love in return. Just as single women can find fulfillment without a husband, so can childless women find fulfillment and be a blessing to the world without a child from her own womb.

CONCLUSION OF PART III

Who Can Find Her?

Is the good wife and mother that has been described in these two chapters a rarity? Are wives and mothers who take their responsibilities to their families seriously and are willing to live unselfishly for others hard to find? The writer of Proverbs apparently thought so, and I am afraid that it may be even more true in our country today.

Many women are saying they want to "find themselves" or "fulfill their secret desires" before they get old. They want to be free to develop all their capabilities. Many think that they must leave their husbands and children to be able to live their own lives and be fulfilled.

God thinks differently. He feels that a woman can find "completeness" as a wife and mother. Yet He is not saying that she has to be tied to her home or be kept in a cage. Proverbs 31:10-31 gives a composite picture of a "complete" woman as she carries out her wife-mother responsibilities; and, at the same time, shows how a woman can be active "outside" the immediate sphere of her home. This passage serves as an appropriate summation of what God intends for women in their wifely and motherly roles as well as leading us into the next section of this book which considers women as leaders:

An excellent wife, who can find? For her worth is far above jewels. The heart of her husband trusts in her, and he will have no lack of gain. She does him good and not evil all the days of her life. She looks for wool and flax, and works with her hands in delight. She is like merchant ships; she brings her food from afar. She rises also while it is still night, and gives food to her household, and portions to her maidens. She considers a field and buys it; from her earnings she plants a vineyard. She girds herself with strength, and makes her arms strong. She senses that her gain is good; her lamp does not go out at night. She stretches out her hands to the distaff, and her hands grasp the spindle. She extends her hand to the poor; and she stretches out her hands to the needy. She is not afraid of the snow for her household, for all her household are clothed with scarlet. She makes coverings for herself; her clothing is fine linen and purple. Her husband is known in the gates, when he sits among the elders of the land. She makes linen garments and sells them and supplies belts to the tradesmen. Strength and dignity are her clothing, and she smiles at the future. She opens her mouth in wisdom, and the teaching of kindness is on her tongue. She looks well to the ways of her household, and does not eat the bread of idleness. Her children rise up and bless her; her husband also, and he praises her, saying: "Many daughters have done nobly, but you excel them all." Charm is deceitful and beauty is vain, but a woman who fears the Lord, she shall be praised. Give her the product of her hands, and let her works praise her in the gates (Proverbs 31:10-31).

Let us consider carefully what this passage teaches us. (1) *The Marriage Relationship.* The wife is honest and upright, so the husband trusts her implicitly (v. 11). He has confidence in the way she manages things at home, for her behavior is consistently trustworthy and she seeks to protect his reputation and character. He knows she will not squander money or waste what he provides for the family. She will not be hiding purchases in the closet or charging things on the credit card without his knowledge. She even helps in earning some of the money to provide for the family's needs (vv. 16, 24).

She is not kind and good only when he gives her love and attention, but also every day of her life (v. 12). She thinks of her husband first; she realizes that she may have to set aside some of her selfish desires at times in order to meet his needs. The wife allows her husband to be the leader in the home and supports his activities as a leader in the community (v. 23). He is known and respected and sits among the elders (leaders) at the main center of the public life (gates).

The husband also considers her needs and does not expect or demand that she stay in the house and cook and clean. He allows her freedom to travel (v. 14), to shop, and to have interests and work outside the confines of the house (vv. 16, 20, 24). He is very appreciative of all her efforts and praises her highly (v. 29).

(2) *Mother-child Relationship.* The mother provides for her children's physical needs (vv. 15, 21, 27) as well as their spiritual needs (v. 26). She prepares food for them, makes their clothes, protects them from the cold, manages the household so that it runs smoothly, and teaches them about wisdom and kindness. She is available to them, even late at night (v. 18). Her children appreciate her, love her, and respect her (v. 28). She evidently practices *agape*-love and uses corrective discipline wisely.

(3) *The Woman's Activities.* She sews and weaves to provide clothing for her family and herself (vv. 13, 19, 21, 22) as well as selling what she makes to the merchant for money (v. 24). She does all her work willingly and joyfully (v. 13). She shops carefully for food (v. 14). She is certainly not lazy (v. 27), rising before dawn to prepare meals (v. 15) and retiring late at night (v. 18). She buys a field and plants a vineyard (v. 16). She helps the needy in the community (v. 20), and tends to her own spiritual relationship with God (v. 30). She takes care of her physical body (v. 17) and seeks to look attractive (v. 22).

(4) *The Woman's Character.* She is honest (v. 11), good (v. 12), strong (vv. 17, 25), intelligent and wise (vv. 16, 18, 26), industrious and a good manager (vv. 15, 18, 27),

compassionate and caring (vv. 12, 20). She does not spend time worrying about her family (v. 21) or fretting about the future (v. 25). She is happy and fulfilled (vv. 13, 25), busy and dependable (v. 11). She respects God and His life-style (v. 30).

(5) *The Woman's Priorities.* It is evident that this woman considers her husband and her children to be the most important areas of her life and expends a great deal of effort to fulfill their needs. Yet she does not forget her responsibility to obey God, she does not neglect her looks, and she is not too busy to reach out into her community and serve others.

We, in no way, get the idea from this description that God expects women to stay at home all the time doing housework. Neither do we get the idea that a wife and mother can go out and pursue a career while leaving the children and husband to fend for themselves. Instead, we have a picture of a happy, busy woman who fulfills all her responsibilities and becomes a well-rounded person, a woman who has "got it all together." Truly such a woman is a treasure of great value to all who know her (v. 10) and will receive a rewarding life (vv. 30, 31).

Who can find such an excellent wife and mother? Who can possibly live up to this goal? Your husband and children can find such a woman in your own home if you seek to follow the principles and precepts found in God's Word!

A Word of Caution. We must remember that this description was about a woman in the Old Testament culture. God does not expect us to weave our own cloth or make clothes for everyone in the family. He does not expect us to get up before dawn or stay up all night if our family's needs can be met within another time period. We will not be planting vineyards, and our husbands will not be sitting at the literal

255

gates of a city. Thus, we are not to take every point literally, but we are to note the main trends and principles that this woman followed.

Neither are we to assume that every woman must be this busy or out buying and selling real estate. We do not know the age of this woman or the age of her children. Certainly a woman with toddlers or with several children would not be expected to be so active outside the home. No woman's talents and capabilities are the same. We are each unique individuals with unique home situations. God does not expect us to be "superwomen," but He does expect us to be His women, doing our best for Him with what interests and abilities we possess.

DISCUSSION QUESTIONS:

1. What do you think are the root causes for the lowering of respect for motherhood in our society today?
2. Discuss the pros and cons of abortion. Is it murder? Should it ever be allowed? What is God's view about abortion?
3. In what ways do you think we are to be as children in order to be citizens of the Kingdom of Heaven?
4. A mother's actions show how she feels about her children. List what her actions would be if she felt as God does about children (that they are precious gifts to be cherished and nurtured).
5. Is it natural for parents to have favorites among their children? Give examples from your own experiences that show the destructiveness of favoritism.
6. Discuss what you feel the author meant by this statement: "a child needs both quantity and quality time."

7. What aspect of *agape*-love is the most difficult for you to practice?

8. Under what conditions should a mother seek for outside employment? Under what conditions should she remain at home?

9. List all the reasons you can think of why the Bible should be the content of our children's instruction.

10. Give examples from personal experience of how children learn from their parents' attitudes.

11. What is God's view about the somewhat popular philosophy that we should be permissive with our children and never spank them?

12. Discuss all the implications of Ephesians 6:1-4:

    a. What is the child's responsibility?
    b. What is the parent's responsibility?
    c. What does nurture mean?
    d. What does admonition mean?
    e. What does "provoke to anger" mean?

13. What causes a child to rebel?

14. List all the aspects of *agape*-love and point out how the woman of Proverbs 31 fulfilled them (could be done in buzz groups).

Part IV

WOMEN AS LEADERS IN
THE CHURCH AND COMMUNITY

To reach their full potential, women should realize that they can be leaders in whatever sphere of life they find themselves and that God is ready to bless them in their efforts.

Introduction

Only in the last few years has America begun to fully realize the tremendous influence women can and do have on society. Because most women have traditionally been in the supportive, behind-the-scenes roles of wives and mothers, their qualities of leadership have been overlooked. Now that more women are entering careers and the "world of work outside the home," their abilities are coming into a clearer focus. Yet most people are still surprised that a woman could become the Prime Minister of Great Britain as Margaret Thatcher has done. Many of us would stand in awe of a woman who was the president of a large company or who was a United States Senator.

What does God think about these new developments? Is He just as happy with a woman who is a movie producer or an executive vice president as He is with a woman who has chosen to be a wife and mother only?

God is not nearly as "behind the times" as many of us are. From our study thus far, we know that God is not against women. He considers women to be very special and important. He expects us to relate to Him personally, and He holds us responsible for our thoughts and actions. He has never been in the dark about our many capabilities.

As highly as He considers the roles of wives and mothers and as necessary as they are to the ongoing of His plan, He has never restricted women to these roles. He knows that some women are extremely capable of leading in various ways in their communities and in their churches; and throughout history He has always encouraged and blessed such women in their endeavors. He has never said by word or by Biblical example that a woman with the interest, talent, and opportunity to be influential in leading should remain at home pushing a broom, working over a hot stove, or bearing children—only. He fully realizes that some women can do it all—career, wife, and mother—while others can fulfill only one responsibility well.

It is up to women individually to find their niche in life; and, of course, it can change from year to year. But we must realize that there is no boogie-man in heaven pointing His judgmental finger at us when we venture into spheres outside the home (as was pointed out in the discussion of the passage in Proverbs 31 in the last chapter). However, our loving Father would be very saddened if we were running away from our commitments and responsibilities as wives and mothers or if we were turning our backs on God's lifestyle and principles.

Chapter Eight

WOMEN AS LEADERS

God has always expected each individual to use all of his or her God-given talents, interests, and abilities in His service, and He expects *only* what each person can give. He expects us to give our best, but not more than what we are capable of giving. And He does not put us on levels of importance as the world does. To Him, a wife and/or mother is just as significant as the President of the United States. To Him, a maid is just as significant as her wealthy employer. To Him, the church janitor is just as significant as the church's preacher.

In the Old Testament, God cared for Hagar, a lowly maidservant, just as He cared for Sarah, the mother of the Jewish nation. He considered the supportive, serving roles of the wives and mothers to be a part of their work for Him. He did not consider the public women leaders such as Deborah or Huldah to be more important than the many wives who worked alongside their husbands in the fields and who lived as nomads in tents, or more important than the mothers who reared children.

When God instituted the church to carry on His work, He did not change His attitude toward women. He desires that each member of the church to do his or her part by using their gifts or abilities to build up the fellowship itself and to evangelize the world. He made it clear through Paul that no member was more important than any other member, regardless of what responsibility he or she fulfilled (I Corinthians 12). The supportive, behind-the-scenes roles are just as significant to the unity and work of the church as the public, out-front roles.

When we studied how God considers women as important individuals, we mentioned the many women who

262

worked in various ways in the church (Chapter Five, pp. 114-120) — those who showed hospitality by opening their homes to the believers (Lydia, the mother of John Mark, Nympha, Apphia), those who were supportive wives and mothers (Acts 21:5), those who delivered communications (Phoebe), and those who did benevolent work, etc. (Dorcas). All of these women were important and doing their best for God.

But to fulfill the purpose of this chapter, I want us to consider in detail the women who were influential leaders in both the Old and New Testaments — not because I think (or because God thinks) they were more important than those who followed and served, but to point out that God expects women to use all of their capabilities for Him, and He blesses them as they do.

In The Old Testament

The first instance of a woman being referred to as a leader in the Bible was after Israel's exodus from Egypt. (1) *Miriam*, Moses' sister, was called a prophetess and was cited as one of the people who led the nation of Israel out of Egypt (Exodus 15:20, Micah 6:4). We can assume then that she was responsible for speaking God's message and leading the people in some way.

(2) *Deborah*. The times of the Judges were wild and confusing. The tribes of Israel had finally arrived in the promised land and were just beginning to settle down, but they were not acting as a united nation. There was feuding between the tribes, and the Israelites were living alongside heathens. There was intermarriage with the heathen neighbors, and some Israelites tried to incorporate the idol worship with

their worship of God. Sexual immorality, violence, and political disputes were prevalent.

God allowed this confusion and the interaction with the neighboring nations to test the Israelites' loyalty and commitment to Him (Judges 3:4). He hoped this time of testing would serve to strengthen and solidify them as a nation. He used every opportunity to demonstrate to them His power and His love for them as well as His justice.

The people would sin and turn away from God; God would then allow a heathen nation to overpower them. The people would realize how much they needed God and would cry out to Him in their anguish because they were ruled and treated harshly by foreigners. God would then raise up deliverers (or judges) to heed the cries of Israel and free them from their enemies.

These judges were gifted individuals upon whom God's Spirit would descend and guide them as they led Israel to victory. They were considered to be spiritual leaders as well as civil and military leaders. They carried a big responsibility on their shoulders.

Deborah was married and a woman, but God chose her to defeat the enemies of Israel—the Canaanites, who had nine hundred chariots of iron and had kept Israel under their thumbs for twenty years. She was a valiant and remarkable woman who was available to God. She was called a wife, a prophetess, and a judge. She would sit under a certain palm tree to counsel and guide people in their problems and disputes (Judges 4:5). God spoke to her directly and gave instructions about how to defeat Jabin's army (Judges 4:6).

Yet she was not an abrasive or pushy woman; she did not come on like "gang-busters." She told Barak of God's directions and told him to carry them out as the leader of the Israelite army. But Barak had such respect for her presence and confidence in her abilities that he wanted her with him: "If you will go with me, then I will go; but if you will not go with me, I will not go" (Judges 4:8). Deborah gave the man the opportunity to take the honor of leading the nation to victory all for himself, but was not afraid or hesitant to help him in the leadership role when asked to do so. Together, they led Israel to victory. Deborah was especially honored in the song of celebration in Judges 5 by being called the "mother of Israel"; yet she never let the people forget that God was responsible for the victory. She was truly a great leader whose devotion and commitment to God was obvious.

(3) *The Woman of Abel Beth-maacah.* Though this woman was not named, she was called wise and was evidently the leader of the people of this city during the reign of King David. She was the main spokesperson and go-between in settling the city's feud with Joab, the commander of David's army (II Samuel 20:16-22). She pointed out to Joab the folly of destroying the Israelite inhabitants of a city in order to get revenge on just one man. Joab agreed and said he would depart if the man was given to him. The woman then spoke of the plan to the people of the city who agreed to deliver the miscreant, Sheba, to Joab. Though this woman had great influence and saved the lives of many people, she was not arrogant or pushy. She referred to herself as a maidservant, she was peace-loving and faithful to God, and she deferred to the authority of Joab (20:17, 19, 21, 22).

(4) *The Queen of Sheba.* This woman was the recognized ruler of Arabia during the reign of Solomon (I Kings 10:1-13). She was very wealthy, independent, and a traveler. She was

intrigued by the reports of Solomon's wisdom and wealth and decided to go take a look for herself to see if the reports were true. She asked a great many questions, and evidently Solomon gave her "a grand tour" of his establishment. After her investigation, she concluded that Solomon was even greater than he was rumored to be. She recognized his good qualities as a person and praised God for making him the king of Israel. She established a type of trade agreement with Israel which any wise leader of a country would do under the circumstances. Even Jesus pointed out her intelligence, sensitivity, and understanding of people:

> The Queen of the South shall rise up with this generation at the judgment and shall condemn it, because she came from the ends of the earth to hear the wisdom of Solomon; and behold, something greater than Solomon is here (Matthew 12:42).

(5) Although we certainly would not want to emulate her, we cannot deny that Jezebel was a very influential leader (I Kings 16-21). She was not officially the ruler of Israel, but she so dominated and manipulated her husband, the king, that in all practicality she was the ruler. If it had not been for God's working through Elijah, Jezebel would probably have converted the whole nation of Israel to the worship of Baal. She had a great intellect and an extremely forceful will. She knew nothing of humility or self-restraint. She was brash, cruel, and licentious; she was evil through and through. There is no quality that commends her except her dedication. She was dedicated, but to the wrong god and to the wrong life-style; and God punished her severely (II Kings 9:30-37). My, just think what she could have done if she had been on God's side rather than against Him!

(6) *The Woman of Shunem* who provided a home for Elisha whenever he was in her city was called a "prominent woman" (II Kings 4:8). We cannot ascertain from the Scriptures in what way she was a leader; but most think she was an affluent woman, considered to be a pillar of the community.

(7) *Huldah.* When King Josiah found the book of the law of the Lord which had been lost in the wreckage of the temple and heard its words, he was sorrowful because he knew the sins of his people were many. He told the priest to find out if the book was genuine and what further message God had for them since they had not followed God's laws for many years.

The priests, scribes, and the king's servants went to a married woman who was well-known for her commitment to God and for her ability to speak for God (a prophetess). Huldah told the king very clearly and specifically God's message (II Kings 22:14-20), and King Josiah acted upon her words immediately by calling the people together to hear the words of God's laws (23:1-3).

(8) *Esther.* Esther was not a leader in the land of Israel, but through a series of circumstances became the Queen of Persia, even though she was a Jewess. Certainly God was a guiding force in her life, for when her cousin Mordecai (who had reared her from a child) told her of Haman's plot to have all Jews in Persia exterminated, she knew what she had to do to save her people.

She asked all the Jews to pray and fast with her so she would have the strength to appear before the King without having been invited, which according to the custom could have meant her death (Esther 4:16). She no doubt felt it was quite possible that the King would not be willing to hear any of her requests or even allow her to talk because of his disdain for women who were willing to speak their minds as was evidenced in his great wrath when Vashti, the former queen, refused to tantalize him and his drunken friends at a party.

When the King did allow her admittance before the throne, Esther showed her intelligence by not "spilling the beans" right away about her Jewishness or about Haman's plot. Instead she invited the King and Haman to a banquet. They had a very pleasant time; she invited them to another banquet at which time she promised to make her requests known. In every way, she retained her femininity, her beauty, and sweetness, but her petition was concise and very pointed. She humbly said she would not have spoken out if the Jews had only been made slaves—they could handle that—but the fact that they were to be utterly destroyed so cruelly caused her to request the King's mercy.

When the King asked who was responsible for such a travesty of justice to her people, she unhesitatingly and with great fervor made clear the wickedness of Haman. Haman was the King's favored man, probably the second-in-command. Would the King listen to a woman? It was obvious that the King was very angry to think that Haman had tricked him. As the King left the room, Haman noted the King's anger. He realized what influence Esther had on the King and proceeded to beg her for mercy for his own behalf. The King returned seeing him on the Queen's couch and became even angrier that Haman would presume to become so familiar with Esther. The King ordered Haman to be hanged, and the lives of the Jews were saved.

Esther has been rightly considered throughout history a brave heroine of Israel. This incident of her bravery and wisdom was so noteworthy that the Jews established a holiday to act as a remembrance of what she had done and how the Jews had been delivered (the days of Purim, Esther 9:30-32).

(9) We know very little about *Isaiah's wife,* except that she was a wife, mother, and a prophetess (Isaiah 8:1-4). It was not the practice to call a wife of a prophet a prophetess, so there is no reason to think it was done here. Evidently, Isaiah's wife not only supported him in his ministry and mothered his child, but also declared messages from God to the people.

In the New Testament

In Jesus' Time

(1) The role of prophetess continued in New Testament times as is evidenced by the reference to *Anna,* a prophetess and a widow, who served "night and day with fastings and prayers" (Luke 2:36-38). She was wholly committed to God and realized that redemption was coming to Israel through the infant Jesus. She did not keep this knowledge to herself, but told "all those who were looking for the redemption of Jerusalem" (2:38).

(2) The *woman at the well* in Samaria (John 4) was sinful, had a bad reputation, was a Samaritan, and a woman — all marks against her in the eyes of the Jewish world. Yet after meeting and talking with Jesus, her life changed completely. She became a personal evangelist. After realizing that Jesus was the Messiah sent from God, she went into the city and testified to the people (who had formerly shunned her) that she had found the Savior (John 4:39-42). Because of her testimony, many Samaritans came out of the city to hear Him and then believed.

It is ironic that the disciples had just been in the same city buying food, but evidently had neglected to tell those Samaritans about the Savior. They had probably let their prejudices blind them to the fact that Samaritans had spiritual needs also. Or perhaps the Samaritans were more ready to believe "one of their own" rather than a Jew. Whatever the situation, we must note that this unnamed woman's willingness to speak out for Christ was instrumental in leading many to the Savior.[1]

In the Early Church

In Romans 12:3-8, Paul listed the different categories of ministries that were utilized in the New Testament Church as follows (the Greek meanings are included in parentheses): prophesying (inspired speaking), ministering (serving, working), teaching (instructing, guiding, causing to understand), exhorting (encouraging, comforting, advising), giving (sharing materially), ruling (standing before, to be set over another —as an organizer, administrator, an elder), showing mercy (lovingkindness, having compassion).

In Ephesians 4:6-16, Paul listed in addition to those mentioned above: apostles (one sent forth, probably on a specific mission), evangelists (a messenger of the good news), and pastor-teachers (a shepherd who guides and feeds the flock—such as the elders).

In I Corinthians 12:28-30, Paul mentioned also miracles, gifts of healing, and tongues (speaking in other languages) as being special ministries.

---

1. See a more detailed description of this woman's character and encounter with Jesus in Chapter Five, pp. 87-91.

270

We will consider the responsibilities which involved women in roles of leadership and serving in the early church.

(1) *Deaconess* (servant, helper). Some believe that this was a specific office in the early church.[2] Others hold that it is used in Romans 16:1 as a general term indicating a servant. If this was an office we do not know for certain what the duties were, but it would probably have involved some type of service to the members of the church.

Phoebe was called a deaconess by Paul (Romans 16:1). She was to be received by the church in Rome "in the Lord in a way worthy of the saints" (see I Thessalonians 5:12, 13). Paul told the people to help her with whatever she needed and called her a "helper" of many, including himself (Romans 16:2). This word for "helper" (*prostatis*) in verse two is not the same word that is used for deaconess in verse one (*diakonos*). The feminine form of the word as used in verse two was often used to refer to a patroness. Perhaps she had acted as a champion for the rights of Paul or others, or perhaps she was Paul's patroness, who helped him financially. (See Luke 8:1-3.)

Some feel that I Timothy 3:11, 12 gives credence to the idea that there was a special group of women with specific functions just as there were the offices of overseer and deacon for the men. Others, however, consider these verses to refer to wives of the deacons. There is a reference in a secular source in Latin (Letters from Pliny) that could be translated "deaconesses." However, we have no Scriptural proof that women held such an office in the early church, unless the reference to Phoebe supports this idea.

---

2. Dorothy R. Pape, *In Search of God's Ideal Woman*, pp. 209-214.

271

(2) *Apostle* (one sent forth). Junias was referred to in Romans 16:7 as Paul's kinsman (one of the same race), fellowprisoner, an apostle, and one who had become a Christian before Paul had. The scholars differ as to whether Junias was a man or woman. A few modern scholars believe this is a case of a woman who was called an apostle.[3] Whatever the case, Junias must have been quite an active Christian and was in prison for a time because of his or her faith.

(3) *Teacher* (one who instructs another). Priscilla was both a supportive wife and a very active member of the church. She and her husband were instrumental in starting the churches at Corinth, Ephesus, and probably Rome. They had a church meeting in their home in Rome (Romans 16:5). She and Aquila were referred to by Paul as his fellowworkers (16:3) — a term which he also applied to Timothy (16:21) and Luke (Philemon 24). Paul mentioned that they both had risked their lives for him and should be thanked by all the churches (Romans 16:4).

While Aquila and Priscilla were in Ephesus, a Jew from Alexandria (Apollos) came to preach in the synagogue. He was no ordinary man. He was a fiery, mighty preacher who thrilled the people with his teaching about the Scriptures. But his knowledge extended only to the baptism of John; he did not know the full good news about Jesus' death and resurrection. After he spoke, Aquila and Priscilla took him aside and taught him about the more complete knowledge (Acts 18:24-26).

Luke affirms that Priscilla, a woman, and Aquila, a man, both were involved in teaching Apollos, a man. Aquila and

---

3. Pape, pp. 217, 218.

Priscilla worked as a team, and we have no way of knowing who did what in that partnership. But it is quite obvious in this case that they *both* taught Apollos.

(4) *Prophetess* (inspired spokeswoman). In his sermon on Pentecost, Peter said that women would be prophesying when the Holy Spirit came as well as men (quoting Joel in Acts 2:17). According to Paul's writings, it is evident that women of the church prayed and prophesied (I Corinthians 11:5). Philip's four daughters were prophetesses (Acts 21:9).

In Revelation, John referred to a woman of the church at Thyatira who called herself a prophetess. John warned the church about her wrong teachings, but he did not say that a woman could not prophesy (Revelation 2:20-24).

Summary

In Summarizing, we can make these observations:

1. There is no Scriptural example of a woman ruling as an elder in the early church.

2. There are no examples of women having the gift of healing or miracles.

3. However, many kinds of ministries were done by women as well as men.[4]

What About Us?

Many people think that the Bible teaches that women are to provide the food for the church fellowship dinners

---

4. It would be profitable at this point to reread the discussion in Chapter Five about the women as believers and workers in the early church and the exegesis of the difficult passages of Paul on women in the church.

and the P.T.A. potlucks and clean up afterwards, teach the elementary school children in Sunday School, be a Cub Scout Den Mother, go door-to-door collecting for the March of Dimes, be regular in worship attendance, keep colorful curtains in the church windows, and bake cookies for the school's bake sale — and that is to be the extent of a woman's activity.

They think the Bible teaches that a woman is not to be campaigning for a political candidate or — horror of horrors — be a candidate herself. She should not stand up and be vocal at the P.T.A. meetings; she should not be circulating petitions or get her picture in the newspaper unless she has been named "Mother of the Year." Many feel that God intends for women to be the bench-warmers and the cleaner-uppers *only* (with the exception of a woman choir director or a single woman on the mission field). Many feel that men are the only ones who should be making the speeches, teaching, and leading out in the community and the church.

There is no indication in the Scriptures that God has ever held these archaic traditions. Even from the very beginning of the Israelite nation, women were leading out, making speeches, and influencing greatly the communities in which they lived. Some restrictions that have been placed upon women throughout history (except for moral restrictions) have come from the minds of sinful men, not from the mind of God.

If in reading this chapter you were hoping for a blueprint of exactly *what* women should do in the church and community, you will not find it because the Bible does not make detailed demands or restrictions in this area. Instead, God's message is "Do whatever you can with whatever abilities you have to make your community and church more Christ-like — always remembering your responsibilities to your husband and children."

But through studying the Biblical examples of women leaders, we can ascertain certain practices and principles that we should follow in our leadership endeavors. We have no commands on *what* we women are to do, but we do have guidelines on *how* we are to work for God.

Be Available. Many of the women leaders in the Bible were simply in the right place at the right time; and when God or the circumstances issued the call, they were available and responded. Deborah was married and led a quiet life, until God decided the bondage under the Canaanites should end and that she should be the leader of Israel. Her life then became very public; she was open to God's directions and was committed to obey Him.

The woman of Abel Beth-maacah was probably a busy wife and mother; but when the situation with Joab arose and her city was in danger, she arose to the occasion. Esther did not become the Queen of Persia with the idea of saving her people; but when the opportunity came, she performed as she knew she should.

Priscilla was willing to uproot and move, seemingly at a moment's notice, to wherever she and her husband could best serve the Lord. She was available and always willing to open her home to groups of Christians in whatever city they were living.

Some women are content to live in the tiny, secure boxes of their lives as wives and mothers. Some are afraid to venture out and get involved in their communities and churches. It is much safer and easier to stay in their own little worlds than to become involved so opportunities to witness can arise, and many of them use their position as wives and mothers as excuses not to do anything else. Being a wife and mother is an important work for God—that is an indisputable truth. And sometimes these roles leave little room for anything else—that is true. But a wife and mother who is doing her job properly cannot help but be involved in church and school activities, not necessarily as an out-front leader, but certainly as an active worker, ready and available to follow God's call.

Often God's call comes in the package of an opportunity to witness for Christ, either on a one-to-one basis or as a Christian involved in community activities. No matter what we do as wives and mothers, whether going to the supermarket, to the P.T.A. meeting, or to the Little League ballgame—we are constantly rubbing shoulders with other people. There are many opportunities for us to speak for Christ; we don't have to wait until we are asked to speak to a large assembly or until we become the P.T.A. president. We need to be continually studying God's Word and have our prayer life in shape, so that we can always be ready and available to talk about Christ as the opportunities arise. We must be willing to open the little boxes of our lives and let our Christian witness influence and shape the world and our Christian service build up the fellowship of the church.

Be Courageous. In order to follow through with God's call and directions, many of the women leaders in the Bible had to have a great deal of courage. Deborah was facing a nation with great military strength, yet she trusted that God would help and guide her and stepped forward with courage.

Esther was risking her life to appear before the King; she had no reason to think that he would actually listen to anything she would say. But with three days of prayer and fasting, asking for God's help, and the people of Israel supporting her, she stepped forward with courage.

The Samaritan woman at the well was looked down upon by the community in which she lived because of her immorality; but when she had discovered the Messiah, she put all reticence aside and spoke to her neighbors about Him.

Priscilla and her husband had been thrown out of Italy because of their faith, and the cities in which they witnessed for Christ with Paul were not exactly cordial to the Christian faith. To become a Christian in the first century was a constant threat to one's job and even one's life. Pagan influences were difficult to overcome, but the hostility of the strict Jews toward Christianity was even worse. To be a leader — either man or woman — in the early church was risky business and took great courage to stick with it.

It also takes courage for us to live as Christians in our world today. We are not often threatened with physical violence as the Christians of the first century were; but we are ridiculed, snubbed, and laughed at, which can make havoc of our self-esteem. It takes courage to speak up when we see another employee stealing from the company or when we see a clear case of child abuse. It takes courage to speak out when the baseball coach is using dishonest tactics. It takes courage to try to get pornography off the newsstands and close down the porno-movie houses. It takes courage to go door-to-door in the slum area of town, calling for Christ. It takes courage to draw up petitions, write letters, and make telephone calls to stop immorality and dishonesty and to make Christian attitudes and principles known and felt in the community.

It is not easy to "make waves" or to induce change in the status quo. Many in the world do not appreciate the

277

Christian influence. But we must not give in or give up. We must continue the struggle, so the world can one day be won for Christ.

Be Humble. Women with influential responsibilities must not lose their humility. Deborah was not only the military leader of Israel, but also was the civil and religious leader. Yet she gave Barak the opportunity to lead the army and receive the resultant honor. When the victory was complete, she gave praise to others who helped, especially to God.

The woman of Abel made clear her wish to serve and deferred to the authority of Joab. The Queen of Sheba praised Solomon and God for the success of Israel and gave no indication that she was arrogant and "tooting her own horn." Esther was submissive and respectful to her cousin Mordecai and to the King, even though she was in the high position of Queen.

The women in the early church were definitely *serving* leaders, willing to open their homes and risk their lives for fellow Christians. Priscilla and her husband could have easily made a public example of Apollos but chose to teach him privately instead.

We can note the negative examples of those who did *not* have humility in order to learn how not to act. Miriam showed disrespect for Moses and was punished for it. Jezebel of the Old Testament was so arrogant and narrow-minded that she continued on her evil way, no matter how much God showed His power. The Jezebel in Revelation was misusing her influence by leading people from the church into paganism, just as her namesake in the Old Testament did.

Even though we accept a different interpretation of the Bible's teaching regarding women in leadership roles, we must act humbly toward those with whom we differ. We should honestly share our views and yet humbly cooperate.

When we do lead out in our churches and communities, we must retain our humility and our serving natures. No matter who we become, we must never think that we are too good to wash dishes after the fellowship dinner at church or to clean up after the all-school party. No matter how much in the public eye we are nor how influential we become, we must continue to be respectful and polite to those around us and be careful not to become puffed up with our own self-importance. We must never misuse our influence to lead others to follow our pet opinions rather than Christ. We must strive to retain our attitudes of submission to God, to our fellow Christians, and to our husbands. We must never think that because we are fully in charge at the office that we are also to be fully in charge at home — the husband is still to be the leader at home.

Be Feminine. The women leaders of the Bible were also peace-loving. They exerted much effort to avoid violence and retain the peace. They were intelligent, even logical, and they applied their intelligence in order to keep the peace (especially the Woman of Abel and Esther). They were also sensitive to the needs of others; they showed much understanding of others' feelings. Deborah was mindful of Barak's feelings, the woman of Abel of Joab's, Esther of the King's, and Priscilla of Apollos'.

In so doing, these women retained their femininity, their distinctive qualities as women. They did not "come on" full force as brutes, running rough-shod on everyone around them. They were not harsh talkers or crude in their actions. At the same time, they did not act impulsively or strictly on the basis of their emotions as some men say all women do. No, their actions were well thought-out, planned, and organized, yet they never lost the sense that they were women — differentiated from the men.

Many women today in their struggle to be free of restrictions and to achieve full equality with men have forgotten that they are women. They have forgotten that they have specific and different contributions to make to society precisely because of their femininity. They have chosen instead to deny their femaleness or at least put it on the shelf for awhile and talk, walk, and act as they perceive men do. They talk rough. They push people around. They have become cold and unfeeling. They are obtusely aggressive and often are obnoxious and loud. They opt for violence rather than peace. They have become a great deal like the Jezebel of I and II Kings. I am not saying that these unlikable qualities are a part of maleness, but many women have interpreted maleness to include them.

Such actions cannot help but hinder a woman's complete fulfillment, for God created her to have special qualities of tenderness and compassion to complement the aggressive qualities of men. God created women to be equal in worth and dignity, in intelligence, and in responsibility. But God did not create women to be just like men in personalities or emotions. It is a great loss to the women themselves as well as to society as a whole when they cease to be womanly.

Have Right Priorities. The women leaders who had families did not neglect the family members. Just as the woman in Proverbs 31, they knew that their first loyalty should be to God and to their families. Yet this is at the very point that many women today fall short. They get so wrapped up in their outside interests that they have no time, energy, or interest left for their families. They don't want to clean house anymore; they don't want to cook anymore; they don't want to take the time to listen to the children tell about their day at school anymore; they don't want to spend time with their husbands anymore.

280

We must realize that there is only so much time to go around, so we must use our time wisely and according to God's will (Ephesians 5:16, 17). We must make the most of our opportunities (Colossians 4:5), but we must not forget who and what are the most important factors in life. We want to influence our communities, but if we suddenly find ourselves dropping out of church activities and services or if we find that there never seems to be any time to be at home with the family, we had better take a second look at our priorities and get our values straight. We cannot do everything; we will have to choose; we will have to line up our priorities. May we do it with the wisdom from God!

Summary

The points emphasized in this chapter are as follows:

1. God intends for women to use their abilities to serve Him in the church and in the community.

2. God has not forbidden women from leading out in church and community but He does expect them to remain mindful of their responsibility to Him.

3. God does provide women with guidelines for their attitudes as they are leading: they should be available, be courageous, be humble, be feminine, and maintain the proper priorities.

DISCUSSION QUESTIONS:

1. What is God's view concerning a woman's leadership in the following areas: (Support your answers with Biblical evidence.)

281

    a. an out-spoken community leader
    b. a preacher
    c. a deaconess
    d. an elder
    e. a teacher in the church
    f. a missionary

2. Why is it important to consider what leadership positions women held in the first-century church? How does that example apply to us?

3. Think about your own church situation. Make two columns on the chalkboard. In the first column list the areas in which women are expected to work and in the second column the areas in which they are not allowed to work. Then decide as a group if these differentiations are valid Scripturally.

4. Think of the women leaders you know. Which Biblical guidelines for leadership do they follow? Which ones do they not follow?

5. In what area of the church life or community life do you think you could be a leader?

6. If the men in your church do not allow women to have the leadership positions that God allows in His Word, how should you change their minds if you go about it in God's way?

7. How does God feel about the attitudes and actions of the militant feminists of today who are demanding their rights? Cite Scripture to prove your answer.

8. Why do we need men in our world today? How does God intend for women to complement them?

Part V

WOMEN, THEIR INNER SELVES

To complete the structure in which women can live happily and securely, we must consider the personal characteristics that women need to fulfill their roles in life and how they can obtain these characteristics.

Introduction

We have discovered that God considers women to be important individuals, just as important as men; and we have studied the principles and guidelines that God desires for women to follow in fulfilling their responsibilities as wives, mothers, and leaders in the church and community. But what about a woman *personally*?

Many people in our world today expect women to be young looking, beautiful, and sensuous; they are mostly concerned about who women are externally. The media help promote this idea, for women's bodies, hair, and faces are stressed overwhelmingly in advertisements, television programming, magazine covers, etc. Women are not expected to be intelligent or strong; they are expected to be vulnerable, soft, pretty, and available to men. Women are many times treated as sexual objects rather than as persons with thoughts and feelings.

But God looks upon the hearts of women, not upon their appearance (I Samuel 16:7). God is concerned about a woman's character—the sum total of her attributes and qualities, her inner self. He is concerned about a woman's essence, the spirit and mind that distinguish her from all others. He is also concerned about the patterns of behavior and speech that emanate from her inner qualities.

God has made clear in His Word what kind of character a woman who wishes to follow Him must strive to have. He told women through His spokesmen what qualities, attitudes, and actions they should develop in order to obtain true joy and contentment in their lives. We will zero in on those New Testament passages that speak specifically to women, we will define the qualities in detail, we will consider the women throughout the Bible who embodied these qualities, and then we will discover how we modern women can incorporate these qualities into our lives.

Chapter Nine

THE CHARACTERS OF GOD'S WOMEN

Today's women want happiness, fulfillment, and success. They want to feel good about themselves and want to function in the world not just adequately, but very well. They want to make waves and leave their marks!

There are many voices being heard as to what character attributes will enable a woman to fulfill her desires. Some say she must be independent and listen only to her inner voice. Some say she must be aggressive and push her way through. Some say she should be satisfied with what she has and be quiet. Some say hard work and being true to herself is the only way. Others say she must take, demand, and enjoy all the world's pleasures that are within her grasp.

As we have already discovered, God's ideas and views are different from those of the modern world. The character attributes that He directs should be a part of a woman's life seem illogical and even undesirable to many modern thinkers. Some people even say that what God wants from women is impossible to attain. Some scoff, and others cringe at the type of persons that God wants us to be. But God has created us, and He knows who we *can* be. He knows what qualities of character will lead us to the happiness and fulfillment that we seek and to the influence on society that we want to be.

God describes in His Word certain foundational characteristics that are needed to get us started on a pattern of Christian growth, and He also includes other attributes that will enable us to become fully mature women of God. As we consider these qualities (those specifically directed at women in the New Testament), we must constantly remind ourselves that they are attainable but they are not achieved overnight. Neither do they descend upon us magically as

285

we rise from the baptismal tank; we must put forth some effort and commitment and realize that the Holy Spirit provides us strength, while the Bible provides us the guidance we need in our Christian growth.

Before we go any further, the point must be made that each of these aspects of character that God has emphasized as pertaining to women were emphasized as pertaining to *all* Christians as well. We can find in many passages of Scripture (that are addressing all Christians) the characteristics that women are told to develop, except being subject to one's husband, being a keeper at home, and attitudes about one's adornment. God was not singling out women in these passages that we will consider because they were weak, inferior, or intellectually deficient and could not understand what had been said to Christians at other times in a general sense. It was not that women had to be told again how to act or who to be because they missed the point the first time, anymore than the male leaders (elders, deacons, etc.) of the church had to be reminded of proper character attributes because they missed the general emphasis. The writers of the Bible simply sought to help with problems that had arisen in the early church and offer certain reminders and admonitions. Since women were very much a part of the early church and its work, it is logical that they would be mentioned in the exhortations also.

At the same time, we must realize that all the qualities that are to be a part of a Christian's life are also to be part of each Christian woman's life whether they were *specifically* directed to the women of the New Testament or not. Women were not specifically told to love others in the *agape*-sense, but we know that all Christians are to do so. Women were not told specifically to forgive others, but we know that all

Christians are to do so. Women were not told specifically to love Jesus and keep His commandments, but we know that Jesus expected that of *all* of His followers.

Keeping these thoughts in mind, let us consider the characteristics that are to be a part of our lives as specifically stated in the New Testament as applying to women.

Humility

The first foundational quality in a woman's character is humility. On the basis of humility the rest of her character can be built. Peter stated that women must be concerned about their inner qualities and that the basic type of spirit they should have is one of gentleness and quietness:

> But let it be the hidden person of the heart, with the imperishable quality of a gentle and quiet spirit, which is precious in the sight of God (I Peter 3:4).

The Greek meaning of the two words "gentle" and "quiet" could best be summed up with the word "humility." It is a quality that comes from within a person, promotes peace, and results in service to others.

As Peter mentioned, God is pleased with those who have humility, for besides being willing to serve others they have an approachability, an open-mindedness, a teachability. A humble person is able to be guided, is not stuck on self or selfish interests, and is willing to yield. God hears the prayers of the humble (Psalm 9:12) and promises to guide the humble in the way He would have them go (Psalm 25:9). He promises to lift up the humble (Matthew 23:12; James 4:10; I Peter 5:6) and to give them grace (Psalm 149:4; Proverbs 3:34; James 4:6), and honor (Psalm 147:6; Proverbs 15:33; 18:12; 22:4; 29:23).

Jesus often taught about the necessity and desirability of humility. In His Sermon on the Mount, the first quality He stressed was being "poor in spirit" which meant being at one's lowest ebb, being impoverished, being so low that one turns to God for the answers. A person who has this attitude of being humble and lowly is on his way to receiving God's richest blessings, even the Kingdom of Heaven (Matthew 5:3).

Jesus also stressed that a person's worship, giving, and praying should not be done as in an attitude of boasting or seeking attention from others but in an attitude of quiet humility before God (Matthew 6:1-6). He told a parable of a Pharisee and a tax-gatherer who were before God in prayer. The Pharisee was proud of his goodness and let God know about it, while the tax-gatherer felt so sinful and lowly that he dared not even raise his eyes. Jesus said God was more pleased with the tax-gatherer because he did not exalt himself, but was humble (Luke 18:13, 14).

When asked how to achieve greatness, Jesus said humble service to others was God's way to greatness (Luke 22:24-27). And He showed in His life that He truly believed those words. He consistently helped others in meeting their needs, whether those needs were physical, emotional, or spiritual.

After the Lord's Supper in the upper room had ended, Jesus took a towel and a basin of water and washed each of the disciples' feet. Washing another's feet was considered to be the lowliest task of all — so low that even a servant could refuse to do it. Yet, Jesus, the Master of all men, lowered Himself in such a way in order to teach the disciples what it meant to be humble and how they must seek to do the same types of service for others (John 13:3-17). Then in the ultimate act of humility, He went to the cross to die. He esteemed all others more highly than Himself, He thought of others' spiritual needs before His own, and was obedient unto death (Philippians 2:4-11). Then God exalted Him, just as God exalts all who are humble.

In direct contrast to Jesus' teaching and example is the proud or haughty person. The book of Proverbs makes clear what God thinks of the proud and what will happen to them:

The Lord will tear down the house of the proud . . . (15:25).

Everyone who is proud in heart is an abomination to the Lord; assuredly, he will not be unpunished (16:5).

Pride goes before destruction, and a haughty spirit before stumbling (16:18).

Before destruction the heart of man is haughty . . . (18:12).

An arrogant man stirs up strife (28:25).

Isaiah also spoke very forcefully of what is ahead for the proud:

For the Lord of hosts will have a day of reckoning against everyone who is proud and lofty, and against everyone who is lifted up, that he may be abased (Isaiah 2:12).

He painted a picture of proud women and their destruction:

Because the daughters of Zion are proud, and walk with heads held high and seductive eyes, and go along with mincing steps, and tinkle the bangles on their feet, therefore the Lord will afflict the scalp of the daughters of Zion with scabs, and the Lord will make their foreheads bare. In that day the Lord will take away the beauty of their anklets, headbands, crescent ornaments, dangling earrings, bracelets, veils, headdresses, ankle chains, sashes, perfume boxes, amulets, finger rings, nose rings, festal robes, outer tunics, cloaks, money purses, hand mirrors, undergarments, turbans, veils. Now it will come about that instead of sweet

289

perfume there will be putrefaction; instead of a belt, a rope; instead of well-set hair, a plucked-out scalp; instead of fine clothes, a donning of sackcloth; and branding instead of beauty (Isaiah 3:16-24).

Because these women crushed and plundered the poor, thought themselves to be better than others, and paraded around in their riches, God promised to punish them by taking away their finery, their beauty, and their security. The proud are always abased and made low in the final analysis.

In the New Testament, Jesus said those who exalted themselves would be made low (Luke 18:14) and that those who sought the honor of the world would receive it but would not receive God's honor (Matthew 6:2, 5).

Paul included the qualities of arrogance and boastfulness in the list of depravities that worldly people take part in (Romans 1:30; II Timothy 3:2) and warned Timothy of how conceited people will not listen to the truth and will have no understanding (I Timothy 6:4). Peter emphasized that all Christians must seek to be humble, for God opposes the proud (I Peter 5:5). Peter also explained so well how humility results in peace and blessings from God and how it is the very basis of our Christian characters and behavior:

> To sum up, let all be harmonious, sympathetic, brotherly, kindhearted, and humble in spirit; not returning evil for evil, or insult for insult, but giving a blessing instead; for you were called for the very purpose that you might inherit a blessing. For "let him who means to love life and see good days refrain his tongue from evil and his lips from speaking guile. And let him turn away from evil and do good; let him seek peace and pursue it. For the eyes of the Lord are upon the righteous, and his ears attend to their prayer, but the face of the Lord is against those who do evil" (I Peter 3:8-12).

Thus, we can conclude that a humble woman realizes who she is in her relationship to God and others; she realizes that she is much less than God but loved by Him and that she is equal to but not better than others. She will not feel she has all the answers, but she will be ready to receive God's guidance and the truth of His Word. She is not hung up on her self-importance and will not be continually demanding her rights be recognized; instead she will think of others' needs and seek to meet those needs. It will not offend her to clean the toilet or to pick up the trash after a child's party. She will not be criticizing others in order to build up herself. She will be willing to go the "second mile" if it will help someone else (Matthew 5:41).

The depth of a woman's humility is seen in part by her willingness to submit. Although submission is a "dirty word" in our American culture and humility seems to be a demeaning quality to many modern women, these qualities were very much a part of the vocabulary of the writers of the Scripture. Every Christian, male and female, was told to submit to one another (Ephesians 5:21); and, of course, the whole basis of the Christian faith is in our humbly submitting to God (which Paul referred to when he told the women to be subject in I Corinthians 14:34). If we are humble, we will submit to God; we will surrender our whole selves to Him.

Women were told many times to be submissive to their husbands (I Corinthians 11:3, 7, 10; Ephesians 5:22, 24, 33; Colossians 3:18; I Timothy 2:11, 12; Titus 2:5; I Peter 3:1, 5, 6).[1] No matter how some people try to take these verses out of context or explain these passages away by

---

1. For more on submission in marriage, see Chapter Six, pp. 167-198.

saying Paul was conditioned by the culture of his time, the repetition of this command is indisputable. Why was there such a heavy emphasis on the wife's submission to her husband? Probably because women in the early church were having a diffiult time living it out. It is the hardest to submit to someone whose faults we know so well and with whom we have such a continuous relationship. And no woman can truly submit to her husband if she is not, first of all, humble.

To help us be humble and submissive in our marriage relationship, we must realize the benefits: peace and harmony in the home and in the church (I Corinthians 14:33; Colossians 3:15-19), win non-Christian husbands to Christ (I Peter 3:1), and present the proper Christian witness in the community (I Corinthians 11; Titus 2:5).

Women also need the quality of humility to be valuable workers in the church fellowship. Paul made clear the foolishness and harsh consequences of being arrogant and haughty in our church relationships. God's kindness toward us as His children will turn to severity if we act conceited, become too proud of ourselves, or feel we are better than others in God's family (Romans 11:15-32). He commanded that we associate with the lowly and not think of ourselves too highly (Romans 12:3, 16). The many problems and factions in the church at Corinth were caused by some of the members feeling superior to others and boasting about their special talents (I Corinthians).

When women in the church either as individuals or in groups begin thinking that they are more holy and righteous than others in the church because of their knowledge of the Scriptures, because of their leadership functions, or because of their ways of service, they lose the basic attribute of humility and soon the rest of their characters will come tumbling down. The church fellowship will be hurt as those women who have been snubbed or ignored by the haughty ones are hurt and sorrowful because the love that should be between Christian sisters was not felt. Consider your own actions individually as well as how your church women's group is behaving. Are your proud or are you humble? Are you always ready to learn new truths or do you feel you know the full truth already? Are you seeking to meet others' needs or are you seeking to do those jobs that will put you "out front" or in the church paper? Do you welcome others into your group, or would you rather just keep your small, elite group? Seek to be humble, serving, loving women, and be alert to the dangers of becoming a close-knit clique.

Biblical Examples. There are many examples in the Bible of women who show us what it means to live humbly:

(1) Jephthah's daughter lived during a period of great turmoil and was the victim of an impulsive vow her father made to God. Jephthah was asked to be the commander of Israel when the nation was threatened by their heathen neighbors, the Ammonites. He tried in vain to establish peace without violence; then he began gathering men for the army. His courage was evidently waning when he considered the huge forces of the enemy, and he made a vow to God that he later regretted:

> If thou wilt indeed give the sons of Ammon into my hand, then it shall be that whatever comes out of the doors of my house to meet me when I return in peace from the sons of Ammon, it shall be the Lord's, or I will offer it up as a burnt offering (Judges 11:31).

We do not know what Jephthah had in mind when he made his vow. Did he expect an animal to be the first out of the door when he returned from the victorious battle? A lamb or a goat perhaps? Or did he expect a servant to come out? He certainly did not expect his only child to be the first out of the door, but she was. She was quite joyous about her father's great victory and came out of the door of his home dancing and playing tambourines (11:34). Jephthah was stricken with sorrow and dismay when he realized that his daughter must pay for a vow he recklessly made (11:35).

Some scholars feel that because of the wording of his vow and the depth of his sorrow when he realized what he had done, he actually sacrificed his daughter upon an altar to the Lord as a literal burnt offering. However, his vow allowed for two possibilities: (a) being given to the Lord (as a person), (b) or offered as a burnt offering (as an animal). The response would depend on who or what came through the door. And considering the rest of the passage, it is much more likely that he was giving his daughter to God to live completely in His service in the tabernacle, much in the same way Hannah dedicated Samuel to God's service. So instead of becoming a wife and mother and continuing the line of Jephthah, she remained unmarried and a virgin (11:39). Jephthah was sorrowful because no heirs would be forthcoming.

Jephthah's daughter so respected God and her father that she insisted the vow be carried out and voluntarily gave of herself:

> My father, you have given your word to the Lord; do to me as you have said, since the Lord has avenged you of your enemies (Judges 11:36).

She asked that she be allowed to go to the mountains with her friends for two months to fortify herself for the commitment she had made (11:37). She thought of the kind of life she had dreamed she could fulfill and wept because her dreams would never come to pass. In that culture, every Jewish girl dreamed of becoming a wife and mother, and the knowledge that she could not be as other women was heartbreaking. But after the crying, she put aside her selfishness and submitted to God and her father. She did not rebel or run away; she willingly gave her whole life to fulfill her father's vow. She would not have done such a sacrificial thing if her basic attitude had not been one of humility. She was considered to be such an example that Israelite women commemorated her action each year (Judges 11:40).

(2) Naomi was a sad, angry, and bitter woman. Life had dealt her some vicious blows. She and her husband left Judah to settle in Moab to escape the hardships of a famine. The Moabites were idol-worshippers, but Naomi and her husband retained their faith and customs. However, tragedy found its way into their lives—Naomi's husband died as well as her two married sons (Ruth 1:3-5).

Naomi felt she had nothing left to live for. She was bereft in every way—she was a foreigner in a strange land, she had no hope that their family would increase and surround her with love, and as a widow she had no economic security. She decided she would return to her homeland where she would at least have acquaintances and be surrounded by the Jewish way of life.

Being faithful to the customs of the time, Ruth and Orpah (the wives of Naomi's sons) accompanied Naomi. Even though Naomi felt her own life was empty and finished, she did not want these young women to suffer. She urged them to go back to their families to remarry and start new lives. Orpah returned to her home, but Ruth clung (the Hebrew word means "stuck like cement") to Naomi and humbly pleaded to be allowed to stay with her (Ruth 1:16, 17).

Ruth must have known that she herself would feel isolated in a strange land and that the Jews hated her people. But she also knew that Naomi as a widow with no family would have no one to protect her or provide for her physical needs. In such a male-dominated culture, the circumstances were serious. So she gave up her thoughts for her own welfare and thought only about caring for Naomi.

Ruth was younger and stronger but always remained respectful to Naomi. She asked for permission to go out into the fields to work for their sustenance (Ruth 2:2). She was respectful and humble before the field hands, requesting permission to pick up the leftovers in the field (2:7). According to Jewish law, widows and poor people could come into the fields after the reapers had harvested the grain and take the loose sheaves that were left at the edges and corners of the field (Deuteronomy 24:19). But Ruth was a Moabite and could not have expected to be treated well in the fields. She was literally putting her life on the line to get food for herself and Naomi as is evident from the directions of Boaz and Naomi's comment about her work (Ruth 2:15, 16, 22).

Ruth fell on her face in gratitude before Boaz when he allowed her to get grain from his fields (2:10). She humbly submitted to Naomi's directions of how to make Boaz aware of their family kinship (3:5, 6), and she followed Boaz's directions as well (3:13-17). Her whole life was characterized by humility and submissiveness. Because of her attitude of being willing to serve others and being respectful to those in authority, she was known by all to be a "woman of exellence" (2:11; 3:11).

(3) Mary, the mother of Jesus, reminds us of Ruth because they both shared a "gentle and quiet spirit," a humble willingness to serve and submit. Mary did not understand

why God chose her to be the mother of the Savior, nor did she understand how it would come to pass without a male counterpart (Luke 1:34). She was troubled and afraid (1:29, 30); she did not know what would happen to her. Pregnant, unmarried women were very much looked down upon, and she no doubt thought of what her fiancee's reaction would be. But she put selfishness aside and submitted (Luke 1:38). She consistently submitted to God's and her husband's leadership throughout her lifetime. And in two separate instances, she submitted to Jesus' guidance when He was a man (John 2:4; Matthew 12:46-49).

Since she was the mother of the Messiah, she could have attracted a lot of attention to herself and demanded that she be treated in a special way. But she never got hung up on her self-importance; instead she quietly blended in with the groups that followed Jesus and in the prayer meeting after His ascension (Acts 1:14). Even though she realized the magnitude of what part she had played in God's plan, she always considered herself to be a lowly handmaiden of the Lord.

(4) The woman who was a "sinner" and came in off the streets into the house of Simon the Pharisee when Jesus was dining there bowed down before Jesus and washed His feet, an action which denoted great humility in that culture. She was highly praised for her humility and devotion in direct contrast to the proud and lofty attitude of Simon who felt he was superior and knew all the answers. Because of her humility, this woman received forgiveness for her sin and could start her life anew. But the Pharisee was too proud to learn from the Master (Luke 7:36-50).

(5) The Canaanite woman came humbly begging Jesus to help her daughter. She made clear her own insignificance

and how powerful and important she felt Jesus was. She recognized His godly connections and felt keenly her own unworthiness since she was not a Jew. She could have gotten angry and demanded that Jesus listen to her because of her rights as a person and as a mother, but she chose instead to be respectful and humble. She was certainly rewarded for her attitude (Matthew 15:22-28).

(6) Jesus had just finished talking about how the scribes liked to parade around in their long robes and make flowery prayers to be seen of men and seem to be quite religious, while they were dishonest and treated the lowly shamefully (reminds us of Isaiah's speech about the proud women of Zion, page 289). Then He sat before the treasury and observed how the rich were proudly putting in large sums; most people would have been so impressed that they would not have even noticed the poor widow who put in two small coins. But Jesus noticed her and called His disciples to Him. He indicated the poor widow who in her humility and dedication to the Lord put in all she owned — yes, even all she had to live on. Jesus was teaching His disciples that God took more note of this woman's humble surrender than of all the huge sums of money others could give (Mark 12:41-44) and was more pleased with her than with the proud scribes (the elite).

For Us. In our current society, these women would probably be considered doormats, puppets, or at least "milk toasts." Yet we must point out that each one chose to do what she did *voluntarily.* These women could have refused to submit; they could have demanded that their own needs and desires be met before they served others, or that they be given more assurance that they would not be sacrificing too much, or that after they had served their time they would be

298

free to go their own way. No, they set down no conditions. They yielded.

Was it because they had no self-esteem? Was it because they were afraid to refuse? Was it because they felt they had no choice? No, each woman yielded because of her love toward God and others and her proper view of herself and her responsibilities. No woman exalted herself, but instead abased herself in service. And if we are to be God's women, we must do the same.

Faithfulness

Issuing out of humility is another important foundational characteristic—faithfulness. Paul told Timothy that the women must be "faithful in all things" (I Timothy 3:11). He also said the young widows would be in danger if they "set aside their previous pledge" (I Tim. 5:12) which would be the opposite of faithfulness. After her conversion, Lydia used the word "faithful" in Acts 16:15: "If you have judged me to be faithful to the Lord, come into my house and stay."

Being faithful refers to being loyal at all times as well as being full of a firm conviction and trust in God. We cannot be faithful or maintain our Christian life through the rough and the good times without having a firm faith in God. Faith is not only an intellectual belief that God exists; it also includes an ever-abiding trust, rooted in the very depths of our beings. It results in hope in the future, peace in our hearts, and a security built on the rock of God's love and power. Even when things get dark and beyond all human understanding, the faithful one stands secure, at peace, and with a positive outlook.

We have faith in God because of what He has done in the past, because we believe what He says, and because of what He has done for us personally. This faith accompanies wisdom (understanding, Hebrews 11:3) and results in obedience and good works (James 2:24-26). Because of faith we become children of God (Galatians 3:26), Christ dwells within us (Ephesians 3:17), and we continue in our Christian walk (Galatians 5:22). Faith can move mountains (Matthew 17:20), can heal our bodies (Mark 5:34), and can purify our hearts (Acts 15:9). Our faith shields us from the advances of the devil and enables us to overcome the world (Ephesians 6:16; I Thessalonians 5:8; I John 5:4). Through faith, we can tap the great power of God.

Biblical Examples. For our instruction, let us consider a few women of the Bible whose faith faltered when times got rough. (1) As long as things were going well, Eve trusted in God and enjoyed the blessing of living in the Garden. But when temptation came—when Satan made the alternative to trusting in God seem quite attractive—Eve doubted and wondered if God was tricking her and her husband because He was afraid they would become as wise as He. She decided that what Satan said made more sense and was more desirable than what God had said. She shifted her loyalties and became disobedient to God. Her lack of faithfulness resulted in much misery and insecurity, for she and Adam were thrown out of the pleasant and secure environment of the Garden (Genesis 3) and their close fellowship with God was marred.

(2) Sarah had been promised repeatedly that she and Abraham would have a son. But year after year went by, and she was still barren. She was getting close to being too old to conceive. She should have had full trust in God's

promise, but instead she was worried, frustrated, and terribly impatient. She had little peace and happiness. She probably prayed everyday that God would fulfill His promise and anxiously waited for the first sign of pregnancy. She probably asked, "What is God waiting for? Doesn't He know how old I'm getting? Has He forgotten about us?"

In her impatience, she convinced Abraham to become sexually intimate with her maidservant Hagar, thinking that they could claim her son as their heir (Genesis 16:1-3). Not only was she causing their marriage covenant to be broken, she was also showing her lack of faith in God's promise. She was not being faithful in her time of trouble. This decision (about Hagar) caused much pain and heartache in their family circle; the two women and thus their two sons could not get along peaceably in the years to come (Genesis 16:4-9; 21:9-14).

(3) Rebekah also had a direct promise from God. God told her that Jacob would become Isaac's heir and a spiritual leader (Genesis 25:23). But like Sarah, Rebekah became worried and impatient; God was taking too long! The situation was looking pretty dismal to her. Isaac was old and sick, but he was determined to give a blessing to his favorite son, Esau. Rebekah thought to herself, "No, this must not happen! My beloved Jacob is to receive the blessing." Instead of trusting in God, she took things into her own hands. She disguised Jacob, so Isaac would think he was Esau and bless him instead. Rather than being faithful, she became deceitful. Isaac was terribly upset and hurt; hatred and threats arose between the brothers; and their family life became a shambles (Genesis 27).

(4) Naomi thought her life was over when her husband and sons died. Instead of enjoying peace and security in

God's love in her time of trial, she became very resentful and bitter. She blamed God for her affliction rather than trusting in Him to care for her and give her life new meaning. When she got back to her homeland of Judah, her acquaintances did not know her because of the change in her looks and attitude — a change for the worst (Ruth 1:19-21) which reflected her lack of faithfulness, her lack of trust in God.

(5) When Job and his wife suffered so many calamities, she was ready to blame God for it all and "throw in the towel" (Job 2:9, 10). She showed that her faith was not firm but ready to topple at the first setback.

From these examples, we discover that without faithfulness, there is no real peace and security. In its place are frustrations, impatience, worry, insecurity, and bitterness.

In contrast to these examples, let us consider women who remained faithful. (1) Even though Sarah's faith faltered at times, her faith matured as she grew older, for she was listed among the faithful in Hebrews 11:11. Just as God had promised, she and Abraham had a son in their old age and loved him greatly. But one day the situation grew bleak, because God told Abraham to sacrifice their son on an altar. How natural it would seem for Sarah to scream, plead, and cry out to God. She could have told Abraham that he must be mistaken about God's directions. After waiting so long for a son and after the promise of a nation to come through them, God could not mean that Isaac was to be sacrificed as an animal! It just would not be logical! But Sarah trusted in God's judgment and guidance and did her part to carry out God's plan, apparently without complaint (Genesis 22:1-18).

(2) Faithfulness often results in courageous acts. Rahab put her life on the line because she believed that God's way

was a better way (Joshua 2). (3) Deborah trusted that God was more powerful than the hundreds of chariots of iron of the Canaanites and led the army of Israel to victory in battle (Judges 4). (4) Hannah was faithful to her promise to give her son to the Lord's service. It would not be easy for a mother to leave her longed-for child in a faraway place and have little contact with him, but she trusted that God would take care of him (I Samuel 1:26-28; 2:11). (5) Esther trusted in God's will and power, so much so that she was ready to die if that was what God desired. She said as she was preparing to appear before the King uninvited: "If I perish, I perish" (Esther 4:16).

(6) Mary, the mother of Jesus, was ready to follow God's directions, even though her reputation could have been in jeopardy, and she could have been stoned for being adulterous—since Joseph knew he was not the father of her child (Luke 1:26-38). (7) The prophetess Anna believed and trusted in God's promise to send a Savior. She showed her faithfulness by never leaving the temple, by serving God night and day there, and by proclaiming the good news (Luke 2:36-38), even though she was quite elderly. (8) Paul commended Eunice and Lois for being faithful in passing on God's truths to Timothy (II Timothy 1:5; 3:14, 15). And Paul praised many other women who were faithful workers for Christ (Romans 16).

These women were secure and confident as they remained trusting in God. They could see the troubles around them in the proper perspective and realized that God would work things out for the best. They were not lured away from God and His way by the worldly philosophies of their time.

For Us. I am sure we can identify with the women of the Bible who worried, who were frustrated, and who were impatient when things were not going the way they thought

303

they should. We have all had faltering faith at times, and we have all been tempted to turn from God's way to the worldly way.

Living in this country of material abundance, we can identify with Eve who yielded to the temptation to fulfill her selfish desires instead of obeying God. And the philosophies of our time — "do what makes you feel good," "do your own thing," and "trust in your own instincts" — sound just like Satan in the Garden of Eden. What the world says and offers sounds so logical and desirable and appeals to our basic lusts so strongly that it takes a great amount of trust in God to turn away from them. And an even greater tragedy is how many people think they can be selfish and enjoy the world's way of life and still be counted as God's children. They do not realize the awful consequences of their alliance with the world anymore than Eve realized the deceitfulness of Satan and the misery that would befall her when she disobeyed God. May we believe in Jesus' words: "No one can serve two masters; for either he will hate the one and love the other, or he will hold to one and despise the other. You cannot serve God and mammon" (Matthew 6:24). May we trust that our true happiness lies in God, not in the world.

We can also identify with Sarah when she worried about her barrenness. She did not trust in God enough to leave the timetable to Him. True, according to man's logic, God was waiting too long but trust means believing in God even when it seems illogical and foolish. When we worry, we are also demonstrating our distrust in God. We may worry about death, about a sickness, about having money to pay the bills, and about a multitude of tragedies that might befall us.

My husband travels a great deal and has been doing so for almost ten years as a part of his job as college professor.

One weekend I allowed my mind to dwell on all the awful things that could happen to him while in an airplane. I pictured in my mind midair collisions, the plane falling into the ocean, the plane bursting into flames, the plane being hijacked by a mad gunman. I was uneasy and anxious; I lost a lot of sleep. When that weekend was over, I learned that all that worrying was a waste of time and energy and was an indication of my selfishness, for all the while I was thinking about how terrible my life would be without him. How much better it is to entrust my husband to God, having faith that He will take care of him as He has for several years.

Worry is not the same as a sincere concern for others that results in compassionate caring and constructive service to others. It is a fretting about people and/or events that might be in danger or might happen or about matters over which we have no control. Such fretting clutters up our minds so that we cannot think clearly. It occupies our thoughts almost constantly and stultifies any constructive thoughts or activities that we would otherwise be thinking or doing. In the Greek, "worry" means "to divide the mind." It gives us the picture of dividing up our mind into little pieces so that we do not have a "wholeness" to devote to anything.

Worry is a strain on us both physically and emotionally. It is the root cause of many headaches, ulcers, high blood pressure, heart trouble, and even colds. It saps our energy so much that we have a hard time facing up to reality; our *imagined* realities can paralyze us so that we cannot operate in the real world adequately. Sometimes we are so caught up in our worries that we do not see the needs of others. Instead we remain in our own selfish little worlds of worry and feel no peace or contentment. It is as the Proverb says, "Anxiety in the heart of a man weighs it down" (Proverbs 12:25).

Of course, it is much easier to *say* "don't worry" than it is to live it out daily, but we must seek to erase this tendency to fret if we are to remain faithful to God. God has made promises to us just as He made promises to the women of the Bible. Here are a few of God's promises that should help us secure our faith:

Do not fear, for I am with you; do not anxiously look about you, for I am your God. I will strengthen you, surely I will help you. Surely I will uphold you with my right hand (Isaiah 41:10).

Do not be anxious for your life, as to what you shall eat, or what you shall drink; nor for your body, as to what you shall put on. Is not life more than food, and the body than clothing? Look at the birds of the air, that they do not sow, neither do they reap, nor gather into barns, and yet your heavenly Father feeds them. Are you not worth much more than they? . . . But seek first His kingdom and His righteousness; and all these things shall be added to you. Therefore do not be anxious for tomorrow; for tomorrow will care for itself. Each day has enough trouble of its own (Matthew 6:25, 26, 33, 34).

Let not your heart be troubled; believe in God believe also in me (John 14:1).

And we know that God causes all things to work together for good to those who love God, to those who are called according to His purpose (Romans 8:28).

Casting all your anxiety upon Him, because He cares for you (I Peter 5:7).

And this is the confidence which we have before Him, that, if we ask anything according to His will, He hears us (I John 5:14).

For whatever is born of God overcomes the world; and this is the victory that has overcome the world — our faith. And who is the one who overcomes the world, but he who believes that Jesus is the Son of God? (I John 5:4, 5).

Are we believing that God cares and loves us and that He wants only the best for us? Are we trusting in God's promises and claiming them for our own? Are we trusting that God forgives us and removes our guilt and fears? Do we refuse to dwell on negative thoughts? Are we continually thanking God for His kindness toward us? Only with this faith can we experience inner peace and security in our sinful and transitory world. Paul expressed these thoughts so eloquently and tells us to replace our worrying with rejoicing, patience, praying, and thankfulness:

> Rejoice in the Lord always; again I will say, rejoice! Let your forbearing spirit be known to all men. The Lord is near. Be anxious for nothing, but in everything by prayer and supplication with thanksgiving let your requests be made known to God. And the peace of God, which surpasses all comprehension, shall guard your hearts and your minds in Christ Jesus (Philippians 4:4-7).

We must realize that there will be bad times in our lives. As long as we live in the world, there will be problems. We don't escape discouragement or trials by becoming Christians. Faith is not like a tranquilizer that enables us to go through life in an unrealistic daze, nor is it a happiness pill that leads to instant happiness and contentment. Faith is not a quick and easy road to peace; it is not like a Valium that takes away the pain of living. No, temptations, pain, suffering, and persecution are all around us, but if we are faithful we can be secure and triumphant amidst those problems.

What does a faithful woman do during troublesome times? She does not look for the easy or selfish way out that the world offers. She does not blame God for the hard times. She does not worry. Instead she maintains an inner peace by trusting in God's promises. She does not become deceitful in order to have things go her way. Instead she turns the problem over to God in prayer and waits. She does not become impatient, but trusts that God will do what is best and in His time. She fulfills her commitments and responsibilities with courage, knowing that as long as she is doing God's will He will be with her.

Discernment

In addition to being humble and faithful, women are to be discerning. Paul directed Titus to have the older women teach the younger women in the early church to be "sensible" (*sophron,* Titus 2:5) which is from the Greek word for wisdom[2] Women were to practice discernment, were to be discreet, and were to be sound-minded.

Women have minds and creative intelligence; they are capable of discernment. Yet many women think of themselves as stupid and have remained passive in that area of life, feeling there is no use to try to better their minds. Perhaps they have been told too long by our man-dominated culture that "women are to be seen (emphasizing physical beauty) but not heard. Men are to tend to the intellectual pursuits."

God has never looked down upon women because they sought to use and improve their minds. The simple, the naive, and the foolish were condemned (Proverbs 1:22;

---

2. Paul used the same word in his directions for the elders of the church, but it is translated "prudent" (I Timothy 3:2). He also used the word when directing the elders, older men, and the younger men in Titus 1:8; 2:2, 6.

9:13), while the discerning women were praised (Proverbs 11:22, 14:1). God fully intends for women to use their intelligence to serve Him and to make the world a better place for all. He expects women to be humble and submissive, but He has never meant by that that women are to sit around looking pretty or serving as simple-minded slaves. He has shown consistently in His Word the influence that intelligent, sensible women have made upon history and how He has blessed those women in their activities.

Biblical Examples. It took a great deal of common sense, intelligence, and dedication to God's way for (1) Jochebed to hide her infant son for three months (how did she conceal a crying infant?) and then devise a plan to save the child as well as become the child's nurse (Exodus). (2) Rahab's plan to secure the safety of the Hebrew spies in Jericho was not only daring, but also quite clever. Her securing an oath that she and her family be saved when the Hebrews took over the land also showed her foresight and her understanding of the power of God (Joshua 2).

(3) Abigail's quick thinking, quick action, and tactfulness preserved her whole household from destruction when her churlish husband insulted David. She wisely gave gifts of food and appealed to David on the basis of peace and mercy and maintained her attitude of respect and humility. She could have cried and beat her breasts, becoming quite emotional as she pled for mercy; but she decided instead to use common sense and tact to influence David (I Samuel 25:1-42).

(4) The unnamed woman of Abel Beth-maacah showed her wisdom in her appeal to Joab to punish only the man they sought and to spare the city (II Samuel 20:16-22). (5) The Queen of Sheba was cited for her understanding

about Solomon and his relationships to God (Matthew 12:42). (6) Esther showed discernment in the way she approached the King of Persia about Haman's plot. First, she gained his respect and trust and got him in a favorable frame of mind; then she revealed how Haman had fooled him (Esther 5-7).

(7) The Samaritan woman at the well showed insight into the purpose of the Messiah and the meaning of Jesus' symbolic language, especially remarkable since she was part Gentile and probably not as familiar with Jewish prophecies (John 4). (8) Mary of Bethany, Martha and Lazarus' sister, was praised by Jesus for her choosing to listen to His words rather than working in the kitchen. Mary was concerned about her mind; she wanted to grow spiritually and knew that such growth must begin with the dedication of her mind to Jesus. She was ready and eager to learn (Luke 10:38-41). She also showed understanding of Jesus' greatness when she anointed His feet, while some of Jesus' disciples had missed the whole point (John 12:1-8).

(9) The Canaanite woman understood Jesus' refusal to help her and in her discernment expressed her complete confidence in His power and assured Him of her pure motives. She recognized Jesus' connection with God and knew He was the only one who could heal her daughter (Matthew 15:21-28). (10) Priscilla showed that she was continuously developing her mind in order to serve the Lord; for when Apollos needed more instruction, she was ready to give it (Acts 18:24-26).

For Us. Discernment involves using and developing our minds so that we can grasp the deep riches of God's truth. It involves filling our minds with the proper thoughts:

Finally brethren, whatever is true, whatever is honorable, whatever is right, whatever is pure, whatever is lovely, whatever is of good repute, if there is any excellence and if anything worthy of praise, let your mind dwell on these things (Philippians 4:8).

It involves being ready to handle any situation that confronts us with tact and sensitivity. It involves relying on good sense and factual information rather than letting our emotions and impulses to rule our actions.

This type of sensibleness proceeds from God, but it does not descend magically upon us as in a mist. It is a quality that must be worked for and developed. We cannot sit idly by and expect God to suddenly enlighten us. We cannot expect God to guide us with dreams and visions. He has created us with minds with great capacities for intelligence, and He has revealed His will for our lives in His Word. It is up to us to be concerned enough to develop our mental capabilities so we can understand and apply the principles of His Word.

It is true that the duties of housework and carting the children around to their various activities do not in and of themselves contribute to one's mind development. A simple-minded person can scrub floors and do the laundry. Anyone can be trained to sweep and dust properly. But it is up to the individual to turn her situation into a mind-expanding experience.

It takes a great deal of intelligence to organize one's housework — to get everything done and still have time to meet the needs of the family members and participate in outside activities as well. It takes a great deal of creativity to plan and prepare meals that are appetizing, varied, well-balanced, and still within a budget. It takes a great amount of understanding and sensitivity to know when one's husband is depressed or the children are troubled or sad and how to help them. It takes an alert and calculating mind to stay within a budget and find the best bargains. It takes creativity to arrange and decorate a house so it is comfortable, practical, and attractive.

Working outside the home has been made to seem quite glamourous and stimulating, but many women who are in that workaday world know that much of what they are doing is just as humdrum as household duties are made out to be and are often more meaningless than what they do at home. They perform the same tasks over and over again — filing papers, typing letters, filling out forms, making entries in a ledger, punching a cash register, marking price tags, stocking shelves, etc. It takes intelligence and creativity for women in such positions to make their jobs interesting, to understand how what they do fits into the whole, to perceive what contribution they are making to the business, and to feel that their jobs are worthwhile. A woman must be intellectually alert, always willing to learn, and have much sensitivity and understanding in order to be a success in what is still considered to be a man's world.

No matter where you are in life, whether you are changing diapers and taking Johnny to piano lessons, or whether you are selling candy in the dimestore, or whether you are a business executive, your world is only as mentally restrictive as you allow it to be. Only you can push back the horizons of your world.

With careful planning and determination, a busy mother can still find time to browse in the library, read the newspaper, read a book, or go to the Bible study group at the church. She can take college courses or attend conferences sponsored by the church at least some time during the year. If she is open and alert, she can learn a great deal by helping her children with their homework and reading their school books.

A wage-earning wife and/or mother can find time to study her Bible; she may have to get up an hour earlier, but she can do it. She can find time to fellowship with Christians and can use her vacation time to revitalize her thinking. As the saying goes, "Where there is a will, there is a way." And there is always a way for a Christian woman to improve herself mentally and accomplish the quality of discernment.

Self-control

A humble, faithful, and discerning woman will develop self-control—an important aspect of character. The writers of the New Testament made many exhortations to women to exercise self-control in various areas of their lives. In Paul's instructions to Timothy, his comments about women learning in "quietness" and remaining "quiet" referred to a life-style of self-restraint (I Timothy 2:11, 12, 15, see detailed exegesis in Chapter Five (pp. 130-132). What is involved in such a life-style?

PURITY. A woman who has self-control will live a pure life. Peter said that a husband could be won to Christ, not only by the wife's submissiveness, but also by her "chaste" (hagnos, pure) behavior (I Peter 3:1, 2). "Chaste" refers to being immaculate, or being without any type of pollution. In writing to Titus, Paul used the same word when he told the older women to teach the younger women to be "pure" (Titus 2:5). In a general sense, the word referred to being free from all evil, being sanctified, being set apart by God to be holy—as all Christians are to be.

313

We are reminded daily of the dangers of a polluted environment. We take the ecologists seriously and seek to do our part to keep our surroundings clean and natural. But how many in our world today take God's Word seriously when God talks of the dangers of polluted inner characters? God expects us to be pure in our thoughts and actions.

Our thoughts are really the keys to the type of persons we are and cause us to do what we do: "For as he thinks within himself, so he is" (Proverbs 23:7). We may be able to fool others around us for awhile about our real selves; but we cannot fool God, for He knows our innermost thoughts. He knows whether we are pure or not (Proverbs 16:2).

Our minds are like computers or storehouses. Whatever comes into our minds stays there. Sometimes it is stored in our subconscious, but it is there; and often arises to our consciousness at the most unexpected moments. That is why God wants us to be careful about what we allow to enter our minds. We are not to think about the things that will defile us. We are not to dwell on the negative, the evil, or the dirty. We should not be reading books that contain dirty language or evil concepts (even if they are on the best seller list), for the thoughts of those books will be stored in our minds. We should not be watching daytime dramas (or the nighttime ones, for that matter) that promote adultery, divorce, and deceit, for those thoughts and concepts will be seeping into our consciousness. We should not be viewing movies that feature indecent language, sexual scenes, or extreme violence, for our sensitivity to immorality and indecency will become dulled.

Instead we should fill our minds with thoughts of the higher things (Colossians 3:2). We should seek to have Christ's thoughts fill our minds (Philippians 2:5). We should read

314

and meditate upon God's Word because it will lead to pure thoughts:

> How can a young man keep his way pure? By keeping it according to Thy word. With all my heart I have sought Thee; do not let me wander from Thy commandments. Thy word I have treasured in my heart, that I may not sin against Thee (Psalm 119:9-11).

In a more specific sense, *hagnos* (pure, chaste) referred to *sexual* purity. If we are to be God's women, certainly we must remain sexually pure. But our society today does not help us much, for we are consistently surrounded by sexual immorality. We are expected to believe that adulterous affairs are exciting and a must to keep our marriages alive. Bedroom scenes are the daily fare on television. Advertisements use sex to sell their products. Recently a half-hour situation comedy program announced that it was increasing its emphasis on sex and showing much more of women's flesh in order to boost the show's sagging ratings. As women who are seeking to add the quality of purity to our characters, we must be aware of these trends and how they are polluting our minds and attitudes.

God created sex for the enjoyment of husbands and wives and for the continuation of the human race. Sex is a healthy and wonderful act within the marriage commitment (see section on sexual relationship in marriage, Chapter Six, pp. 198-204). But Satan uses this good God-given desire to entice us to sin, to lead us outside of God's intentions for the use of sex. Women who commit adultery and fornication are living outside God's will (Hebrews 13:4), and such actions will create havoc in their lives. Women who use sex to manipulate men to get their own way or who seek to stimulate men sexually (just for the fun of it) by the way they dress and move bodily are not using sex according to God's wishes. Women who deprive their husband of sexual intimacy are also walking along Satan's path, for such action can propel men into sexual immorality because of their strong desires that are not being satisfied within marriage (I Corinthians 7:1-5).

God has always been concerned about a woman's sexual purity. When because of Abraham's deceitfulness, the Pharaoh took Sarah into his house to be numbered among his concubines, God intervened by sending plagues upon the land and elicited Sarah's release. God was concerned that she remain pure (Genesis 12:14-20). He repeated His intervention on her behalf when Abraham pulled a similar stunt with another king. God told the king in a dream why he could not touch Sarah and warned him of dire consequences if he did not return her to her husband (Genesis 20:2, 6, 7, 18).

God's strict restrictions in the Mosaic Law also point out His concern for purity. He did not allow for pre-marital, extra-marital, or perverted sex (Leviticus 20). The book of Proverbs makes quite clear the harmful consequences of adultery (Proverbs 6, 7, 9:17, 18). Jesus' teachings also stressed the need for sexual purity, not only in behavior but in thoughts as well (Matthew 5:27-32). Paul made clear that God abhors sexual immorality and will punish those who engage in it (I Corinthians 6:9; Galatians 5:19; Hebrews 13:4).

Biblical Examples. We not only have these direct commands and teachings, we also have living examples in the Bible of women who were *not* pure in their sexual behavior and the disastrous results.

(1) Judah's two sons died before they could provide any heirs through Tamar, and he kept putting off allowing

316

her to marry his third son which the levirate law directed that he do (the brother is to marry the dead brother's wife to provide an heir). Tamar was disgusted at his failure to do right by her. She must have known of her father-in-law's wayward habits, for when he went to have his sheep sheared and visit a friend, she disguised herself and posed as a harlot and lured him into a tent. She asked for payment and took some of his possessions as a pledge that she would be paid later. They were sexually intimate, and she conceived.

When Judah was informed that she was with child and ordered her put to death for her indiscretion, she sent to him the possessions that he had given the "harlot" as a pledge. He immediately knew what had happened and said she was within her rights because he had done wrong to her. Her life was spared, and she bore two sons (Genesis 38:6-30).

Tamar was as desperate as she was clever. In the culture in which she lived, she felt she had no other choice than to assert herself in this impure manner. Even though she had been wronged, her sexual manipulation and the commission of incest did not please God.

(2) Joseph was sold into slavery by his own brothers; but in the foreign land of Egypt, with God's protection and guidance, he prospered. He served in the house of Potiphar, a captain of the Pharaoh's bodyguard. He was very successful, gained the confidence of his master, and was promoted to the position of overseer of Potiphar's whole household (Genesis 39:5, 6).

Potiphar's wife noticed how handsome and capable Joseph was and desired him. She flirted, sought to seduce him, and asked him to go to bed with her. Joseph told her that such an action would be a sin against Potiphar and against

God, and he refused her (39:8, 9). But she persisted day after day with the same entreaty. He avoided her presence and continually refused (39:10). One day when no one else was around the house, she grabbed at Joseph in a frenzy and made her intentions known again. She tore at his clothes; he fled leaving the pieces of his garment in her hands.

She was enraged at his refusal and concocted a story to tell her husband, using Joseph's garment as proof that he tried to force himself upon her sexually (Genesis 39:17, 18). The lie had its intended effect; Joseph lost his job and was thrown into jail. God worked good for Joseph out of the despicable situation, but the harm that unrestrained sexual lust causes is apparent.

(3) Delilah did not have uncontrolled sexual desire as Potiphar's wife did, but she did use sex to fulfill her uncontrolled lust for money. Samson's weakness was beautiful women, so she used her beauty and sexual attentions to manipulate him to tell the secret of his strength. She then told his enemies, and they gave her money for the information (Judges 16:5, 18).

Samson loved Delilah and was so blinded by her beauty and sensuousness that he continued with her even when it was obvious that she was keeping soldiers in her home to capture him when his physical powers left him. It is hard to understand how a thinking person could be so taken in by her deceit and not realize her evil intentions, but the power of a woman's physical beauty upon a man must never be underestimated.

The results of Delilah's sexual manipulation were devastating. Samson was captured, blinded, and imprisoned; the leader of Israel was reduced to slavery because of a physically desirable, deceitful woman. After much time had passed,

318

his captors called him out so they could mock him at one of their pagan celebrations. Samson stood between two pillars of the building, prayed that God would restore his strength, and brought death down around the ears of all those present, including himself and no doubt Delilah, by shaking the pillars loose and destroying the building (Judges 16:25-30). How tragic! God blessed this woman with great physical beauty, but she misused her gift and perverted the God-given desire for sex.

(4) King David had chosen not to go to battle, but sent his commander and soldiers out while he remained in Jerusalem (II Samuel 11:1). In the evening as he walked upon his roof, he saw a woman bathing—Bathsheba. She was beautiful and he desired her. He found out who she was and had her come to his palace; they were sexually intimate, and she became pregnant (11:4, 5). When David could not make it look like the child was Uriah's (Bathsheba's husband), he arranged for Uriah's death, and took Bathsheba as his wife (11:6-27).

The Bible is not clear as to how much of this incident was Bathsheba's fault, but we can note the following: (a) Why did she bathe immodestly on her roof? A woman of purity would have taken the proper precautions so that no one could see her. (b) It is doubtful that even though David was the King that he could force a woman to be sexually intimate with him against her will. If she was true to her marriage commitment, she probably could have refused David's attentions. (c) She did not seem surprised or become guilt-ridden that her husband was murdered (surely she knew of David's actions), but moved into David's house. (d) Certainly Bathsheba was not an innocent victim, for God punished them both by taking the life of the child conceived in their illicit union (II Samuel 12:15-23).

It seems evident that both David and Bathsheba allowed Satan to entice them into sexual sin; their selfish desires took precedence over their common sense and their consideration of others. Bathsheba must have repented of her sin (as David repented of his), for God gave them a son and her life was blessed from then on. Even though the story ended happily, we must remember all the pain, the sorrow, and the sinfulness that was caused by the sexual indiscretion.

(5) Gomer was a flagrantly wayward and unfaithful wife. Her husband Hosea was a prophet of God. Because of the agony he experienced as the result of his wife's liaisons with several lovers, he was able to understand God's sorrow over the wayward nation of Israel.

Their marriage resulted in three children (Hosea 1), but evidently Gomer was not satisfied with her life as a wife and mother. She sought after lovers and the gifts they could give her (2:5). She danced about in gaiety, had much food and drink, probably went from party to party, wore fancy jewelry, and forgot her husband and her marriage vows (2:13).

She had a "high time" of pleasure for awhile. But her "sweet life" turned sour suddenly when one of her lovers sold her at an auction as a slave. He had evidently tired of her and decided to use her to make some money (3:1, 2). Even in the light of her shameful actions and as she was in the depths of sin, Hosea still loved her. He bought her at the auction, brought her back home, and admonished her to be the proper wife to him. Gomer was finally humbled to realize her responsibilities and where her true happiness could be found — at home with her loving husband.

Yes, sexual immorality may be exciting and pleasurable for a time, but the depths of shame and degradation, not to mention the physical and emotional scars that such actions leave on a person, are awful prices to pay for a few moments of pleasure.

(6) Herodias was living in adultery with Herod. The fact that John the Baptist, a popular preacher, boldly made her immorality public caused her to want John's imprisonment and death (Mark 6:19). Deep down in her consciousness, she must have known of the depths of her sin. Why else would she be so enraged at a Jewish preacher? Her guilt was showing.

Herod, on the other hand, respected John and enjoyed hearing him speak (Mark 6:20). He did put him in prison to please Herodias (6:17), but he was not planning to kill him. Herodias knew Herod's weakness for pretty women and instructed her beautiful daughter to dance seductively at Herod's birthday banquet. Her scheme worked; Herod offered to give the young girl what she desired (6:22, 23). Prompted by her mother, she asked for the beheading of John the Baptist (6:24, 25). Herod realized too late that he had been manipulated; but to save face, he murdered the preacher (6:26-28).

Consider all the people whom Herodias' immoral actions touched — her former husband, Herod, her daughter, and John the Baptist — and the pain, the sorrow, and the death that she caused. There is nothing good or pretty that results from illicit sexual liaisons or sexual manipulations.

For Us. God did not put these incidents in the Bible to titillate us or to shock us but to instruct us. He is warning us of the awful results of sexual immorality and manipulation. He wants us to realize that sexual impurities are sin and selfishness, and that Christian women are to have no part with them. He expects us to control our desires and

321

remain immaculate, regardless of how polluted our environment is.

As distasteful and abhorrent as sexual impurities are, we must not forget that they are forgivable and that God is always waiting with arms outstretched to receive the repentant one. While Jesus went about His ministry, He met many sexually impure women: Samaritan woman at the well (John 4), the woman caught in adultery (John 8), and the harlot who came in off the street to wash Jesus' feet (Luke 7:36-50). In each instance, He treated the women with respect and compassion. Through His words and attitudes, they knew they were forgiven, could put their pasts behind them, and begin new lives of purity with God's blessing. We can know this same cleansing forgiveness and hope today if we repent and turn to God.

CONTROL OF THE TONGUE. Another aspect of self-control that New Testament writers stressed when speaking to women was the necessity for them to control the use of their tongues. Paul told Timothy that women must not be "malicious gossips" (*diabolos,* I Timothy 3:11) and that widows should not be "gossips and busybodies, talking about things not proper to mention" (I Timothy 5:13). In writing to Titus, Paul said the older women should not be "malicious gossips" or "slanderers" (*diabolos,* Titus 2:3).

The Greek word *diabolos* means an accuser, one who finds fault and spreads talk of it, one who uses harsh and critical words, one who gossips and spreads lies. Proverbs makes clear the harm that results from harsh words and lies:

> There are six things which the Lord hates . . . a lying tongue . . . a false witness who utters lies, and one who spreads strife among brothers (6:16, 17, 19).

He who spreads slander is a fool (10:18).

With his mouth the godless man destroys his neighbor (11:9).

He who goes about as a talebearer reveals secrets, but he who is trustworthy conceals a matter (11:13).

There is one who speaks rashly like the thrusts of a sword, but the tongue of the wise brings healing (12:18).

A harsh word stirs up anger (15:1).

A slanderer separates intimate friends (16:28).

He who repeats a matter separates intimate friends (17:9).

A fool's lips bring strife and his mouth calls for blows. A fool's mouth is his ruin and his lips the snare of his soul. The words of a whisperer are like dainty morsels and they go down into the innermost parts of the body (18:6-8).

A brother offended is harder to be won than a strong city (18:19).

Death and life are in the power of the tongue (18:21).

Do not associate with a gossip (20:19).

A lying tongue hates those it crushes, and a flattering mouth works ruin (26:28).

Harsh words cut into others like a sword into the inner parts of a person; they offend and separate friends; they cause strife and anger. Lies and gossip crush and destroy others and reveal confidences that should be kept secret. Not only are we not to gossip ourselves, we are not to associate with anyone who does; for before we know it, we would be listening and participating in the harm that gossip promotes.

James spoke clearly about the devastating power of our tongues and how difficult but necessary it is to control them:

If anyone does not stumble in what he says, he is a perfect man, able to bridle the whole body as well. Now if we put

323

the bits into the horses' mouths so that they may obey us, we direct their entire body as well. Behold the ships also, though they are so great and are driven by strong winds, are still directed by a very small rudder, wherever the inclination of the pilot desires, So also the tongue is a small part of the body, and yet it boasts of great things. Behold, how great a forest is set aflame by such a small fire! And the tongue is a fire, the very world of iniquity; the tongue is set among our members as that which defiles the entire body, and sets on fire the course of life, and is set on fire by hell (James 3:2-6).

Biblical Examples. The Bible provides us with several illustrations of the harm a woman's uncontrolled tongue caused: (1) Bitterness and strife between Hagar and Sarah (Genesis 16:1, 2, 4, 5; 21:9, 10). (2) Strife between Rachel and Leah (Genesis 30:1, 2, 14, 15). (3) Imprisonment of Joseph caused by Potiphar's wife's lie (Genesis 39:11-20). (4) Miriam was punished because of her words of bitterness and jealousy against Moses (Numbers 12). (5) Sorrow and frustration in Elkanah's home because of the strife and bitterness between his two wives (I Samuel 1:2, 6, 7). (6) Death of Naboth because of the witnesses Jezebel caused to lie about him (I Kings 21:1-14). (7) At a time when Job needed comfort and support because he had lost his wealth, children, and his health, his wife spoke harsh and bitter words against him and God (Job 2:9, 10). (8) Sapphira was punished because of her lie to God (Acts 5:1-10).

In contrast to the lack of restraint in this area of life, we also have illustrations of women who used their tongues to help others: (1) Deborah counseled and prophesied (Judges 4). (2) Ruth's words of loyalty and kindness aided Naomi (book of Ruth). (3) Abigail spoke for peace (I Samuel 25).

(4) The woman from Tekoa spoke of family love and loyalty restoring happiness to King David (II Samuel 14:1-20). (5) The woman of Abel saved a city because of her wise words (II Samuel 20:16-22). (6) Naaman's maid directed him to Elisha so he could be healed (II Kings 5:1-19). (7) Huldah spoke out for God (II Kings 22:14-20). (8) Esther saved her people with her words (book of Esther). (9) Mary and Elizabeth supported each other with words of praise (Luke 1). (10) Anna blessed others with her words from God (Luke 2:36-38). (11) The Samaritan woman led others to the Messiah with her words (John 4). (12) Priscilla instructed Apollos about Christ (Acts 18:26).

For Us. Our words reveal how righteous and self-controlled we are or how out-of-control we are. They reveal whether we are contented, happy, and peace-loving or whether we are complainers with negative attitudes and argumentative natures. Our words show whether we are wise or foolish, humble, or proud. And how we use our words reveals whether we truly love others or not.

We are not loving others if we spread their secrets or pass on rumors about them. We are not loving others if we speak harshly and critically, always emphasizing others' faults. Words spoken in haste and without thought often hurt another's feelings terribly and are difficult wounds to heal, no matter how apologetic we are.

We must realize that the devil can use our tongues to destroy and crush others' reputations and self-esteem; our tongues can even cause sickness and death. If we so hurt people that they have no desire to continue living, we have destroyed their very essence.

We must constantly be aware of the need to control ourselves in the way we speak. We cannot always control the gossip we hear, but we can control the gossip we spread. Once lying or harsh words are out of our mouths, they are out of our control and are unleashed to do their damage. We may think that passing on juicy tidbits will not hurt us, but we are digging our own pits. Friends will cease to be friends, and it will not be long before no one will trust us or have confidence in what we say. Just consider how you feel about the woman in your town who is constantly on the telephone whispering about others. She has very little respect from anyone. We don't want to fit her mold!

Instead let us concentrate on complimenting and praising others, sharing God's truths, uttering words of kindness and comfort, and showing restraint when we become angry or frustrated.

TEMPERANCE. Being temperate is another important aspect of self-control. Paul told Titus that the older women were not to be "enslaved to much wine" (Titus 2:3) which is a part of being temperate. Paul was saying, "Don't let wine rule your life." He knew that wine could become addictive and was cautioning the women against becoming a slave of the drink.

Life for women in the first century was not easy, and many of them turned to drink to relieve the pain and unhappiness with which they lived. It is likely that some of these women had become Christians, so Paul was reminding them of their witness in their community and how they could not be glorifying God if they were drunkards (Titus 2:11-13; I Timothy 3:14-16).

God makes clear to us in His Word the destructiveness of drunkenness:

Who has woe? Who has sorrow? Who has contentions? Who has complaining? Who has wounds without cause? Who has

326

redness of eyes? Those who linger long over wine, those who go to taste mixed wine. Do not look on the wine when it is red, when it sparkles in the cup, when it goes down smoothly; at the last it bites like a serpent, and stings like a viper. Your eyes will see strange things, and your mind will utter perverse things. And you will be like one who lies down in the middle of the sea, or like one who lies down on the top of a mast. They struck me, but I did not become ill; they beat me, but I did not know it. When shall I awake? I will seek another drink (Proverbs 23:29-35).

It results in sorrow, strife, loss of physical and mental health, destroys one's appearance, and is responsible for uncontrolled words. It causes one to see things, to feel nothing, to sleep instead of work, and to feel as if he is drowning with no defense.

Other passages tell us that wine is deceiving (Proverbs 20:1), causes one to stagger (Psalm 60:3), causes one to forget and use poor judgment (Proverbs 31:4, 5; Isaiah 28:7), and is often associated with sexual impurity (Hosea 4:11). We cannot point to any specific incidents of women being drunk in the Bible, but Amos mentioned certain women whose love for drink was one of their vices:

Hear this word, you cows of Bashan who are on the mountain of Samaria, who oppress the poor, who crush the needy, who say to your husbands, "Bring now, that we may drink!" (Amos 4:1).

When used in the general sense, temperance means being restrained, alert, and watchful so as not to be over-indulgent. Paul used the word in this sense when he told Timothy that women were to be "temperate" (I Timothy 3:11).[3]

---

3. Elders, deacons, and all Christians were admonished to be temperate: I Timothy 3:2; Titus 1:7, 8; II Peter 1:5; Romans 14:21; Ephesians 5:18.

Proverbs also speaks of other types of intemperance (other than drunkenness):

> Do not be with heavy drinkers of wine, or with gluttonous eaters of meat; for the heavy drinker and the glutton will come to poverty, and drowsiness will clothe a man with rags (Proverbs 23:20, 21).

Paul warned that we should not make provisions for the flesh or fulfill its lusts, meaning we should not be over-indulgent (Romans 13:14), and said that if we control ourselves we will be temperate (I Corinthians 9:25). He said we must bring our bodies into subjection (I Corinthians 9:27), and we should be known for our moderation (Philippians 4:5).

For Us. We live in a fast-paced, affluent, and competitive society that causes us to be afflicted by pressures, frustrations, confusion, and insecurities. The world's cure for these maladies is often over-indulgence and selfishness. We are told to fulfill all our desires, to partake of all the world's pleasures, and to do whatever feels good so the pain of living will go away. Often we over-indulge in pleasures in order to block out the confusion and the insecurity, in order to relax from tension, or in order to cover up our frustrations.

As women seek to compete with men in the career world, they find that they are facing more pressures and tension. They have guilt feelings about leaving their children in the care of others while they work outside the home. They worry about whether they can really "make it" in an outside job. Women who choose to remain full-time homemakers are sometimes confused and frustrated when other women treat them as uninteresting or inferior. Many women are afraid that they cannot measure up to the "superwoman" image that is being promoted today — the woman who has a family, a career, is a community activist, is involved in church, and is a beauty queen — all rolled into one.

328

To escape these realities or to help release the tensions, some women (an alarmingly increasing number) turn to alcohol, drugs (uppers, downers, sleeping pills, etc.), and/or cigarettes. They become addicted to these crutches which they feel are helping them to cope. Some women begin drinking socially to "fit in" with the crowd at work and to build up their confidence in themselves or begin smoking to relieve their nervousness.

Since women are surrounded by food daily, are usually responsible for buying it and preparing it, and consider it a more acceptable way to release tension and cover up insecurities, many turn to over-eating. They feel inadequacies gnawing away at them on the inside; so they eat, hoping the pains will go away. And they fool themselves into thinking that unlike alcohol and cigarettes, food is good for them. Many have to have food in their mouths constantly and encourage everyone around them to eat also. Their conversations revolve around food; their social activities revolve around food; they even dream about food.

Then there are other women who are bored, confused, or lacking self-esteem who become addicted to spending money. Their every waking thought is about what they want to buy next. They shop almost everyday and cannot turn away from a sale. Their conversation is only about what they bought or what they plan to buy.

Still other women become over-involved in order to shut out their thoughts of confusion and frustration. They become ultra-busy with community, church, and/or career activities. They are going from early morning till late at night. They become physically drained. They become irritable and defensive. They become so heavily scheduled that they can never find the time to relax, to talk with their family members, or to even take a leisurely walk.

All of these over-indulgences can become serious addictions and can become the masters over our lives. We can become just as much a slave to "busyness" or "food" as we can to drink. Our appetites for these things are good; but when they become uncontrolled and used selfishly, we can never be satisfied or fulfilled. We will always be wanting more and more. Soon all of our time and energies will be expended on temporary, material things or pursuits.

Certainly Christian women are not immune to the tensions and pressures of daily living; neither are they immune from the tendencies to over-indulge. It is as James warned us: "But each one is tempted when he is carried away and enticed by his own lust. Then when lust has conceived, it gives birth to sin; and when sin is accomplished, it brings forth death" (James 1:14, 15).

The fight against over-indulgence is a constant one, but it is a battle that we can win. We must remain alert to the pressures and temptations. We must exercise control and caution. We must remember that our confidence and security rest in God, not in the transitory things of the world. Our reality rests in our hope and trust in a loving Father and a compassionate Savior; we need no crutches to help us escape. We have the strength of the Holy Spirit within us to help us control our desires and appetites so they can be used for constructive purposes. We must be determined not to become slaves to bad habits or unrestrained appetites that can destroy us.

OUTWARD APPEARANCE. Another aspect of self-control is in the way a woman dresses and adorns herself. Paul wrote to Timothy:

> Likewise I want women to adorn themselves with proper clothing, modestly and discreetly, not with braided hair and gold or pearls or costly garments (I Timothy 2:9).

330

In the Greek, "proper" (*kosmios*) meant orderly or decent; "modest" (*aidos*) meant refraining from doing anything unworthy; "discreet" (*sophrosune*) meant coming from wisdom, using good judgment. Paul was not saying that Christian women must be "plain Janes," or be sheepish and shy, or that they are never to be attractive physically. He was speaking of their inner qualities — their strength of character, their inner self-government, their restraint from fulfilling selfish desires — that would be seen in their attitudes (2:10, 11) and in the way they presented themselves outwardly as witnesses of Christ in public.

In the context of wives being submissive to their husbands and to God, Peter told the women: "And let not your adornment be external only — braiding the hair and wearing gold jewelry, and putting on dresses; but let it be the hidden person of the heart . . ." (I Peter 3:3). Such an attitude of modesty would proceed from humility and a controlled life (3:1-3). Peter was not saying women were not to be concerned about their appearance (notice the presence of the word "only"). It is not sinful to fix one's hair, wear jewelry, or wear pretty clothes. But he was saying, "Be sure your inner character is more important to you and takes more of your time and energy than your physical body. Don't allow the way you look and what you wear to become a top priority in your life."

According to secular histories of that time, women were spending hours on elaborate hair-dos, weaving jewels into their braids, and trying to outdo one another in the clothing they wore. They tried to have the most expensive, the most colorful, or the most unusual dress. Paul and Peter were telling the Christian women to not be sucked into these types of pursuits and to not seek to draw attention to themselves.

331

Putting it simply, they were telling the women to use good sense, not to go to extremes, and to have the right priorities.

The Bible very seldom went into detail about a woman's outward appearance or her efforts in that area. Some women were called beautiful: Sarah (Genesis 12:11), Rachel (29:17), Abigail (I Samuel 25:3), Bathsheba (II Samuel 11:2), Tamar (II Samuel 14:27), Abishag (I Kings 1:3, 4), Esther (Esther 2:7), the wife in the Song of Solomon (1:15, 16; 4:1-7), and evidently brides adorned themselves for their weddings (Isaiah 61:10; Revelation 21:2). We read of Jezebel who painted her eyes and adorned her head when she heard that Jehu had come to town and that he was seeking to kill her. Perhaps she knew that her death was near and wanted to look her best, or perhaps she thought Jehu might change his mind if he saw her attired and adorned as a queen (II Kings 9:30-35). Nowhere do we read that women are not to try to look attractive, unless they are doing it for evil reasons as with the adulteress in Proverbs (6:24, 25; 7:5-27) or letting their personal adornment become a matter of pride or a consuming passion.

For Us. Living in such a materialistic culture where we are bombarded constantly with the idea that we are to buy things in order to make ourselves look better and smell better and with the philosophy that a woman's worth is found in her youth and beauty, it is very tempting — even for Christian women — to spend too much time, thought, and money on physical appearance. Some women even pride themselves on their new hair-dos and new clothes and love to show them off to the others at church. It is important that we are clean, that we smell good, and that we look attractive, but we must restrain ourselves from making these earthly things more important than spiritual considerations.

Which is more important—having a huge wardrobe of fancy clothes or helping a Christian sister who is in need? Which is more important—getting a new hair-do or using the time and money to take your child on an outing? Do we spend as much time in Bible study and prayer as we do on our hair, our nails, our make-up, and our clothes? It is not that we are not to be concerned about our looks—we are; it is important for our witness in this looks-conscious society. But we must be aware of how much these physical aspects mean to us and not yield to the temptation to make them more important than our relationships with others or with God. Our behavior and how we spend our time and our money will show where our values lie. Be careful!

Good Works

In addition to being humble, faithful, discerning, and self-controlled, we are to be known for our good works. Paul said a woman should be doing good works instead of becoming overly concerned about her appearance (I Timothy 2:9, 10). He said an older widow should have a "reputation for good works" and "devote herself to every good work" if she were to be put on the list of widows who were to receive special help or do a special work in the church (I Timothy 5:10). He told Titus to have the older women teach the younger how to do good (Titus 2:3).

Good works are seeable actions that proceed from an attitude and mind-set of *agape*-love—the love that seeks the well-being of all others, whether we receive anything in return or not. But what specific activities does the term "good works" include? Considering all the references to the work of Christian women in other than leadership roles, "good works" can be listed in three categories: (1) work at home, (2) hospitality to others, (3) and benevolence.

AT HOME. Some would scoff at the idea that the work of a wife and mother was considered by God to be a good work. But God has never thought that working at home was to be just a by-line, something a woman does on the side. He truly desires for it to be the full-time job of most women, for He knows the majority of women were created for this work and find their fulfillment in it.

When instructing Timothy about older widows who are to be put on "the list," Paul mentioned that they should have "been the wife of one man . . . brought up children" (I Timothy 5:9b, 10) in the same breath that he spoke of good works. When giving instructions about the younger widows, Paul thought it best that they "get married, bear children, keep house" so they would not become idle busybodies and so they would not cause reproach to come upon Christ because of their witness (5:13b, 14). He also told the older women to teach the young women to "love" their husbands and children with a particularly warm affection, be submissive to their husbands, and be "workers at home" (*oikourgos*, Titus 2:4, 5). Paul was not saying that working at home as a wife and mother was *all* that a woman could or should do, but he was making the point that it is a good, desirable, and honorable work to do for the Lord.

The Greek word for "workers" (*oikourgos*) literally means "keeper," one who protects, preserves, and watches. As we have already studied (in Chapters Six and Seven), the responsibilities of wives and mothers are very serious and demanding. All that a woman does in these capacities is with a view to keeping her home as a happy and peaceful environment for her husband and children so they can function as God desires for them to. It is definitely a protection and a haven that she provides.

Such an emphasis on home responsibilities is consistent with all of Scripture. God's Word definitely makes clear to us that a married woman's home and family are to be her first priority, both through the examples of godly women (such as Sarah, Jochebed, Abigail, Hannah, Mary, Elizabeth, etc.) and through the direct teaching of the Law, Proverbs 31:10ff., and the New Testament epistles.

For Us. The work of wives and mothers has pretty well been dragged through the mud in our nation in the past few years. In some circles, it is not even considered "work." A housewife is pictured as an overweight slob eating candy and watching television all day. She is considered to be a passive leech who wears curlers in her hair, yells at the kids, and expects her husband to take care of her while she does nothing.

Some of those who consider a wife and mother's position as involving work say it is only menial labor fit for slaves, not for women of intelligence, character, and ambition. They say it is a boring, tasteless, and never-ending job. Many call it being "chained to a stove or to a mop handle." With such ideas floating around freely, it is no wonder that many housewives and mothers who had been happy and fulfilled are now beginning to doubt their own value, are wondering if they have been missing out on real life, and are suddenly dissatisfied and ashamed to admit that they "don't work anywhere."

God's view is so different from the present world view. He considers the home to be a woman's highest calling and should be listed among those things that are considered as "good works" of a Christian woman. There is certainly no reason for a woman to be ashamed of being a wife and mother, for in God's view she is to be honored and praised. Perhaps we wives and mothers need to remind ourselves often of our great and awesome responsibility before God and never allow the world's view to intrude on our thoughts about what we know to be an honorable and noble profession.

Perhaps we should take time to consider for a moment what all is involved in being a wife and mother. We serve as paramedics and nurses. We are teachers and counsellors. We are interior decorators, fashion designers and/or consultants, seamstresses, housekeepers, cooks, and caterers. We are hairdressers, administrators of budgets and schedules, cosmetologists, and laundresses. We are chauffeurs and sometimes plumbers and electricians. We may be house painters and gardeners. We may mow lawns and take out the garbage. We care for sick dogs and help bury the dead turtle. We are public relations agents. We are bookkeepers and accountants. We are buyers and sellers. We can organize fund drives, bake sales, and community clubs. We can run a scout pack, coach ball teams, and even move whole households across the country. On and on the list could go. There is really no more varied, time-consuming, and energy-consuming job. And very few works can compete with it for its importance and necessity. So pick up your chins — we are greatly privileged!

HOSPITALITY TO OTHERS. Paul said the older widows should have "shown hospitality to strangers" and "washed the saints' feet" (I Timothy 5:10). This referred to receiving people in one's home, washing their feet of the dust from the streets, and giving them food and lodging. It would include a willingness to be unselfish and share one's material blessings with others. The duty of hospitality was stressed by Jesus when He sent out His disciples:

> And into whatever city or village you enter, inquire who is worthy in it; and abide there until you go away. And as you enter the house, give it your greeting, and if the house is worthy, let your greeting of peace come upon it; but if it is not worthy, let your greeting of peace return to you. And whoever does not receive you, nor heed your words, as you go out of that house or that city, shake off the dust of your feet. Truly I say to you, it will be more tolerable for the land of Sodom and Gomorrah in the day of judgment, than for that city (Matthew 10:11-15).

It was also stressed many times in the epistles:

> Contributing to the needs of the saints, practicing hospitality (Romans 12:13).

> An overseer, then, must be above reproach, the husband of one wife, temperate, prudent, respectable, hospitable, able to teach (I Timothy 3:2).

> For the overseer must be . . . hospitable, . . . (Titus 1:7, 8).

> Let love of the brethren continue. Do not neglect to show hospitality to strangers, for by this some have entertained angels without knowing it (Hebrews 13:1, 2).

Be hospitable to one another without complaint (I Peter 4:9). And, of course, hospitality would greatly affect the women of a household because they would prepare the food and get the beds ready.

Biblical Examples. The Bible abounds with examples of hospitality because it was a common custom in those times. A woman knew that entertaining overnight guests was her duty and would probably happen often. We must remember that there were no motels or hotels every few miles then as there are today. The few inns they did have were noisy, violent places, known for their drunken clientele. The majority of people walked from place to place, so travel was not fast and was quite tiring.

We remember how hospitable Abraham and Sarah were to the spokesmen from God (Genesis 18), and we cannot forget Rahab who risked her own life to provide lodging for the Israelite spies (Joshua 2:1-16). The widow of Zarephath, even though she was at the "end of her ropes," unselfishly shared with Elijah who was in need of food and lodging (I Kings 17:10-24). The woman of Shunem prepared a special room in her home for Elisha to stay in whenever he was in that city (II Kings 4:8).

We must also note Peter's mother-in-law's eager desire to serve guests in her home, even though she had been sick (Matthew 8:14, 15); Mary and Martha of Bethany who opened their home to Jesus and His disciples many times (Luke 10:38ff.; John 12:1ff.); Mary, the mother of Mark, who opened her home for a prayer meeting (Acts 12:12); Lydia, who besought Paul and his company to stay in her home and also hosted the church meetings in Philippi (Acts 16:15, 40); Priscilla who had church meetings in her home and was hospitable to Paul (Acts 18:1-3; Romans 16:3-5; I Corinthians 16:19); and Nympha who had a church in her home (Colossians 4:15). Each of these women was blessed by God for her unselfishness shown in hospitality.

For Us. Was hospitality just for those people of the Bible times because of their culture? Surely, there is no need today with our speed and frequency of travel and the abundance of public lodging places! Since we wear shoes and have paved roads, there is probably no need for us to be washing the feet of others. However, there is a great need to restore hospitality and the humble service to others that washing the feet signifies. Hospitality has almost become a lost art in our culture, and it is to our detriment as Christians.

Our society today is greatly impersonal. We are parts of groups, not individuals. We are numbers, not persons. We are treated as just another body in the line or on the list. The church, however, should counteract this depersonalization by engendering close fellowship, concern, and caring for one another. The church should be the one place where a person feels like a person of value. There is no better way to engender such closeness and caring than through hospitality. Through opening our homes and sharing with Christians in a meal, fellowship is greatly enhanced. There is no better way to help a visiting evangelist or a traveling missionary than to give them food and lodging. There is no better way to foster friendships than to share one's home with those in temporary need.

Of course, there is work and sacrifice involved. The house must be cleaned, the meals cooked, schedules organized, the bed linens washed, etc. It truly is an act of lowly service, but it is often repaid with newly made friendships, warm feelings, and gratitude from one Christian to another. And we must know surely that God will bless us in our unselfishness. Peter's admonition that we should be hospitable "without complaint" (I Peter 4:9) is so timely and appropriate. Humble service means we will not be griping and complaining about having people in our homes; for no matter how much we smile, the guests will sense they are not truly welcome and then the whole point of being hospitable will be lost.

Of course, as with everything else, we must be hospitable in moderation. Constantly having others in one's home would be very disruptive to family life and leave one devastated—financially, physically, and emotionally. As months

339

go by and more and more people are coming, bitterness and resentment will take over one's life instead of the spirit of giving and serving. So we must be sensible and not go to extremes. We must seek to spread the joys (and work) of hospitality to all the members of the church family.

Many women offer excuses about the condition of their homes or their lack of cooking ability in order to by-pass the service of hospitality. There are a few exceptions to the following rule; but as a whole, people expect only a clean bed and a little food. They do not expect elaborate meals or a private room and bath. They do not expect fancy furnishings or great entertainment. They are usually most grateful simply to share what you have; they don't expect you to clean all week or cook all day for them.

BENEVOLENCE. Benevolence refers to doing kind and gracious deeds for others. Paul mentioned "assisting those in distress" (I Timothy 5:10) and being "kind" (Titus 2:5, *agathos,* which meant in Greek doing good and generous deeds) when speaking about important works of women. "Distress" referred to those who were suffering.

Jesus referred to benevolence when He talked about feeding the hungry, giving drink to the thirsty, clothing the naked, helping the sick, and visiting those in prison (Matthew 25:35, 36) and made clear how important such good deeds are to God. James also stressed the need for the *action* of benevolence when he said:

> If a brother or sister is without clothing and in need of daily food, and one of you says to them, "Go in peace, be warmed and be filled," and yet you do not give them what is necessary for their body, what use is that? (James 2:15, 16).

Biblical Examples. (1) We cannot forget Ruth when we think of kindness and good works, for she reached out to

340

Naomi who was in distress. Naomi had lost her husband and sons and was feeling sorry for herself. She was depressed, had a very negative outlook, and allowed her circumstances to control her (Ruth 1:19-22). Even though Naomi thought she wanted to be left alone in her bitterness, Ruth knew that she needed help and refused to leave her. She looked beyond Naomi's words and selfish attitude and saw her real needs. She wasted no time in going out to work to get food for them (Ruth 2:1-3). Before long Naomi's spirits lifted and she began to see the positive side of life. She anxiously asked Ruth about Ruth's work in the fields and was exuberant about her meeting Boaz (2:19-23). Because of Ruth, Naomi found her life worth living again.

(2) The wife and mother of Proverbs 31 was also benevolent: "extends her hand to the poor; and she stretches out her hands to the needy" (v. 20). (3) Dorcas, who was brought back to life by Peter, was "abounding with deeds of kindness and charity, which she continually did" (Acts 9:36). When Peter arrived after her death, the room was filled with weeping widows who showed all the garments that Dorcas had made for them (9:39).

For Us. The needs that Christian women can meet are as varied as the individuals around us. Our main task is to be alert, to be ready to see what is needed, and be caring enough to use our abilities to meet the needs. Opportunities to serve will arise in the natural course of living; we must be ready and willing to seize them and use them to Christ's glory.

The neighbor may need a baby-sitter; the people down the street may need clothing; the elderly man across town may need a hot meal. The sick may need a visit or a meal or help with the laundry. The family may need some meals brought in while the mother is in the hospital. The widow may need her house painted or lawn mowed. The new family in town may need a friend and a smiling welcome. The young divorcee may need financial aid; the widower may need help with the children. The young child may need a hug and a kind word. People's needs abound, and so should our giving, serving natures.

Dignified Behavior

The woman who develops all the characteristics thus far mentioned will have a godly character which will be displayed in her dignified behavior. Peter said respectful behavior was expected of women (I Peter 3:2). Paul mentioned that this type of behavior should emanate from women:[4] (1) "as befits women making a claim to godliness" (I Timothy 2:10); (2) "Women must likewise be dignified" (I Timothy 3:11); (3) "older women likewise are to be reverent in their behavior" (Titus 2:3).

The Greek word for "dignified" (*semnos*) referred to observable conduct that was honorable and worthy of respect. It is behavior that is above reproach. It means that others see how the Christian woman acts and reacts in various situations and realizes that she is a good example, an upright citizen of the community, one who has a spotless reputation, and one who deserves the highest respect. She will be courteous and respectful of others' rights and authority. She will not be "bad mouthing" others or breaking laws. She will always seek to "build up" rather than "tear down."

---

4. Also applied to elders (I Timothy 3:2, Titus 1:6), older men (Titus 2:2), deacons (I Timothy 3:8), and all believers (II Timothy 2:2).

342

When a woman develops the proper inner qualities, thought-patterns, and attitudes, her behavior will show it. What she is on the inside will show on the outside. Dignified behavior is, in essence, the "topping" on the woman's character, the "roof" atop the building blocks, or the "icing" on top of the basic ingredients.

When we think of Sarah, Deborah, Ruth, Hannah, Abigail, Esther, the wife of Proverbs 31, Mary, Elizabeth, Anna, Mary and Martha, Eunice and Lois, Priscilla, etc., we automatically think of how they followed in God's way and how respected they have been all throughout history. Each woman could have been called dignified as she fulfilled her responsibilities as God's woman.

For Us. We can test our success in developing the Christian character that God wishes for us to have by considering what our image is in our homes, our churches, and our communities:

1. Do your husband and your children respect you and consider you to be a person of high value?

2. Do the people of the church and community consider you to be a good citizen of high moral character?

3. Do people come to you for advice about spiritual matters?

4. Does your husband trust you with his money and have confidence in your ideas?

5. Does your husband have full confidence that you are and always will be faithful to him?

6. Do your children know that you keep your promises?

7. Does your employer have full confidence in your abilities and trust that you will be honest and pure?

8. Do the people of the church know you will carry through with your commitments?

9. Do they consider you a good example for the youth?

Of course, it is possible to fool the people of the church and the community about your real motives and your true inner feelings. You may have some secret, hidden sins. It is harder to fool your family, but it can be done. But it is impossible to fool God. He will know of a surety if your inside character corresponds to your outer behavior.

God's Woman — A Wise Woman

The woman who continually seeks to develop these attributes of character and to practice these behavior patterns would be called from God's vocabulary — a woman full of wisdom. This is the "wisdom from above" that James spoke of, not the wisdom from the world: "But the wisdom from above is first pure, then peaceable, gentle, reasonable, full of mercy and good fruits, unwavering, without hypocrisy" (James 3:17). Notice that the qualities that James listed are the ones that we have considered in his chapter — purity, humility, discernment, doing good works, etc.

Proverbs also makes clear to us what a person of wisdom is like. Notice how these qualities are similar to the ones we have studied: (1) A wise person seeks knowledge and wants to increase in learning (discernment, Proverbs 1:5; 18:15). (2) A wise person will listen to others' advice (humility 1:5; 9:9; 12:15; 15:14). (3) A wise person spreads knowledge and good things (good works, 15:7; 16:23). (4) A wise person understands and appreciates rebukes and discipline (humility, discernment, and self-control, 9:8; 12:1; 15:31; 17:10; 19:25). (5) A wise person is understanding and sensitive, not believing all he or she hears (discernment, 10:13; 14:15). (6) A wise person knows that wisdom comes from the Lord, from respecting Him, and from obeying His commands (humility, faithfulness, self-control, and dignified behavior, 1:7; 2:6; 9:10; 10:8; 15:32). (7) A wise person is humble (humility, 11:2). (8) A wise person shows restraint in every area of life (self-control, 10:19; 17:27, 28). (9) A wise person seeks peace (humility, 15:14). (10) A wise person is cautious and keeps away from evil (self-control, 14:16; 22:3). (11) A wise person will feel secure and confident (faithfulness, 3:21-26; 4:6).

The truly wise woman is the one who follows in God's way and learns from His Word. She is promised that joy and peace will be the results of such a life (Galatians 5:22, 23). There is no need for us to seek for happiness and fulfillment in any other place than what God has made clear to us in His Word—in His will, in His life-style, the same will and life-style that Jesus revealed to us through His example and teachings.

Summary

The following points have been stressed in this chapter: The *Foundational* Qualities of God's Women's Characters:

a. Humility, which is characterized by a gentle, peaceable, submissive spirit.

b. Faithfulness, which is maintaining loyalty to God both in the good and in the tough times.

The Important *Building Blocks* of God's Women's Characters:

c. Discernment, which refers to understanding, sensitivity, and a soundness of mind.

d. Self-control, which includes purity, control of the tongue, temperance, and modest outward appearance.

e. Doing good works from a heart filled with *agape*.

The *Topping* of God's Women's Characters:

   f. Dignified behavior, which signifies conduct that is worthy of the highest respect and emanates from a godly character.

The Overall *Result:* A WISE WOMAN

DISCUSSION QUESTIONS:

1. How do the view of the world and the view of God differ in respect to the meaning of greatness? To the meaning of humility?

2. Why do you think the author discussed the quality of submission under the topic of humility?

3. List the problems that can result in a church if the quality of humility is not lived out (see I Corinthians).

4. Some say that humility shows you have no self-esteem. What do you think?

5. Define these terms: belief, faith, trust, obedience. Differentiate between each and then show how they are related.

6. Relate the parable of the wise and foolish man that Jesus told in Matthew 7:24-27 to the results of faithfulness as discussed in this chapter.

7. Discuss the meaning of these statements: "Faith is not a happiness pill that leads to instant happiness. It is not a quick and easy road to peace. It is not like a Valium that takes away the pain of living."

8. Develop your own plan for mental improvement for the next month. Be specific and indicate the time budgeted for each activity. Share with the class.

9. Why should a Christian's mental improvement be closely tied in with his/her spiritual growth in order to develop discernment?

346

10. What can you change in your habits right now to promote the quality of purity in your character?

11. Discuss how women today sexually manipulate men and vice versa.

12. Relate some of your own experiences concerning how words hurt a person's self-esteem.

13. List all the forms of over-indulgence that are prevalent today. Why do you think people become slaves to these habits?

14. List the guiding principles that we should abide by in deciding how we should dress or adorn ourselves.

15. Illustrate how culture determines what *modest* apparel or appearance· is.

16. List all the reasons why being a homemaker is to be considered a "good work."

17. Why do you think hospitality is important? Is it a lost art in your church?

18. What can you or your class do to reinstate hospitality in your church family?

19. Make a list of the benevolent things you did last week. Then make a list of what benevolence you plan to do next week.

20. What questions would you add to the list that evaluates whether your behavior is dignified or not (p. 343)?

21. Summarize what is meant by "wisdom" (from God's view).

Chapter Ten

BECOMING GOD'S WOMEN

According to the Scriptures, God desires for a woman to be an upright, fulfilled person, a person who truly "has it all together," and a person who has God's type of wisdom. And He fully expects her to become that kind of person.

But as each woman evaluates her own life, she sees her many weaknesses and failures. She realizes that her character has many blemishes upon it: she is not always submissive to her husband when she should be. She passes on gossip. She may have lustful thoughts about her neighbor's husband. She does not always *want* to be a wife and mother. Sometimes she thinks only of her own needs. Many times she is thoughtless and careless about others' feelings. She complains and nags at times. She is irritable and grouchy sometimes. It is not difficult to understand why a woman might say, "There is no way I can ever be the way God wants me to be. I just don't have the control or the strength."

God replies, "THERE IS A WAY!" God has clearly outlined in His Word the way for every person to become fully *His* person; consequently, every woman can become *His* woman.

The First Step

In order to become fully mature women and be *His*, we must first become His children. Become a child to become mature? Sounds paradoxical, but it is true. We become as children and surrender our wills, our minds, and our hearts to God. We must give up our selfish desires or what we want for ourselves to become His. We must be willing to revert to childlikeness, in that our minds and hearts will be open and teachable. We will be ready to receive God's ideas and feelings and be ready to fully trust that God's way is best for us, just as a child trusts that his parents know what is best for him and are teaching him properly. We must be humble, realizing that we are not such "hot stuff," that by ourselves we are nothing, and that we need God's guidance.

The Actions

But what do we do specifically to become a child of God spiritually? There are many examples of men and women in the Bible that show us what we are to do. By considering the first instance of those who became Christians in the first century (in Acts 2), we can derive a number of consecutive steps to becoming a child of God:

(1) They heard the presentation of the gospel, the declaration that Jesus is the Son of God (Acts 2:14; Romans 10:14).

(2) They believed what they heard. They believed in God's power and in Jesus' Sonship (Acts 2:36). They received Peter's words, which were a communication from God.

(3) They were ready to act upon their belief. They were pierced to the heart (2:37); they realized their own feelings and were sorry for their wrongs. They wanted to change their lives. They were ready to surrender to God. They asked, "What shall we do?" (2:37).

(4) They were told that they must repent (Acts 2:38). They must be fully determined to turn away from the world and turn to God.

(5) Then to show their belief, their commitment, their decision to surrender and repent, they were told to be baptized (2:38). In that baptism, they would die to their old way of

living and be raised to walk in a newness of life (Romans 6:3, 4).

(6) The people in Jerusalem who heard Peter that day took the appropriate action (repentance, baptism, Acts 2:41). Then they began participating in the Christian way of life: "And they were continually devoting themselves to the apostles' teaching and to fellowship, to the breaking of bread and to prayer" (Acts 2:42). They shared their lives (even their possessions) fully with each other and praised God (2:44-47) in their living day by day.

These people became children of God by receiving Jesus and by believing in Him as God's Son (John 1:12; I John 5:1, 2). They repented of their wrongs and were baptized. Then God adopted them, and they became His children, His heirs, and fellow-heirs with Christ (Romans 8:14-17; Galatians 3:29; 4:5-7). They began a new life as spiritual babies (John 3:3-7; I Corinthians 3:1).

These basic steps were repeated in each recorded conversion of a person to Christianity. As we read of the Ethiopian eunuch (Acts 8:27-39); Saul (9:1-22); Cornelius (10); Lydia (16:13-15), and the Philippian jailer (16:25-34), we can note that they all heard and believed in Jesus, decided to change their lives, were baptized, and became involved in the Christian life either in rejoicing and/or in doing good deeds and/or witnessing to others.

We must emphasize that as these people became children of God, they did not become spiritually mature instantly. They still had faults and weaknesses. Just as it takes a long time for a physical baby to grow to maturity, it takes time for a spiritual baby to fully become God's person. Part of being a child both physically and spiritually is being beset with selfishness, having doubts, worrying about one's behavior, being defensive, being resentful, etc. But as the

350

days go by, the child learns what is right and wrong. And if the spiritual babe truly seeks to become God's person, he will grow (Ephesians 4:14, 15). He will not remain a spiritual infant. He will be constantly aiming toward the goal of spiritual maturity (Philippians 3:12-16; I Peter 2:2).

The Gifts

Two things do happen instantly, however, when we become children of God — we receive forgiveness of sin and the gift of the Holy Spirit (Acts 2:38). Because of Jesus' death and sacrifice and in the shedding of His blood, God completely wipes out of His memory all of our past sins when we accept what Jesus has done for us. Our spiritual lives are truly new. It is as if we had never sinned. The slate is wiped clean. Our old way of life is emptied out of the bowl of our characters. It is as if we begin life again with a fresh page. But God does not leave us as *empty* bowls or as *blank* pages. He fills us with the capacity and the strength for a new way of life. He fills us with the Holy Spirit, who is His very presence.

God's presence came to earth in the form of man (John 1:14); He was called Jesus, and He explained God to man through His words and actions (John 1:18). When His time on earth was over, He went back to heaven. To take His place, so mankind would not be left without a help and guide, God sent another form of His presence, His Spirit. This Spirit — God's own character — lives within each child of God. The Spirit is not a mysterious whiff of wind, but He is a real presence within us.

The Holy Spirit is a precious gift from God to His children, but what does the Holy Spirit do besides fill us for our new

351

life? The Holy Spirit is a magnificent gift; let us consider what the Scripture says about what He does:

(1) The Holy Spirit was promised to be a helper and a comforter to the apostles, would guide them into all truth, and would teach them all things (John 14:17; 15:26; 16:14; 14:26). Inspired by the Spirit, these apostles wrote the New Testament (all those who wrote the rest of the Bible were also inspired by this same Spirit, II Timothy 3:16, 17).

(2) The Holy Spirit abides and dwells within us (I Corinthians 3:16, 17; 6:19; II Corinthians 6:16-18; Ephesians 2:22; II Timothy 1:14; James 4:5).

(3) The Holy Spirit enables the love of God to pour forth in our hearts (Romans 5:5).

(4) The Holy Spirit gives us life and leads us to righteousness (Romans 8:11-13).

(5) The Holy Spirit bears witness that we are children of God and adopted as sons (Romans 8:16; Galatians 4:5-7).

(6) The Holy Spirit helps us in our weakness, interceding before God with groanings (Romans 8:26).

(7) The Holy Spirit enables us to abound in hope (Romans 15:13).

(8) The Holy Spirit sanctifies us; that is, He sets us aside to pure living (Romans 15:16; I Thessalonians 4:3-7; I Peter 1:2).

(9) The Holy Spirit gives us the power to witness and speak for Christ (Romans 15:19).

(10) The Holy Spirit enables us to know the thoughts of God (I Corinthians 2:10, 11).

(11) The Holy Spirit justifies us, makes us righteous before God (I Corinthians 6:11).

(12) The Holy Spirit gives us individual gifts (abilities) which enable us to work in unity for the building up of the church (I Corinthians 12; Ephesians 4).

(13) The Holy Spirit is God's pledge and seal to us that we are heirs and will receive our inheritance (heaven, eternal life, II Corinthians 1:22; 5:5; Ephesians 1:13; 4:30).

(14) The Holy Spirit gives us liberty (II Corinthians 3:17).

(15) The Holy Spirit strengthens us with power (Ephesians 3:16).

(16) The Holy Spirit makes us new persons, renews us (Titus 3:5).

(17) The Holy Spirit enables us to turn away from the world and its temptations (Galatians 5:16) and to live for God continuously (Galatians 5:22, 23).

(18) The Holy Spirit enables us to abide in Jesus — in His love, in His words, and in His way of life (I John 4:13).

God certainly knows what we need to start out on the right foot and to grow properly; that is why He makes available to us the forgiveness for our sins and the presence of the Holy Spirit when we become His children. Having received these precious gifts, we can proceed to live a new life. Our lives can be changed. The following chart helps us to fully realize how our lives change after we become children of God:

BEFORE	AFTER
1. We were enemies of God	Now we are reconciled, made to be friends with God (II Corinthians 5:18; Colossians 1:21, 22; Romans 5:10).
2. We were slaves to sin	Now we are slaves of righteousness (Romans 6:6, 18).
3. We were dead in sin	Now we are alive in Christ Jesus and walking in a new life (Romans 6:4, 6, 11; Ephesians 2:5; Colossians 2:13).

4. We lived in darkness and did
deeds of darkness . . . . Now we have put on light, live in the light of the Lord, and walk in the light (Romans 13:12; Colossians 1:13; Ephesians 5:8; I John 1:6, 7; 2:8-11).

5. We were not a part of the
family of God . . . . Now we are sons and heirs of God (Galatians 4:6, 7).

6. We were under the Law . . . . . . Now we are led by the Holy Spirit (Galatians 5:18).

7. We were separated and far
off from God. . . . . Now we are brought near to God and united to Him in peace (Ephesians 2:12-14).

8. We were strangers and aliens. . . Now we are fellow citizens (Ephesians 2:19).

9. We lived in the old way, a life
of deceit and lust. . . . . Now we are renewed in our minds and have put on new selves (Ephesians 4:22-24; II Corinthians 5:17).

The Second Step

Now that we have become children of God and have begun living a new life, the most difficult step lies ahead — maintaining the Christian life, the actual day-to-day practice of living righteously (I John 2:29; 3:9, 10).

Just as we are not forced to become a child of God — it is a decision we must make with our minds and then fulfill it in the obedience of our wills — neither are we forced to maintain our status as God's children. We can decide at any time to turn our backs on God and go back to our old way of living. The Holy Spirit comes to reside in us upon our invitation at baptism, but He does not instantly and automatically take us over. He gives us strength and guidance only as we allow Him to. We are not puppets being manipulated by an unseen entity within us. We are still in control of our minds and wills. Of course, it would be easier for God if we were machines, and He could just push our buttons to make us live righteously. But that is not God's way. He wants us to choose of our own free will to live as His person. God does warn us however about what will happen if after becoming children we turn away from Him:

> For if after they have escaped the defilements of the world by the knowledge of the Lord and Savior Jesus Christ, they are again entangled in them and are overcome, the last state has become worse for them than the first. For it would be better for them not to have known the way of righteousness, than having known it, to turn away from the holy commandment delivered to them. It has happened to them according to the true proverb, "a dog returns to its own vomit," and, "a sow, after washing, returns to wallowing in the mire" (II Peter 2:20-22).

God has set up the goal we are to reach—maturity in Christ (Ephesians 4:13-15). He has provided us with a helper and guide—the Holy Spirit (through His presence and the Word)—but only we ourselves can decide how our future will be. Our own growth and development is greatly aided by God's Spirit within us and by our study of the Word, but only we ourselves can have the determination to live out the Christian life daily.

How Do We Do It?

(1) Before we can faithfully maintain a life of righteousness, we must fully realize what such a life entails. We must have in our minds a clear picture of our goal.

355

In the past chapters, we have studied about God's way of living and what kind of persons we need to be. We know that our ways are to be different from the ways of the world. We know that we are to love Jesus, which is shown by keeping His Word and commandments (John 14:15, 23; 15:10; I John 2:3-6; 3:22, 23), and to abide in Jesus (remain in Him), which results in bearing fruit (John 15:2, 4; I John 2:27-29; 4:13).

Jesus' main commandment is summed up in "Love one another" (John 15:12, 17; I John 2:10, 11; 3:11, 23; 4:7, 11, 21), and the practical aspects of how we are to think, feel, and act are made clear in the Sermon on the Mount (Matthew 5-7). Paul repeated these same practical aspects of living and called them the fruit of the Spirit (Galatians 5:22, 23). In Romans 12, he gave the same practical teaching in a series of admonitions. Peter taught of similar aspects of growing as Christians:

> Now for this very reason also, applying all diligence, in your faith supply moral excellence, and in your moral excellence, knowledge; and in your knowledge, self-control, and in your self-control, perserverance, and in your perserverance, godliness, brotherly kindness, and in your brotherly kindness, Christian love. For if these qualities are yours and are increasing, they render you neither useless nor unfruitful in the true knowledge of our Lord Jesus Christ (II Peter 1:5-8).

The results of living such a life are: full, complete joy (John 15:11; 16:24); peace, not living in worry or fear (John 14:27; 16:33; Romans 5:1); having access to God's blessings (Matthew 5:3-11; John 15:7; 14:13; 16:24); being kept from stumbling (John 16:1; II Peter 1:10); being able to overcome sin and the world (I John 5:4); being secure and firm, even though troubles assault us (Matthew 7:24, 25); and entrance into heaven (II Peter 1:10, 11).

(2) Now that our goal is clearly in mind (and surely we realize the desirability of that goal), we must understand the process of growth and be convinced that we can grow and change. Maturing spiritually is a continuous process, not unlike physical maturation. It is very seldom marked by greatly dramatic or exciting events; it is usually a day-by-day moving along, learning from people and situations as we meet them. It is a slow process, often taking years; although there are periods of rapid growth spurts. We will be fooling ourselves and facing much frustration if we expect to be the "perfect" person from the time of baptism onward. We will fail many times, but it is the growth that can result from our failures that is important.

Sarah provides us with a good example of slowly growing and maturing spiritually. When God first told her of His plan for her and Abraham, her faith and trust in God was not mature. When Abraham asked her to pose as his sister, she did so, not fully realizing the strength of God to care for her. As she was approaching old age and still had no child, she got impatient and took things into her own hands. She did not fully trust God. Later when the messengers came saying she would conceive and have a child, she laughed, for she and Abraham were quite old. She was thinking as a person with the world's view, not with God's view. But when God told Abraham to sacrifice their beloved son on the altar, neither she nor Abraham wavered in their faith. God had fulfilled so many promises, and Sarah had learned through her past failures that He was a God to be fully trusted. She fully surrendered to God's will; she became spiritually mature and was praised in the Scripture (Hebrews 11:11).

We must never feel that "we are who we are" and that we cannot change. Anyone can change with the determination to do so and the help of God's Spirit. Rahab exemplifies this point well. She was a harlot (prostitute) and a Gentile. Most people would have thought she was hopelessly enmeshed in her pagan culture. But she had heard of God and His power; a seed of faith had been sown. She acted upon this faith by risking her life and protecting God's men. She asked that she and her family be spared when Israel took over their land. She was saved, and she chose to live with the Israelites the rest of her life. She chose to do things God's way. She left her life of sin to follow God. She changed. She married an Israelite, is listed as an ancestor of Jesus (Matthew 1:5), and is listed among the faithful followers in Hebrews 11 (v. 31)! Change is indeed possible.

We should also remember the woman at the well in John 4. She was also a Gentile, living in sin. But after talking to Jesus, she believed, went into the town, and evangelized for His name. A drastic change took place in her life in just a few hours!

Paul's life clearly illustrates how a person can change. He was in the elite Jewish sect—a Pharisee. He had the best lineage, the best education, and the best record for being a righteous Jew. Yet he fought against Christianity and against any talk of Christ:

> I thought to myself that I had to do many things hostile to the name of Jesus of Nazareth . . . not only did I lock up many of the saints in prisons, having received authority from the chief priests, but also when they were being put to death I cast my vote against them. And as I punished them often in all the synagogues, I tried to force them to blaspheme, and being furiously enraged at them, I kept pursuing them even to foreign cities (Acts 26:9-11).

358

But after Jesus appeared to him on the road to Damascus, he changed from a persecutor of Christians to an ambassador for Christ. He counted his Jewish life as rubbish compared to his new Christian life:

> If anyone else has a mind to put confidence in the flesh, I far more; circumcised the eighth day, of the nation of Israel, of the tribe of Benjamin, a Hebrew of Hebrews; as to the Law, a Pharisee; as to zeal, a persecutor of the church; as to righteousness which is the Law, found blameless. But whatever things were gain to me, those things I have counted as loss for the sake of Christ. More than that, I count all things to be loss in view of the surpassing value of knowing Christ Jesus my Lord, for whom I have suffered the loss of all things, and count them but rubbish in order that I may gain Christ (Philippians 3:4b-8).

If these people could change, so can YOU!

(3) We have our goal ahead of us, we desire it, and we know we can reach it, though it is a slow process. But desire and determination are not all that is needed. We also must seek the proper nourishment to enable us to mature. We need spiritual food in order to maintain growth in our spiritual natures and in order to allow the Holy Spirit to do His work within us (just as physical food is a necessity for our physical growth).

That spiritual food is God's Word, the Bible. The Bible is one means that God has chosen to make clear His intentions and will for our lives. He communicated to the world through His spokesmen in the Old Testament and through Jesus and the apostles in the New Testament. Through the guidance and inspiration of the Holy Spirit, the words and activities of God's Son and His spokesmen were recorded for our benefit (II Peter 1:20, 21). We can know what God has thought and desired from the very beginning of the world, how His power has been felt throughout history, how He really feels about us through Jesus' words and actions, and how we are to respond to all that God has done for us. Thus, we cannot expect to become God's women, unless we know what He wants of us through a study of His Word.

The Psalmist stressed the guidance God's Word offers:

How blessed is the man who does not walk in the counsel of the wicked, nor stand in the path of sinners, nor sit in the seat of the scoffers! But his delight is in the law of the Lord, and in His law he meditates day and night. And he will be like a tree firmly planted by streams of water, which yields its fruit in its season, and its leaf does not wither; and in whatever he does, he prospers (Psalm 1:1-3).

Thy word is a lamp to my feet, and a light to my path (Psalm 119:105).

Jesus also taught the importance of God's Word: "Blessed are those who hear the word of God, and observe it" (Luke 11:28). He said the wise person will act upon His words (Matthew 7:24, 25). We cannot really know His words well enough to act upon them just from listening to sermons or Bible School lessons. We must study for ourselves for the real, intimate knowledge that we need to nourish us to maturity.

Jesus said if we love Him, we will keep His commandments (John 14:15). We will not love Jesus in all His fullness without a study of the Word. And how will we know His commands? Are we to trust what someone else tells us are His commands? When the people of Jesus' time left the reading and interpreting of God's Word to the religious elite, their understanding of God's intentions diminished steadily. They allowed the elite to burden them down with many extra rules and regulations of the Law which God never intended. They were led astray, and even had their minds so clouded that they did not know the Messiah when He did come. Jesus said they erred because they did not understand the Scriptures (Matthew 22:29). We, too, can be led astray or misunderstand God's will if we are not studying the Scriptures for ourselves.

Just as physical babies need nourishment to get the proper growth pattern started, so we as spiritual babies need the proper nourishment of the Word. Peter stressed the importance of the Word at this stage of our growth: "Long for the pure milk of the word, that by it you may grow in respect to salvation" (I Peter 2:2).

Paul told Timothy the importance of the Scripture for the on-going of spiritual growth:

> All Scripture is inspired by God and profitable for teaching, for reproof, for correction, for training in righteousness; that the man of God may be adequate, equipped for every good work (II Timothy 3:16, 17).

Without a study of the Bible, we cannot expect to grow or to maintain our Christian life-style in a world that is beset with sin and strife. Oh, yes, the Holy Spirit will guide us, but He does not do so apart from the Word. The Word is the means the Spirit uses to speak to our hearts and minds with truth (Ephesians 6:17).

Knowing we should study the Bible and actually doing it are often two very different things, but it need not be. Each person can study and understand the Bible. The Bible was written for the "little people" like you and me, not just for the scholars. Oh yes, there will be some verses you won't understand; but everyone can understand the basic truths and principles that God wants to communicate. And as far as finding the time to study, we all know that we will find time for those things that we really feel are important.

There are many books available sharing different methods of Bible study, so there is no need for me to go into great detail here. However, the following hints have been helpful to me, so I will pass them on:

a. Find a translation of the Bible that you feel comfortable with and enjoy reading. Use it for your basic reading, but keep other translations close by to compare on difficult passages.

b. Set aside a time each day or week to read and meditate upon the Bible. Many people devote fifteen to thirty minutes a day. I find that reading in large blocks of time (two to three hours) once or twice a week is more profitable to me because I can read a whole book at one sitting, and my understanding of the major principles and emphases of the author is more greatly enhanced than if I read a chapter or a series of verses each day. Reading in bits and pieces makes it easy to take verses out of context and to miss the whole point the author is making. But whatever your preference, find *some* time to read the Bible.

c. Take notes, underline, outline, paraphrase — whatever helps you remember what you read.

d. Make a personal application at each reading. Ask, "What does this mean to me now?" "How should I be living differently?" "How does this apply to the current philosophies and activities of my community?"

e. Use additional tools to broaden views and enlighten your mind after your reading and meditating habit is well established. You will find that the more you read, the more you will want to study. Use the concordance to find the literal translation of the words and other verses that contain the words to get a clearer idea of certain word meanings. Use a Bible dictionary to do research; it is an encyclopedia of information about many Biblical terms. Consult maps to find the places that are mentioned; they will help you get the right perspective of distances and locations and make the reading come alive. Read books that cover the cultural and historical background of Bible times to help you understand the customs, holidays, dress, etc.

f. After reading the Bible completely through, you might enjoy studying the lives of certain persons or researching various topics (such as, faith, love, anger, pride, etc.). A topical Bible or a concordance would be helpful for this type of study.

(4) Another source of strength and nourishment that enables us to maintain Christian growth is prayer. The leaders of Israel prayed often for strength and guidance. Jesus, our example in everything, prayed often (Mark 1:35; 6:46; Luke 5:16; 6:12; 9:18; 11:1). We are told in Proverbs that God delights in our prayers (Proverbs 15:8). We are encouraged to make our requests known unto God through prayer (Philippians 4:6).

Through the Holy Spirit and the Scriptures, God has opportunity to talk with us. We seek a unity and oneness with God; we cannot have that if the communication is only one-way. It is true that God knows our every thought and need, but He also knows how our asking Him and our expression of our thoughts to Him draw us closer into a more intimate relationship with Him.

If we want to make a friend or want to have a deep relationship with someone, we know that we have to communicate with them. We have to share of ourselves through our words.

How long would a friendship or a marriage last if the people involved did not communicate with each other? It is much the same with God. Our relationship with Him will be enriched and strengthened as long as there is two-way communication going on. Our growth as a Christian will wane and become weak if we do not maintain that communication.

Most of the prayers in the Bible are those of petition, asking God for help. Those who were praying realized their inadequacies in situations and asked God to help them out.

Solomon asked God for wisdom, for understanding, and discernment (I Kings 3:7-14) — a request that was very pleasing to God. We know how much we need wisdom in order to develop the proper character; and through the avenue of prayer, we can ask for it and receive it (James 1:5).

We can ask God for help when we or our loved ones are facing death (Genesis 20:7; II Kings 4:32, 33; 20:2). We can ask for help when we are frustrated or in danger (I Samuel 1:10, 12; Jonah 2:1; Matthew 26:53).

When we have done wrong, we can confess our sins (Ezra 10:1; Nehemiah 1:6; I John 1:9), and ask for forgiveness (I Kings 8:30; II Chronicles 7:14; Matthew 6:12; Acts 8:22). When we are sick, we can ask for healing (Acts 9:40; 28:8; James 5:14). When others threaten or persecute us, we can ask for help in dealing with them (II Kings 19:4; Psalm 55:16-18). When fears and doubts assail us, we can ask for peace (Psalm 122:6). When trials and suffering come, we can ask for strength (Luke 21:36). We can ask for opportunities to witness to arise (Colossians 4:3), and then we can ask for boldness to deal with those opportunities (Acts 4:29-31). When we have tough decisions to make, we can ask for God's will to be done (Matthew 26:39-42; Acts 1:24). When the devil tempts us, we can ask God to help us live righteously (II Corinthians 13:7; Matthew 6:13). In essence, we can share *any* problem or anxiety we have with God and ask for Him to help us carry the burden. What a privilege!

However, God does not promise to hear every prayer that is uttered, so we must consider how our prayers can be most effective. Jesus gave much guidance on this point: (a) He said we are not to pray to make an impression on others; we are to pray with pure motives (Matthew 6:7, 8). (b) We are to believe (really trust) in God and believe that He will answer (Mark 11:24; Hebrews 11:6; James 1:5-7). (c) We are to pray in humility and submission (Luke 18:9-14). (d) We are to pray with persistence (Luke 11:5-13; 18:1-8). (e) We are to pray with forgiving spirits (Mark 11:25; Matthew 6:12, 14, 15).

Paul said we should pray continuously (Ephesians 6:18; I Thessalonians 3:9, 10; 5:17), which means having a constant alertness and consciousness of communication with God. Paul also stressed that we should pray without anger or divisiveness (I Timothy 2:8). Peter added that having the proper marriage relationship was important to prayer effectiveness (I Peter 3:7). John wrote that we will receive what we ask for if we are keeping the commandments and pleasing God (I John 3:22).

The Bible also abounds with instances of Christians and people of God praying for others. Many Bible leaders made prayers of intercession for their people (Numbers 11:2; 21:7; Deuteronomy 9:20; I Samuel 7:5; Nehemiah 1:6; Jeremiah 29:7; Luke 22:32; John 17:9). Jesus said we should pray for more workers (Matthew 9:38) and for our enemies (Matthew 5:44; Luke 6:28). The people in the early church prayed for help for Christian brothers and sisters (Acts 8:15; 12:5; I Thessalonians 3:10; Ephesians 6:18; James 5:13, 16). Thus we know that our prayers must not always be directed toward our own selves but also have the needs of others in mind.

Prayer is vital to a Christian's growth and should be taken seriously. It is an avenue of help, guidance, and strength to us. We can know that God will hear and honor our prayers if we are becoming the type of persons He wishes us to be.

(5) Another important source of strength and nourishment for our spiritual growth is our fellowship with other Christians. When Jesus left the earth, God not only sent His presence (Holy Spirit) to guide and strengthen Jesus' followers, but He also started a new community in which His followers could share — the church. Those who believed in Christ and who lived with His life-style could draw strength and counsel from each other.

In the first century, this community was characterized by love and sharing. Those who had possessions sold them in order to help their fellow Christians who did not have the physical necessities of food and clothing (Acts 2:44, 45). They were continually rejoicing, acting in unity, sharing meals, and witnessing to others (Acts 2:46, 47).

This community (the church) was beset with problems and persecution from without as well as from factions and false teaching from within, but the members were constantly reminded that they were to support one another (especially the immature, the spiritual babies, Acts 20:35; Romans 15:1), to comfort one another (Romans 1:12; I Thessalonians 4:18), not to cause one another to stumble (Romans 14:13), to edify one another (Romans 14:19; 15:2), to be of one mind and live in unity not divisions (I Corinthians 1:10; 10:16, 17; 12:13), to bear one another's burdens

366

(Galatians 6:2), to walk in love (Ephesians 5:2), to worship God together (Ephesians 5:19), to teach and admonish one another (Colossians 3:16; Hebrews 3:13), to encourage one another to do good and to assemble together (Hebrews 10:24, 25), to confess and pray together (James 5:16), and to realize that they were all in the same family (I John 4:7) and members of the same body (I Corinthians 12:25-27).

The church is still thriving today. It still draws its strength from the Word of God, from the foundation of Jesus, and from the working and sharing together of Jesus' followers. God did not create us to live in our own little boxes, living independently of everyone else. He not only expects and intends for us to commune with Him and learn of His Word, He also intends for us to fellowship and work with other Christians. He does not draw us to Him in order to isolate us; instead He draws us into a family of people who care for one another and who are willing to share their gifts (abilities) of the Holy Spirit with each other in order to better witness and win the outside world to Christ (I Corinthians 12, Ephesians 4).

Included in this fellowship should be the elements that were included in the first century church: assembling together for worship, the teaching of the Scriptures, the caring for one another's needs, and then scattering to every area of the land to win others to Christ. Without this involvement, we cannot hope to become God's women.

We need to make our worship meaningful. True, we can commune with God by a river bank or in our kitchens, but we cannot gain strength and comfort from others unless we assemble with them. We need to study the Scriptures privately, but to know the full wealth of God's Word is to discuss and share with others about it. Your insights help them, and theirs enlighten you.

We also must realize that we are not to be always *drinking in* God's blessings; we are to *give them out* as well. We cannot do so effectively without knowing and communicating with our brothers and sisters in Christ and without being involved in the community, for how can we know others' needs or those of the community? We cannot sit alone in our living rooms with the Bible on our laps and expect God to send us a vision of what our fellow Christians need or what issue in the community we need to investigate. The only way we can know needs is to get involved with others.

But still the work of the church is not finished. For the purpose of the church is not only to maintain and encourage its members, but also to reach out to the lost of the world. We cannot expect to grow to maturity unless we are doing our part in this work of witnessing for Christ. We have been given a gift or gifts by the Holy Spirit living within us — gifts to enable us to witness, to worship, to help others, and to take part in some portion of the church's program of reaching out to the lost. God expects us to use those gifts to His glory, not for our own glory or to fulfill our own selfish desires.

We are all to participate by giving money to the church's program of evangelism, to support the spiritual leaders of the congregations, and to help those who are in need (I Corinthians 9:9-14; II Corinthians 8, 9). We are to participate by praying for one another, encouraging each other, comforting each other in time of trouble and sorrow, counseling and teaching each other, rejoicing with each other, and by witnessing to all those we contact.

Now to get specific. In what ways can women participate in the program and purposes of the church? Here are some suggestions:[1]

---

1. Reread section under GOOD WORKS in Chapter Nine for other ideas.

For Fellow Christians

Sponsor a youth group

Teach a Sunday School class or Bible Study group or be a member

Make phone calls, visits, or send cards to the sick, shut-in, or those with special needs

Be available for counseling

Be a friend to others

Smile and be gracious

Open your home for parties and fellowships

Volunteer to help wherever needed

Help make the church building attractive

Be specific in your prayers

Use your money wisely and be a cheerful giver

Encourage the church leaders

Allow others to help you

For The Lost

Start a neighborhood Bible Study for couples, women, or children

Be friendly and pleasant to all

Speak up for Christ when opportunities arise

Use your special gifts and interests to contact others for Christ

Call door-to-door with your husband or another woman

Be a good example in honesty and purity

Help others who have needs — a visit to the lonely, food and clothing to the poor, etc.

Give to the mission program

Cultivate one-to-one relationships

The church — a community that is a source of comfort, that gives physical as well as spiritual help, and is a sharing fellowship that all people need; a community that gives strength and depth to the Christians, who in turn go out into the world ready and willing to bring the lost to Christ; a continuously expanding community that reaches upward to God, inward to its members, and outward to the world — what a splendid plan it is that God has devised! And what a privilege for us all to be able to participate and be active citizens of God's community!

Conclusion

We are constantly becoming. Who we are becoming depends upon our own wills and how we allow God to work within us. Are we becoming strong and righteous women who are sources of joy and comfort to all who know us? Are we becoming caring and serving women who reach out to all without bitterness or prejudice? Are we witnessing women who are winning others to Christ?

Or are we allowing our characters to become weakened by our lack of Bible study, church attendance, and communication with God? Are our characters about to collapse in shambles around us because of our negative attitudes? Are our lives marked by sinfulness and failures? Are we burdens instead of blessings to all who know us? Are we shut up in a box, rather than witnessing for Christ?

Only we can decide who we are to become. As for me, I will strive to become God's woman, knowing full well that it is a slow process and a lifelong commitment but one of true fulfillment and joy. How about you?

Summary

The main points of this chapter can be summarized as follows:

1. We *can* become God's women.
2. The first step is to become children of God through belief, repentance, and baptism.
3. As God's children, we receive forgiveness and the Holy Spirit who guides us.
4. The second step is to maintain a righteous life which can be done by:

a. Clarifying our goal and desiring it.
b. Realizing we can change, but that it is a slow process.
c. Taking in the proper nourishment of God's Word.
d. Maintaining contact with God through prayer.
e. Involving ourselves in the church and its program and purposes.

DISCUSSION QUESTIONS:

1. Make as many comparisons as you can between a physical baby and a spiritual baby.
2. Explain in your own words who the Holy Spirit is and what He does for us.
3. Which action of the Holy Spirit means the most to you?
4. Cite evidence that we are not puppets or machines manipulated by God.
5. In twenty-five words or less, what is to be our goal as Christians?
6. List the things we know about the process of spiritual maturation.
7. How would you reply to a person who said, "I am who I am. I cannot change. Just accept me the way I am"?
8. Why is it necessary for us to study the Bible?
9. Why is prayer important?
10. How would you react to this statement — "Prayer should be for praising God, not for asking for things"?
11. In what ways are you presently involved in the church's program?
    a. How are you helping your spiritual brothers and sisters?
    b. How are you reaching the lost?

371

12. Share with the class how the church strengthens you in your Christian life.
13. Devise your own spiritual improvement program, noting what areas you need to work on in this next week.

Bibliography

Deen, Edith. *All of the Women of the Bible*. New York: Harper and Brothers Publishers, 1955.

DeJong, Peter and Donald R. Wilson. *Husband and Wife*. Grand Rapids, Michigan: Zondervan Publishing House, 1978.

Doely, Sarah Bentley (editor). *Women's Liberation and the Church*. New York: Association Press, 1970.

Edersheim, Alfred. *Sketches of Jewish Social Life*. Grand Rapids, Michigan: Wm. B. Eerdmans Publishing Company, 1976.

Jeremias, Joachin. *Jerusalem in the Time of Jesus*. London: SCM Press, 1969.

Lockyer, Herbert. *The Women of the Bible*. Grand Rapids, Michigan: Zondervan Publishing House, 1971.

Miles, Herbert J. and Fern Harrington. *Husband Wife Equality*. New Jersey: Fleming H. Revell Company, 1978.

Pape, Dorothy R. *In Search of God's Ideal Woman*. Downers Grove, Illinois: InterVarsity Press, 1976.

Scanzoni, Letha and Nancy Hardesty. *All We're Meant To Be*. Waco, Texas: Word Books, 1974.

Stagg, Frank and Evelyn. *Woman in the World of Jesus*. Philadelphia: Westminster Press, 1973.

Tenney, Merrill C. *New Testament Times*. Grand Rapids, Michigan: Wm. B. Eerdmans Publishing Company, 1965.

Whiston, William (translator). *Josephus' Complete Works*. Grand Rapids, Michigan: Kregel Publications, 1974.

On Word Meanings:

Brown, Francis (editor). *A Hebrew and English Lexicon of the Old Testament*. Oxford: Clarendon Press, 1978.

Kittel, Gerhard (editor). *Theological Dictionary of the New Testament.* Grand Rapids, Michigan: Wm. B. Eerdmans Publishing Company, 1964.

Vine, W. E. *An Expository Dictionary of New Testament Words.* New Jersey: Fleming H. Revell Company, 1966.

TOPICAL INDEX FOR *WHAT THE BIBLE SAYS ABOUT WOMEN*

As arranged in *Monser's Topical Index and Digest of the Bible* edited by Harold E. Monser with A. T. Robertson, D. R. Dungan and Others.

ANNA. An aged prophetess at the time of the birth of Jesus. — Lu. 2:36.

BATHSHEBA. Daughter of Eliam or Ammiel, wife of David and mother of Solomon; called also *Bathshua.* — II Sam. 11:3; 12:24; I Ki. 1:11-31; 2:13-19; Ps. 51 title.

BERNICE. Acts 25:13, 23, 30.

BETROTHAL. Espousal among the Hebrews was something more than a marriage engagement is with us. It was the beginning of marriage, was as legally binding as marriage itself, and could be broken off only by a bill of divorce. Hence we find that Joseph is called the husband of Mary — Mt. 1:18, 19. Parents chose the companion — Gen. 21:21; 34:4-6; 38:6; Deut. 22:16.

The marriage was not consummated for some time after the betrothal. — Ju. 14:7-8. Brothers were consulted — Gen. 24:58.

The betrothal was accompanied with gifts. — Gen. 24:53; 34:12. A dowry was given — I Sam. 18:25.

The bride remained at her home till taken by the bridegroom. — Deut. 20:7.

The friend of bridegroom kept up communication between the two. — John 3:29. Compulsory betrothal — Ex. 22:16; Deut. 22:28-29. Violated betrothal — Lev. 19:20; Deut. 22:23. A blameless woman — Deut. 22:25.

CANDACE. Queen of Ethiopia, whose treasurer was the Ethiopian eunuch. — Acts 8:27.

CHASTE, CHASTITY. Tit. 2:5; I Pet. 2:3; Eccl. 7:26. Enjoined — Pr. 21:3; Acts 15:20; Rom. 13:13; I Cor. 6:13-18; Col. 3:5; I Thess. 4:3; Tit. 2:5; Heb. 13:4; I Pet. 4:1-3. Heart, In — Pr. 6:24, 25. Look, In — Job 31:1; Mt. 5:28. Speech, In — Eph. 5:3. Unchaste shall not enter heaven — Eph. 5:5, 6; Heb. 13:4; Rev. 22:14. Unchaste, Shun company of — Pr. 5:3-11; 7:10-27; 22:14; Eccl. 7:26; I Cor. 5:11; I Pet. 3:1, 2. Wicked are not — Eph. 4:19; II Pet. 2:14; Jude 8.

CHILDREN: The chosen type of the kingdom. — Mt. 18:2-5; 19:14; Mk. 10:14, 15; Lu. 18:17; I Cor. 14:20; I Pet. 2:2.

Promised as an inducement to righteousness. — Gen. 15:5; 22:17; Ex. 32:13; Lev. 26:9; Deut. 7:12-14; 13:17; 30:5; Job 5:24, 25; Ps. 45:16, 17; 128:1-6; Is. 44:3, 4; 48:18, 19; Jer. 33:22; Rom. 4:18.

Come from God. — Gen. 4:1, 25; 17:20; 29:31-35; 30:2, 6, 17-20; 33:5; 48:9; Deut. 7:13; Ruth 4:13; I Sam. 1:19, 20; Ps. 107:41; 113:9; 127:3-5; 128:1-6.

Children a blessing. — Gen. 5:29; Ps. 113:9; 127:3-5; Pr. 10:1; 15:20; 17:6; 23:24; 27:11; 29:3.

Childlessness an affliction. — Gen. 15:2, 3; 30:1; I Sam. 1:6, 7; Jer. 20:30; 22:30; Lu. 1:25.

Given in answer to prayer. — Gen. 15:2-5; 25:21; I Sam. 1:10-20, 27; Lu. 1:13.

By special appointment. — Isaac — Gen. 15:2-6; 17:16; 21:1-3. Jacob and Esau — Gen. 15:21-26. Samuel — I Sam. 1:11, 19, 20. John the Baptist — Lu. 1:13-25, 57-80; Lu. 1:26-42. Jesus — Mt.1:18-23; Lu. 1:26-38.

Children taken away in punishment. — Ex. 12:29, 30; Deut. 28:32, 41; II Sam. 12:14, 15; Job 27:14, 15; Ps. 21:10, 11; Hos. 9:12.

Covenant of circumcision. — Gen. 17:10-14; Lev. 12:3; Phil. 3:5.

Named. — Gen. 21:3; 30:6, 8, 10, 13, 18, 20, 21, 24; 41:51, 52; Ex. 2:22. Ruth 4:17; I Sam. 4:21. At circumcision — Lu. 1:59; 2:21. After relatives — Lu. 1:59, 61. From remarkable events — Gen. 21:3, 6; 18:13; Ex. 2:10; 18:3, 4. From circumstances connected with their birth — Gen. 25:25, 26; 35:18; I Chr. 4:9. Named by God — Is. 8:3; Hos. 1:4, 6, 9; Lu. ʻ1:31.

Treatment at birth. — Ez. 16:4-6; Lu. 2:7, 12.

Brought early to the house of the Lord. — I Sam. 1:24.

Weaning of. — Gen. 21:8; I Sam. 1: 22-24; I Ki. 11:20; Ps. 131:2; Is. 11:8; 28:9.

Nurses of. — Gen. 24:59; Ex. 2:7, 9; Ruth 4:16; II Sam. 4:4; II Ki. 11:2.

Adopted. — Gen. 48:5, 6; Ex. 2:10.

Education of. — Gen. 18:19; Ex. 10: 2; 13:8-10; Deut. 4:9; 11:19; 31: 12, 13; Ps. 78:3-8; Pr. 4:1-22; 13: 1, 24; 22:6, 15; Is. 28:9, 10; Lu. 2:46; II Tim. 3:14, 15.

Training of. — Pr. 22:6, 15; 29:17; Eph. 6:4.

Parental authority. — Gen. 9:24, 25; 18:19; 21:14; 38:24; Pr. 13:1, 24.

Parental indulgence. — Gen. 27:6-17, 42-45; 37:3, 4. Indulgence forbidden — Deut. 21:15-17.

Parental example. — Gen. 18:19; II Tim. 1:5.

Duties of children to parents. — Ex. 20:12; 21:15, 17; Lev. 19:3; 20: 9; Deut. 5:16; 27:16; Pr. 1:8; 6: 20; 15:5; 23:22; 24:21; Is. 45:10; Eph. 6:2, 3; Col. 3:20; I Tim. 5:4; I Pet. 5:5.

Penalty for disobedience. — Deut. 21: 18-21; Pr. 30:17.

Prosperity of, greatly depended on obedience of parents. — Deut. 4: 40; 12:25, 28; Ps. 128:1-3.

Amusements. — Job 21:11; Zech. 8: 5; Mt. 11:16, 17; Lu. 7:31, 32.

Fellowship with parents. — Gen. 6: 18; 13:15-16; Lev. 26:45.

Children sacrificed to idols. — Lev. 18:21; 20:2-5; Deut. 12:29-31; 18: 10; II Ki. 17:31; II Chr. 28:3; 33: 6; Ez. 16:20, 21.

Prayers for. — Gen. 17:18; I Chr. 29: 19.

Discriminations: Male. — Redeemed as belonging to God — Ex. 13:13-15. Under care of tutors — II Ki. 10: 1; Acts 22:3; Gal. 4:1, 2. Inherited possessions of their fathers — Deut. 21:16, 17; Lu. 12:13, 14. Received paternal blessing — Gen. 27:1-4; 48: 15; 49:1-33.

Female. — Drawers of water — Gen. 24:13; Ex. 2:16. Inheritors of property in default of sons — Num. 27: 1-8; Josh. 17:1-16. Were given in marriage by father, eldest preferred — Gen. 29:16-29. Being debarred from marriage a reproach — Jer. 11: 37; Is. 4:1.

Illegitimate. — Disregarded by father — Heb. 12:8. Despised by brothers — Ju. 11:2. Excluded from congregation — Deut. 23:2. Exiled from family — Gen. 21:14; 25:6. Had no inheritance — Gen. 21:10-14; Gal. 4:30.

Good children. — Obey parents — Gen. 28:7; 47:29-31; Ex. 20:12; Pr. 10:1; 13:1; Col. 3:20. Observe the law of God — Ps. 119:9, 99; Pr. 28:7. Submit to discipline — Pr. 8:32-36; Heb. 12:9. Honor and care for parents — Gen. 45:9-11; 46:29; 47:12; Pr. 10:1; 29:17. Respect the aged — Lev. 19:32.

Examples of. — Shem and Japheth — Gen. 9:23. Isaac — Gen. 22:6. Judah — Gen. 4:32. Joseph — Gen. 37:13; 46:29. Jacob's sons — Gen. 50:12. Jephthah's daughter — Ju. 11:36. Samuel — I Sam. 3:19; 22:6. David — I Sam. 17:20; Ps. 71:5. Solomon — II Ki. 2:19. Josiah — II Chr. 34:3. Esther — 2:20. The Rechabites — Jer. 35:5-10. Daniel — 1:6. Jesus — Lu. 2:51. Timothy — II Tim. 3:15.

Wicked children. — To their parents — Gen. 26:34, 35; Deut. 27:16; I Sam. 2:25; II Sam. 15:10-15; I Ki. 1:5-10; Pr. 15:5, 20; 19:26; 28:24; 29:15; 30:11; Ez. 22:7. To their leaders — II Ki. 2:23, 24; Job 19:18. Not restrained by parents — I Sam. 3:11-14. Sons of Belial — I Sam. 2:12-17, 22-25; 8:1-3.

Punishment of. — Ex. 21:15; Deut. 21:18, 21; 27:16; II Ki. 2:23; Pr. 28:24; 30:17; Mk. 7:10.

Fondness and care of mothers for. — Ex. 2:2-10; I Sam. 2:19; I Ki. 3:27; Is. 49:15; I Thess. 2:7, 8.

Grief occasioned by loss of. — Gen. 37:35; 44:27-29; II Sam. 13:37; Jer. 6:26; 31:15.

Consequences of sin entailed on children in this world. — Ex. 20:5; 34:7; Lev. 26:39, 40; Num. 14:33; Deut. 5:9; I Ki. 14:9-10; Job 5:3-7; Ps. 21:10; 37:28; Is. 1:4; 13:16; 14:20-22; Jer. 32:18; Lam. 5:7; Mt. 23:32-36; John 9:2, 3, 34.

Children not punished for sins of parents. — Deut. 24:16; II Ki. 14:6; II Chr. 25:4; Jer. 31:29, 30; 32:18; Ez. 18:2-4, 20; Mt. 19:13, 14; Mk. 10:13-15; Lu. 18:15-17.

Children of God. — Heb. 12:5-9; I Pet. 1:14.

Children of light. — Lu. 16:8; John 12:36; Eph. 5:8; I Thess. 5:5.

CONCUBINE. Hebrew concubinage grew out of a desire for offspring as associated with the hope of the promised Redeemer. The children were adopted as if the wife's own offspring — Gen. 30:1-24. Husband could take any of his own slaves as concubines, but could not take any of his wife's slaves without her consent — Gen. 16:2, 3; 30:3, 4, 9. Not illegal, but supplementary. Abraham sent Ishmael away to guard the rights of Isaac — Gen. 17:20, 21.

Laws concerning. — Ex. 21:7-11; Lev. 19:20-22; Deut. 21:9-14. Concubines called wives — Gen. 37:2; Ju. 19:1-4. Children, but not heirs — Gen. Ch. 49.

Incest with concubines. — Gen. 35:22; 49:4; I Chr. 5:1; II Sam. 16:21, 22.

Concubinage not right as we see it, but permitted for the time. — Acts

17:30; Mt. 19:3-12. Since Christ, fornication a sin against one's own body—I Cor. 6:15-20.

Examples in. — Abraham—Gen. 16: 3; 25:6; I Chr. 1:32. Nahor—Gen. 22:24. Jacob—Gen. 30:4; 35:22; 49:4; I Chr. 5:1. Eliphaz—Gen. 36: 12. Gideon—Ju. 8:31. Caleb—I Chr. 2:46. Manasseh—I Chr. 7:14. Saul—II Sam. 3:7; 21:11. David —II Sam. 5:13; 15:16; 19:5; 20: 3; I Chr. 3:9. Solomon—I Ki. 11: 3. Rehoboam—II Chr. 11:21. Belshazzar—Dan. 5:3.

DAUGHTERS OF. Babylon—Ps. 137:8; Is. 47:1; Jer. 50:42; 51:33; Zech. 2:7. Backsliding—Jer. 49:4. Canaanites—Gen. 24:3; 38:2. Chaldeans—Is. 47:1, 5. Dibon—Jer. 48:18. Edom—Lam. 4:22. Egypt— Jer. 46:11, 19, 24. Foreign gods —Mal. 2:11. Gallim—Is. 10:30. Herodias—Mt. 14:6; Mk. 6:22. Jephthah—Ju. 11:34-40. Jerusalem—Is. 22:4; 37:22; Jer. 4:11; 8:11, 19, 21, 22; 9:1, 7; 31:22; Lam. 2:11, 13, 15; 3:48; 4:3, 6, 10; Zeph. 3:10, 14; Zech. 9:9. Judah—Lam. 1:15; 2:2, 4, 5. Lebanon—II Ki. 14:9; II Chr. 25: 18. Kings—Ps. 45:9, 13; Dan. 11: 6. Pharaoh—Ex. 2:2-10; I Ki. 3:1; 7:8; 9:16, 24; 11:1; I Chr. 4:18; II Chr. 8:11; Acts 7:21; Heb. 11: 24. Princes—Num. 25:18; Song of Sol. 7:1. Rabbah—Jer. 49:2, 3. Sidon—Is. 23:12. Tarshish—Is. 23: 10. Troops—Mic. 5:1. Tyre—Ps. 45:12. Zion—II Ki. 19:21; Ps. 9: 14; Is. 10:32; 16:1; 37:22; 52:2; 62:11; Jer. 4:31; 6:2, 23; Lam. 1: 6; 2:1, 8, 10, 18; 4:21, 22; Mic.

1:13; 4:8, 10, 13; Zeph. 3:14; Zech. 2:10; 9:9; Mt. 21:5; John 12:15.

Hearken, O daughter.—Ps. 45:10.

Laws concerning. — Ex. 1:16, 22; 20: 10; 21:7, 31; Lev. 18:9, 10, 11, 17; 19:29; 20:17; 21:2, 9; 22:12, 13; Deut. 5:14; 7:3; 12:18; 13:6; 16:11, 14; 18:10; 22:16, 17; 27: 22; 28:56. That no man might make his son or daughter to pass through fire to Molech—II Ki. 23:10; Ez. 44:25.

Purification of.—Lev. 12:6.

Inheritance determined.—Num. 27: 6, 36.

Prophecies concerning.—Ez. 14:20; 16:44, 45; 22:11. Shall give daughters of women—Dan. 11:17. And ye shall be to me—II Cor. 6:18.

Riseth against her mother.—Mic. 7: 6; Mt. 10:35; Lu. 12:53.

Care of.—Mt. 9:18, 22; 15:22, 28; Mk. 5:23, 34; 7:25, 26, 29; Lu. 8: 42, 48.

He that loveth daughter more than me.—Mt. 10:37.

Figurative.—As a daughter—II Sam. 12:3.

DAUGHTER-IN-LAW. Gen. 38:16. Arose with—Ruth 1:6. Loveth— Ruth 4:15. Mother-in-law, Against —Mt. 10:35; Lu. 12:53. Naomi said unto—Ruth 1:8. Ruth—Ruth 1:22; 2:22. Sarai—Gen. 11:31. Tamar— Gen. 38:11.

DEACONESS. Rom. 16:1, 2.

DEBORAH. (1) **Rebekah's nurse.** —Gen. 35:8. (2) **One of the judges.** —Ju. 4:4. Song of—Ju. Ch. 5.

DIVORCE. Ex. 21:7-11; Deut. 21: 14; 22:13-19, 28, 29; 24:1-4; 28: 1-4; Mt. 5:31, 32; 19:3-9; Mk. 10: 2-12; Lu. 16:18; Rom. 7:2, 3; I Cor.

7:10-17. Moses allowed divorce because of the hardness of heart of the Jew—Mt. 19:8. Adultery breaks the marriage bond—Mt. 19:9.

DORCAS. A female disciple who was charitable to the poor, restored to life by Peter.—Acts 9:36-40.

FAMILY. Divinely established—Gen. 1:28; 2:18, 22.

Laws of.—Gen. 29:21; Lev. 18:18; Num. 36:12.

Promise to.—Gen. 12:3; 28:14; Ps. 68:6; Is. 59:21; 65:23; Jer. 31:1.

Prophecies concerning families of the north.—Jer. 1:15; 25:9. Of Israel—Jer. 2:4; 31:1.

Heads of.—Called chiefs, heads, Elders and householders—Gen. 36:40; 47:12; Ex. 6:14-25; 12:21; Num. 36:1.

Inheritance allotted according to.—Josh. Chas. 13-17.

Families as servants.—Ex. 21:2-5; Lev. 25:45.

Punished for worship of.—Molech—Lev. 20:5. Wood and stone—Ez. 20:32-34.

Warriors numbered.—Num. 1:2, 18-42; 2:34. Levites—Num. 3:15-39.

Numbering the people.—Num. 4:2, 18-46; 26:7, 12-58.

In year of jubilee every man returned to.—Lev. 25:10, 41.

A man may be redeemed by.—Lev. 25:49.

Punishment of.—Jer. 10:25; Zech. 14:18.

Families of the earth.—Amos 3:2.

Sells families through witchcrafts.—Nah. 3:4.

Contempt of families terrified.—Job 31:34.

Noah and his family saved.—Gen. 7:13, 23.

Terah and his family moved to the land of Canaan.—Gen. 11:31.

Figurative.—Like flocks—Ps. 107:41. Family of God—Eph. 3:14.

GIRL. Joel 3:3; Zech. 8:5.

GRANDCHILDREN. I Tim. 5:4.

GRANDMOTHER. II Tim. 5:4.

HAGAR. Handmaid of Sarai—Gen. 16:1. Taken as legal concubine at Sarai's suggestion—Gen. 16:2, 3. Hagar despises Sarai—Gen. 16:5. Causes trouble—Gen. 16:5, 6. Hagar flees into wilderness, but is sent back by an angel—Gen. 16:7-9. Her seed to be multiplied—Gen. 16:10; 17:20; 21:18. Descendants—Gen. 16:12, 15, 25; 12-18; I Chr. 5:10, 19, 20; 27:31; Ps. 83:6. Descendants described—Gen. 16:12. Ishmael born—Gen. 16:11-16. Hagar recognizes Jehovah—Gen. 16:13. Hagar sent away—Gen. 21:9:16. God appears unto Hagar—Gen. 21:17-20.

Figurative.—Gal. 4:24-25.

HANDMAID. Word used broadly.—Ruth 3:9; II Sam. 14:6.

Applied to bondservants.—Hagar—Gen. 16:1; Gal. 4:22. Maids of Leah and Rachel—Gen. 29:24, 29.

Voluntary servitude.—Mary—Lu. 1:38. Hannah—I Sam. 1:11.

Expressive of humility.—Bathsheba—I Ki. 1:11-31. Esther—Esth. 5:1-8. Ruth—Ruth 3:9.

An unbearable heirship.—Pr. 30:23. Sarah and Hagar—Gen. 21:10; Gal. 4:30.

HARLOT. For hire.—Gen. 34:21; Num. 25:1, 6; Ju. 11:1; 16:1; 19:2, 25; I Ki. 3:16; Amos 2:7.

In heathen worship. — Gen. 38:21; Ex. 34:15, 16; Hos. 4:14.

Legislation against. — Common — Lev. 19:29; Deut. 23:18. Religious — Ex. 34:12-16; Lev. 21:7, 9, 14; Deut. 23:17; Hos. 1:2; 4:12; Ez. 16:26.

Warnings. — Pr. 6:26; 7:7-23; 23:27; 29:3; Hos. 4:11-14.

Punishment. — Burned or stoned to death — Gen. 38:24; Lev. 20:10-12; Deut. 22:22-25; John 8:5.

The New Covenant demands purity of heart and life. — Mt. 5:8, 27, 28, 31, 32; Acts 15:20, 29; I Cor. 6:9, 10, 13-20; Eph. 5:3-5; Col. 3:5-8; Tit. 1:15; 2:12; Jas. 4:4, 8.

HOME. At home. — I Ki. 5:14; Lam. 1:20. **Going, coming, bringing home.** — Gen. 39:16; 43:26; Ex. 9:19; Ju. 11:9; 19:9; Ruth 1:21; I Sam. 18:2; 24:22; I Ki. 13:15; I Chr. 13:12; Jer. 39:14; John 19:27; 20:10.

Government of. — Gen. 3:16. Controlling children — Gen. 18:19; I Tim. 3:4. Giving honor to husbands — Esth. 1:20-22; I Pet. 3:1-6.

References. — Protected from invasion by creditors — Deut. 24:10-11. Preparing for a home — Deut. 21:10-14. Infelicity at — Pr. 14:1; 15:17. Blessing bestowed upon — I Sam. 2:20. Purifying home by sacrifices — Job 1:5. Good conduct at — Ps. 101:2. Jealousy among children caused by favoritism — Gen. 27:5-46. Must provide for — I Tim. 5:8. Jesus' compassion on those He dismisses — Mk. 8:3, 26. Home rejoicing for sheep finding — Lu. 15:6. John takes Jesus' mother to — John 19:27. Broke bread at home — Acts 2:46. Taught at — Acts 5:42. Hungry disciples must not devour the Lord's Supper — I Cor. 11:34. At home in body, with the Lord — II Cor. 5:6. Workers at home — Tit. 2:5.

Unhappiness caused by plurality of women. — Gen. 16:5; 21:10-11; 29:30-34. By contemptuous conduct — I Sam. 6:16, 20-23. By riotous life — Esth. 1:10-22.

Home, as future abode. — Eccl. 12:5; II Cor. 5:8. See Job 17:13; 30:23.

HULDAH. A prophetess in the days of Josiah. — II Ki. 22:14; II Chr. 34:22.

HUSBAND. Laws concerning. — Ex. 21:22; Lev. 19:20; 21:3, 7; Num. 30:6-16; Deut. 22:22, 23; 24:5; 25:11; 28:56; Ez. 44:25. Jealousy — Num. 5:13, 19, 29-31. Marriage of captive women — Deut. 21:13. Bishops — I Tim. 3:2. Elders — Tit. 1:6. Divorce — Deut. 24:3, 4; Mt. 5:31, 32; 19:3-9; Mk. 10:12; Lu. 16:18; Rom. 7:2, 3.

Duties of. — Deut. 24:5; Pr. 5:18; I Cor. 7:2-4, 10, 16, 34, 39; Eph. 5:23-33; Col. 3:19; I Tim. 5:8; I Pet. 3:7.

Exhortation to. — Eccl. 9:9; Eph. 5:23-33; Col. 3:19; I Tim. 5:8; I Pet. 3:7.

Making husbands contemptible. — Esth. 1:17.

Prophecy concerning. — Jer. 6:11.

Figurative. — Is. 54:5; Jer. 31:32; II Cor. 11:2; Gal. 4:27. Christ the husband of His people — Eph. 5:25-32; Rev. 19:7f.

Illustrative. — Jer. 3:1; Ez. 16:32, 45; Hos. 2:2, 7; Joel 1:8; Rev. 21:2.

Mention of. — Adam to Eve — Gen. 2:18, 23, 24; 3:6, 16. Abraham to Sarai — Gen. 16:3. Isaac to Rebekah

—Gen. 24:67. Jacob to Leah— Gen. 29:32, 34; 30:15, 18, 20. Manoah—Ju. 13:6, 9, 10. Samson to Philistine woman—Ju. 14:15. Elimelech to Naomi—Ruth 1:3, 5, 12. Of Ruth—Ruth 1:9, 12; 2:11. Of Orpah—Ruth 1:9, 12. Elkanah to Hannah—I Sam. 1:8, 22, 23; 2:19-21. Phinehas as—I Sam. 4: 19, 21. Nabal to Abigail—I Sam. 25:19. Paltiel to Michal—II Sam. 3:15, 16. Uriah to Bathsheba—II Sam. 11:26. To woman of Tekoa —II Sam. 14:5, 7. To the Shunammite woman—II Ki. 4:9, 14, 22, 26. Sons of prophets were—II Ki. 4:1. Of a worthy woman—Pr. 12: 4; 31:11, 23, 28. To Samaritan— John 4:16-18. Zacharias to Elizabeth —Lu. 1:5, 13, 39, 40. Joseph to Mary—Mt. 1:16, 19. To Anna—Lu. 2:36. Ananias to Sapphira—Acts 5:9, 10. Aquila to Priscilla—Acts 18:24-28; I Cor. 16:19.

Husband head of the house.—Esth. 1:22; Eph. 5:23; Col. 3:18.

INSTRUCTION: Parents.—Abraham —Gen. 18:19. Jonadab—Jer. 35: 6, 8, 18. The law—Ex. 12:26, 27; 13:8, 14, 15; Deut. 4:9, 10; 6:7, 20-25; 11:19; Pr. 1:8; 4:1-4, 11; 6:20; 13:1; 30:17; 31:1; Song of Sol. 8:2; Joel 1:3; II Tim. 3: 14; Tit. 2:3.

JAEL. Wife of Heber, who slays Sisera.—Ju. 4:17-22; 5:6, 24.

JEZEBEL. Born and reared an idolater.—I Ki. 16:31.

Married Ahab, king of Israel.—I Ki. 16:31. Strongminded—I Ki. 19:1, 2; 21:7. Induced Ahab to build a temple and altar to Baal—I Ki. 16:

32; 21:25, 26. Wicked—II Ki. 9: 22. Zealous in idolatry—I Ki. 18:4, 13, 19; 19:1, 2. Caused murder of Naboth—I Ki. 21:5-16. Her death foretold—I Ki. 21:23; II Ki. 9:10. Fulfilled—II Ki. 9:30-37. Her name a synonym for seduction to idolatry —Rev. 2:20.

JOANNA. A female disciple, wife of Ahuza, an officer under Herod. One of the women who went to Jesus's tomb—Lu. 8:3; 24:10.

JOCHEBED, Wife of Amram, mother of Moses and Aaron.—Ex. 6:20; 26:59.

KETURAH. Wife of Abraham.— Gen. 25:1, 4; I Chr. 1:32, 33.

LADY. Ju. 5:29; II John 1.

LEAH. Rachel's sister, and daughter of Laban.—Gen. 29:16. Tender-eyed—Gen. 29:17. Married to Jacob—Gen. 29:23-26. Laban gives Zilpah to—Gen. 29:24. Children of—Gen. 29:31-35; 30:9-13, 17-21; 35:26. Reuben brings mandrakes to—Gen. 30:14, 16. In field—Gen. 31:4. Asks father for portion—Gen. 31:14. Flees with Jacob—Gen. 31: 19-21; 32:1, 22-23; 33:1-18. Daughter defiled—Gen. 34:1. Death of —Gen. 35:19; 49:31. Leah and Rachel referred to by Boaz as builders of house of Israel—Ruth 4:11.

LOVE. Love for children. —Gen. 22: 2; 30:1; 44:20; II Sam. 1:23; 18: 33; Ps. 127:3-5; Is. 2:17-18; Mk. 10:13-16; Lu. 18:15-17; Tit. 2:4.

Love of man and woman.—Gen. 24: 67; 29:18-20, 30, 32; 34:3, 12; Ju. 16:4; Ruth Chs. 2-4; I Sam. 1:5; II Sam. 13:1; I Ki. 11:1; II Chr. 11: 21; Esth. 2:17; Song of Sol. 1:4, 7;

2:4-8; 3:2; 4:1, 7-10; 5:1, 9, 16; Hos. 3:1; John 11:5, 36; Eph. 5: 25, 28-31; Col. 3:19; Tit. 2:4.

MAID. Ps. 123:2; Mt. 26:69; Acts 12: 13; 16:16.

MAIDEN. Ex. 2:5; Ruth 2:8; II Ki. 5: 2; Esth. 2:7.

MAID-SERVANT. Ex. 20:10; II Sam. 17:17; Lu. 12:45.

MAN: Is created by God. —Gen. 2: 7; Deut. 4:32; Job 4:17; 10:3, 8; 14:15; 31:15, 32:22; 33:4; 34:19; 35:10; 36:3; Ps. 95:6; 100:3; 119: 73; 138:8; 139:15, 16; Pr. 14:31; 22:2; Eccl. 7:29; Is. 17:7; 45:12; Jer. 27:5; Hos. 8:14.

Man made in the image of God. — Gen. 1:26, 27; 5:1, 2; 9:6; I Cor. 11:7; Jas. 3:9.

Man formed from the dust of the earth. —Gen. 2:7; 3:19; Job 4:19; 10:9; 33:6; Is. 29:16; 45:9; 64:8; Jer. 18:6; Rom. 9:20, 21; II Cor. 4:7.

God gives to man the breath of life— The Father of his spirit—Gen. 2:7; Num. 16:22; 27:16; Job 12:10; 27: 3; 33:4; 34:14; Is. 42:5; 57:16; Dan. 5:23; Ez. 37:5, 6, 9, 10; Zech. 12:1; Acts 17:25; Heb. 12:9; Rev. 22:6.

Man consists of body (*Heb.* Basar. *Gr.* Soma). —**Soul** (*Heb.* Nephesh. *Gr.* Psuche). **Spirit** (*Heb.* Ruach, Neshama. *Gr.* Pneuma). Gen. 2:7; Job 32:8, 18; 34:14; Ps. 31:9; Is. 10:18; Mt. 10:28; II Cor. 5:6, 8; I Thess. 5:23; Heb. 4:12.

Man is the completion of creation. — Gen. 1:28; 2:4-7; Ps. 8:4-8; Heb. 2:6-8.

Made but a little lower than God. — Ps. 8:5. **Than angels.** —Heb. 2:7.

Granted dominion over the earth. —Gen. 1:26, 28; Ps. 8:6-8; 49:14; 72:8.

Wonderfully made. —Job 10:8-11; Ps. 149:14-16; Eccl. 11:5. A puzzled saint—Job 12:4-6; Rom. 7:15-24. Thwarted plans—Ps. 33:10-19.

Differs from everything else living. —I Cor. 15:39.

Male and female represented in. — Gen. 1:26-28; 5:2; Mt. 19:4; Mk. 10:6.

Endowed with intellect. —Job 13:3, 15; Is. 1:18; 41:1, 21; 43:26; Jer. 12:1; Mt. 11:25; 16:7.

Endowed with affections. —Gen. 3: 16; Lev. 19:18; Deut. 18:6; I Chr. 29:3; Mt. 19:19; John 13:34; Rom. 12:10; 13:9, 10; Col. 3:12; I Thess. 4:9; Heb. 13:1; I Pet. 1:22; I John 3:14.

Man made to toil. —Gen. 1:28; 2:5, 15; 3:19; 31:42; Ex. 31:16; Ps. 104:23; Pr. 13:11; 14:23.

Full liberty granted with but one restriction. —Gen. 2:16, 17; 3:2, 3.

Fall of. —Gen. 3:1-8; Eccl. 7:27-29; Rom. 5:12-19; I Cor. 15:21, 22.

Enticed by the tempter. —Gen. 3:4, 5, 13; Pr. 1:10-19; 12:26; 16:29; John 8:44; II Cor. 11:3; I Tim. 2: 14; I Thess. 3:5; I Tim. 2:14; Jas. 1:13-15; I John 2:16, 17; Rev. 12: 9, 13.

Sinfulness of. —Gen. 6:5, 6, 12; 8: 21; I Ki. 8:46; Job 15:14-16; Ps. 14:1-3; 51:5; Pr. 20:9; Eccl. 7:20; 9:3; Is. 53:6; Jer. 17:9; Mk. 7:21-23; John 3:19; 7:7; Rom. 3:9-18; 7:18; Gal. 5:17; Jas. 1:13-15; I John 1:8. Gen. 3:6.

Imperfection and weakness of. —Job 4:17-21; Ps. 39:5-13; Is. 41:21-

382

24; Mt. 6:27; Rom. 9:16; II Cor. 3:5; Gal. 6:3.

Man subject to suffering. — Gen. 3: 17-19; Job 5:7; 14:1, 2; Rom. 8: 22, 23.

Man rebuked for perversity. — Is. 59: 1-15; John 8:21-24, 38-48.

Vanity of man's life. — Job 7:7-10, 16; Ps. 103:14-16; Eccl. Chs. 1; 2; 7:15; 12:1-8; I Pet. 1:24.

Equality of. — I Sam. 2:7; Job 21:23-26; Ps. 49:6-14; Pr. 22:2; 29:13; Acts 10:34-35; Gal. 3:28; Eph. 6: 5-9; Jas. 2:1-9.

The shortness of his life. — Job 14: 1-22; Ps. 39:5; 49:6-14; 89:48; 90: 5-10; Eccl. 1:4; 12:1-8; Heb. 9:27.

Man is great, though in ruins. — Lu. 15:17-24; 19:7-10; Rom. 5:7-8.

Man honored in the assumption of humanity by Jesus. — I Cor. 15: 45-49; Eph. 1:19-23; Phil. 2:5-9; Col. 1:12-20; Heb. 2:5-18.

Man's salvation provided for from the beginning. — Gen. 3:15; 12: 3; Is. 53:1-12; Mt. 25:34; Rom. 16: 25; Eph. 1:3-14; 3:1-11; II Thess. 2:13, 14; II Tim. 1:9, 10; Tit. 1:2, 3; II Pet. 1:10-12, 18-20; Rev. 13:8.

Man at his best when following Christ. — Mt. 4:19; 19:28, 29; II Cor. 3: 18; 5:17; Eph. 2:4-7, 10; 4:11-13.

Man's individuality respected. — Lu. 12:57; John 8:15; 12:47; 15:14-16; Rev. 3:20, 21.

Man obtains enlargement of life. — John 1:4; 5:21-26; 6:33-35; 10: 10; 17:2, 3; 20:31; I John 3:1-3.

Endowed with will. — John 7:17; Rom. 7:18; I Cor. 9:17; Phil. 2:13; Rev. 22:17.

Value of. — Mt. 10:31; 12:12; 16:26; Mk. 2:27; John 3:16; I Cor. 11:7.

Whole duty of. — Deut. 10:12; Eccl. 12:13; Mic. 6:8; I John 3:18-22.

Man proposes, but God disposes. — I Sam. 17:47; II Chr. 20:15; Eccl. 9:11; Is. 10:11; 47:1-15; Jer. 9: 23, 24; Amos 2:14-16; Lu. 12:16-21.

Obtains an advocate in time of trouble. — Rom. 8:34; I Tim. 2:5, 6; Heb. 7:25; 9:24-28; I John 2:1, 2.

Man the partaker of the divine nature. — John 1:16; Eph. 3:19; 4:13, 24; Heb. 3:1, 14; 6:4; 12:10; II Pet. 1: 4; I John 3:2.

He shall be recompensed according to his works. — Deut. Chs. 27; 28; Job 34:1, 12, 25; Ps. 62:12; Pr. 12: 14; 24:12; Is. 3:10, 11; Jer. 32:19; Mt. 7:15-27; 16:27; John 5:29; Rom. 2:5, 6; 6:20-23; 14:12; I Cor. 3:8; II Cor. 5:10; Eph. 6:8; Col. 3:25; Rev. 2:23-27; 20:12, 13; 21:7, 8; 22:12.

MARRIAGE: Ordained of God. — Gen. 2:18, 24; Mt. 19:5, 6; Mk. 10:7, 8; I Cor. 6:16; 11:11, 12; Eph. 5:31; Heb. 13:4.

Expressed by. — Joining together — Mt. 19:6; Mk. 10:9. Making affinity — I Ki. 3:1; 7:8; 9:16; II Chr. 8:11. Taking to wife — Ex. 2:1; Ruth 4: 13. Giving daughters to sons, and sons to daughters — Deut. 7:2; Ezra 9:12.

Commended. — Pr. 18:22; 31:10-12; Jer. 29:6; I Tim. 5:14, 15.

For this life only. — Mt. 22:30; Mk. 12:23; Lu. 20:27-36.

Marriage of near relatives. — Abraham and Sarai were half brother and sister — Gen. 20:12. The mother of Moses and Aaron was the aunt of

383

her husband—Ex. 6:20. Of cousins—Gen. 24:50-67; 28:2; Num. 36:1-12.

Marriages contracted by parents.—Gen. 21:21; 24:1-67; 34:4-10; 38:6; Ex. 21:7; 22:17; Ju. 1:12; 14:2, 3; I Sam. 17:25; 18:17-27.

Father gave daughters in marriage.—Ex. 22:17; Deut. 7:3; Josh. 15:16, 17; Ju. 14:20; 15:1-6; I Sam. 18:17-21; 25:44. Eldest daughter usually given first—Gen. 29:26. A dowry given to woman's parents before marriage—Gen. 24:53; 29:18; 34:12; Deut. 22:29; I Sam. 18:25-28; Hos. 3:2.

Consent of parties necessary.—Gen. 24:57, 58; I Sam. 18:20, 21; 25:40, 41.

Marriage contract made at gate of city.—Ruth 4:1-11.

Marriage laws of the Jews: Concerning near relatives.—Lev. 18:6-18, 24; 20:11-21; Deut. 22:30; 27:20-23; Mk. 6:17-19. **After seduction.**—Deut. 22:28, 29; Ex. 22:16.

Levirate marriage.—In case a man died without an heir—Brother or near kinsman to marry widow—Gen. 38:8-11; Deut. 25:5-10; Ruth 2:1, 10-13; 3:2-18; 4:1-13; Mt. 22:24-28; Mk. 12:19-23; Lu. 20:28-33.

Marriages were to be between members of the same tribe.—Ex. 2:1; Num. 36:6-12.

Marriages of priests.—Lev. 21:7, 13, 14; Ez. 44:22.

Marriages with Gentiles forbidden because of idolatry.—Gen. 24:3-6; 27:46; 28:1, 2, 6-9; 34:13, 14; Ex. 34:13-16; Deut. 7:3, 4; Num. 25:6-15; Josh. 23:12, 13; I Ki. 11:2; 16:31; Ezra 9:11, 12; Neh. 10:30; 13:23-30.

Marriages made with Gentiles.—Jer. 14:1-5; I Ki. 11:1; Neh. 13:23-30.

Marriage of captives.—Deut. 21:10-14.

Married man exempted from going to war for one year after marriage.—Deut. 20:7; 24:5.

Infidelity of those contracted in marriage same as if married.—Deut. 22:23, 24; Mt. 1:19. Tokens of virginity—Deut. 22:13-21.

Not to be married considered a calamity.—Ju. 11:37, 38; Ps. 78:63.

Weddings.—Celebrated with feasting—Gen. 29:22; Ju. 14:10-12; Esther 2:18; Jer. 16:8, 9; 33:11; John 2:1-10. Feasting lasted seven days—Gen. 29:27; Ju. 14:12. Garments provided for guests at the wedding—Mt. 22:12. Christ attends the wedding feast in Cana—John 2:1-10.

The bride.—The bath and anointing—Ruth 3:3. Receives presents—Gen. 24:53. Given a handmaid—Gen. 24:59; 29:24, 29. Adorned—Ps. 45:13, 14; Is. 49:18; Jer. 2:32; Rev. 19:7, 8. *With jewels*—Is. 61:10. Attended by bridesmaids—Ps. 45:9. Stood on right hand of bridegroom—Ps. 45:9. Receives benediction—Gen. 24:60; Ruth 4:11, 12. Must forget father's house and people—Ruth 1:8-17; Ps. 45:10.

Bridegroom.—Specially clothed—Is. 61:10. Attended by many friends—Ju. 14:11; John 3:29. Crowned with garlands—Song of Sol. 3:11; Is. 61:10. Rejoices over bride—Ps. 19:5; Is. 62:5. Returns with bride to his house at night—Mt. 25:1-6.

384

Paul's teaching concerning — Advises marriage. — I Tim. 5:14, 15. For the sake of chastity — I Cor. 7:1-6, 9. Lawful in all — I Cor. 7:8-40; 9:5. Rebukes those who advise against marriage — I Tim. 4:3. Elders or bishops and deacons to be husbands of one wife — I Tim. 3:2, 12. **Should be only in the Lord.** — I Cor. 7:39. **Honorable in all.** — Heb. 13:4. **Seems to think that to remain unmarried and virtuous is better, because of persecution of that time.** — I Cor. 7:8, 17, 25-40.

Be not unequally yoked with unbelievers. — II Cor. 6:14, 17.

Marriage of widows. — Rom. 7:1-3; I Cor. 7:39, 40.

Monogamy taught in the Bible. — Wife singular number — Mt. 19:5. God gave Adam one wife — Gen. 2:18-24. Each man had one wife in the ark — Gen. 7:13. Gen. 2:24; Mal. 2:15; Mt. 19:5, 6; Mk. 10:7, 8; I Cor. 11:11, 12; Eph. 5:31; I Tim. 3:2, 12.

Polygamy and concubinage practised. — Lamech the first polygamist — Gen. 4:19. Abraham — Gen. 12:5; 16:1-6; 25:1, 6. Jacob — Gen. 29: 25-30. Esau — Gen. 36:2, 3. Gideon the judge — Ju. 8:30, 31. Elkanah the father of Samuel — I Sam. 1:2. Saul — II Sam. 3:7. David — I Sam. 27:3; II Sam. 5:13; I Chr. 14:3. Solomon — I Ki. 11:1-3; Song of Sol. 6:8. Rehoboam — II Chr. 11: 21.

Marriage figurative. — Symbolizes: Idolatry — Mal. 2:11. God's union with the Jews — Is. 54:5; Jer. 3:14; Hos. 2:19, 20. Christ's union with the church — Mt. 22:1-14; 25:1-10; Rom. 7:4; Eph. 5:23, 24, 32; Rev. 19:7.

Jesus' teaching on marriage. — Mt. 19:4-9; 24:38; Mk. 10:5-12; Lu. 14:20; 17:27. No marriage in heaven — Mt. 22:30; Mk. 12:25; Lu. 20: 34, 35. Marriage feast — Mt. 22:1-14; 25:1-10; Lu. 12:36; 14:8. Committing adultery — Mt. 5:32; 19:9; Mk. 10:11; Lu. 16:18.

MARY. Heb. Mariam (1) **The virgin mother of Jesus.** — Mt. 1:18-21; Lu. 1:30-38; John 2:1; Acts 1:14. **Descendant of House of David.** — Lu. 1:27; Rom. 1:3. Sister to the wife of Clopas — John 19:25. Betrothed to Joseph — Mt. 1:18-22. Annunciation of Gabriel — Lu. 1:36-38. Conception of Jesus by the Holy Spirit — Mt. 1:18-20. Mary honored by Joseph — Mt. 1:20, 25. Visits Elizabeth — Lu. 1:39, 40. Magnifies the Lord in wonderful hymns — Lu. 1: 46-55. Returned to Nazareth — Lu. 1:56. Journeys with Joseph to Bethlehem, because of the enrollment under Cyrenius — Lu. 2:1-5. Gives birth to the Child Jesus in a manger — Lu. 2:7. Ponders eagerly the message of the shepherds — Lu. 2:19. Marvels at the words of Simeon — Lu. 2:33. Warned of her sorrows — Lu. 2:34, 35. Gave Jesus careful training — Lu. 2:41. Taught Him the Scriptures — Lu. 2:40. Her sorrows begin — Lu. 2:43-49. Questions Jesus about His absence — Lu. 2: 48. Still holds control — Lu. 2:51. Ponders the strange words of the Boy Jesus — Lu. 2:51. Addressed as woman — John 2:4; 19:26. Work of the Messiah not under her control —John 2:4. Her relation to Jesus changes: Doubt comes as to His sanity, due to His unexpected conduct —Mt. 12:46-50; Mk. 3:31-35; Lu. 8:19-21. Committed to the care of the Apostle John—John 19:25-27. Attendant at the Cross—Mt. 27: 56; Mk. 15:40; John 19:25-27. Was among earliest believers, after the resurrection of Jesus—Acts 1:14.

(2) **Mary Magdalene** (*Or*, of Magdala). —Seven demons cast out of her— Mk. 16:9; Lu. 8:2. Accompanied Jesus through Galilee—Lu. 8:1, 2. Ministered to Jesus' wants—Lu. 8: 2. Also accompanied Jesus on last journey to Jerusalem—Mt. 27:55; Mk. 15:41; Lu. 23:55; 24:10. Lingered at the cross—Mt. 27:56; Lu. 23:33; John 19:25. Watched the tomb on Friday afternoon after the burial of Jesus—Mt. 27:61; Mk. 15:47. Visits the sepulchre, Saturday afternoon—Mt. 28:1. Brought spices after the sabbath was past— Mk. 16:1. Came early Sunday morning to anoint the body of Jesus— Mk. 16:2; John 20:1. Runs to tell Peter and John of the empty tomb —John 20:1-10. Weeps beside the tomb, and sees two angels—John 20:11-15. Recognizes Jesus after the resurrection—John 20:16, 17. Testifies to the resurrection of Jesus —John 20:18.

(3) **Mary of Bethany, the sister of Lazarus.**—Her family shared their home with Jesus—Mt. 21:17; 26: 6; Mk. 11:1; Lu. 19:29; John 12:1. Sat at Jesus' feet as learner—Lu. 10:39. Implores Jesus concerning Lazarus—John 11:31, 32. Anointed

the head and feet of Jesus—Mt. 26: 6-13; Mk. 14:3; Lu. 7:36-38; John 12:3-7.

(4) **Mary, wife of Clopas.** — Sister of Jesus' mother—John 19:25. Followed Jesus in His journeys—Lu. 8:1-3. Watched at sepulchre of Jesus —Mt. 27:61; Mk. 15:47. Visited sepulchre, late on sabbath day—Mt. 28:1. Brought spices after the sabbath passed, about sunrise on Sunday to anoint the body of Jesus—Mk. 16:2.

(5) **Mary the mother of John Mark.** —Acts 12:12. Peter resorts thither on being released from prison — Acts 12:12. Her house a house of prayer —Acts 12:12-17.

(6) **Mary the friend of Paul.**—Rom. 16:6. (This enumeration of the Marys presents difficulties of identification and is not agreed to by all scholars.)

MIDWIVES. Gen. 35:17; 38:28; Ex. 1:15-21.

MIND: Image and likeness of God. —Gen. 1:26, 27; 5:1. Reference is to mind, not body, else animals would also be in image of God. **Man** is superior—Ps. 8:6-8. A little lower than God—Ps. 8:5. Or angels— Heb. 2:7. God without form—Deut. 4:15, 16. Mind speedily created— Gen. 2:7. In Christ there is a new creation, also in the image of God —Rom. 6:4; 7:6; II Cor. 5:17; Eph. 4:24; Col. 3:10. Man is responsible because he can reason and choose —Deut. 30:15-20; Josh. 24:15, 22; Ju. 10:14; I Ki. 18:21; Pr. 1: 29-31; John 10:42; Acts 5:4; Phil. 1:22; Heb. 11:25. Mind as a field —Mt. 13:19-23; Mk. 4:14-20; John 4:35; I Cor. 3:6-9.

A storehouse of thoughts and purposes. — Job 12:5; Ps. 10:4; 33: 11; 92:5; 94:11, 19; Pr. 12:5; 24: 9; Is. 59:7; 65:2; 66:18; Jer. 4:14; Dan. 4:5, 36; Mic. 4:12; Mk. 12: 30; Lu. 2:35, 47; 10:27; Acts 14: 2; I Cor. 1:19; II Cor. 4:3; 10:5; Eph. 1:18; Heb. 8:10; 10:16; II Pet. 3:1; I John 5:20; Rev. 17:9.

The mind perceives. — Ez. 11:5; 20: 32; Lu. 9:47; 24:38, 45; II Tim. 2: 7; Rev. 13:18.

The mind remembers. — Deut. 30:1; Neh. 9:17; Ps. 8:4; 31:12; 111:5; 115:12; Is. 17:10; 46:8; 65:17; Jer. 3:16; 32:35; 44:21; 51:50; Lam. 3:21; Mk. 14:72; Tit. 3:1; Heb. 2:6.

The mind reasons. — Job 4:13; 13:6; 20:2; Ps. 8:4; 31:12; 111:5; 115: 12; 139:23; Dan. 2:29, 30; 4:19; 5:6, 10; Amos 4:13; Mt. 9:4; 12: 25; 15:17; 16:7-9, 11; 21:25; 24: 15; Mk. 2:6-8; 8:16, 17; 11:31; 12:28; Lu. 3:15; 5:21, 22; 9:46; 20:5, 14; 24:15, 45; John 12:40; Acts 8:22; Rom. 1:20; 2:15; 7:23, 25; I Cor. 3:20; 14:14; Eph. 3:4; I Tim. 1:7; Heb. 4:12; 11:3.

Feels. — Sorrow — Gen. 26:35; Deut. 28:65; I Sam. 9:5. Worry — I Sam. 9:20; Mt. 6:25, 27, 28, 31, 34; 10: 19; Mk. 13:11; Lu. 12:11, 22, 25, 26. Anger — II Sam. 17:8. Hate — Col. 1:21. Love — Rom. 8:5; 12: 16; Phil. 3:15, 19; Heb. 11:15.

Plans, forms a purpose. — Deut. 15: 9; I Sam. 2:35; II Ki. 9:15; I Chr. 22:7; II Chr. 24:4; Job 17:11; 21: 27; Ps. 40:5; 56:5; 146:4; Pr. 16: 3; 21:5; Is. 55:7-9; Jer. 6:19; 19:5; 29:11; Ez. 24:25; 38:10; Mt. 1:19; John 5:15; Rom. 8:27; 15:5, 6; I Cor. 2:16; II Cor. 1:15, 17; 13:11;

Gal. 5:10; Phil. 2:2, 5; 3:15; 4:2; II Thess. 2:2; I Pet. 3:8; 4:1; Rev. 17:13.

Desires. — Deut. 18:6; Neh. 4:6; Acts 13:22; Eph. 2:3; I Pet. 4:3.

Decides. — I Chr. 28:9; Lu. 12:29; Acts 28:6; Rom. 7:23; Phil. 1:27; I Pet. 1:13.

Consents. — Gen. 23:8; Rom. 7:25; Phil. 1:14.

Can be persuaded. — Jer. 15:1; Acts 28:23, 24.

Can be humble. — Acts 20:19; Phil. 2:3.

Imagines. — Gen. 6:5; I Chr. 28:9; 29:18.

Obeys or refuses. — Num. 16:28; 24: 13; Rom. 6:12.

Should seek God. — Deut. 4:29; 10: 12; Acts 17:27.

Can grow worse. — Ps. 119:113; Pr. 21:27; Ez. 38:10; Rom. 1:28; 8:6, 7; II Cor. 3:14; 4:4; 11:3; Eph. 4: 17, 18; Col. 2:18; I Tim. 6:5; II Tim. 3:8; Tit. 1:15; Heb. 12:3.

Can grow better. — Mk. 5:15; Lu. 8: 35; Rom. 8:6; 12:2; Eph. 4:23, 24; Col. 1:9, 2:2, 3, 10.

MIRIAM. (1) Sister of Moses and Aaron — Ex. 15:20. Watches over Moses while in the ark — Ex. 2:4-8. Called "The prophetess" — Ex. 15:20. Ranks with Moses and Aaron — Mic. 6:4. Led the women in a song of deliverance — Ex. 15:20, 21. Stricken for being jealous of Moses — Num. Ch. 12; Deut. 24:9. Dies and is buried at Kadesh — Num. 20:1.

(2) **A daughter of Ezra.** — I Chr. 4: 17.

MISTRESS. II Ki. 5:3; Ps. 123:2; Pr. 30:23; Is. 24:2. Despise — Gen. 16: 4. Flee from — Gen. 10:8. House,

Of the—I Ki. 17:17. Kingdoms, Of —Is. 47:5. Return to—Gen. 16:9. Witchcrafts, Of—Nah. 3:4.

MOTHER. Must honor her—Ex. 20: 12; Deut. 5:16; Pr. 1:8; 23:22; Mt. 15:4;19:19; Mk. 7:10; 10:19; Lu. 18:20; Eph. 6:2. Eve, the mother of all—Gen. 3:20. Love of mothers contrasted with God's—Is. 49:15. Sarah a mother of nations—Gen. 17:16. Punishment for maltreatment of—Ex. 21:15, 17; Lev. 18:7; 20: 9; Pr 30:11; 30:17. Foolish son heaviness of—Pr. 10:1. Despise not, when old—Pr. 23:22. He that loveth, more than Me—Mt. 10:37. Mother of Lord come to Me—Lu. 1:43. Mother of Jesus was there— John 2:1. Peter's wife's mother— Mt. 8:14; Lu. 4:38. Who is my mother?—Mt. 12:48; Mk. 3:34. Mary, Mother of Jesus, steadfast— Acts 1:14. Can a man enter second time, etc.—John 3:4. Entreat elderly women as mothers—I Tim. 5:2.

MOTHER-IN-LAW. Not to be defiled —Lev. 18:17; 20:14; Deut. 27:23. Ruth's affection for—Ruth 1:14-17. Dwelt with—Ruth 2:23. Boaz provides for—Ruth 3:17. Rising up against—Mic. 7:6; Mt. 10:35; Lu. 12:53. Peter's mother-in-law healed by Jesus—Mk. 1:30-31.

NAOMI. Mother-in-law of Ruth— Ruth 1:6-18; 3:1, 16, 17. Wife of Elimelech—Ruth 1:2. Husband dies —Ruth 1:3. Women in Bethlehem did not know Naomi—Ruth 1:20, 21. Came to Bethlehem in barley harvest—Ruth 1:22. Her kinsman —Ruth 2:1, 20, 22; 4:3. Buying Naomi's field—Ruth 4:5, 9. The women said to Naomi, "Blessed be Jehovah"—Ruth 4:14.

NURSE. Gen. 24:59. Became—Ruth 4:16. Cherisheth children—I Thess. 2:7. Child—Ex. 2:7, 9. Rebekah's —Gen. 35:8. Stole away—II Ki. 11:2; II Chr. 22:11. Took him up —II Sam. 4:4.

PARENTS: The father.—Father was the priest of the family group—Gen. 31:53; 32:9; I Sam. 20:6. As such, Reverence due him—Ex. 21:15, 17; Mt. 15:4-6; Mk. 7:10-13.

House.—Fathers constituted elders of Hebrew communities—Ex. 3:16, 18; 4:29; 12:21; 17:5; 18:12; 24: 1, 9. Ruled the household—Gen. 18:19; Pr. 3:12; 13:24; I Tim. 3: 4, 5, 12; Tit. 1:6; Heb. 12:7. Decided on marriages of children—Gen. 24:4, 28:2; Ju. 14:2. Sold daughters to bridegrooms—Ex. 21: 7; Neh. 5:5.

Wives and mothers.—Wives were bought and paid for; thus legally property of husband—Gen. 29:18-30; 31:41; Ex. 20:17. Wife not a mere chattel. Wife largely the provider—Pr. 31:10-29. Superior to concubine in that her children were preferred—Gen. 17:18-21. Law sympathetic to wife—Ex. 21:2, 12; Deut. 21:14.

Mother.—To be childless a disgrace —Gen. 30:1; I Sam. 1:5-7; Is. 4:1. To possess children a great joy— Gen. Ch. 30. Mother to be honored —Ex. 20:12; 21:15; Lev. 19:3; Mt. 15:4; 19:19; Eph. 6:2. Beloved by children—Pr. 31:28. Comforts her children—Is. 66:13.

Parents: Responsibilities of.—To maintain children—Pr. 19:14; II Cor. 12:14. To educate—Gen. 18:19; Ex. 12:26, 27; 13:8; Deut. 6:6, 7;

388

Eph. 6:4. Sons depend on fathers after passing from mother's control — Pr. 1:8; 3:12; 4:1; 13:1.

Further duties of parents. — To love — Tit. 2:4. To train children up for God — Deut. 4:9; 11:19; Pr. 22:6; Is. 38:19; Eph. 6:4. To command obedience to God — Deut. 32:46; I Chr. 28:9. To teach them God's power — Ex. 10:2; Ps. 78:4. His judgments — Joel 1:3, 4. To pity them — Ps. 103:13. To bless them — Gen. 48:15; Heb. 11:20. To provide for them — Job 42:15; II Cor. 12:14; I Tim. 5:8. To correct them — Pr. 13:24; 19:18; 23:13; 29:17; Heb. 12:7. Not to provoke them — Eph. 6:4; Col. 3:21. Not to make unholy connections for them — Gen. 24:1-4; 28:1-2. To impress divine deeds and commands upon them — Deut. 4:9; 6:6; 11:19; 32:46; Ps. 44:2; 78:3-6.

PRINCESSES. — I Ki. 11:3; Lam. 1:1.

PROPHETESSES. — Miriam — Ex. 15:20. Deborah — Ju. 4:4. Huldah — II Ki. 22:14. Anna — Lu. 2:36. Joel 2:28; Acts 2:17-21.

QUEEN: Queen of Egypt. — Tahpenes — I Ki. 11:19. Queen of Sheba — I Ki. 10:1, 4, 10, 13; II Chr. 9:1, 3, 9, 12; Mt. 12:42; Lu. 11:31.

Queen of Persia. — (1) Vashti — Esth. 1:9, 11, 12, 15-17. (2) Esther — Esth. 2:17, 22; 4:4; 5:2, 3, 12; 7:1-8; 8:1, 7; 9:12, 29, 31. (3) Neh. 2:6.

Queen of the Chaldeans. — Dan. 5:10.

Queen of Ethiopia. — Acts 8:27.

Figurative. — Ps. 45:9; Rev. 18:7.

In Song. — Song of Sol. 6:8, 9.

Queen mother. — I Ki. 15:13; II Ki. 10:13; 11:3; II Chr. 15:16; Jer. 13:18; 29:2.

Queen of heaven. — Venus — Jer. 7:18; 44:17-19, 25.

RACHEL. Wife of Jacob and daughter of Laban — Gen. 29:6, 9, 10, 12, 16, 18, 29. Jacob serves 7 years for her — Gen. 29:20, 25. and yet 7 more — Gen. 29:30. Laban gives Bilhah to — Gen. 29:29. Envies Leah — Gen. 30:1. Jacob angry with — Gen. 30:2. Blessed with sons — Gen. 30:6, 8, 24; 46:22, 25. Meets Jacob in field — Gen. 31:14. Asks father for portion — Gen. 31:14. Flees with Jacob — Gen. 30:25. Steals teraphim — Gen. 31:19, 32-35. Rachel and son follow company — Gen. 33:1, 2, 7. Rachel dies in travail — 35:16, 19. Jacob mourns for Rachel — 48:7. Leah and Rachel referred to by Boaz as builders of house of Israel — Ruth 4:11.

RUTH, *Friend.* **Daughter-in-law of Naomi.** — Ruth 1:4, 6. Lived in Bethlehem — Ruth 1:19. Refused to leave Naomi — Ruth 1:14, 16-17. Gleans in Boaz's field — Ruth 2:2-3. Boaz recognizes her — Ruth 2:5-9. Presents for consideration a kinsman's duty — Ruth 3:1-9. Boaz submits and marries — Ruth 4:1-13. Obed, a son, is born, who in time begets Jesse, the father of David — Ruth 4:13, 17, 21, 22; Mt. 1:5-6. Ancestress of Jesus — Lu. 3:32.

SARAH. Wife of Abraham. — Gen. 11:29, 31. Is barren — Gen. 11:30; 16:1.

Also Abraham's half sister. — Gen. 12:13; 20:2, 5, 12. Goes out with others from Ur — Gen. 11:41. Dwells in Haran — Gen. 11:31. **Sarai goes with husband into Egypt.** — Gen. 12:10.

389

Is persuaded to pass as sister.—Gen. 12:15. Beholding her beauty, Pharaoh takes her as his wife—Gen. 12:15; Jehovah plagued Pharaoh and he releases Sarai—Gen. 12:17-20. **Sarai gives Hagar as a concubine to Abraham.**—Gen. 16:1-3. Hagar despises Sarai—Gen. 16:4. Sarai drives her out—Gen. 16:6. Angel of Jehovah bids her return—Gen. 16:7-9. Ishmael is born to Hagar—Gen. 16:15. **Sarai's name changed to Sarah.**—Gen. 17:15. **Sarah is promised a son.**—Gen. 17:16-19; 18:10-15. Entertains messengers of God—Gen. 18:1-15. **Sarah visits Gerar with her husband and is taken into harem by Abimelech.**—Gen. 20:2. God warns him concerning his act and Sarah is restored—Gen. 20:3-18. **Isaac is born.**—Gen. 21:1-7. **Demands that Hagar be cast out.**—Gen. 21:9-13; Gal. 4:23-30. **Sarah dies in Hebron at the age of 127 years.**—Gen. 23:1, 2. **Buried in the cave of Machpelah.**—Gen. 23:3-19. **The faith of Sarah.**—Heb. 11:11. **Obeyed Abraham.**—I Pet. 3:5, 6. **Justified in casting out Hagar.**—Gal. 4:23-31. **SERVANT. Early mention of.**—Gen. 9:25-26.

Divided into: Male—Gen. 24:34. Female—Gen. 16:6. Bond—Gen. 43:18; Lev. 25:46. Hired—Mk. 1:20; Lu. 15:17. Called hirelings—John 10:12-13. **Servitude under the patriarchs.**—Was of two kinds, born in the house, and bought with money—Gen. 17:

13. Abraham formed an army out of his 318—Gen. 14:1-16. Those born in house had large privileges—Gen. 15:2-3; 24:2-9; 17:12-14. Jacob bought his wives with labor—Gen. 29:16-23. Joseph was sold into Egypt—Gen. 37:27-28. **Egyptian bondage.**—Egyptians had servants—Ex. 8:21, 24; 9:14, 20, 21; 11:5. Israelites not distributed among Egyptians—Gen. 46:33-34; Ex. 8:21-24; 9:23. Service required of the males by taskmasters—Ex. 1:8-14; 5:4-21. **Servitude under Moses.**—Laws of Moses concerning—Ex. 21:1-11, 20-32; Lev. 19:20-22; 25:6, 10, 44-54; Deut. 15:12-18. **Israelites were no men-stealers.**—Ex. 21:16; Deut. 24:7. Service either voluntarily or judicially imposed—Lev. 25:39, 47; Ex. 21:7; 22:3, 4; Deut. 20:14. Strangers, only, might be purchased—Lev. 25:44-46. Not to be oppressed—Deut. 24:14-15. Could change his master—Deut. 23:16. If abused he went free—Ex. 21:26-27. Term limited—Deut. 15:12. **Privileges of.**—Admitted into covenant with God—Deut. 29:10, 13. Took part at festivals—Ex. 12:43, 44; Deut. 12:18; 16:10-16. **Instructed in conduct of life.**—Deut. 31:10-13; Josh. 8:33-35; II Chr. 17:8-9; 34:30. Under same law as masters—Deut. 1:16, 17; 27:19; Lev. 19:15; 24:22. Rights the same—Num. 15:15, 16, 29. Intermarried with master's family—Gen. 16:1, 2, 6; 30:3, 9. **Hired.**—Engaged by the day—Mt. 20:2. By the year—Lev. 25:53; Is. 16:

14. To be paid when work is done —Lev. 19:13; Deut. 24:15. To be esteemed worthy of wages—Lu. 10: 7. To partake of produce of land in Sabbatical year—Lev. 25:6. If foreigners, not allowed to partake of holy things—Ex. 12:45; Lev. 22:10.

Bondservants.—Bought and sold—Gen. 17:13, 27; 37:28, 36; 39:17; Lev. 22:11; Deut. 28:68; Esth. 7: 4; Ez. 27:13; Joel 3:6; Rev. 18:13.

Captives of war made slaves.—II Ki. 5:2; II Chr. 28:8-10. Portion of captives given to priests and Levites—Num. 31:28-47.

Other classes made slaves.—Sojourners—Lev. 25:45. Belonging to foreign nations—Lev. 25:44. Unable to pay debts—II Ki. 4:1; Neh. 5:4-5; Mt. 18:25. Thieves unable to make restitution—Ex. 22:3.

Kindness enjoined.—Lev. 25:43; Eph. 6:9.

Shown by Job.—Job 31:13-14. By Boaz—Ruth 2:4. By Centurion—Mt. 8:8-13. In redeeming them—Neh. 5:8. Emancipation—II Chr. 36:23; Ezra 1:1-4; Jer. 34:8-16; Acts 6:9; I Cor. 7:21.

New Testament principles.—Cannot serve two masters—Mt. 6:24; Lu. 16:13. He that serves is greatest—Mt. 20:26-28; 23:11; Mk. 9:35; 10: 43, 44. Advance from servants to friends—John 15:15. To serve one another—Gal. 5:13. Render justice to servants—Col. 4:1. Must not be eye-servers—Col. 3:22. Obedience becomes servants—Eph. 6:5. Believing masters to be honored—I Tim. 6:1-2. Must not purloin from or gainsay—Tit. 2:9-10. Must treat believing servants as brothers and sisters —I Cor. 7:20-22. Philemon 16.

Term servant used by people to express courtesy.—Gen. 18:3; 32: 5; 33:5; I Sam. 20:7; I Ki. 20:32.

Examples of good.—Eliezer—Gen. 24:10. Jacob—Gen. 31:36-42. Joseph—Gen. 39:5; 41:39; Acts 7:10. Boaz—Ruth 2:4. Jonathan's —I Sam. 14:6-7. Abigail's—I Sam. 25:14-17. David's—II Sam. 12:18. Naaman's—II Ki. 5:2-13. Centurion's —Mt. 8:9. Cornelius—Acts 10:7. Phoebe—Rom. 16:1. Onesimus—Phil. 11.

Examples of bad: Hagar—Gen. 16: 4. Of Abraham and Lot—Gen. 13: 7. Of Abimelech—Gen. 21:25. Of Absalom—II Sam. 13:28-29; 14: 30. Ziba—II Sam. 16:1-4. Zimri—I Ki. 16:9. Gehazi—II Ki. 5:20. Of Joash—II Ki. 12:19-21. Of Amon —II Ki. 21:23. See also Mt. 18:28; 25:14-30; Lu. 19:12-26.

SERVICE. Acts 24:14. As deacons—I Tim. 3:10. Choose, whom ye will —Josh. 24:15. Cumbered about much—Lu. 10:40. God, Unto—Mal. 3:14; John 16:2. Grievous—II Chr. 10:4. Hard—Ex. 1:14. Most of heaven—Acts 7:42. King's—Esth. 8:10. Lord—Acts 20:19. Nations shall—Ps. 72:11. One another—I Pet. 5:5. Perfect heart, With—I Chr. 28:9. Seed shall—Ps. 22:30. Spiritual—Rom. 12:1. Two masters —Mt. 6:24. War, In—I Chr. 7:40. Whom should I—II Sam. 16:19.

SUBJECTION. I Cor. 14:34; Gal. 2:5. All things in—I Cor. 15:27; Heb. 2:8. Brought into—Ps. 106:42; Jer. 34:11, 16. Children, In—I Tim. 3:4. Father, Unto—Heb. 12:9. Masters, To—I Pet. 2:18. Must needs be in —Rom. 13:5. Wives, Of—Eph. 5: 22; Tit. 2:5; I Pet. 3:1, 5. Women, Of—I Tim. 2:11.

WIDOW. Under God's protection—Deut. 10:18; Ps. 68:5; 146:9; Pr. 15:25; Jer. 49:11. Laws relating to marriage—Deut., 25:5; Lev. 21:14; Ez. 44:22; Mk. 12:19. See also I Cor. 7:8.

Laws respecting: Not to be oppressed—Ex. 22:22; Deut. 27:19; Is. 1:17, 23; 10:2; Jer. 22:3; Zech. 7:10; Mal. 3:5. Creditors not to take raiment—Deut. 24:17. Bound to perform their vows—Num. 30:9. To be allowed to glean in fields—Deut. 24:19. To have a share of triennial tithe—Deut. 14:28-29; 26:12-13. To share in public rejoicings—Deut. 16:11-14.

When childless, to be married to husband's nearest kin.—Deut. 25:8-10; Ruth 3:10-13; 4:4-5; Mt. 22:24-26.

Widows to be cared for by church.—Acts 6:1; I Tim. 5:3-5, 9-16; Jas. 1:27.

WIFE: Laws concerning.—Ex. 20:17; 21:3-5; 22:16; Lev. 18:8, 11, 14-16, 18, 20; 20:10, 11, 14, 21; 21:7, 13, 14; Num. 5:11-31; 30:16; 36:8; Deut. 5:21; 13:6; 20:7; 21:11-14; 22:13, 30; 24:5. Divorce—Deut. 24:1, 3, 4; Mt. 5:31, 32; 19:3-10; Mk. 10:2-12; Lu. 16:18; I Cor. 7:32-40.

Proverbs concerning.—Pr. 12:4; 18:22; 31:10.

Duties of.—Gen. 3:16; Rom. 7:2; I Cor. 7:2-4, 10, 11, 13, 14, 16; Eph. 5:22, 24, 33; Col. 3:18; Tit. 2:4, 5; I Pet. 3:1. Honoring husbands—Esth. 1:20.

Illustrative.—Jer. 3:1, 20; Ez. 16:32; Eph. 5:25-27, 29, 33; Rev. 19:7; 21:9.

WOMAN, *i.e.,* **Taken out of man.**—Gen. 2:23. Created—Gen. 1:27; 2:21, 22. Blessed of God—Gen. 1:28. The function of—Gen. 1:28. A helpmeet to man—Gen. 2:18. Led astray by Satan—Gen. 3:1-7; II Cor. 11:3; I Tim. 2:14. Curse pronounced on—Gen. 3:16.

Had separate dwelling.—Gen. 24:67; 31:33. Esth. 2:9, 11.

Had a court in the tabernacle assigned to them.—Ex. 38:8; I Sam. 2:22.

Dress.—II Sam. 13:18; Is. 3:16-23; I Tim. 2:9; I Pet. 3:3-5. May not wear man's clothing—Deut. 22:5. Wore a veil—Gen. 24:65; 38:14; I Cor. 11:5-7, 13. Often went unveiled—Gen. 12:14; 24:16, 21. Wore long hair—I Cor. 11:5, 6, 14, 15. Wore hair plaited and adorned with gold and pearls—Is. 3:24; I Tim. 2:9; I Pet. 3:3. Had head covered—I Cor. 11:5-7, 13. Wore Ornaments—Is. 3:16-23; I Tim. 2:9. Earrings—Gen. 24:47; 35:4; Ez. 16:12. Nose jewels—Is. 3:21. Bracelets—Gen. 24:47; Ex. 35:22; Is. 3:9; Ez. 6:11. Armlets—Is. 3:18. Signet rings—Ex. 35:22. Anklets—Is. 3:18. Amulets—Is. 3:20.

Abiding as virgins.—I Cor. 7:25-38. Spared in war—Num. 31:18, 35; Deut. 21:14. Wives for the tribe of Benjamin—Ju. 21:12-14. Apparel of king's daughters—II Sam. 13:18. Nurtured by kings' wives—Esth. 2:8-13. No marriage without father's consent—Gen. 34:6-8; Ex. 22:17. Non-marriage a calamity—Ju. 11:37; Ps. 78:63. Punishment for corrupting betrothed—Deut. 22:23, 24. When not betrothed—Ex. 22:16, 17; Deut. 22:28, 29. Kingdom of heaven likened to—Mt. 25:1-12. Typify saints in heaven—Rev. 14:4.

Duties of women.—Subject to husband—Gen. 3:16; I Cor. 7:39; 11: 8, 9; Eph. 5:22-24; Col. 3:18; Tit. 1:5; I Pet. 3:1-6. Helper of husband. —Pr. 31:11-29. Housekeeping—Gen. 18:6; Pr. 31:15-21, 27. Spinning—Ex. 35:25, 26; Pr. 31:19. Tending flocks and herds—Gen. 29: 9; Ex. 2:16. Gleaning—Ruth 2:7, 8, 15-23. Drawing and carrying water—Gen. 24:11-16; I Sam. 9:11; John 4:7. Work in fields—Is. 27: 11; Ez. 26:6, 8. Grinding corn—Mt. 24:41; Lu. 17:35.

Social status of.—Esth. 1:10-22; Dan. 5:1, 2, 10-12; Acts 8:27; 24:24; 25:13, 23. Take part in public affairs —Ex. 15:20, 21; Ju. 4:4-22; 9:50-54; 11:24; I Sam. 18:6, 7; II Sam. 20:14-22; I Ki. 1:15-21; 10:1-13; 21:7-15; II Ki. 11:1-3; II Chr. 9:1-9; 21:6; 22:3; Ps. 68:25; Dan. 5: 9-13.

In business.—I Chr. 7:24; Pr. 31:14, 16; Acts 16:14.

Required to attend the reading of the law.—Deut. 31:12; Josh. 8:35.

Celebrants of victories.—Ex. 15:20-21; I Sam. 18:6-7.

Mourners at funerals.—Jer. 9:17, 20.

Property rights.—Num. 27:1-9; Josh. 17:3-6; Ruth 4:3-9; Job 42:15. Wife sold for husband's debts—Mt. 18: 25. Aid to widows—Deut. 14:29; II Ki. 4:1-7; Ps. 146:9; Acts 6:1; I Tim. 5:3, 16.

Characteristics.—Fair and graceful—Gen. 12:11; 24:16; Song of Sol. 1:8. Haughty—Is. 3:16. Ambitious —Mt. 20:20, 21. Wise—II Sam. 14: 2; Pr. 31:26. Weaker than man—I Pet. 3:7. Timid—Is. 19:16; Jer. 51:30; Nah. 3:13. Silly and easily led into error—II Tim. 3:6. Loving and affectionate—II Sam. 1:26.

Clings to her children—Is. 49:15. Virtuous—Ruth 3:11. Fond of dress and ornaments—Is. 3:17-21; I Tim. 2:9. Mirthful—Ju. 11:34; 21:21; Jer. 31:13. Patriotic—Ex. 15:20-21; Ju. 4:4-22; 5:24-27; 9:53, 54; I Sam. 18:6; II Sam. 20:16-22; Esth. 5:1-8; 7:1-4; Prophetic: *Deborah* —Ju. 4:4. *Hannah*—I Sam. 2:1-10. *Huldah*—II Ki. 22:14-20. *Elizabeth*—Lu. 1:41-43. *Philip's daughters*—Acts 21:9.

Woman's vows.—Num. 30:3-16.

Woman, charged with adultery, to be tried.—Num. 5:12-31.

Taken captive.—Num. 31:9, 15, 17, 18, 35; Deut. 28:32, 41; Ju. 5:30; Lam. 1:18; Ez. 30:18.

Treated with cruelty in war.—Is. 13: 16; Lam. 5:11. Zech. 14:2.

Purification of.—Lev. Ch. 12; 15:19-33; II Sam. 11:4; Lu. 2:22-24.

Punishment of.—Ex. 22:16, 17; Deut. 22:23-27, 28, 29.

Religious privileges in N.T.—Lu. 2: 36-38; Acts 1:14; 12:12-17; 21:9; I Cor. 11:5; 14:34, 35; Gal. 3:28; Phil. 4:3; I Tim. 2:12; 5:2-11; Tit. 2:3-5.

Church workers.—Phil. 4:3. Lydia—Acts 16:14-15. Dorcas—Acts 9:36. Priscilla—Acts 18:26. Phoebe——Rom. 16:1, 2. Julia—Rom. 16:5. Mary—Rom. 16:6.

Paul's teaching concerning.—I Cor. 11:5-15; Eph. 5:22-24; Col. 3:18; I Tim. 3:11; 5:2-16; Tit. 2:3-5. Concerning public speaking—I Cor. 11: 13; 14:34, 35; Gal. 3:28; I Tim. 2: 12, 13. Paul welcomes women as church workers—Acts 16:13-15; 18:2, 3; Rom. 16:1-16.

First at the sepulchre.—Mk. 15:46, 47; 16:1-6; Lu. 23:55, 56; 24:1-10; John 20:1.

Christ appears to the.—Mt. 28:8, 10; Mk. 16:8, 10; Lu. 24:9, 10, 22; John 20:2, 18. To Mary Magdalene—Mk. 16:9; John 20:14-17.

Precepts concerning: Seduction— Pr. 2:16, 19; 5:3-11; 6:25-29; 7: 4-27; 23:27. Housekeeping—Pr. 14:1; 18:22; 31:10-31; Lu. 10:38-42. Keepers at home, sober—Tit. 2:1-5; Virtue—Pr. 12:4; 31:10-31. Contentiousness—Pr. 19:13; 21: 9, 19; 25:24; 27:15, 16; I Cor. 14: 34. Prudence—Pr. 19:14. Idlers and tattlers—I Tim. 5:13. Examples to the younger—Tit. 2:3-5. Modesty —I Cor. 11:5, 6; 14:34, 35.

Two remarkable conversions.—Samaritan woman—John 4:7-39. Lydia—Acts 16:13-15.

Noted women—Good: Deborah—Ju. 4:5-16; 5:1-31; Mother of Samson —Ju. 13:23; Naomi—Ruth 1:1-22; 2:1-3, 18-22; 3:1; 4:14-17. Ruth —Ruth 1:4-22; Chs. 2-4. Hannah, the mother of Samuel—I Sam. 1:2-28; Abigail—I Sam. 25:14-37. Widow of Zarephath, who fed Elijah— I Ki. 17:8-24. The Shunammite woman—II Ki. 4:8-38. Vashti—Esth. 1:9-22; 2:1-4. Esther—Esth. 2:5-23; 4:4-17; 5:1-14; 7:1-10; 8:1-17. Mary, mother of Jesus—Mt. 1: 18-25; 2:11-15; 12:46, 47; Mk. 3: 31; Lu. 1:26-56; 2:4-7, 16-19, 34, 35; 8:19; John 2:3-5; 19:25-27; Acts 1:14. Mary Magdalene—Mt. 27:56, 61; 28:1-10; Mk. 15:40, 47; 16:1-9; Lu. 8:2, 3; 23:55, 56; 24: 1-7; John 19:25; 20:1, 11-18. Mary, sister of Lazarus—Mt. 26:7-13; Mk. 14:3-9; Lu. 10:38-42; John 11:1, 2, 5, 29; 12:3. Mary, wife of Clopas —Mt. 27:55; Mk. 15:47; John 19: 25. Mother of John Mark—Acts 12:

12. Elizabeth—Lu. 1:6, 41-45. Anna —Lu. 2:37, 38; Widow with two mites—Mk. 12:41-44; Lu. 21:2-4. Joanna and Susanna—Lu. 8:3. Martha—Lu. 10:38-42; John 11: 1-5, 17-40. Pilate's wife—Mt. 27: 19. Dorcas—Acts 9:36-39. Lydia —Acts 16:14, 15. Priscilla—Acts 18:26; Rom. 16:3, 4. Phoebe— Rom. 16:1, 2. Julia—Rom. 16:15. Lois and Eunice—II Tim. 1:5.

Wicked women: Eve—Gen. 3:6; I Tim. 2:14. Lot's wife—Gen. 19:26; Lu. 17:32. The daughters of Lot—Gen. 19:31-38. Tamar—Gen. 38:14-24. Potiphar's wife—Gen. 39:7-21. Samson's wife—Ju. 14:15-19. Delilah —Ju. 16:4-22. Michal—II Sam. 6: 16-23. Jezebel—I Ki. 18:4; 19:1, 2; 21:1-29; II Ki. 9:30; Rev. 2:20. Athaliah—II Ki. 11:1-16. Herodias and her daughter—Mt. 14:3-11; Mk. 6:17-28; Lu. 3:19, 20. The woman of Samaria—John 4:7-29. Woman taken in adultery—John 8:1-11. The woman who was a sinner—Lu. 7:36-49. Sapphira—Acts 5:2-10.

WOMB. Barren—Pr. 30:16; Lu. 23: 29; Rom. 4:19. Formed from—Job 31:15; Is. 44:2, 24; 49:5. Fruit of —Gen. 30:2; Is. 13:18; Hos 9:16. Jesus concerned in—Lu. 1:31, 41, 42, 44; 2:21, 23. Lame from—Mt. 19:12; Acts 3:2; 14:8. Miscarrying —Hos. 9:14. Nazirite from—Ju. 13: 5, 7; 10:17. Open—Gen. 29:31; 30:22; Ex. 13:2; Num. 8:16; Ez. 20:26; Lu. 2:23. Second time in —John 3:4. Shut—Gen. 20:18; I Sam. 1:5, 6; Is. 66:9. Sons in— Ruth 1:11. Two nations in—Gen. 25:23, 24; 38:27.

ZIPPORAH. Wife of Moses.—Ex. 2: 21; 4:25; 18:2.

Index of Bible Women

Abigail 72, 195, 196, 309, 324, 332, 335, 343

Abishag 77, 332

Anna 82, 269, 303, 325, 343

Apphia 116

Athaliah 76

Bathsheba 76, 165, 234, 319, 320, 332

Chloe 116, 119

Claudia 116

Damaris 116

Deborah 70, 262-265, 275-279, 303, 324, 343

Delilah 318, 319

Dorcas 116, 118, 341

Elizabeth 81, 82, 213, 214, 215, 240, 325, 335, 343

Esther 74, 75, 267-269, 275, 276, 278, 279, 303, 310, 325, 332, 343

Eunice 116, 240, 303, 343

Euodia 116, 119

Eve 7-16, 18-21, 25-27, 47, 48, 130, 131, 161, 165, 188, 189, 212, 300, 304

Gilead's wife 227

Gomer 77, 159, 320

Hagar 50, 51, 52, 53, 161, 162, 213, 233, 262, 301, 324

Hannah 71, 72, 161, 166, 213, 251, 303, 324, 335, 343

Harlots before King Solomon . . . 234, 235

Hebrew midwives 55

Herodias 321

Herodias' daughter 321

Huldah 71, 262, 267, 325

Isaiah's wife 269

Jehosheba 74

Jephthah's daughter . . . 69, 293-295

Jezebel, the prophetess . . . 119, 273, 278

Jezebel, the Queen . . . 76, 155, 192, 193, 266, 278, 280, 324, 332

Joanna 106, 107

Job's wife 302, 324

Jochebed 56, 57, 234, 309, 335

Julia 116

Junias 116

Leah . . 54, 151, 161, 194, 195, 324

Lois 116, 240, 303, 343

Lot's wife 53

Lydia 118, 338, 350

Manoah's wife 70, 244

Martha . . . 103, 104, 105, 106, 310, 338, 343

Mary Magdalene 106, 107, 108

Mary, mother of James and Joses . . . 106

Mary, mother of Jesus . . . 80, 81, 84-87, 188, 213, 214, 215, 235, 249, 296, 297, 303, 325, 335, 343

Mary, mother of Mark 118, 338

Mary of Bethany 103, 104, 105, 106, 111, 310, 338, 343

Mary (the other) 106

Michal 77, 165, 191

Miriam 67, 263, 278, 324

Naaman's maid 73, 325

Naomi 187, 295, 296, 301, 302, 324, 341

Narcissus 116

Noah's wife 48

Nympha 116, 118, 338

Peninnah 161, 324

Persis 116

Peter's mother-in-law 96, 338

Philip's daughters 119, 273

Phoebe 116, 118, 271

Potiphar's wife 317, 318, 324

Priscilla . . . 116, 118, 119, 122, 156, 272, 273, 275, 277, 278, 279, 325, 338, 343

Queen of Sheba 114, 265, 266, 278, 309

395

Rachel 54, 161, 194, 195, 213, 324, 332
Rahab . . 68, 69, 302, 303, 309, 338, 358
Rebekah 53, 54, 162, 165, 190, 200, 215, 219, 301
Rizpah 77, 234
Ruth 295, 296, 324, 340, 343
Salome 106, 107, 235
Samaritan woman 87-91, 167, 269, 270, 277, 310, 322, 325, 358
Sapphira . . 117, 134, 193, 194, 324
Sarah . . 29, 48, 49, 50, 51, 52, 161, 162, 165, 186, 187, 189, 199, 213, 233, 262, 300, 301, 302, 304, 324, 332, 335, 338, 343, 357
Slave girl 122
Susanna 106
Syntyche 116, 119
Tamar 65, 77, 316, 317, 332
Tryphena 116

Tryphosa 116
Vashti 196, 197
Widow at the Treasury 111, 298
Widow of Nain 96, 97
Widow of Zarephath . . . 75, 235, 338
Wife of Cleophas 106
Woman bent double 101, 102
Woman caught in adultery . . . 93-95, 167, 322
Woman of Abel . . 73, 265, 275, 278, 279, 309, 325
Woman of Shunem . . . 73, 235, 267, 338
Woman of Syro-Phoenecia 99, 100, 101, 111, 236, 297, 298, 310
Woman of Tekoa 72, 325
Woman of the street 91-93, 111, 297, 322
Women of Zion 289, 290, 298
Woman with issue of blood . . . 97, 98
Zelophehad's daughters 65
Zipporah 162, 165

Index of Scriptures

Genesis

Reference	Page
1:27	7
1:28	8, 19, 21, 199, 211
1:31	8
2:15	8
2:16	13
2:17	13
2:18	8, 11, 184
2:20	7
2:23	9
2:24	9, 135, 151, 161, 198, 202, 208
3	300
3:2	13, 14
3:3	14
3:6	14, 15, 161
3:7	18
3:8	13, 18
3:12	18
3:13	18
3:15	26, 48, 211
3:16	18, 19, 20, 21, 24
3:17	16, 25
3:18	25
3:19	25
3:20-24	25
4:1	20, 21, 26, 212
4:19	161
4:25	212
5	30
5:2	10
12:10	162
12:11	31, 50, 332
12:12, 13	31, 50, 162
12:14-20	31, 50, 316
13:10	50
13:14	53
16:1	213, 301, 324
16:2	162, 213, 301, 324
16:3	213, 301, 324
16:4	213, 324
16:5-7	213, 324
16:8	52, 213, 324

Genesis

Reference	Page
16:9	52
17:15, 16	49
18:4, 5	187, 338
18:6	33, 186, 187, 338
18:7, 8	187, 338
18:10	49
18:12	186, 199, 213
18:13, 14	51
19:17	53
19:26	53
20:1	31, 50
20:2	31, 50, 316
20:3	31, 50
20:6	316
20:7	316, 364
20:18	250, 316
21:1, 2	50
21:6, 7	213
21:9	50, 233, 301, 324
21:10	50, 187, 233, 301, 324
21:11	301
21:12, 13	51, 301
21:14	301
21:16	234
21:17-19	52
21:20, 21	53
22	187
22:1-18	302
24:11	33
24:15, 16	33
24:17-19	33, 190
24:20	33
24:67	200
25:22	215
25:23	54, 215, 301
25:28	220
27	162, 190, 301
27:41	220
29	194
29:6	33

Genesis

Reference	Page
29:17	332
29:31	54, 213
29:32	194
29:34	152, 194
30:1	195, 213, 324
30:2	324
30:8	195
30:14, 15	324
30:20	194
30:22	54
30:23	213
31:19	195
37:3, 4	220
38	65
38:6-30	317
39:5, 6	317
39:8-10	318
39:11-16	324
39:17, 18	318, 324
39:19, 20	324

Exodus

1:8	55
1:15-21	55
2:1	234
2:2	56, 234
2:3-11	234
4:24-26	162
13:14	237
15:20	67, 263
18:5, 6	162
19, 20	59
20:12	60, 212
20:14	60
20:17	61
21	62
21:15-17	60
21:20	63
21:22	63, 214
21:23	214
21:26	63

Exodus

Reference	Page
21:28-32	63
22:16	63
22:22	63
32	59
35:26	33
38:8	66

Leviticus

12:1-8	66
15	66
15:19-24	34
15:25	34, 97
15:26-33	34
18	66, 67
18&20	63
19:3	60, 212
19:29	66, 67
20	66, 67, 316
20:10	63, 67, 94, 163, 202
20:11, 12	163
20:13	163
20:14	163, 202
20:15, 16	163
20:21	202
20:27	67
21:9	67

Numbers

6:2	66
11:2	365
12	324
12:5, 10, 15	67
21:7	365
25:3	151
27:1-11	65
30:3	66
30:5, 8	66
31	63
36:1-13	65

Deuteronomy

Reference	Page
5:16	60
5:18	60
5:21	61
9:20	365
11:18, 19	238, 239
11:20, 21	239
21	63
22:13-21	63, 164
22:22	63, 66, 163
22:23-27	66
22:28, 29	66, 164
22:30	66
24:1	63, 163
24:2, 4	64
24:5	199
24:6	33
25:5, 6	65
30:11-18	58

Joshua

Reference	Page
1:14	59
2:1-16	302, 309, 338
2:6	68
6:25	69
24:19-25	59

Judges

Reference	Page
3:4	264
4	303, 324
4:5	70, 264
4:6	70, 238, 264
4:7	238
4:8	70, 265
4:18	33
4:21, 22	238
5	265
9:53	33
11	69
11:1-3	227
11:31	293

Judges

Reference	Page
11:34	294
11:35-39	294
11:40	295
13:3-5, 10-14	70
14:2, 3	244
14:9	244
15:1	244
16:1	244
16:4ff	244
16:5, 18	318
16:25, 30	319
19:20, 21	31, 69

Ruth

Reference	Page
1:1	187
1:3-5	295
1:6, 7	188
1:16, 17	295
1:19-21	302, 341
2:1	341
2:2	33, 296, 341
2:3	341
2:7	296
2:10	296
2:11	296
2:15, 16	296
2:19-21	341
2:22	296, 341
2:23	341
3:5, 6, 11	296
3:13-17	296

I Samuel

Reference	Page
1	213
1:2, 6, 7	324
1:8	213
1:10	71, 364
1:11	71
1:12	364
1:19	72
1:26-28	303

I Samuel

Reference	Page
2:1-10	72, 213
2:11	303
2:19	33
7:5	365
9:11	33
16:7	284
18:20, 21	77, 191
18:22-28	191
19:11-17	191
25:1	309, 324
25:2	309, 324
25:3	195, 309, 324, 332
25:4	309, 324
25:5-8, 10, 11	195, 309, 324
25:9-17	309, 324
25:18	33, 309, 324
25:19-24	309, 324
25:25	195, 309, 324
25:26-35	309, 324
25:26	195, 309, 324
25:37, 38	309, 324
25:39	72, 309, 324
25:40-42	309, 324

II Samuel

Reference	Page
3:13, 14	191
5:13	161
6:16-23	191
11	76
11:1	319
11:2	332
11:4, 5	319
11:6-27	319
12:15-23	319
13	77
13:8	33
14:1-20	73, 324
14:27	332
20:16-22	73, 265, 309, 324
21	77
21:8-14	234
23:3	22

I Kings

Reference	Page
1	77
1:3, 4	332
1:17, 18, 21	234
3:7-14	364
3:16-27	235
8:30	364
10:1-13	265
11:1-3	161
11:4	76
16	266
17	75, 266
17:12	235
17:10-16	338
17:17-24	235, 338
18	155, 266
18:4, 13	192
19-21	266
21:1-6	324
21:7	192, 324
21:8-14	324
21:25	192
21:27-29	155

II Kings

Reference	Page
4:1-7	75
4:8-10	33, 73, 267, 338
4:27	235
4:32, 33	364
5:1-19	74, 324
8:10-12	214
8:26	76
9	192
9:30-37	266, 332
11:2, 3	74, 76
15:16-18	214
19:4	364
20:2	364
22:14-20	74, 267, 325
23:1-3	267

I Chronicles

Reference	Page
15:29	191

II Chronicles

7:14	364

Ezra

10:1	364

Nehemiah

1:6	364, 365
5	77
6:14	77

Esther

1:5-7	196
2:7	332
4:16	75, 267, 303
5-7	310
9:30-32	269

Job

2:9, 10	302, 324
19:20	151
31:15	215
41:24	33

Psalms

1:1-3	360
2:9	243
9:12	287
22:10	215
22:15	151
25:9	287
55:16-18	364
60:3	327
78:5-8	238
119:9-11	315
119:31	151
119:105	360
122:6	364

Psalms

Reference	Page
127:3-5	215
128:3, 4	216
139:13	215
144:12	75, 216
144:13-15	216
147:6	287
149:4	287

Proverbs

1:1-4	248
1:5	248, 344
1:6	248
1:7	248, 345
1:8	75, 212, 248
1:9	248
1:22	308
2:1	248
2:2-5	75, 248
2:6	345
2:16	77, 203
2:17-19	203
3:1, 2	248
3:13-18	75
3:21-26	345
3:34	287
4:6	75, 345
5:1, 2	202, 203
5:3	77, 203
5:4, 5	203
5:6	77, 203
5:8	203
5:15-17	202
5:18-20	75, 200
6	316
6:2	204
6:7	21
6:16, 17, 19	322
6:20	75, 212
6:23	202
6:24	77, 332
6:25	77, 204, 332

Proverbs

Reference	Page
6:26-29	77, 203
6:30, 31	77
6:32, 33	77, 203
6:34, 35	77
7	77, 316
7:1-4	202
7:5	202, 204, 332
7:6-9	332
7:10	204, 332
7:11-15	332
7:16-18	204, 332
7:19, 20	332
7:21, 22	204
8:1, 11	75
9:1-6	75
9:8, 9	344
9:10	345
9:13	309
9:17, 18	203, 316
10:1	75, 212, 248
10:8	345
10:13	344
10:18	323
10:19	345
11:2	345
11:9, 13	323
11:16	75
11:22	309
12:1	344
12:4	75
12:15	344
12:18	323
12:25	305
14:1	75, 309
14:15	344
14:16	345
15:1	323
15:7	344
15:8	363
15:10	241
15:14	344, 345

Proverbs

Reference	Page
15:20	75, 212, 248
15:25	289
15:31	344
15:32	345
15:33	287
16:2	314
16:5	289
16:18	289
16:23	344
16:28	323
17:9	323
17:10	344
17:25	75, 212, 248
17:27, 28	345
18:6-8	323
18:12	287, 289
18:15	344
18:19, 21	323
18:22	75
19:14	75
19:18	241
19:20	241, 248
19:25	344
19:26	75, 212, 248
20:1	327
20:19	323
20:20	212, 248
22:3	345
22:4	287
22:6	238, 248
22:14	77
22:15	242
23:7	314
23:13, 14	242
23:20, 21	328
23:22	75, 212
23:27, 28	77
23:29-35	327
26:28	323
28:15	22
28:25	289

INDEX OF SCRIPTURES

Proverbs

Reference	Page
29:2	22
29:15	75, 242
29:17	242
29:23	287
30:11	75
20:17	212
30:20	77
31	280
31:4, 5	327
31:10	76, 252, 253, 255, 335
31:11-13	76, 252-255, 335
31:14	76, 252, 253, 254, 335
31:15	33, 76, 252, 253, 254, 335
31:16-18	76, 252, 253, 254, 335
31:19	33, 76, 252, 253, 254, 335
31:20	76, 252, 253, 254, 255, 335, 341
31:21	76, 252, 253, 254, 255, 335
31:22-24	76, 252, 253, 254, 335
31:25	76, 252, 253, 254, 255, 335
31:26-29	76, 252, 253, 254, 335
31:30, 31	76, 252, 253, 254, 255, 335

Ecclesiastes

4:9-12	153
9:9	208

Song of Solomon

1:15, 16	332
4:1-7	332
4:9, 11	199
6:1-9	199
7:1-10	199

Isaiah

1:17	75
2:12	289
3:16-24	289, 290

Isaiah

Reference	Page
8:1-4	269
10:5	242
11:4	242
28:7	327
41:10	306
47:1-15	77
49:13-15	223
51:2	51
54:4-8	158
61:10	332
62:4, 5	159
66:13	223

Jeremiah

1:5	215
3:1	159
7:6	75
13:11	151
29:7	365
31:32	159

Ezekiel

13:17, 18	77
16:32	159
20:37	242
29:4	151

Hosea

1	320
1:1-11	159
2:5	320
2:13	320
2:19	159
3:1, 2	159, 320
3:3-5	159
4:11	327

Amos

1:13	214
4:1	327

Jonah

2:1	364

Micah
Reference	Page
6:4	67, 263

Nahum
3:5, 10	77

Malachi
2:14, 15	159
2:16	159, 166

Matthew
1	31
1:5	69, 358
2:13-15	235
5	356
5:3	288, 356
5:4-11	356
5:27-30	111, 112, 316
5:31, 32	111, 112, 164, 316
5:41	291
5:44	365
6	356
6:1	288
6:2	288, 290
6:3, 4	288
6:5	288, 290
6:6	288
6:7, 8	365
6:12	364, 365
6:13-15	365
6:24	304
6:25, 26	306
6:33, 34	306
7	356
7:9-11	217, 218
7:24, 25	346, 356, 360
7:26, 27	346
8:14, 15	110, 338
8:27	168
9:15	159
9:38	365
10:11-15	337

Matthew
Reference	Page
12:42	266, 310
12:46	86, 297
12:47, 48	297
12:49	86, 297
12:50	86
13:33	114
15:21-28	99, 100, 236, 298, 310
17:20	300
18:1-16	216
19:3	112, 113
19:4	20, 64, 112, 113, 164
19:5	20, 64, 112, 113, 152, 164
19:6	10, 112, 113, 152, 164
19:7	112, 113, 164
19:8	64, 112, 113, 164
19:9	112, 113, 202
19:10-12	112, 113, 205
20:20-23	107, 236
20:24	236
20:25-28	22
22:29	361
23:12	287
23:14	113
24:40	114
24:41	33, 114
25:35, 36	340
26:13	106
26:17-19	110
26:39-42	364
26:53	364
27:56	106
28:18-20	114

Mark
1:27	168
1:35	363
3:21	86, 235
3:31-35	235
5:26	97
5:34	300
6:17	321

INDEX OF SCRIPTURES

Mark

Reference	Page
6:19, 20	321
6:22-28	321
6:46	363
7:6-8	28
7:24-30	99, 100, 236
10:13	113
10:14	113, 216
10:15, 16	216
10:35-40	107, 236
11:24, 25	365
12:41, 42	298
12:43, 44	111, 298
15:41	108
15:47	106, 108
16:11	108

Luke

Reference	Page
1	325
1:5	81
1:6	81, 240
1:13, 14	82
1:15	82, 215
1:16	82
1:25	82, 213
1:26, 27	303
1:28	80, 81, 303
1:29	297, 303
1:30	80, 81, 297, 303
1:31-33	303
1:34	81, 297, 303
1:35	81, 303
1:36	81, 215, 303
1:37	81, 303
1:38	188, 240, 297, 303
1:41	215
1:42	81, 82, 215
1:43-45	81, 82
1:46	213
1:47-49	80, 213
1:50-53	213
1:54, 55	80, 213

Luke

Reference	Page
2:4-6	188
2:36-38	82, 269, 303, 325
2:48, 49	84, 235
2:51	84, 240, 249
2:52	84, 240
4:38-40	96
5:16	363
6:12	363
6:28	365
7:11-18	91, 96, 97
7:36-50	91-93, 297, 322
8:1-3	106, 110, 271
8:43-48	97, 98
9:18	363
10:38	103, 110, 310, 338
10:40, 41	103, 104, 110, 310
10:42	103, 104, 110
11:1	363
11:5-13	365
11:27	113
11:28	113, 360
11:29-32	114
12:51, 53	114
13:10-13	101
13:14, 15	102
13:16	98, 102
13:19-21	114
15:8-10	114
15:11-32	249
18:1-8	114, 365
18:9-12	365
18:13	288, 365
18:14	288, 290, 365
21:36	364
22:8-13	110
22:24-27	288
22:32	365
22:42	168
23:27-29	109
23:55, 56	107
24:10	107

John

Reference	Page
1:1	83
1:9	83
1:12	350
1:14	351
1:18	83, 351
2:4	85, 297
2:12	86
3:3-7	350
3:29	159
4	87, 167, 310, 322, 325, 358
4:7	33
4:9	88
4:10	89
4:15	89
4:16-18	88, 89
4:19	89
4:21-25	90
4:26	91
4:27	88
4:29	91
4:39-42	269
5:30	83
6:11-13	110
8:1-11	93-95, 164, 167, 322
8:38	83
11:3	104
11:5	103
11:11-16	105
11:20, 21, 23	105
11:24-27	104, 105
11:28	105
11:33-35	106
11:37	105
11:45	105
12:1	310, 338
12:2	33, 106, 110, 310
12:3	104, 310
12:4, 5	106, 110, 310
12:6	310
12:7, 8	106, 110, 310

John

Reference	Page
12:49	83
13	111
13:3-12	288
13:13-15	23, 288
13:16, 17	288
13:33	222
14:1	306
14:13	356
14:15	356, 360
14:17	352
14:23	356
14:26	352
14:29	356
15:2, 4, 7	356
15:10-12, 17	356
15:26	352
16:1	356
16:14	352
16:20, 21	114
16:24	356
16:33	356
17:9	365
19:25-27	87
20:1-17	108
21:9	111

Acts

Reference	Page
1:6	107
1:14	115, 118, 297
1:24	364
2:14	349
2:15, 16	119
2:17	119, 273
2:18	119
2:36, 37	349
2:38	249, 351
2:41	115, 350
2:42	117, 350
2:43	117
2:44-47	117, 350, 366
4:29-31	364

INDEX OF SCRIPTURES

Acts

Reference	Page
4:34-37	117
5:1-10	117, 134, 194, 324
5:14	115
6:1-3	120
8:1	119
8:3	116
8:4	119
8:12	115
8:15	366
8:22	364
8:27-39	350
9:1	350
9:2	116, 350
9:3-22, 35	116
9:36	118, 341
9:37, 38	118
9:39	33, 118, 341
9:40	364
9:41, 42	116
10	350
11:14	116
12:5	366
12:12	118, 338
15:9	300
16:1	116, 240
16:2	240
16:13	350
16:14	116, 350
16:15	116, 118, 299, 338, 350
16:16-19	122
16:25-32	350
16:33	116, 350
16:34	350
16:40	118, 338
17:4, 12	116
17:34	116
18:1	338
18:2	119, 156, 338
18:3	156, 338
18:8	116
18:18	119, 156

Acts

Reference	Page
18:24, 25	272, 310
18:26	119, 156, 272, 310, 325
20:31	248
20:35	366
21:5	119, 263
21:9	119, 273
22:4	116
26:9-11	358
28:8	364

Romans

Reference	Page
1:12	366
1:26, 27	202
1:30	290
3:23	117
5:1	356
5:5	352
5:10	353
5:12-21	15
6:3	350
6:4	350, 353
6:6, 11, 18	353
7:2, 3	164
8:7	168
8:11-13	352
8:14, 15	350
8:16	350, 352
8:17	350
8:26	352
8:28	306
9:9	49
9:10-13	54
10:3	168
10:14	349
11:15-32	292
12	122, 356
12:1, 2	40
12:3	117, 270, 292
12:4, 5	117, 270
12:6	117, 208, 270
12:7, 8	117, 270

Romans

Reference	Page
12:9	151
12:13	337
12:16	292
13:1, 5	168
13:12	354
13:14	328
14:13, 19	366
14:21	327
15:1, 2	366
15:13, 16, 19	352
16	116, 303
16:1	271
16:2	118, 271
16:3	119, 122, 156, 272, 338
16:4	122, 156, 272, 338
16:5	118, 119, 156, 272, 338
16:7	272
16:21	122, 272

I Corinthians

Reference	Page
1:10	152, 366
1:11	116, 119
2:10, 11	352
3:1	350
3:16, 17	352
6:9	203, 316
6:11	352
6:16	198
6:19	352
7:1-3	123, 200, 316
7:4	10, 123, 199, 200, 316
7:5	123, 200, 316
7:8, 9	124, 206
7:10-13	125
7:14, 15	125, 165
7:16	125
7:17	125, 206
7:18-24	206
7:25-27	125
7:28-35	125, 207
7:37, 38	125

I Corinthians

Reference	Page
7:39	124, 152
7:40	124
9:9-14	368
9:25, 27	328
10:1-10	29
10:11	29, 248
10:13	185, 202
10:16, 17	366
10:31-33	127
11	292
11:3	125, 126, 134, 171, 291
11:4	125
11:5	119, 125-128, 130, 273
11:6	125-128
11:7	125-128, 291
11:8, 9	11, 13, 15, 24, 32, 125-128
11:10	11, 13, 15, 24, 32, 125-128, 291
11:11	11, 13, 15, 24, 32, 125, 128, 164
11:12	11, 13, 15, 24, 43, 125, 128
11:13-15	125, 128
11:16	128
12	122, 262, 352, 367
12:13	366
12:25-27	367
12:28-30	270
13:4-8	177, 220
14:1-5	130
14:12	129
14:17-23	129
14:24-26	129, 130
14:29, 31	130
14:33	120, 129, 292
14:34	120, 129, 130, 291
14:35	120, 129, 130
15:22	117
15:28	168
16:16	168
16:19	118, 119, 338

II Corinthians

Reference	Page
1:22	353
3:17	353
5:5	353
5:17	354
5:18	353
6:14	152
6:16-18	352
8, 9	368
9:13	168
12:14	218
12:15	219
13:7	365

Galatians

Reference	Page
3:26	300
3:27	117
3:28	117, 122
3:29	350
4:5-7	350, 352, 354
4:19	222
4:22, 24, 28, 30, 31	52
5:16	352
5:18	354
5:19	203, 316
5:22	300, 345, 353, 356
5:23	345, 353, 356
6:2	367

Ephesians

Reference	Page
1:13	353
2:5	353
2:12-14	354
2:19	354
2:22	352
3:10	129
3:16	353
3:17	300
4:6-12	117, 270, 352, 367
4:13	117, 270, 352, 355, 367
4:14, 15	117, 270, 351, 352, 355, 367

Ephesians

Reference	Page
4:16	117, 270, 352, 367
4:22-24	354
4:26	229
4:30	353
5:2	367
5:8	354
5:16, 17	281
5:18	327
5:19	367
5:21	120, 133, 168, 172, 175, 291
5:22	12, 24, 120, 133, 134, 160, 169, 291
5:23	23, 133, 172, 173
5:24	168, 172, 291
5:25	23, 133, 172, 173, 177
5:26	23, 133, 172, 173
5:27	23, 133, 173
5:28, 29	23, 133, 135, 173
5:30	23, 133
5:31, 32	23, 133, 159
5:33	23, 24, 133, 134, 160, 174, 291
6:1	169, 246, 248
6:2, 3	246, 248
6:4	246, 247
6:5	168
6:16	300
6:17	316
6:18	365, 366

Philippians

Reference	Page
2:3	167
2:4	289
2:5	168, 289, 314
2:6-8	168, 289
2:9-11	289
3:4-7	359
3:8	121, 359
3:12-16	351
4:2	116, 119

Philippians

Reference	Page
4:4	307
4:5	307, 328
4:6	307, 363
4:7	307
4:8	203, 311

Colossians

1:13	354
1:21, 22	353
2:13	353
3:2	314
3:15	292
3:16	248, 292, 367
3:17	292
3:18	120, 132, 134, 169, 291, 292
3:19	120, 132, 134, 292
3:20	169, 248
4:3	364
4:5	281
4:15	116, 118, 338

I Thessalonians

2:7, 8	222
3:9	365
3:10	365, 366
4:3-7	352
4:18	366
5:8	300
5:12, 13	118, 271
5:17	365

II Thessalonians

| 3:12 | 132 |

I Timothy

2:2	132
2:5, 6	117
2:8	365
2:9	120, 130, 131, 330, 333
2:10	120, 130, 331, 333, 342

I Timothy

Reference	Page
2:11	15, 120, 130, 131, 169, 174, 291, 313, 331
2:12	12, 15, 120, 130, 131, 174, 291, 313
2:13, 14	15, 120, 130, 131
2:15	130, 131, 313
3:1	24
3:2	24, 161, 308, 327, 337, 342
3:3	24
3:4	24, 169
3:5-7	24
3:8	342
3:11	271, 299, 322, 327, 342
3:12	118, 161, 271
3:14-16	326
4:1, 2	200
4:3	200, 208
4:4, 5	208
5:9	118, 135, 334
5:10	118, 135, 333, 334, 336, 340
5:11	118, 135
5:12	113, 135, 299
5:13	135, 322, 334
5:14	135, 334
5:15	135
5:16	136
5:17	118
6:4	290

II Timothy

1:5	116, 240, 303
1:14	352
2:2	342
3:2	290
3:14	238, 303
3:15	238, 240, 303
3:16, 17	352, 361
4:19	119
4:21	116

410

Titus

Reference	Page
1:6	161, 342
1:7	327, 337
1:8	308, 327, 337
2:1	120, 136, 137
2:2	120, 136, 137, 308, 342
2:3	120, 136, 137, 160, 322, 326, 333, 342
2:4	120, 136, 137, 170, 179, 222, 334
2:5	120, 136, 137, 169, 229, 291, 292, 308, 313, 334, 340
2:6	120, 137, 308
2:7, 8	120, 137
2:9	120, 168
2:10	120
2:11-13	326
3:1	168
3:5	353

Philemon

2	116
24	122, 272

Hebrews

3:13	367
10:24, 25	367
11:3	300
11:6	365
11:8	168
11:11	51, 302, 357
11:23	57
11:31	358
12:5	245, 248
12:6-10	245
12:11	245, 246
13:1, 2	337
13:4	202, 203, 315, 316
13:17	168

James

Reference	Page
1:5	237, 364, 365
1:6, 7	365
1:14, 15	330
1:19	229
1:27	120
2:15, 16	340
2:24	300
2:25	69, 300
2:26	300
3:2-6	324
3:17	344
4:5	352
4:6	287
4:7	168, 203
4:10	287
5:13	366
5:14	364
5:16	366, 367

I Peter

1:2	352
1:12	129
1:14	168
1:22	168
2:2	351, 361
2:13	120, 168
2:14-17	120
2:18	120, 168
2:19-25	120
3:1	120, 130, 169, 197, 291, 292, 313, 331
3:2	120, 130, 134, 174, 197, 313, 331, 342
3:3	120, 130, 197, 331
3:4	120, 130, 197, 287
3:5	52, 120, 130, 169, 291
3:6	52, 120, 130, 186, 291
3:7	117, 120, 160, 173, 365
3:8-12	290
3:22	168

I Peter

Reference	Page
4:9	337, 339
5:3	24
5:5	168, 290
5:6	287
5:7	306

II Peter

1:5	327, 356
1:6-8	356
1:10, 11	356
1:20, 21	359
2:20-22	355

I John

1:6, 7	354
1:9	364
2:1	222
2:3-6	356
2:8, 9	354
2:10, 11	354, 356
2:12	222
2:27	356
2:28	356, 222
2:29	354, 356
3:9, 10	354

I John

Reference	Page
3:11	356
3:18	219
3:22	356, 365
3:23	356
4:7	356, 367
4:11	356
4:13	353, 356
4:21	356
5:1, 2	350
5:4	300, 307, 356
5:5	307
5:14	306

II John

1	116

Revelation

2:20-24	119, 273
2:27	243
10:10	133
19:7-10	160
19:15	243
21:2	332
22:17	160